BAD MEDIEVALISM AND THE MODERNITY PROBLEM

Bad Medievalism and the Modernity Problem

Kathy Lavezzo

FORDHAM UNIVERSITY PRESS   NEW YORK 2026

Copyright © 2026 Fordham University Press

All rights reserved. No part of this publication may be reproduced, stored in a retrieval system, or transmitted in any form or by any means—electronic, mechanical, photocopy, recording, or any other—except for brief quotations in printed reviews, without the prior permission of the publisher.

Fordham University Press has no responsibility for the persistence or accuracy of URLs for external or third-party Internet websites referred to in this publication and does not guarantee that any content on such websites is, or will remain, accurate or appropriate.

Fordham University Press also publishes its books in a variety of electronic formats. Some content that appears in print may not be available in electronic books.

Visit us online at www.fordhampress.com.

For EU safety / GPSR concerns: Mare Nostrum Group B.V., Mauritskade 21D, 1091 GC Amsterdam, The Netherlands, gpsr@mare-nostrum.co.uk

Library of Congress Cataloging-in-Publication Data available online at https://catalog.loc.gov.

Printed in the United States of America
28 27 26   5 4 3 2 1
First edition

Contents

PREFACE   vii

Introduction: Race, Affect, Periodization   1

Part I. White Mythologies of History

1 Modernity, the Medieval, and the Feel of Periodization   37

2 "Between Then and Now": The Veil of Periodization   76

Part II. Tolkien vs. Hall: White Heritage Fantasy and Diasporic Critique

3 Whiteness, Medievalism, Immigration: Rethinking Tolkien through Stuart Hall   109

4 Stuart Hall's *Piers Plowman*   141

Part III. Black Feminist Modernism, Black Feminist Medievalism

5 High Theory, Low Feelings: Gloria Naylor's *Bailey's Cafe*   181

6 Tradition and the Individual Black Talent: Contesting Malory and Modernism in *The Fisher King*   216

ACKNOWLEDGMENTS 249

APPENDIX: STUART HALL'S FIRST PUBLICATION 253

NOTES 259

INDEX 323

Preface

Bad Medievalism and the Modernity Problem pursues the upsetting twists and turns through which periodization—namely, the West's obsessive division of humans into superstitious medievals and rational moderns—has supported a debilitating *longue durée* of whiteness. This dialectical project balances scrutiny of the dangerously feel-good racializations at work in white approaches to periods with an exploration of the productively feel-bad historicisms of contemporary intellectuals of color. This book centers on an episode that witnesses the dangers of a white medievalism, the moment in the 1950s when J. R. R. Tolkien dissuaded a young Stuart Hall from becoming a medievalist.

I never intended to write a book about affect, modernity, Stuart Hall, Gloria Naylor, and Paule Marshall. After publishing my second monograph in 2016, my plan was to write a student-oriented book on race in medieval Europe modeled on Ruth Mazo Karras's marvelous *Sexuality in Medieval Europe* (2005). But a confluence of factors compelled me to change course.

That shift began about eight years ago when I immersed myself in the work of Stuart Hall. At the time, I was formulating a methodology for my approach to race in that original third book project, and my partner, Americanist Harry Stecopoulos, suggested that I begin with Hall. From the moment I began reading Hall's 1988 essay "New Ethnicities," I became passionately interested in his approach, and especially his delivery of difficult concepts in a notably clear manner. Soon after that, my colleague Deborah Whaley, having learned about my budding Hall attachment, invited me to join a University of Iowa working group on Hall. The working group spawned a new digital journal about Hall and his impact. I agreed to write a short piece for the volume about my rationale for incorporating Hall into a book about medieval Europe.

To prepare for that essay, I read Hall's posthumous memoir, *Familiar Stranger: A Life between Two Islands* (2017), hot off the press from Duke. I picked up *Familiar Stranger* with an eye toward Hall's comments on method but quickly became drawn into his compelling account of the years before his birth as a New Left intellectual. To my surprise, Hall's memoir described not only his time reading English at Oxford University but also his love of medieval English literature and even his interest in doing graduate work on William Langland's late medieval English poem *Piers Plowman*. My contribution to Deborah's journal ceased to center on methodology and instead engaged Hall's abandoned medievalism.

During fall 2018, as I drafted my essay, I became increasingly curious about a detail from Hall's anecdote regarding his interest in medieval study. Hall describes how his "South African language professor" rejected his approach to medieval texts. I began an online inquiry into professors at Hall's college, Merton, during his time there in the 1950s. My heart skipped a beat when I learned that the single South African–born instructor at Merton was none other than J. R. R. Tolkien.

I followed up on my hunch about Tolkien via email missives to contacts at Oxford, who confirmed that the epic fantasy creator was the only candidate for Hall's anonymous teacher. The discovery prompted a radical shift in my research. The meaning of both Tolkien's gatekeeping and Hall's medievalism now drew my concerted attention. While I am one of those rare medievalists who never loved Tolkien's works, I took a deep dive into his entire corpus, published and unpublished, finished pieces and fragments. My new project also licensed a rewarding immersion in Hall's life and work; I explored his ideas of history, literature, and especially the medieval.

Coincidentally, I had agreed during this period to begin teaching an introduction to the English major course at the University of Iowa. I chose to center the class on the category of the "human" from Chaucer's *Miller's Tale* to Toni Morrison's *Sula*. Teaching this class—my first large lecture course after two decades of small-classroom teaching—was truly a trial by fire. But my preparatory research for the class—namely, an exploration of periodization and discourses of the human—prompted two additional shifts in my scholarship. On the one hand, I became fascinated by the remarkable similarity of medieval and postmedieval white discourses. The continuities—and especially the racializing continuities—were, to my mind, undeniable. On the other hand, I grew equally fascinated by how writers of color, such as Olaudah Equiano, Jean Toomer, and Toni Morrison, acutely unsettled those white discourses. Morrison particularly spurred me to read as many works by U.S. Black women writers as possible. In effect, starting in 2018, I commenced an independent extended study of African American women's writing—Morrison, Gwendolyn Brooks, Paule Marshall, Gloria Naylor, Ann Petry, and others—that is ongoing. That research served me well, as it led to my encounter, for the first time, with the incisive responses to white medieval discourse respectively performed by Naylor and Marshall. The final step in my "road to Damascus" conversion to Black studies has been teaching, regularly since spring 2022, the first courses in critical race theory offered in my department. The opportunity to put Hall into conversation with thinkers including the Combahee River Collective, W. E. B. Du Bois, Frantz Fanon, Cheryl Harris, bell hooks, Saidiya Hartman, Jennifer Nash, and Hortense Spillers for cohorts of always curious, rigorous, and committed undergraduates has been deeply rewarding. All of which is to say, since 2017, this medievalist has been inching her way toward this unusual book.

My project might appear neither fish nor fowl. With its close attention to writers as diverse as Hall and Tolkien, Chaucer and Naylor, Malory and Marshall, Saul/Paul and Du Bois, Marx and Huizinga, *Bad Medievalism* resists placement in a scholarly box. But, if anything, my research on this book has reminded me of the danger of "cleaning up"—or, as Foucault would say, "cutting"—a messy and upsetting reality on behalf of "knowledge." Honing expertise within rigorously narrow frames can risk supporting the white discourse that construed those categories in the first place.

BAD MEDIEVALISM AND THE MODERNITY PROBLEM

Introduction
Race, Affect, Periodization

After a conference banquet, two white keynoters saunter to a cemetery in Oxford, Mississippi, where the elderly men pour whiskey over William Faulkner's grave. A cool white nerd dissertating on Thomas Pynchon gets the Trystero muted post-horn tattooed on his bicep. A Black feminist scholar relishes a badass Sula and mourns with Nel the end of an intimate friendship. An Anglo-Jewish scholar of high modernism identifies with the angst, and is dismayed by the antisemitism, of T. S. Eliot. A white Oxbridge medievalist from South Africa thrills at the *Beowulf* poet's account of northern European heroism. The same don shudders at the thought of his West Indian student adopting new critical approaches to medieval English texts. The would-be medievalist never enters the field.[1]

What are the affective premises of literary criticism? More precisely, how do questions of identity and belonging, of selfhood and alterity, determine assemblages of feeling in a scholarly imaginary? In what ways do the politics of representation spur, block, or modify an academic cathexis to a text, an author, or a period? What feelings undergird work on canonical versus marginalized and under-recognized writers? How can a hegemonic component of a literary work hinder attachment for some scholars or, conversely, open horizons of passionate connection for others? To what extent do sentiments determine how, why, and what works are read and govern what readers (and what readings) matter?

Such questions and hypothetical scenarios might seem ill-conceived to anyone who views academic work as an unsentimental fact-finding mission. For those who oppose cognition and feeling, the very idea of critical sentiment contradicts the scholarly enterprise. However, multiple factors counter the notion that, in Rita Felski and Susan Fraiman's words, "academic argument is entirely free of affect."[2] Examples abound in the West of intellectual feeling, from the Renaissance melancholia anatomized by Richard Burton to the romantic sublimity celebrated by Kant.[3] Moreover, at least since the 1960s, an array of thinkers—within areas that include the history of science, structuralism, Black studies, Indigenous studies, feminism, and postcolonial and decolonial studies—have persuasively upended the myth of the emotionally detached scholar by demonstrating the contingent relationship of analysis and sentiment. Lorraine Daston and Peter Galison, for example, have tracked the history of a "scientific" self since the nineteenth century, revealing how ideals of objectivity are constituted in and through shifting valuations of an emotive subject.[4] And thinkers such as Sara Ahmed, Lauren Berlant, Felski, and Fraiman have made clear how mood and related affects are "not optional, but a prerequisite for any kind of intellectual engagement; critical dispassion is not an absence of mood, but one manifestation of it."[5] While many works of literary criticism might put forth a stance of cold detachment, in practice a scholar's relation to a text, an author, a genre, or a period encompasses numerous additional and often changing sentiments. Scholarly feeling can be positive, negative, or ambivalent. It can reverse itself, alter, or be put to a stop by a host of human and nonhuman catalysts that arise both within and without a text. How a scholar feels—or desires to feel—about their object of inquiry fundamentally impacts the scope, aims, methods, and outcomes of academic work.

In literary and cultural studies, this home truth applies to not only how academics feel about the persons, events, and cultural forms they study but also scholarly sentiment about periods and periodization. Notions of periodization are as emotionally charged as they are indispensable. As Marshall Brown puts it, "periods are entities we love to hate," based on their status as artificial categories that one nevertheless "cannot do without."[6] Whatever they might be (western or non-western; classical, Victorian, Vedic, Edo), periods can't help but epitomize Michel Foucault's dictum that "knowledge is not made for understanding; it is made for cutting."[7] Insofar as the production of knowledge always excises what does not belong in an episteme, that intellectual dynamic especially pertains to how temporal categories annihilate the rich messiness of history. And yet, however much one might dislike it, "one cannot not periodize," in the words of Fredric Jameson.[8]

Of all western literary periods, that of the medieval offers an especially fruitful site for revisiting debates about emotion and scholarship. As the dialectical obverse of western modernity—or what Paul Freedman and Gabrielle Spiegel call "the West's shadowy 'other'"—the medieval is indispensable to any inquiry into the affective dynamics of humanities scholarship.[9] One can readily gauge the uniquely charged position of the medieval by comparing it to that other era to which moderns have compared themselves: Greek and Roman antiquity. As Hans Robert Jauss demonstrates, European moderns of all sorts—from Cassiodorus to the participants in the *querelle des anciens et des modernes* and beyond—have long understood their moment in relation to the classical West.[10] But unlike *antiquitas*, which "was always," in Jürgen Habermas's words, "regarded as the normative model to be imitated" up to (and in some circles, well after) the European Enlightenment, the medieval emerged not as an exemplar of human perfection but rather as a dark and barbarous gap between (classical and modern) civilizations.[11]

Like the French *médiéval* and the Italian *medievale*, "medieval" is a modern word. From its first appearance in the language in the nineteenth century, the word "medieval" has, from the start, designated a cluster of negative attributes that oppose the values of modernity. The *Oxford English Dictionary* defines "medieval" both as "a period of time intervening between (periods designated as) ancient and modern" and, in a colloquial or popular register, "the severity or illiberality ascribed to [that] former age; cruel, barbarous"; while in the *Collins English Thesaurus*, "medieval" is synonymous with "primitive."[12] "Bad" in my title partly refers to the singularly negative reputation of the medieval.

The negative feelings directed at the medieval urge its relevance to an inquiry into academic feeling. Denigrations of that period often encompass questions of sentiment—that is, the association of the medieval with passionate irrationality. Bad feelings about the medieval hinge on claims about its relationship to feeling and thus its alterity to modern objective thought. The very idea of cognitive neutrality embraced by academic work comprises one of the western virtues that supposedly broke from a fervent—and thus inferior—medieval worldview. As L. O. Aranye Fradenburg puts it, "The alterity of the Middle Ages continues to secure, for modernity, its intelligibility to itself—continues, as it were, to produce, if only by way of negativity, the enlightenment discourse of science, and its disavowals of passion."[13] Consider, for example, David Harvey's account of visual art and cartography in *The Condition of Postmodernity* (1989). There, he describes both how the "'coldly geometrical' and 'systematic' sense of space" made possible by a linear perspective "broke radically with the practices of mediaeval art and architecture" and how maps, "stripped of all elements of fantasy and religious belief," became "abstract and strictly functional systems for the factual ordering of phenomena in space."[14] Reflecting received truisms about perspective and Ptolemaic geography, Harvey supports the idea of a dispassionate modern turn to natural truths that "broke radically" with passionate medieval attachments to the enchanted and the supernatural.

Insofar as the idea of a detached modern lucidity arose in tandem with the notion of an emotion-saturated medieval superstitiousness, a full critique of the former concept demands a critical engagement with the latter. *Bad Medievalism and the Modernity Problem* tracks and analyzes the relationship between affect and analysis—between feeling and critique—in work on the medieval-modern binary by medievalists, scholars of modernity, and twentieth-century novelists. A central aim of this book is countering feel-good trends pertaining to what Wallace Ferguson has called "the revolt of the medievalists."[15] Based on the notion that modernity broke the shackles of a backward and irrational medieval age, medievalists' field imaginary is uniquely burdened with a hefty amount of negative emotional baggage. "There can be no denying," as Margreta de Grazia puts it, "that the modern divide has been hard on medievalists."[16] In response to their bad reputation, scholars of the European Middle Ages have long claimed to find in their period versions of the wonders of modernity. If the titles of two recent publications—*The Light Ages* and *The Bright Ages*—are any indication, far from a dark age, the medieval seems sunnier than ever.[17]

To be sure, stereotypes of superstition and savagery reveal little, if anything, about the long and complicated thousand-year period in Europe called the Middle Ages. But so too do happy accounts of a proto-modern medieval period fail to tell the whole story about that era. This book contends that a full account of the Middle Ages and modernity requires not evacuating sentiment in the manner of the neutral intellectual but rather embracing affect in a slew of new forms. To put it another way, the problem with studying the medieval West and its modern obverse isn't so much the presence of sentiment per se but rather the kinds of sentiments that such work demands. To that end, along with its other resonances, "bad" in my title also affirms my espousal of a "feel-bad" scholarship. *Bad Medievalism* embraces the critical benefits that accrue to academic work informed by a range of negative emotions.

Crucially, the negative sentiments I advocate pertain not to "bad medievalism" as usually conceived—that is, denigrating the Middle Ages as modernity's other. Rather, the array of negative feelings showcased in this book arises from the depressing realization that the European Middle Ages enabled—and even laid the groundwork for—a western modernity whose claims of objectivity, emancipation, and progress are in many respects unfounded. I argue that a full understanding of the Middle Ages demands a negative assessment in line with the failures of modernity. Thus, instead of yoking the Middle Ages to a modernity understood as an admirable phenomenon or, in the case of nostalgic and anti-modernist medievalism, sundering the Middle Ages from a modernity understood as a deplorable phenomenon, I urge linking a bad modernity to a bad medieval period. Drawing on the critical pessimisms of writers of color such as Hortense Spillers, Sylvia Wynter, and Alexander Weheliye, as well as work on negative affect by feminist and queer theorists such as Ahmed, Sianne Ngai, Anne Anlin Cheng, Berlant, Jennifer Nash, and Heather Love, this book urges an understanding of periodization that is informed by sentiments such as disappointment, rage, nausea, pain, and disgust.[18]

Bad Medievalism responds to Wynter's call for "the un/writing of our present normative defining of the secular mode of the Subject" by analyzing how ideas of modern objectivity support a white "genre" of humanity with disturbing medieval roots.[19] *Bad Medievalism* interrogates how the medieval-modern binary both misrepresents and is complicit in a *longue durée* of white supremacist thought and practice. In other words, this book performs a feel-bad inquiry into the affective and periodizing antimonies of whiteness. It confronts disturbing and affectively charged irrationalities about white subjecthood that bind the European Middle Ages to modernity, undermine received ideas of modern neutrality, and shape the idea of period division itself. This book also balances its critique of western ideas of the medieval-modern divide with an engagement with alternate discourses and temporalities generated by persons situated in fraught relation to the West.

At the heart of this project is a charged scholarly encounter that concerns modernity as much as it does the Middle Ages: the moment in the 1950s when future cultural studies pioneer Stuart Hall (1932–2014) contemplated graduate work in medieval studies, only to be swayed from that path by epic fantasy founder J. R. R. Tolkien (1892–1973). As Hall puts it in his posthumous memoir, *Familiar Stranger: A Life between Two Islands* (2017), upon his arrival at Oxford as a Rhodes Scholar from Jamaica, he was "plunge[d]" into the "icy depths" of a belletristic and racialized English culture.[20] Hall would warm, though, both to a Leavisite "counter tradition" that he passionately "proselytized" and to the medieval English texts he was required to read.[21] Regarding the latter, medieval attachment, Hall states, "I loved some of the poetry—*Beowulf, Sir Gawain and the Green Knight, The Wanderer, The Seafarer*—and at one point I planned to do graduate work on Langland's *Piers Plowman*." But Hall's "ascetic South African language professor"—none other than Tolkien, an Oxford don—felt otherwise.[22] A blood-and-soil believer in "the profound appeal" of medieval texts to the English readers with whom they share an "essential kinship," Tolkien was distressed at the thought of a West Indian student adopting new critical approaches to *Piers*.[23] "In a pained tone," Tolkien told Hall, "this was not the point of the exercise."[24] Tolkien deterred Hall from joining a field whose medieval materials the don cherished as part of a white cultural heritage capable of compensating for his modern western anomie. But Hall would go on to generate a corpus of transnational modernist scholarship whose multiple dimensions include contesting and dismantling "feel-good" white heritage medievalisms.

The central chapters of *Bad Medievalism* investigate the significance and implications of the Hall-Tolkien encounter. I frame my analysis of Hall and Tolkien with chapters that both consider white western periodization and engage alternate medievalisms and modernisms produced by writers who are, like Hall, complexly positioned within and without the West.[25] Taken together, the six chapters of this book juxtapose an initial critique of the white supremacist sentiments that all too often hinder a full account of western history with an exploration of the productively "feel-bad" modernisms and medievalisms of diasporic intellectuals. *Bad Medievalism* thus aims at a dialectical analysis of the affective politics of periodization. This book affirms the depressing reality—articulated by scholars including Jacqueline de Weever, Geraldine Heng, Wan-Chuan Kao, Cord Whitaker, and Wynter—that racial formations in medieval Europe adumbrated and informed their modern counterparts.[26] I argue that this disturbing continuity demands consideration in tandem with the white supremacist apparatus that puts pressure on, activates, troubles, and reverses ideas of modernity and the Middle Ages. A radical revisionist history requires holding in mind both the presence of an overarching racial discourse from which medieval and postmedieval agents drew *and* the racialized shifts and contradictions witnessed in various assessments and deployments of periodization. To put it another way, by charting feel-bad continuities between medieval and modern racisms, I intend not to synthesize but illuminate the paradoxical shifts that produce a "modern" and "medieval" opposition. Employing a dialectical and race-conscious look at Eurocentric and diasporic ideas of the medieval and modern, I argue, provides a new vantage point on both terms, where they appear as not hard, monolithic opposites but strategies of human empowerment and denigration that travel in complex ways across time, backward and forward. Ultimately, this volume looks to the feel-bad literary medievalisms and modernisms of writers of color to discover genres of human identity and modes of historicism that counter the white subjects and white temporalities that often dominate scholarship. "Bad" in my title thus also refers to the badass (that is, bracing and provocative, unsettling and defiant) alternate worlds and alternate models of the human charted by writers such as Hall, Gloria Naylor, and Paule Marshall. Thanks partly to the critical vantage point afforded by their shifting and fraught location within and without the West, these writers theorize a more authentic concept of humanity, one that isn't bound to mythic claims about individual periods and historical rupture.

Scholarly Feeling

By "affect" and related terms—for instance, "emotion," "sentiment," and "feeling"—I refer to embodied phenomena that, to all intents and purposes, are inextricably tied to signs and representations. A sizeable interdisciplinary body of scholarship has emerged in recent decades that concerns itself with affect as a phenomenon distinct from emotion and that at times understands affect as preconscious and preverbal.[27] This book does not approach emotion as a discrete entity that is separable from language. I do not consider feeling in terms of "the expressive hypothesis," according to which affects originate from within persons and flow out of those subjects to reveal their authentic selfhood.[28] Instead, I follow critics such as Raymond Williams, Ngai, and Ahmed in seeing emotion—which I treat as interchangeable with affect—as a phenomenon that surfaces and travels in and through systems of meaning.[29]

Williams's idea of "structures of feeling" provides an early and important account of the discursive and social components of emotion.[30] Rather than defining affect as that which exists "beneath, alongside, or generally other than conscious knowing," Williams highlights the

> specifically affective elements of consciousness and relationships: not feeling against thought, but thought as felt and feeling as thought: practical consciousness of a present kind, in a living and interrelating continuity. We are then defining these elements as a "structure": as a set, with specific internal relations, at once interlocking and in tension. Yet we are also defining a social experience which is still in process, often indeed not yet recognized as social but taken to be private, idiosyncratic, and even isolating, but which in analysis (though rarely otherwise) has its emergent, connecting, and dominant characteristics, indeed its specific hierarchies.[31]

Williams's association of affect with social hierarchy anticipates Ahmed's stress on how "language works as a form of power in which emotions align some bodies with others, as well as stick different figures together, by the way they move us."[32] Ahmed describes emotion as a "doing" that "is bound up" with "the sticky relation between signs and bodies," that is, how systems of meaning or discourses "work on and in relation to bodies."[33] Feelings pertain to "the sensational nature" of how a dominant discourse liberates, organizes, or freezes persons and collectives, as well as the sentimental components of formations that critique, challenge, and resist dominant discourse.[34]

Analyses of the confluence of affect, aesthetics, and the sociopolitical often yield productively ambivalent results. In *Cruel Optimism*, Berlant tracks the fraught emotional content of the aesthetic contracts through which inhabitants of the U.S. and Europe are called on to represent, comprehend, and hopefully consent to a cruel and disabling relation to capitalist democracies. Berlant specifically problematizes the alignment of optimism with a happy belief in best outcomes. She interrogates optimism as "a scene of negotiated sustenance" and "a social relation involving attachments that organize the present," making "life bearable as it presents itself ambivalently, unevenly, incoherently."[35] Similarly, Ngai analyzes emotions that trouble any idea of a "good" and "bad" affective binary. Her 2005 book *Ugly Feelings* explores how the weak or minor sentiments portrayed in late modern writings provide telling indices of "the predicaments posed by a general state of obstructed agency with respect to other human actors or to the social as such" (3). Drawing on Baruch Spinoza and Hannah Arendt, Ngai's "ugly feelings" are "wavering[s] of the mind" closely bound to dilemmas of action that are "charged with political meaning" (2).

Ahmed, Ngai, and Berlant contribute to an extensive and long-standing body of work on affect that, at times, considers academic sentiment.[36] Ahmed, for example, theorizes Edmund Husserl's white academic comfort as well as "feminist wonder" and hope.[37] Ngai, analyzing antagonisms within feminism, considers how "the affective dimension of feminism, including all its ugly feelings," should "be taken far more seriously than it has been so far" (164). And Berlant, in an essay on Eve Sedgwick's "grandiosity," addresses how "critical theory," for all its skepticism, "dark" suspiciousness, and "exhausting anxiety" about the value of thought, nevertheless is compelled "to repeat optimism" and hazard "having to survive, once again, disappointment, and depression."[38]

Work on academic affect tends to highlight contemporary issues. But medievalists offer an arguably more revealing instance of what academic feelings do and how they circulate, thanks to the charged and complex interrelationship of the Middle Ages and modernity. Many scholars have already gone far in tracking some of those affective dimensions of medieval studies, particularly vis-à-vis "desire," a psychoanalytic term with important affective valences. Fradenburg tracks how medievalists have "kept themselves desiring" via a melancholic stance toward a medieval past that is irretrievably gone yet also recoverable for the scholar who toils, with rigorous rationality, to acquire the "appropriate" skill set.[39] The desire of medievalists for a unrecoverable past, as critics including Fradenburg, Kathleen Biddick, Donna Beth Ellard, Tom Prendergast, and Stephanie Trigg demonstrate, has led to an array of sentiments, such as disdain for amateurs, discontent over historical alterity, nostalgia (however disavowed) for a lost medieval organicism, queasiness over anachronistic and controversial methodologies, and enjoyment of the sacrifices their profession demands.[40]

Work on medievalist desire queries received notions of both the medieval-modern divide and scholarly affect. By showing how desire—and its attending sentiments—have *always* been central to medieval studies, even to its philologists, paleographers, and other rigorously "professional" practitioners, medievalists challenge notions of academic disinterest. But frequently that work by medievalists on academic feeling rejects or occludes the generative benefits of negative emotions. In lieu of the pain, melancholia, and discontent that typically accompany medievalist practice, many of those scholars urge a more positive and explicitly enjoyable relation to the past. Helpfully inverting the dynamic of a privileged modern rigor and disavowed medieval enjoyment at play in academia, these scholars map out not just an explicitly desiring scholarship but even at times a loving field formation.

The loving medievalism advocated by scholars gains additional traction based on an aspect of medieval studies that sets it apart from other scholarly formations and their related affects: the ongoing and widespread fandom of the Middle Ages. No other field—classics, art history, American studies, Victorian studies, modernism, even Renaissance studies—enjoys the level of public adoration witnessed by the *Legend of Zelda* video games, the drama *Game of Thrones*, or Tolkien's fantasy epics. Thanks to its massive scale (for instance, the viewership of the *Lord of the Rings* film trilogy), medieval fan culture exceeds that of, say, Civil War reenactors, Shakespeare's Globe attendees, or owners of reproductions of *Starry Night*. Increasingly, academics have come to value amateur medievalism. Many influential medievalists have urged their fellow professionals to not spurn but instead embrace and tap into a rich and thriving pop medievalism. Engaging with such explicitly loving amateur medievalisms, those scholars contend, can not only provide medieval studies with a sorely needed relevance during a time of academic crisis but also enhance and deepen both the intellectual and the political terms of medieval scholarship.[41]

The contradictions of scholarly desire tracked by medievalists are undeniable, as are medievalists' important work on the multiplicity of history and the utility of certain feel-good approaches to academe. At the same time, however, as several medievalists make clear, a scholar's relationship to the medieval European past can't always be happy or loving. Lisa Lampert-Weissig, for example, situates medieval antisemitism in relation to a lachrymal or mournful scholarship at work in Jewish historiography.[42] And Carolyn Dinshaw has pondered how the "intricate relationships between West and East, and between literature and colonization," generate a complex cluster of affects that inform her work as a medievalist possessed of a "particularly diasporic queerness."[43] More recently, scholars including Whitaker, Jonathan Hsy, Shokoofeh Rajabzadeh, Kao, and Kavita Mudan Finn have expanded on Dinshaw's turn-of-the-millennium response to the intersection of race, religion, and emotion in early texts and their subsequent readers.[44] In a telling example, Finn asks, "Happy for whom"? of those medieval romances where "the pagan knight wins the Christian princess, he converts, and his prior sins—and sometimes his skin colour itself—are washed away as part of a happy ending." Finn's account of how "this particular strain of medieval romance has always sat uncomfortably with me, a woman of color" echoes the sentiments of other scholars.[45]

In this book, I build on and complicate those medievalists' insights on scholarship and feeling through an engagement with theorists such as Wynter, Spillers, W. E. B. Du Bois, and Frantz Fanon. That work clarifies how oppositions of modern vs. medieval, professional rigor vs. lay inaccuracy require not just rearrangement, deconstruction, or reversal but also a larger, systemic reassessment. Instead of working within ideas of a rational modernity and the emotional medieval, Wyner et al. query the basis of those ideas in white modes of subjectivity and world making. Fanon, for example, shifts attention from the contradictions of desiring western subjects to how, within the world conjured by western thinkers, only certain humans enjoy the role of a desiring subject in the first place. "I came into the world," Fanon writes, "imbued with the will to find a meaning in things, my spirit filled with the desire to attain to the source of the world, and then I found that I was an object in the midst of other objects."[46] Serious examination of affect and periodization requires both confronting the whiteness that often mobilizes medievalists' good feelings and taking seriously the pessimistic medievalisms and modernisms of writers of color, as well as others denied full humanity under a white western regime.

Modernity and the Shifting Configurations of Race and the Medieval

My reassessment of scholarly affect, race, and the medieval-modern divide has its challenges, in no small part because of the unwieldy nature of those concepts. Indubitably, the sheer enormity of terms like "modernity," "medieval," and "race" makes them resistant to any sort of brief overview. Nevertheless, to help clarify my use of those concepts, I hazard in what follows a short account of my working understanding of those terms and their interrelationships. Modernity, to begin, is a notoriously slippery and ambiguous idea. Felski's survey of definitions, for example, demonstrates a notable "semantic confusion that derives from the complicated and many-faceted aspects of modern development," as well as the various positionalities—ethnic, political, disciplinary—of commentators on the modern.⁴⁷ Meanings of modernity can include: the spread of capitalism and related colonizing and dehumanizing practices; the replacement of religious ideologies of divine or supernatural agency with secular ideologies of human potential, achievement, and progress; the substitution of feudal, tribal, and other political collectives with the state and/or nation; the rise of cities; the use of the scientific method and the attending proliferation of technologies of innovation (that is, modernization) that heighten the tempo and broaden the scale of human existence as well as rationalize spheres of life into autonomous domains possessed of unique epistemologies; and aesthetic and intellectual commentaries (that is, modernisms) on the problems and potentials that inform secularization, a profit economy, utilitarianism, scientific "advances," and other phenomena.⁴⁸

Rendering modernity especially unwieldy is its temporal and spatial multiplicity. With respect to the former dynamic, Jauss tracks the history of the word "modern" in the West, starting with its origins in the Late Latin use of *modernus* during the fifth-century "period of transition from ancient Rome to the new Christian world."⁴⁹ Among the multiple western modernities Jauss describes are the *modernitas* of twelfth-century scholastics "sitting on the shoulders" of classical "giants" (and thus inhabiting a "present [that] can see farther than the past"), the historical distance and acuity claimed by Renaissance humanist *moderni* with respect to Greece and Rome, and "the open horizon of the future's budding perfection" claimed by "enlightened *modernes*."⁵⁰

While Jauss evokes the many modernities that have circulated over time in the West, other scholars track the spatial multiplicity of modernity. Upending the received idea that the story of modernity is synonymous with the story of the West and its geopolitical and cultural exceptionalism, those thinkers chart non-western "modernities" taking place in different sites (and different times). Examples of non-western modernities include the "rationalization processes" of the Tang dynasty described by Alexander Woodside, the Mongol modernities discussed by Susan Stanford Friedman, and the debates about the Japanese Pure Film Movement studied by Aaron Gerow.⁵¹ Indeed, in Friedman's *Planetary Modernisms* (2015), the proliferations of modernity carry the potential to occur throughout the planet, at any location, and at any moment.

Modernity, or, rather, moderni*ties*, are thus radically multiple phenomena that can assume many guises, appear in a host of locations, and occur during a variety of historical moments. But there is a common thread woven into all those definitions of the modern, even those linked to non-western sites and non-modern times: what Felski identifies as the "distinctive rhetorical power" of modernity as "an enunciation of a process of differentiation, an act of separation from the past."[52] Regardless of their particular understanding of modernity, most thinkers define it in terms of a sharp break from a former way of living, thinking, and being. Even Friedman, who hopes "to break away from periodization altogether" in her notably wide-ranging and cross-temporal account of "planetary modernisms," locates modernity across various places and times specifically as instances of "sharpened change, radical ruptures, accelerated mobilities."[53] Ultimately, for all her pluralism, Friedman endorses the idea that "the adjective 'modern,'" in Bruno Latour's words, "designates a new regime, an acceleration, a rupture, a revolution in time."[54]

By "modernity," I primarily refer in this book to ideas and practices linked to "Europe" around and after 1500 CE and their radiating impact on (and always contingent relationship with) sites and persons located both inside and outside the West. I do not deny that non-western modernities have occurred and are occurring elsewhere and at other times, independently of any "developments" in the West. But modernity in this book isn't something that other sites and persons get to have or deserve the right to claim for themselves but rather a problematic phenomenon needful of critique. I'm concerned, as my title indicates, with what literary critic Jennifer Fleissner, following philosopher Robert Pippin, calls the modernity problem, and especially the damaging and close relationship of discourses of western modernity to racism and related dehumanizing representations and practices.[55] As Felski, Latour, and other critics affirm, modernity primarily concerns ideas of rupture. But I'm specifically interested in how those ruptures encompass not just massive economic, scientific, technological, and other changes that break from prior modes of living but also deleterious, violent, and irrational divisions of persons into fully human beings and less-than or nonhuman figures.

Understanding the modernity problem as a matter of mistaken and in many ways lethal claims about humans unsettles its alignment with hard breaks and clean ruptures. In its guise as a practice of dehumanization, modernity multiplies and doubles back on itself in ways that expose its defining quality of rupture not so much as a hard "fact" about historical change but rather as a dangerous myth. A case in point is how, as work on colonization by Edward Said, Johannes Fabian, Dipesh Chakrabarty, and Kathleen Davis stresses, those harmful practices are themselves powerfully mobilized by claims about the "modernity" of western agents.[56] Insofar as modernity is a concept inexorably tied to ideas of temporal breaks, any celebration of it—any happy hailing of modernity as a welcome change—can't help but invoke politically charged ideas of difference and hierarchy. As Chakrabarty maintains, "If modernity is to be a definable, delimited concept, we must identify some people or practices as non-modern."⁵⁷ Notions of modern innovation, relevance, and growth depend for their legibility on ideas of a prior backwardness, irrelevance, and stagnation.

Delving into racialized deployments of historical rupture necessitates defining race and racism. Conceptualizing and analyzing those concepts pose formidable challenges, as both terms shift between the universal and the particular, between subjectivity and objecthood, and between the abstract and the material. Thanks to the dialectical approach that analyzing race demands, no account of it can ever rest on a single formulation but rather must always alter its directionality and adjust its claims. My approach relies heavily on that of Hall, whose "significance . . . in shaping the field of racial and ethnic studies in the past four decades," as Claire Alexander puts it in a still-accurate 2009 statement, "is almost impossible to overestimate."⁵⁸

Hall adopts a structural approach that stresses how racism, like every identity formation and indeed all the representations through which life is rendered meaningful, is constituted in and through discourse. Hall stresses the utility of a discursive approach because as

> hateful as racism may be as a historical fact, it is nevertheless also a system of meaning, a way of organizing and meaningfully classifying the world. Thus, any attempt to contest racism or to diminish its human and social effects depends on understanding how exactly this system of meaning works, and why the classificatory order it represents has so powerful a hold on the human imagination.⁵⁹

Like other essentialist discourses, racism constructs supposedly insuperable lines that separate and hierarchize humans. As Hall demonstrates in works such as *The Fateful Triangle: Race, Ethnicity, Nation* (2017), understanding and analyzing those discourses demands attending to how they generate meaning via a system of signs that coordinate a grid-like assemblage of binary oppositions. Through oppositions like "them and us, primitive and civilized, light and dark," racist discourse restricts certain groups to one side of the binary because of purportedly innate and fundamental traits (98). With its claims about real and unchanging essences, race functions as a "major or master" trope that fixes such signs within a discursive "world of Manichean opposites" (32, 98).

Racism asserts mythic claims about unchanging, absolute, and essential aspects of a group identity. But identity, as Hall stresses, is "an open and differential phenomenon" that entails multiplicities, contingencies, and instabilities (72). Far from something stable, natural, inherent, and autonomous, identity is a stylized and creative cultural practice. In other words, the claims about identity marshaled by racists are completely different from the way identity in fact works. Identity is mobile, plural, changing, and grounded in difference. Identities can encode a host of meanings, significations that may support—or contest—white western hegemony.

One indicator of the shifting nature of identity pertains to the mobility and impermanence of who is racialized. Examples include the shifting positioning of Jews in thirteenth-century England, the German Reich, and the post-1945 U.S.; the "intermediate race" status of nineteenth-century Irish and Italian U.S. immigrants; and the whiteness bestowed on "the nonslaveholding poor" in the U.S. Confederacy as a "blessing" more valuable than slaveholding.[60] The way certain groups have shifted in and out of "race" radically undermines racist claims about unchanging essences. The changing objects of racialization also speak to an instability at the core of racial discourse: the supposedly essential, unchanging, and natural traits it asserts are cultural constructs and linguistic tropes, metaphors that don't describe but misrepresent the world and its inhabitants. The orderly and stable account of life presented by an essentializing discourse—through neat metonymic dichotomies and patterns in all sorts of arenas, such as religion, medicine, politics, literature, history, law, visual art, music, and education—radically misrepresents the world, which is, in reality, defined by a messy and "fluctuating contingency."[61] What might seem in racial discourse to be factual is instead part of a signifying grid, a discursive creation, an invocation of binary categories of "natural" absolutes and universals. As Hall puts it with respect to the racisms directed at members of the Black Atlantic, "What precisely tends to fix race in its obviousness and visibility—in physical characteristics of 'color, hair and bone'—are themselves nothing but the signifiers of an invisible code that writes difference upon the black body" (63).[62]

And yet, racism, however fictive its claims, has proven deeply pertinent to lived experience. For racist fictions have enjoyed tremendous historical agency. As Hall puts it in *The Fateful Triangle*, false and essentializing binary oppositions of racist discourse have long allocated "wealth, resources and knowledge differentially across societies and between groups" (43). Thus the true dividing line in racial discourse concerns not any supposedly natural or unchanging differences between human collectives but rather how an *artificial* account of what is unchanging naturalizes and legitimates *real* historical differences "between belonging and otherness."[63] The interpenetration of racist representations and racializing historical practices has had very real material, psychological, and biological effects on social groups, thanks to its impact on major political, legal, economic, and other systems. Examples within the contemporary U.S. context include how, thanks to their multiple jeopardy, "Black women continue to experience excess mortality relative to other US women, including—despite overall improvements among Black women—shorter life expectancies and higher rates of maternal mortality"; and how a "new Jim Crow" continues to subject Black men in the U.S. "to legalized discrimination in [voting rights,] employment, housing, education, public benefits, and jury service."[64]

The ongoing discrimination faced by Black women and men in the U.S. makes abundantly clear how rejecting race as a false and mythic construct, as many westerners have done at least since 1945, hardly puts a stop to racism. Depressingly and infuriatingly, regardless of its fictive nature, racism remains powerful as a result of its legitimization of deeply entrenched material and political inequities. Moreover, thanks to its capacity to function as what Hall calls a "sliding signifier," racism creeps into discourses that overtly disavow it; representations of ethnic, religious, and other identities that explicitly reject racism often slip or slide into racial thinking any time they center a white perspective and/or intimate—however subtly, however faintly—what is "natural" or fundamental or intrinsic to a group (108–9).

Sensitive to those slippages, Hall models a neo-Gramscian, conjunctural methodology for analyzing race that stresses how it is never straightforward, monolithic, or inevitable but rather part of a "social formation" composed of various and multiple linkages that are joined together or, to invoke Hall's Althusserian terminology, "articulated" at specific moments in time and in specific places.[65] Race is never autonomous but joins a host of disciplines, such as law, education, entertainment, and culture. Race penetrates unevenly, even within a particular social formation. Race overlaps, works alongside, and/or emerges in contingent relation to other categories of identity such as gender, sexuality, and class.[66] A full analysis of race thus asks, "What are the specific conditions which make this form of distinction socially pertinent, historically active?" and what concrete historical "work" does racism perform?[67] With respect to the modernity problem and related questions of periodization, analyzing race entails asking what kind of historiographic work racism enables, and, conversely, what ideas of race shape the production of knowledge with respect to modernity, the medieval, and other notions of time.

The "medieval," from the moment of its emergence as a historical period and object of scholarly study, has been intimately tied to race. In England, for example, the discipline of Anglo-Saxon studies emerged during the nineteenth century to support happy claims about blood and soil linking northern Europeans to their ostensibly heroic Germanic ancestors. Scholars including Mary Rambaran-Olm and Ellard have tracked how early English scholars such as Benjamin Thorpe (1789–1870) and John Mitchell Kemble (1807–57) examined texts like *Beowulf* to discover a wondrous white northern European past.[68] Inside and outside the academy, racial ideas of white medieval ancestry would persist into the twentieth century and beyond. For example, in her wide-ranging study of Réunionnais-born scholar Joseph Bédier (1864–1938), Michelle Warren describes how the singularly influential French medievalist strove to reconcile contradictions pertaining to his "creole" status by promoting racial and national ideas of medieval heritage as found in a "culturally pure and Francocentric" text like the *Song of Roland*.[69] And Adam Miyashiro has described how U.S. historian and Medieval Academy president Lynn White (1907–87) asserted in a 1965 essay links between the American Wild West and medieval Europe to promote a discourse of "American modernity and exceptionalism."[70] A still more recent example of a racializing academic medievalism appears in Rambaran-Olm's account of how, in a 1985 essay, Michael Lapidge (b. 1942) supports "Western notions of superiority" and rejects "scholarship highlighting" non-western influences on early England because they are "outside the framework of Eurocentrism" he espouses.[71] Warren, Miyashiro, Rambaran-Olm, and other scholars demonstrate how insidious heritage elements of white academic medievalist practice are complexly "intertwined with the global colonial" and racializing project, a program that includes the recent violent medievalisms on the part of the far right.[72]

The medieval is a particularly unstable signifier when it comes to the intersection of its racializing and affective dimensions. While, as the previous examples affirm, white conservative academics and extremist groups have invoked the medieval for their own feel-good white supremacist ends, other hegemonic authorities deploy the medieval to denigrate, control, and oppress those they deem other. Instead of fantasies about heritage essences shared with medieval forebears, such claims hinge on myths about a "spirit" essential to whites that enables their advancement from a benighted medieval past to a shining modernity. At least since the eighteenth century, white western elites have used the term "medieval" to "deny coevalness" (that is, modernity) to those whom they sought to colonize, enslave, and/or exterminate.[73] Ideas of a medieval-modern divide and related notions of stadial progression, human maturation, and other schemas of periodization have legitimated colonization, enslavement, and genocide. Kathleen Davis, focusing specifically on modern imperialism, has led the way in identifying and analyzing such invocations of the medieval as "one of colonialism's most cherished stories."[74] Davis and other scholars, such as Nadia Altschul, demonstrate how western agents gained legitimacy by constructing themselves as fully modern—having moved on from an atavistic medieval past—and representing non-western persons as mired in a medieval or primitive temporality.[75] Focusing on the colonial sphere, Ananya Jahanara Kabir analyzes instances of that practice in British representations of India. Her examples include an education manual that contrasts a singularly learned Britain with the "stalled movement" or "barely improved" positioning of Hindus and Muslims, and Scottish missionary Alexander Duff's claim that "arguing with the Brahmins, you find yourself transported back to the days of European darkness" and scholastic "fine-spun distinctions."[76] Turning to France and "the *mission civilisatrice* that drove French colonial ideology for much of the nineteenth and early twentieth centuries," Michelle Warren describes how "French anthropologists" went so far as "to prove morphological similarities between contemporary Africans and medieval Europeans (to the detriment of both groups)."[77] And, in the case of the Atlantic slave trade, Simon Gikandi relates how, by the end of the seventeenth century, Europeans began to construct Africans as objects of enslavement by rendering them members of "an imaginary culture of the Middle Ages."[78] In the colonial discourse in which "the African unmodern came to operate under the sign of medievalism," Gikandi explains, "European agents on the so-called Africa gold and slave coasts" widely used descriptors identical to those deployed by Jacob Burckhardt, the hugely influential Swiss historian who associated medieval Europeans with "superstition, childishness, [and] despotism."[79]

From roughly 1870 to 1920, white westerners marshaled the full force of Enlightenment disciplines—for instance, natural philosophy, new biology, anthropology, linguistics, and philology—to articulate unabashedly racist claims about primitive or "medieval" others. Those western "experts" used modern methods—science—to proclaim their white supremacy and deny coevalness to racialized others. But the explicitly racist use of phrenology, eugenics, and other sciences foundered over time, especially in the wake of World War II. Critiques of those racializing sciences were of long stead, particularly "in the writings of those stereotyped by the sciences of the day."[80] But the Holocaust—a genocide that took place in the heart of Europe—prompted official rejections on a global scale. Echoing Frederick Douglass's claims about the "absurdity" of craniology a hundred years earlier, a 1950 UNESCO statement affirmed that "'race' is . . . a social myth."[81] As a result of their overt grounding in white supremacy, academic fields like craniology and anthropometry were no longer loci of pride but rather became sources of embarrassment, ridicule, and condemnation. Scientific racism—and, in certain white circles, any explicit statement of white supremacy, even uttering the word "race"—became anathema.

This shift marks yet another conjunction of modernity, medievalism, and race in addition to western denigrations of contemporary others as medieval and ancestral myths celebrating medieval origins. By the mid-twentieth century, racism had itself become an object of a periodizing knowledge. Instead of celebrating their premodern forebears or denigrating racialized others as primitive, moderns now rejected racism as backward. Racism, in effect, became medieval.

Douglass, who, as we have seen, anticipated critiques of scientific racism by a century, also adumbrated associations of the medieval with racism. In *My Bondage and My Freedom* (1855), the second of three autobiographies he would write, Douglass cannily critiques slave plantations as medieval and backward. Exemplifying what Matthew Vernon describes as "the potency of the Middle Ages as a metaphor used to understand American mythologies of race," Douglass compares the plantation owned by one-time Maryland governor Edward Lloyd (1779–1834) to "the baronial domains . . . during the middle ages in Europe."[82] Douglass continues, "Grim, cold, and unapproachable by all genial influences from communities without, *there it stands*; full three hundred years behind the age, in all that relates to humanity and morals."[83] Southern plantations have long been associated with feudalism. But Douglass offers an ingeniously antiracist version of that trend. By describing how the plantation South is medieval in its racism, Douglass upends white efforts to demonize non-western persons as unmodern.

For those who still understand modernity as progress, phenomena like slavery and scientific racism figure as aberrant primitivisms—that is, as instances of a regrettable medieval atavism that bears little relation to the generally progressive nature of humans' achievements since at least the sixteenth century. An example of this view emerged in the aftermath of the January 6, 2021, attack on the U.S. Capitol. Perpetrators included white supremacist rioters who were tattooed with Norse symbols and had donned Viking garb, evincing a right extremist love of the medieval.[84] While the far-right attackers embraced their white medieval "roots," others condemned the episode *as* medieval. A police officer present during the attack called on the received equation of the medieval with barbarism when he reported that it was "like something from a medieval battle."[85] Even the newly elected U.S. president, Joe Biden, reiterated the stereotype when he described how "law enforcement officers were subject to the medieval hell."[86]

Whiteness and a *longue durée* of Race

Comments like those of Biden and the policeman exemplify a tendency to use the medieval to separate white supremacist discourse from the overall structure of contemporary U.S. life, which has presumably moved on and transcended racism. But, as thinkers located within and without the West have demonstrated, racism has a complex relation to history that makes it as entangled with the modern as it is linked to the medieval. Nancy Leys Stepan and Sander Gilman's critique of the supposed aberrance of scientific racism is instructive. Often scientific racism is called a pseudoscience, a label that reflects received ideas about the universality of science as *"the* nonpolitical, unbiased arena of knowledge" in modernity. But the very concept of value neutrality was itself "a social outcome of a process whereby science was historically and materially constituted to have certain meanings, functions and interests." The "complex series of innovations" that gave rise to "science's epistemological claims"—like those of other modern professions like law, medicine, and academia—entailed a host of phenomena including the politics of class, gender, and race.[87] Many—if not most—modern epistemologies and practices, including science, have been "inherently political" from the point of their emergence to the present day.[88]

Discerning the politics of ostensibly fair and objective elements of modern life requires shifting attention from explicit instances of racism (or sexism, ablism, etc.) to how the *totality* of modern social forms serve a *particular* construction of human identity. In other words, a full account of race in modernity necessitates attention to whiteness. By whiteness, I refer not just to white skin and ideas of biological inheritance but also to what Ahmed calls "the skin of the social"—that is, a systemic practice of world-building that takes place on behalf of, and thus is oriented toward, a certain group of persons.[89] Hall clarifies how whiteness embeds race at the center of modernity by querying the West's "transcendental claims to speak for everyone, while being itself everywhere and nowhere" and embracing identities "predicated on difference and diversity" and situated specifically in space and time.[90] The critical attention to whiteness that Hall helped inaugurate moves beyond identifying Manichean binaries to adopting a larger view on the totality or "world" to which they contribute. That wider framework recognizes how essentializing chains of semantic opposition and equivalence are woven into a discursive whole oriented around an unrecognized white location, from which pseudo-facts about the nature of the world are identified and manipulated. Whiteness, as a discursive world or cosmos, organizes itself on behalf of the figure at the hidden center of that totality (usually an elite, heterosexual western male), whom it elevates as an arbiter of a normative and universal humanity. Whiteness thus refers to how western culture, in all its nuances, contradictions, and twists, serves white privilege and empowerment in social, political, and cultural life. Whiteness empowers only certain groups as fully human while disempowering others and delimiting them within the boundaries of certain sites within that white world.

Analyses of whiteness locate a despicable and dangerous irrationality at the core of modern forms of cognition—the ludicrous and offensive notion that certain humans aren't fully human or aren't human at all—that upends its self-misrecognition as universal, objective, and just. These studies show how racist discourses, along with abhorrent practices such as genocide, settler colonialism, and chattel slavery, are not marginal but central to the emergence of modernity. As the invaluable work generated by theorists including Hall, Cheryl Harris, Saidiya Hartman, Spillers, and others affirms, whiteness subtends and organizes the institutions that define modernity in the West.[91] The dominance of whiteness clarifies how racism is not a backward "medieval" belief with which moderns have finally done away but rather is embedded everywhere in the West in its economic, academic, and other social spheres, as well as in the discourses that support them. In Gikandi's words, "That a powerful racial ideology was central to the theories and practices of modernity is not in doubt."[92]

Modernity is thoroughly bound up with race. Yet the intimate connection between modernity and race doesn't remove the medieval from the equation. To chart the meaning of race across 1500 CE, one must jettison the stubbornly persistent narrative of historical rupture.[93] This work is already well underway. For decades, scholars working in both medieval studies and later periods have amassed evidence charting a *longue durée* of race that overturns arguments about a medieval-modern divide. Their work analyzes both medieval practices of colonization, anti-Jewishness, and racism and the white dehumanizing discourses that perpetrators used to authorize those reprehensible acts against fellow human beings. With respect to the latter discursive phenomenon, a multitude of cognitive dichotomies—good over evil, civilized over savage, beautiful over ugly, high over low, white over Black, and more—were deployed in specific ways at different times and in different places in the medieval West to dehumanize, reject, and attack non-Christian and other marginalized groups. Fanon famously wrote that the modern image of the Black man is "woven out of a thousand details, anecdotes, and stories," and, as medievalist Robert Sturges affirms, medieval texts "must be included among those details and stories."[94] In a more intersectional register, representations of "the black woman warrior" as, in de Weever's words, "giant, monster, wild woman, and vice, all rolled into one" in texts produced as early as the twelfth century support discursive patterns that are taken up and repurposed in modern constructions of Indigenous American, African, and other non-western persons who lived under the sign of woman.[95] As Richard Sévère avers, the "evidence of medieval racism" uncovered by medievalists is, in a word, "overwhelming."[96] Taken together, this important and growing body of scholarship on race makes clear that while, as Heng puts it, "the *grand récit* of Western temporality" understands the Middle Ages as "a politically unintelligible time, because it lacks the signifying apparatus expressive of, and witnessing modernity," the opposite is actually the case.[97]

Ultimately, scholarship on medieval race makes visible what Heng describes as "that strange creature who is nowhere yet everywhere in cultural discourse:

the white Christian European in medieval time."[98] And that construction of the human at the heart of medieval western culture—that is, the white, heterosexual, Christian, aristocratic, able-bodied man—is, unquestionably, all too akin to the "human" at the center of western modernity. The modern white idea of the human and the modern demonization of persons as less-than human or nonhuman are intimately connected to medieval discourses and practices. As Bruno Latour should have put it, "we" (that is, white Europeans) have always been modern.

To examine the racializing white concepts and projects that cross over and muddy the lines dividing the medieval and the modern in the West, I will often refer to those periods in their most basic terms—that is, as pragmatic temporal markers, not as signifiers of social and cultural formations. "Modernity" in this book thus often signals only a period that begins roughly around 1500 CE and continues up to the current moment, while the "medieval" refers only to the years 500–1500 CE.[99] My definition of modernity as a basic temporal designator may seem retrograde. For one thing, it ignores the sorts of Enlightenment and post-Enlightenment processes—economic, political, cultural—widely identified as hallmarks of the modern. I don't mean to underestimate the differences between modernity and the medieval. To be sure, a modern "now" is distinguished from a medieval western "then" with respect to phenomena such as industrialization, information technologies, travel, capitalism, and politics. And there is no denying that the massive scale of horrors such as the Holocaust, the genocide of Indigenous Americans, and the African slave trade sets modern racism apart from medieval European counterparts. Moreover, racializing practices indisputably are themselves heterogeneous; they involve articulations and conjunctures that differ over time and space. Racism is a messy and variegated affair. My project rejects any reification of the term "white" and affirms, with Kao, that "whiteness is not a thing but an operation" whose workings are not inevitable.[100] This project is not calling for a renewed lachrymal history. And finally, my critical attention to how offensive western misconceptions about persons bridge the medieval and modern eras is not meant to deny or negate the multitude of other discursive formations and practices enacted in various places and at various times.[101] To turn to an oft-debated example for medievalists, to link Dante to a long history of othering, as Said does in *Orientalism* (1978) isn't to deny how "Islam is inside from the start" of the West or to occlude the ethical interactions that have taken place between others over time.[102]

Alongside all those exceptions, though, there exists a damaging and oppressive white through line that binds the medieval and the modern West. Modernity is a rupture, to be sure, but the manifold new guises of modernity also possess deep political dimensions that are aligned with white medieval biases. Horrific medieval practices—for instance, pogroms, expulsions, colonization, and crusades—were legitimized via white totalizing systems whose dynamics persist in the white discourses studied by Hall, Ahmed, and many other theorists and thinkers. This book confronts how offensive white western "knowledges" generated and oppressions performed after 1500 CE didn't break from but rather continued and elaborated prior racializing actions and mentalities. I contend that manifold benefits accrue to not letting go or getting over a long history of racism and enacting an affectively negative or melancholic confrontation with it.

The Benefits of a Killjoy Historicism,

The feel-bad approach to academic study I advocate is not new to the humanities. A case in point is the new American studies. Since the 1980s, Americanists have incorporated critical theory and identity politics into their work in ways that have redefined the discipline, shifting it from a celebratory stance to a far more critical attitude toward U.S. literature and culture. As Robyn Wiegman puts it, the new American studies' "practice of critique" bespeaks a "disidentification" with both the prior generation of Cold War practitioners of American studies and "the primary object of its field, 'America.'"[103] While Americanists often understood themselves as participants in a national, even patriotic, project, the New Americanists turn from supporting ideologies of American exceptionalism to indicting the crimes that premise and are cloaked by such nationalist claims.

Medieval studies, too, has had its share of feel-bad practitioners, at least since the arrival of work by second-wave feminists in the '80s and the publication of R. I. Moore's Weberian take on high medieval institutions, *The Formation of a Persecuting Society* (1987). An ethical investment in telling the history of marginalized persons and groups has prompted a critical assessment of hegemonic structures (such as monarchies or the Christian church) and agents (such as emperors, princes, popes, preachers, burghers, and mobs), along with the negative feelings, such as repulsion and dismay, to which such analyses give rise. Miri Rubin tracks the "horrible violence" wrought during the 1389 pogrom in Prague; Peter Haidu calls "profoundly repugnant" the "religious absolutism" at play in the *Song of Roland*; and Jo Ann McNamara describes how the high medieval "fus[ion of] personhood with manhood . . . was a tragedy for women," anyone deemed less-than masculine, and "the psychologically maimed creatures the system produced."[104]

The negative turn in American studies, medieval studies, and other disciplines is not singular and monolithic. On occasion, however, tight overlaps emerge. A case in point is medievalist and New Americanist scholarship on the medievalisms that have authorized racism in the U.S. South. More broadly, much of the scholarship by medievalists, New Americanists, and other "feel-bad" academics is united by its imbrication of negative sentiment with an optimistic investment in progressive politics. Whether their object of inquiry is, say, an emerging separate-sphere discourse in thirteenth-century England or the plight of the citizen under late capitalism in the U.S., scholars combine a hatred for and critical assessment of oppressive structures with a desire and hope for social justice.

That scholarly binding of affect and ethics has not been welcomed on all fronts. In the case of medieval and American studies, certain scholars reject methodologies they label reductive and anti-intellectual. American studies practitioners claim that New Americanists witness a "hatred for America so visceral" that, for them, "American history" is "a highlight film of outrages" in which virtually "nothing makes [America] great."[105] And medievalists warn both that "critical work that tends to particularly invoke a strident emotional vocabulary in the pursuit of its ethical positions" risks undoing "our scholarly subject" altogether by "reducing the text under study to a type of historical hate crime," and that the overall "affective turn in medieval studies" has "come at the cost of a creeping anti-intellectualism."[106] Such critiques reflect a more widespread sense that emotionally charged and politically driven scholarship occludes the richness, depth, and complexity of the object of study.

Often such complaints are issued by defenders of hegemonic field formations who implicitly or explicitly contrast what they see as an emotional and political anti-intellectualism with the more nuanced scholarly work made possible from their own seemingly calm, apolitical, and rational positioning. However, politics is never optional, and emotions are never separable from politics. All critics write from a subject positioning that reflects their affective allegiances with respect to identity and power. It is only when, as medievalist Tarren Andrews puts it, "scholarship overtly or covertly supports hegemonic structures" that "it is rarely classified as 'political.'" That masking of the political, Andrews continues, "has generally been the case for medieval studies, which has enjoyed the privileges of a close relationship to dominant political and cultural discourses, making it easier for some medieval studies scholars to understand their work as 'apolitical.'"[107] Similarly, while certain scholars have advocated an "Arnoldian disinterestedness" enabled by the "decentering of the political," such a yoking of the "apolitical" with detachment demonstrates how hegemonic identification permits a neutral tone.[108] Thanks to their political affiliation, scholars aligned with the power elite enjoy the comfort of knowing that their field of study is as it "should be"—that is, oriented around and organized on behalf of dominance. The hegemonic scholar can identify nuances and contradictions in a calm manner because those complexities ultimately support a larger totalizing structure in which that white scholar is centered. One of the aims of this project is to dislodge whiteness from its privileged centrality and shift white readers who enjoy a position of acritical comfort regarding medieval anglophone culture (for instance, Euro-American, white, male, heterosexual, Christian, and/or elite readers) to a position of productive discomfort. If white scholarship has all too often been premised on beliefs in the universality, objectivity, and thus invisibility of whiteness, this book endeavors to attack and undo those white assumptions, including my own.[109]

Bad Medievalism seeks to unsettle whiteness by engaging work by scholars situated both inside and outside the western hegemonic formations. Those scholars haven't cornered the market on ugly feelings (witness the outrage of white conservative academics at left-leaning methodologies). But they also exhibit how negative sentiments like anger, sorrow, disgust, and horror can contribute to critical disidentifications with dominant politics. Those intellectuals have leveraged brilliant analyses and critiques of modernity. Indeed, as Barbara Christian puts in a withering take-down of white "neutral humanist" advocates of theory in the 1980s, members of the Black diaspora "have survived . . . the assault on our bodies, social institutions, countries, our very humanity" via an acute "theorizing" that is "dynamic rather than fixed."[110] More recently, and with respect to the particular example of Black studies, Weheliye affirms how the field "represents a substantial critique of western modernity and a sizeable archive of social, political, and cultural alternatives."[111] Weheliye singles out Wynter and Spillers as hallmarks of how "black feminism" has "sustained African American cultural theory at the same time as it has grounded the institutional existence of black studies for the last few decades."[112] In keeping with the insights of Weheliye, Christian, and other scholars, this book honors and engages the insights of persons situated at a remove from white supremacy—and thus uniquely poised to critique, resist, and even annihilate the white subject served by western discourse. My intent is not to essentialize those scholars as figures grounded in a fixed and privileged standpoint (which would reify the Enlightenment autonomous self) but rather to engage the critiques made available from their fraught, dialectical, and critical relation to dominant formations like the West.

I refer here not only to work in Black studies or in other fields centered on non-western populations (like postcolonial studies, Indigenous studies, and Latinx studies) but also to scholarship by persons, including white persons, working in fields (such as Jewish studies, feminism, and queer theory) that consider persons and groups that white heteropatriarchal capitalism rejects, dehumanizes, and disempowers. That important body of work indicates how multiple advantages accrue to analyzing historical and cultural phenomena that offend and disturb. To trope on Ahmed's *The Promise of Happiness*, being a medievalist and/or modernist "killjoy" can be a good thing. For example, Love's important account of "feeling backward" with respect to queer history details the advantages of inhabiting bad feelings. Love, to be sure, acknowledges that "it might seem like a good idea to leave . . . behind . . . an identity that cannot be uncoupled from violence, suffering, and loss" (30). Queer persons, Love admits, might want to look away from a past that—embarrassingly, painfully, offensively, and depressingly—showcases homophobic representations and anti-gay historical violence. Such a rejection of a feel-bad historicism echoes similar stances assumed by other groups, such as Jewish studies scholars' critique of a "lachrymose history" of Jewish oppression and Black studies scholars' turn away from Afropessimism to an affirmation of Black joy.

However, as Love contends, in a lesbian-specific claim with implications for other marginalized groups, the feel-bad practice of "clinging to ruined identities and to histories of injury" is nevertheless important. "Moving on" from a feel-bad past to a feel-good present or feel-good future problematically can entail dismissing many aspects of the past, and especially the lives of "the most vulnerable, the least presentable, and all the dead." Though they are risky and possibly traumatic, "backward feelings serve as an index to the ruined state of the social world," including the persistence of earlier "structures of inequality" in the present (30). Love draws on literary critic D. A. Miller to stress how "important connection exists between" historical and contemporary "queer experience" (20). Love avers, in a riff on Marx, that because "the dead can bury the dead all day long and still not be done," doing "justice to the difficulties of queer experience" demands "a politics of the past" (1). Furthermore, drawing on Sedgwick's and other scholars' work on shame, Love stresses how bad feelings can "articulate 'collectivities of the shamed'" in "*salons des refusés*, where the most heterogeneous people are brought into great intimacy by their common experience of being despised and rejected in a world of norms that they now recognize as false morality" (14).

Love stresses the affiliations between a feel-bad lesbian history and other oppositional critiques that lay "bare the conditions of exclusion and inequality"

(29). That feel-bad work includes Ngai's important account of how ugly feelings "mediat[e] between the aesthetic and the political" in late modern writing and thought (3). Ngai suggests how affects like disgust "might be recuperated for critical praxis in general" and considers how negative affect can support a productively "negative thinking," which Ngai notes is "Herbert Marcuse's shorthand for ideology critique in the dialectical tradition" (8). Cheng's work on racial melancholy similarly suggests the critical benefits of bad feelings. Cheng demonstrates how racial melancholy, with its sad doublings and over-identifications, isn't so much a disease but rather a generatively feel-bad "disease of location" and memory. Such "a place of political discomfort," Cheng contends, can offer "the most intense examination of what it means to adopt a political stance."[113]

Hall's work resides within the orbit of this body of work and marks an early and invaluable delineation of a feel-bad perspective on race, modernity, and violence. For example, in "Culture, the Media, and the 'Ideological Effect'" (1977), Hall engages in a neo-Marxist, Gramscian analysis of how the various sides of the political issues debated within the British mass media are—like other aspects of the world conjured on behalf of the dominant groups—based on biased ideas of what counts as rational or irrational, reasonable or extreme.[114] Feminist literary critic Gayatri Spivak calls Hall's searing exposure of the white limits of "debates" in the British press his "fighting words," alerting us to the aggression, rage, and disgust bound up with his critique.[115] Exposing the contradictions, repressions, and particularity of a world generated on behalf of white dominance, Hall's negative critique, to trope on Fanon, "shakes the world in a very necessary manner."[116]

Scholarship by both self-avowed Afropessimists such as Jared Sexton, Calvin Warren, Frank Wilderson, and David Marriott and Black feminists such as Hartman, Harris, Nash, and Spillers takes up a version of Hall's world-shaking confrontation with a totalizing society structured in dominance.[117] Those scholars stress how an effective and honest critical methodology cannot simply take up and reformulate received western ideas of betterment and progress. Warren, for example, queries positive "humanist affect (the good feeling we get from hopeful solutions)," since those good feelings "will not translate into freedom, justice, recognition, or resolution."[118] Identifying the foundational role of racism in modern worldmaking, this work replaces notions of progress with wrenching narratives of "innovations" that perpetuate earlier and more overt strategies of dehumanization. As this work affirms, as long as the modern world is premised on white formations—formations that reject alternate views as irrational even as they themselves endorse irrational racisms—"progress" is impossible.

Diasporic Literature, and a Transformative Politics of Representation

> Thus the ethical situation can only be figured in the ethical experience of the impossible. And literature, as a play of figures, can give us imaginative access to the experience.
> —GAYATRI SPIVAK, "THINKING CULTURAL QUESTIONS IN 'PURE' LITERARY TERMS"

My engagement with scholarship by Afropessimists and other critics, in part, involves a new temporal orientation and scope. Often such feel-bad work limits itself to a post-1500 CE historical purview. For example, Afropessimists like Wilderson premise their critiques on the centrality of the Atlantic slave trade (and thus the social death of Africans) to the birth of modernity.[119] And scholars like Hartman and Harris redefine post-"emancipation" history by charting the systematic exclusions that perpetuate racism. In contrast, I direct my critical pessimism to the worlds structured in white dominance not just after but also before 1500 CE. While the years after watershed modern events demand a negative assessment, so too does premodernity itself require reexamination along pessimistic lines. Confining one's object of study to modernity means remaining within its temporal politics; a fuller critique necessitates jettisoning that period division and looking at the other side of 1500 CE.

Crucially, though, this book does more than confront a *longue durée* of white supremacy. Alongside its pessimism, *Bad Medievalism* recognizes the critical agency and intellectual achievements of figures like the scholars covered in the previous section. Even the Afropessimists, for all their claims about white ideas of Black nonbeing and objecthood, at some level defy whiteness through their very scholarship. While the message of figures such as Wilderson and Calvin Warren is bleak in the extreme, their own critical brilliance and stunning academic interventions are cause for a certain celebration.

This book also extends its admiration of feel-bad writing beyond academic pieces to literary texts by persons who, "by historical definition, not essence, relate differently or obliquely to" modernity and the West.[120] While the hermeneutic encounter with a literary text can of course support hegemonic affects and allegiances, the literary also holds transformative potential. In the same piece where she recounts the "comfort" she finds in Hall's "fighting words," Spivak asserts that "rhetorical reading practices ... can be an ethical motor that undermines the [white] ideological field."[121] Through a reading of Antiguan-American novelist Jamaica Kincaid's *Lucy*, Spivak demonstrates how "literature, as a play of figures, can give us imaginative access to the experience" of different discursive worlds, containing rich and complex alternatives to received ideas of identity and society.[122] Like Spivak, Felski also embraces what is singularly literary, but in the "context" of an actor-network theory–driven essay with important implications for periodization. Contra those who "cast [literary texts] into coffinlike containers called periods"—such as the Middle Ages or modernity—Felski advocates a close, respectful, and attentive engagement with "texts" as entities that "have things to say on questions that matter."[123] Indeed, she continues, careful attention to the literary can generate new knowledge, information that "mess[es] up the tidiness of our periodizing schemes, forcing us to acknowledge affinity and proximity alongside difference, to grapple with the coevalness and connectedness of past and present."[124] Spivak and Felski each urge a hermeneutic practice driven not by preestablished "facts" about the nature of identities, periods, etc. but rather by individual literary texts as wellsprings of new information and modes of understanding.

Spivak, Felski, and other like-minded critics identify a means of enacting, through literature and literary studies, the kind of critical and generative work called for by pessimistic theorists. Certainly, the very totalizing scale of white modernity radically frustrates both the project of eradicating it and the effort to replace it with any sort of alternative. Nash, in a discussion of the resonances that link Afropessimism and dominant feminism, clarifies the monumental and even apocalyptic work called for by their feel-bad criticism, stating that "both theories—in their totalising conceptions of the world—remind us that nothing short of the destruction of the universe will facilitate something closer to what we might call freedom."[125] How can one, to cite Audre Lorde, "dismantle . . . the master's house" when the master's home possesses worldly or even universal dimensions?[126] The sociopolitical task is overwhelming. Yet one can also "believe," with Spivak, "in an irrational, utopian, and impractical way," that literary texts hold the potential to perform a different politics of representation. Questions of aesthetics can support strategies of resistance.[127]

The final chapters of this book closely engage two such transformative texts, each penned by a Black U.S. writer: *Bailey's Cafe*, a 1992 novel by Gloria Naylor (1950–2016), and *The Fisher King*, a 2000 novel by Paule Marshall (1929–2019). I closely engage each text for the particular lessons it offers on questions of periodization and race. *Bailey's Cafe* and *The Fisher King* brilliantly revise hegemonic worldviews. In lieu of feel-good myths of white supremacy, these novels lay bare the difficult positioning of their Black characters in a white world order. At the same time, Naylor and Marshall rewrite the world as it appears from the vantage point of Black persons who embody a complex, heterogeneous, and contingent humanity, an identity unloosed from dominant ideas of history and personhood. Crucially, for my purposes, both works engage the medieval roots of the white world order they upend. *Bailey's Cafe* responds to the *Canterbury Tales* and *The Fisher King* responds to medieval grail lore. Naylor and Marshall explode the white discursive worlds manifested by medieval texts, repurposing fragments of those premodern western works for distinctively transformative and complex diasporic ends.

Chapter Overview

Part I, "White Mythologies of History," analyzes the politics of scholarly emotion in work on modernity and the Middle Ages. After highlighting Eurocentric conceptions of modernity and the medieval by dominant white scholars, I engage major reconsiderations of periodization by intellectuals historically located within the racial zones demarcated by whiteness. Drawing especially on the work of W. E. B. Du Bois and Sylvia Wynter, the second chapter addresses both the feel and import of history before and after c. 1500 and clarifies how white understandings of the medieval-modern divide not only have supported damaging and offensive constructions of human identity but also betray the medieval roots of modern racism.

Chapter 1, "Modernity, the Medieval, and the Feel of Periodization," tracks the white feelings central to some of the most influential western theories of modernity and periodization penned over the last two centuries. Insofar as whiteness, especially for whites, is hard to grasp due to the invisibility bestowed upon it by its identification with the universal and normative, attending to the emotional import of Eurocentric historicisms assists in visualizing its white contours. Their distinctive affects expose the particularity of white historians. I contend that serious analysis of the white feel of modernity necessitates attention to its constitutive other, the Middle Ages. Examining theories of modernity by critics including Jacob Burckhardt, Karl Marx, and Fredric Jameson, I track how the fixation with relevance that runs through their analyses—that is, what Margreta de Grazia describes as "a massive value judgment, determining what matters and what does not"—is fueled via its opposition to a quiescent medieval past.[128] For white European and U.S. modernists, cathexis to modernity as an object of fascination—a cause for excitement, fear, hope, love, and alarm—hinges on ideas of medieval outmodedness that provide the present with its pertinence. Then, turning to major interpretations of periodization by white medievalists, I track how their abiding attachment to western modernity—whether as an object of ardent affirmation or equally fervent negation—circumscribes the feel and politics of their medievalisms. From the modernist nostalgia of Johan Huizinga and Caroline Bynum to the proto-modernizing claims about the medieval asserted by Charles Haskins and his inheritors, white medievalists frequently work within the same affective trajectory adopted by their modern studies counterparts. Medievalists often confine their inquiry to a rebuttal of their field's denigration by scholars of modernity. Seeking nothing more than an inversion of the status quo, medievalists prove only capable of understanding their object of study in positive terms, as a worthy object of admiration and even love.

Chapter 2, "'Between Then and Now': The Veil of Periodization," engages the acute and abidingly pessimistic assessments of modernity penned by academics complexly positioned both inside and outside the West. Thinkers such as W. E. B. Du Bois, Paul Gilroy, and Sylvia Wynter expose the mutual constitution of modernity with settler colonialism, chattel slavery, and other abhorrent crimes against humanity and the planet. Moreover, their work offers a uniquely compelling means of problematizing the received modes of periodization outlined in Chapter 1. Taking Du Bois's foundational metaphor for racism—the veil—as my touchstone, I reassess periodization, arguing that the specifically temporal implications of the veil shed light on a host of denials of coevalness that undo the idea of a medieval-modern divide, especially as it appears in Burckhardt's influential formulation. In keeping with its touchstone, Du Bois's dialectics of the veil, this chapter traces a dialectical path that moves from the whiteness of canonical medieval texts by Geoffrey Chaucer and Thomas Malory, to the medieval Christian antisemitic veil, and finally to Saul/Paul and the "spirit" of European modernity.

Part II, "Tolkien vs. Hall: White Heritage Fantasy and Diasporic Critique," turns to the instance of academic gatekeeping at the core of this book, insofar as it encapsulates the deleterious effects of a white "feel-good" medievalism: the moment in 1954 when Stuart Hall experienced how modernity, medievalism, and racism could collide in modern life.

Chapter 3, "Whiteness, Medievalism, Immigration: Rethinking Tolkien through Stuart Hall," unpacks the multiple linkages at play in the conjuncture articulated in the Tolkien-Hall encounter. My contextualization of Tolkien's actions includes the Oxford don's South African roots, the white politics of medieval study at Oxford, Tolkien's modernist contempt for his mechanized and globalized milieu, and the British response to the arrival of the Windrush generation in the "motherland." I argue that Tolkien's white medievalism contains his most deeply felt racist formations, which both shaped his fiction and informed his life in a university town populated by West Indian immigrants. After examining Tolkien's essentialist and nostalgic approach to medieval study, I examine how the don believed that his innate knowledge about his ancestors' language and myths enabled him to create a national mythology (that is, *The Lord of the Rings* trilogy) and how his fantasy fiction depicts its heroes' inheritance of their shared ancestral tongue and temperament. I conclude the chapter by discussing how, while Tolkien's epic fantasies may be appropriated successfully for oppositional ends, they present unique challenges for a significant component of Tolkien's readership, medievalists.

Chapter 4, "Stuart Hall's *Piers Plowman*," turns to Hall and the Langland dissertation he never wrote. Any consideration of a Hallian reading of *Piers Plowman* is necessarily speculative. Yet I contend that an imaginative recovery of that aborted project is well worth pursuing for what it reveals about both Hall and Langland, as well as related issues of race, affect, and periodization. I conjecture that, by planning to write on *Piers*, Hall might have been poised to unsettle the politics of belonging that had long informed left engagements with Langland and the English literary tradition more broadly. In much the same way that the conservative Tolkien bound medieval texts like *Beowulf* to a blood-and-soil English heroic identity, left writers and scholars claimed *Piers* on behalf of a populist Englishness defined by rebellion and working-class values. The chapter reads against the grain of Hall's body of work, revisiting his important analyses of modernity, identity, and the West with an eye to questions of periodization, the medieval, and even *Piers* itself. In a view that spans his first publication—the under-analyzed "Our Literary Heritage" (1953)— and later pieces such as "The West and the Rest" (1992), "The Spectacle of the Other" (1997), "'In but Not Of Europe'" (2002), and "Whose Heritage?" (2005), I recover Hall's marked interest in how medieval modes of othering unsettle English fantasies of heritage. The chapter then offers a hypothetical reading of Langland à la Hall, focusing on the critical account of England in Passus 15 of the B-text of *Piers*. I argue that Langland's episodic and penetrating approach to questions of social justice adumbrates (and possibly even may have prepared Hall) for his work on Englishness and difference, as well as his renowned dialectical and destabilizing methodology. At the same time, however, I postulate that a mature Hall might have critiqued *Piers* in much the same way he rejected racist and nationalist aspects of his own moment. My speculative vision of Stuart Hall's *Piers Plowman* thus ambivalently considers both a young Hall's possible attraction to and a later Hall's critical assessment of Langland.

Part III of this book, "Black Feminist Modernism, Black Feminist Medievalism," interprets the pessimistic and incisive forms of medievalism and modernism at work in two late twentieth-century novels. Gloria Naylor's *Bailey's Cafe* offers an intricate and destabilizing representation of Black identity, gender, and sexuality in twentieth-century sites within and without the U.S. prior to the civil rights movement. Paule Marshall's *The Fisher King* is a compact and deeply intertextual portrayal of the fraught identities and relationships of the transnational family to which an eight-year-old boy belongs. In each work, Naylor and Marshall critique and unsettle the white politics of the *Canterbury Tales* and *Le Morte Darthur*, two canonical Middle English texts I discuss in Chapter 2.

Chapter 5, "High Theory, Low Feelings: Gloria Naylor's *Bailey's Cafe*," recovers the poststructuralist dimensions of both Naylor's vision of modernity and her revision of the medieval in *Bailey's Cafe*. I argue that a full appreciation of the politics of representation in that novel requires attending to Naylor's academic affiliations and especially her ties to "high theory." In *Bailey's*, Naylor puts deconstruction into conversation with Black feminism to masterfully contest Chaucer via the alternate Black world order represented in the novel. This chapter unpacks Naylor's poststructuralist Black feminist project as it specifically emerges in the two tales that bookend *Bailey's*: that of Sadie, an elderly, indigent, and alcoholic prostitute; and that of Miss Maple/Stanley, a cross-dressing and talented man raised in privilege and isolation in California. The chapter culminates in a reading of the end of Maple/Stanley's tale, which features a tour-de-force Black poststructuralist contestation of Chaucer's General Prologue.

Chapter 6, "Tradition and the Individual Black Talent: Contesting Malory and Modernism in *The Fisher King*," concludes the book by revisiting the widely lauded diasporic modernism of Paule Marshall. I argue that *The Fisher King* contributes in crucial ways to Marshall's diasporic vision insofar as it engages her ongoing critical conversation with T. S. Eliot and his white medievalism. In interviews, Marshall had long registered how the Arthurian "red rock" of tradition embraced by Eliot served for her as a burdensome white literary tradition from which she sought liberation. In this chapter I track how, in *The Fisher King*, Marshall unsettles the white masculine politics of a text important to Eliot's notion of western tradition, Thomas Malory's *Le Morte Darthur*, through her representation of the fraught relations between a transnational group of complexly rendered Black men and women. For Marshall, like Naylor, a dark and fraught depiction of Black identity, history, and society emerges through her revolutionary response to English literary history. The chapter ends by considering how Marshall encodes in *The Fisher King* metacommentaries on the powers of Black art, including her own.

Ultimately, the linked examples of Naylor's and Marshall's novels offer multilayered arguments for pessimistic assessments of the present and the past and the crucial role of the literary in such reckonings. On one hand, both *Bailey's Cafe* and *The Fisher King* demonstrate how confronting the nefarious politics of the western canon doesn't demand jettisoning it altogether. To be sure, the dense literary workings of texts like the *Canterbury Tales* and *Le Morte*

Darthur potentially exceed any offensive and damaging content. The hermeneutic encounter with those texts might lead to new knowledge that resists western hegemonic forms. But on the other hand, much like *The Narrative of Arthur Gordon Pym* and the other early American texts analyzed by Toni Morrison in *Playing in the Dark*, Chaucer and Malory merit attention as documents of the complex dynamics of whiteness.[129] Morrison clarifies how attending to the racial intricacies of a western text, far from reducing it, opens a window onto contradiction and complexity. The *Canterbury Tales* and *Le Morte Darthur* call for close attention not as objects of a post-critical celebration but rather as the focus of searching critiques akin to those enacted by *Bailey's Cafe* and *The Fisher King*. Cognizant that, as Calvin Warren and Heather Love respectively stress, "hopeful solutions" and comforting "narratives of progress" are themselves part and parcel of the modernity problem, both *Bailey's Cafe* and *The Fisher King* evince, as Anne Anlin Cheng puts it, how the work of resistance doesn't generate a new *terra firma*, with stable identities and firm answers, but rather opens up a melancholic space devoid of "ideologies of authenticity" and stable selves.[130] Such honest, if grim and disconsolate, visions model a praxis for academic work and artistic practice that doesn't so much cancel as interrogate, thus moving, in Hall's words, from a "struggle over the relations of representation" (although such a struggle is ongoing and remains necessary) "to a politics of representation itself."[131] Both novels offer, to cite Barbara Christian, the "possibility of the integration of feeling/knowledge, rather than the split between the abstract and the emotional in which western philosophy inevitably indulged."[132] Via the acute worldmaking performed by their novels, Naylor and Marshall appropriate and transform the medieval western archive for Black feminist ends that meet the difficult challenges described by counterhegemonic scholars.

PART I
White Mythologies of History

1
Modernity, the Medieval, and the Feel of Periodization

In an important essay on Caroline Bynum's groundbreaking *Holy Feast and Holy Fast: The Religious Significance of Food to Medieval Women* (1988), Nicholas Watson discerns within medievalist scholarship an unacknowledged sentimental dimension. Watson asserts that, far from emptying their work of "irrational" feelings, scholars should explicitly engage their emotions. Embracing affect as a telling "mode of knowing" during both the past and present, Watson urges medievalists to consider the relationship between their feelings and those of medieval thinkers themselves.[1] Watson marshals as evidence his own dynamic relation to the emotional intelligence of mystics Hadewijch and Julian of Norwich, urging scholars to "devise historiographic models that are self-conscious about their incorporation of affect" (72). Benefits accrue, Watson contends, to approaching texts like Julian's *Showings* as "theoretical essays in affective historicity" (93). In the case of Watson, such an inquiry revealed to him the "shock[ing]" truth of "how far [his] approach to the past had become infused, through a sort of hermeneutic osmosis, with [Julian's] own" (93–94).

Watson links medievalist emotion to the Middle Ages by describing how medieval Christian affects and historical sensibilities spill into and shape contemporary academic feeling and historicism. Addressing his community of medievalists, he advocates "taking into ourselves . . . the full force of" a "passionate" circuitry that obtains when medievalists engage figures like mystic Richard Rolle and experience a "mingl[ing]" of desires between author, subject and reader (97). I would go further, arguing that to "think clearly," as Watson urges, "about the way all" medieval study "has emotional designs on its object" necessitates extending one's historical purview beyond the western period deemed "medieval" (61). The question of how scholars and intellectuals feel about the centuries before 1500 CE in Europe exceeds that era and ineluctably pertains to the question of *modern* affect. Namely, thanks to the nineteenth-century creation of the Middle Ages as the other of modernity (or, following Ernesto Laclau and Chantal Mouffe, its "constitutive outside"), the feel of the one period is always bound up with that of the other.[2] For both medievalists and modernists, discerning scholarly affect requires attending to both sides of the medieval-modern binary.

This chapter investigates the underappreciated role played by feelings in major theories of the Middle Ages and modernity. My focus is not the emotions that circulated during the medieval and modern eras, a topic on which both medievalists and modernists have produced an abundance of crucial work.[3] Neither am I primarily concerned in this chapter with popular and artistic engagements with those two periods.[4] Rather, my concern is how major medievalists and scholars of modernity feel about both their object of study and the medieval-modern binary. How a scholar feels—or seeks to feel—about their object of inquiry comprises an important impetus for the scope, aims, methods, and outcomes of academic work. Emotions play a key role in, for example, strategies of scholarly persuasion, authorial orientations, and the discourses—racial, gendered, national, colonial—a scholar seeks to support or resist.

The converse is true, as well. That is, just as one can learn a good deal about scholarly affect by looking at periodization, one can also learn much about periodization by considering academic feeling. It is now a widely acknowledged truism, with roots that extend at least to the work of Edward Said and Johannes Fabian, that social and geopolitical inequalities are authorized via "knowledge" about historical categories.[5] But less understood is how the politics of time functions through all sorts of emotions. Attending to feelings helps clarify the stakes of periodization and its long-standing allure—that is, how claims about the medieval-modern relation deform and misrepresent history, persons, and places, even as they succeed in "hooking" (that is, cultivating attachment from) academics and non-academics alike.[6] Moreover, juxtaposing the emotional investments of scholars of modernity *and* scholars of the Middle Ages offers an important means of grasping how profoundly those periods are conceptually and politically entangled. For example, and as I demonstrate in further detail in this chapter, a Eurocentric investment in and/or anxiety over the status accorded modernity has long governed how white medievalists feel about their period. And, as Chapter 2 will explore, a willingness to feel the "worst" about the West (that is, Western modernity) can shed light onto disturbing ties connecting either side of 1500 CE, ties that encompass, but are not limited to, the very opposition of a modern era of progress and a time of "medieval" backwardness.

This chapter considers scholarship on periodization by northern European and U.S. academics who have enjoyed considerable prestige and influence in scholarly circles and beyond since the mid-nineteenth century. Space precludes me from anything approaching a comprehensive survey; what follows is a necessarily incomplete and somewhat idiosyncratic genealogy. Most notably, this chapter concerns, by and large, white men, hailing from Europe and former European colonies, who have long enjoyed prominence in academia. I aim through this focus to contribute to the necessary project of critiquing the patriarchal white formations that have dominated the academy and still exert widespread influence. Just as modernity has long been understood as the provenance of white men, so too have understandings of the medieval and periodization been dominated by, in Mary Rambaran-Olm's words, "white men grounded in classical and/or Christian learning."[7] By specifically attending to the *feel* of those scholars' claims about periodization, I follow Richard Dyer in stressing how "mak[ing] sense of white people" entails both the "cerebral" meaning of "sense" and "the full affective, sensuous weight of the word."[8] To dislodge whiteness from invisibility demands tracking white affects. As Dyer contends, in an observation that clearly applies to white academia, "absence of affect" comprises "the essence of the aspiration of whiteness."[9] But, as we shall see, white scholarship on modernity and the Middle Ages is far from a purely cerebral and unsentimental matter and instead engages palpable structures of feeling.

This is not to say, however, that only white male academics are implicated in the patterns of scholarly feeling I analyze. Thanks partly to their dominance of and influence within scholarship, those scholars' affective formations exceed them. As my inclusion of Bynum in this chapter and my discussion of white feminist medievalists in Chapter 5 indicate, white female (and feminist) academics—and even other persons aligned with different identity categories—have participated in the trend I trace. In other words, it behooves all scholars to ponder just how much their feelings about their object of study reflexively assume a feel-good turn, thanks to long-standing white constructions of modernity and its denigrated medieval other.

The remainder of this chapter moves, diptych-like, from considering how scholars of modernity feel about both their object of study and the medieval to examining medievalist affect vis-à-vis the Middle Ages and modernity. My modernists are Jacob Burckhardt (1818–97), Stephen Greenblatt (b. 1943), Karl Marx (1818–83), Marshall Berman (1940–2013), and Fredric Jameson (1934–2024). As we shall see, those critics adopt complex and heterogeneous sentiments toward the years after 1500 CE. Burckhardt hails modernity as the time when European men first activated their rich potential as human agents capable of perfecting themselves and the world around them. Burckhardt's inheritor, Greenblatt, shares that view in his most public-facing work, and even Burckhardt's contemporary Marx maintains a certain faith in the progress of mankind. Berman occupies more of a middle ground insofar as he highlights the wonders *and* failures wrought by modern men, even as he shares with Burckhardt a celebratory outlook toward the expansive intellects of great modern thinkers like Marx and Nietzsche. Jameson, in contrast, follows feel-bad theorists like Max Weber (1864–1920) and Michel Foucault (1926–84) in asserting the vast and totalizing reach of capitalist oppression in the West.

For all their differences, these writers all agree on one claim: the Middle Ages are fundamentally opposed and thus completely irrelevant to their period of study. Scholars from Burckhardt to Jameson understand the medieval era as a superstitious and enchanted time devoid of the rationality, secularism, and ideas of progress that, for better or for worse, encapsulate modernity. The utter alterity of the medieval proves attractive as a means of delineating the nuances, contours, and contradictions of the modern; but it also fixes 500–1500 CE in Europe as always already "medieval" (backward, superstitious), a known quantity whose defining feature is its sheer inconsequence. Thus, while affective attachment toward the pressing pertinence of their moment prompts scholars of modernity to assess the merits and problems of modernity, their belief in the complete irrelevance of an irrational and enchanted medieval era to the now—to the present—licenses a detachment so complete as to preclude serious intellectual inquiry altogether.

The chapter then turns to medievalists, including Johan Huizinga (1872–1945), Charles Homer Haskins (1870–1937), Richard Southern (1912–2001), James Simpson (b. 1954), and Watson's focus, Bynum (b. 1941). I contend that a full assessment of those medievalists also demands broaching them as modernists—that is, as figures caught up in a western historical discourse in which the meaning of their object of inquiry, the years in Europe between 500 and 1500 CE, necessarily hinges on its relation to the category of "modernity." As a result, those medievalists share with their modernist counterparts a vested interest in just what modernity entails. Like white theorists of the modern, white medievalists manifest toward modernity a variety of sentiments. Some of them—for example, Haskins and Southern—share with Burckhardt and his inheritors a celebratory stance toward modernity as a time that liberated human potential. Other scholars, such as Huizinga, Bynum, and Simpson, adopt a more pessimistic take on modern life.

Those medievalist scholars' investment in modernity prompts them to echo not only white modernists' vacillating affects toward the modern but also modernists' one-dimensional understanding of the medieval. The only difference between the unvarying understanding of the medieval adopted by scholars of modernity and scholars of the Middle Ages is the substitution of derogatory dismissal with celebratory rescue. In other words, the endorsement of received narratives of temporality by medievalists traps them into a circumscribed intellectual purview regarding their own object of study. As a result, while scholars of modernity prove capable of critique when it comes to their period and medievalists as well prove capable of critique with respect to modernity, the latter group often finds it hard to critically consider—in affective terms, feel badly about—their own medieval object of scholarly inquiry. On the contrary, the insistent othering of the medieval by moderns prompts an equally unrelenting effort to discover praiseworthy aspects of 500–1500 CE and save their period of study from irrelevance and disregard.[10]

In short, modernists and medievalists both remain passionately attached to western ideas of periodization. Regardless of whether they love it or hate it, those scholars are deeply invested in the concept of "modernity" as a historical rubric. And that attachment precludes a more complete and accurate scholarly investigation. Conventional western periodicity, far from figuring as an object of critical investigation, instead shapes their analyses, thus hampering a deeper and more telling analysis of the relationship between the history of ideas and practices before and after 1500 CE. Alternate phenomena, situated outside the medieval-modern hermeneutic, including trends that crisscross the 1500 CE divide, also escape consideration.

The Reveal and the Swerve: Burckhardt, Greenblatt, and the Medieval Suppression of the Human

In his influential account of western periodization, the Swiss historian Jacob Burckhardt weaves a dramatic tale about the thrilling birth of "modern man."[11] Burckhardt opens "The Development of the Individual"—the second part of *The Civilization of the Renaissance in Italy* (1860)—by recounting how a tragically long period of dormant humanity abruptly and wondrously ended:

> In the Middle Ages both sides of human consciousness—that which was turned within as that which was turned without—lay dreaming or half awake beneath a common veil. The veil was woven of faith, illusion, and childish prepossession, through which the world and history were seen clad in strange hues. Man was conscious of himself only as member of a race, people, party, family, or corporation—only through

some general category. In Italy this veil first melted into air; an *objective* treatment and consideration of the state and of all the things of this world became possible. The *subjective* side at the same time asserted itself with corresponding emphasis; man became a spiritual *individual*, and recognized himself as such. (70, emphasis original)

Burckhardt's medieval man is tragically incapable of apprehending the earthly wonders without and the spiritual wonders within himself, thanks to his metaphorical veiling by an ideological cloth composed of colors that are strange or alien to reality. According to Burckhardt, the tremendous influence of a corporate Christian perspective on life, as well as a host of lingering primitive superstitions and fears regarding the nature of existence, reduced medieval people to a quasi-comatose state that blocked them from anything approaching a rational perspective on the worlds located outside or inside themselves. But finally, after a thousand years of somnolence, the human inside homo sapiens began to stir. In Italy, during the time of Dante, the lengthy arrested development of medieval Europeans came to an end.

It's no surprise that medievalists, annoyed by the marginalization of their period, have long directed at Burckhardt their frustration and ire. His vision of modernity hinges not just on a temporal rupture or breaking away from an atavistic, childlike, and superstitious Middle Ages but on an utter disappearing or stripping away of the medieval altogether. The onset of modernity is, for him, also the vanishing of the Middle Ages: Burckhardt's modernity depends upon the very "melt[ing] into air"—in German, "verweht ... in die Lüfte" (blown away into the air)—of medieval forms that prevented human development.[12] That dynamic renders the prospect of any rapprochement between the two eras unthinkable, dooming medieval Europe to irrelevance and inconsequence.

As Julia Reinhard Lupton puts it, "Burckhardt's 1860 *Die Kultur der Renaissance in Italien* succeeded in establishing if not inventing the mythos of the Renaissance as the birth of modern secular individualism."[13] Published in German in 1860 and translated into English by S. G. C. Middlemore in 1878, Burckhardt's tale of the birth of the human in Renaissance Italy still enjoys wide influence. To medievalists' chagrin, the account of modernity in *Civilization* has remained as "decisive" in scholarly circles as it was when Wallace Ferguson first applied that adjective to Burckhardt in his important 1948 book about Renaissance historiography.[14]

Ferguson understands Burckhardt's prominence in terms of the Swiss historian's capacity as a "historical artist" to masterfully synthesize claims that "had been in the air for some years."[15] But equally central to Burckhardt's influence is the emotional payoff of his narrative. With its sensational image of the dissolution of the veil separating medieval man from his human potential, *Civilization* offers the singular affective pleasures of what I call the "reveal," a word whose relation to veils emerges in its origins in the Latin *revelare*, to unveil.[16] Like a movie makeover or a contemporary home improvement program that unearths the long-buried beauty of an ugly duckling, Burckhardt prompts in his reader sentiments of invigoration, liberation, and awe by describing what is, in anthropocentric terms, the ultimate reveal: the disclosure of the human itself.

Reveals depend for their emotional impact on a temporal contrast—that is, the radical difference between an inferior "before," when hidden treasures remained unseen, and the superior "now" of their revelation. In the case of *Civilization*, the human quiescence of medieval man serves as a foil to the modern awakening of human potential. Making Burckhardt's reveal all the more emotionally satisfying is its grand, one-thousand-year delay. The pleasure of discovery is singularly gratifying when the treasure has been buried, not just for many years, but for centuries. The epic length of the medieval period heightens Burckhardt's capacity to "hook" his reader, to cite Rita Felski's formulation of literary attachment.

However, for Burckhardt, modernity is no uniformly happy affair. A Basel native who witnessed whirlwind demographic, sociopolitical, cultural, and economic changes in that city, Burckhardt was an aristocratic liberal and former Calvinist who critiqued modernity and rejected its ideology of progress.[17] Burckhardt's study of thirteenth-century Italy comprises part of his emphatically ambivalent brand of modernism. While Burckhardt's modern self enjoys access to lucid scrutiny of the world, that vision does not equate with the betterment of humans or life on earth. Rather, the melting of the medieval veil of superstition is a mixed blessing. While medieval people regrettably possess an immature and suppressed humanity, the "many-sided men" of modernity aren't without a dark side (73). The liberation of the human in modernity also accompanies unheard-of oppressions that reflect how Renaissance man had a "fundamental vice" that "was at the same time a condition of its greatness— namely excessive individualism" (237).

The initial, political chapters of *Civilization* describe how the power vacuum created by the failure of medieval papal and imperial political formations opened a space filled by horrible Italian despots in whom individualism was first "fostered in the highest degree" (71). Burckhardt details how the "tyrants" of Renaissance Italy "destroyed the freedom of most of the cities" (34), the Italian mercenaries known as *Condottieri* committed "monstrous iniquit[ies]" (12), and a "monstrous capital of cruelty and cowardice ... accumulated from generation to generation" in the house of the despotic Visconti of Milan (7). Ultimately, the emotional impact of *Civilization* entails not simply the revelation of a wondrous humanity and its creative heights but also a nightmarish thrill over the egotistical depths of the modern man birthed in Renaissance Italy.

Perhaps Burckhardt's most prominent contemporary Anglophone inheritor is the eminent Shakespearean and cofounder of New Historicism, Stephen Greenblatt. That claim may surprise those readers who associate Greenblatt with a pessimistic Foucauldian account of the early modern English containment of subversive social forces. But Greenblatt has long adopted a feel-good and quasi-Burckhardtian approach to his object of study, starting with his structuralist and dialectical take on Burckhardt's autonomous modern individual in *Renaissance Self-Fashioning* (1980). Moreover, Greenblatt persistently has worn his heart on his sleeve in ways that reveal his deep attachment to the worldview Burckhardt calls modern. Greenblatt's famous opening line of *Shakespearean Negotiations* (1988)—"I began with a desire to speak with the dead"—indicates his abiding attraction to the lives and accomplishments of humans on earth, and especially their finest cultural creations.[18] And he prefaces his most public-facing publication—*The Swerve: How the World Became Modern* (2011)—with an account of how Renaissance Epicureanism helped him overcome a mortality complex stemming from his mother's "obsessive fear" of death and embrace his own limited time on earth to the fullest.[19] A passion for life as an opportunity, albeit fleeting, for human achievement undergirds Greenblatt's scholarship.[20]

The Swerve is deeply Burckhardtian. It rehashes Burckhardt's argument verbatim and even retains particulars of the Swiss historian's locutions, such as his characterization in *Civilization* of modern man as "many-sided."[21] However, Greenblatt never employs the Swiss historian's veil metaphor. Instead, he opts for his titular "swerve" terminology to convey the feel of modernity. "Swerve" in the book speaks to two related phenomena. On one hand, it refers to the theory of random atomic movement (or swerving) postulated by the ancient thinker Lucretius. On the other, it denotes how fifteenth-century Italian book-hunter Poggio Bracciolini's rediscovery of Lucretius led to a swerving (or sudden veering away) from a prior medieval spiritual mindset to an earthly worldview. Instead of the bracing feel of the reveal, Greenblatt conveys modernity through a startling jolt away from a staid medieval religiosity toward the rush and outpouring of a new and secular human creativity. During the Renaissance "something . . . *surged up* against the constraints that centuries had constructed around curiosity, desire, individuality"; classicism, a key part of that *Rinascimento* "surge," was "*propelled . . . forward*" as never before.[22] *The*

Swerve offers readers a thrill akin to the American movie trope of a character hopping on a motorcycle (or bus, rocket, or train) to escape a closed-minded and oppressive Christian milieu.

If anything sets Greenblatt's approach to modernity apart from that of Burckhardt, it is the former scholar's optimism. As we have seen, in *Civilization*, the "many-sided men" who awoke from their long medieval slumber were capable not only of great achievements but also of horribly oppressive actions. Greenblatt, however, omits this dark component of Renaissance man and describes just his heroic side. Thanks largely to its focus on humanism (and not such fraught components of early modernity as politics, the state, and despotism), *The Swerve* primarily serves up to readers happy feelings and, above all, "the deepest wonder" that arises from "knowing the way things are" in the material world.[23]

Greenblatt and Burckhardt, to be sure, highlight objectivity. The birth of modernity during the Renaissance makes possible "knowing the way things are" and an "*objective* treatment and consideration of the state and of all the things of this world." But, crucially, in the two scholars' respective narratives of the European *rinascimento*, objectivity functions as a trope possessed of crucial affective dimensions: the excitement of the reveal and the swerve. A neutral assessment of facts paradoxically offers significant emotional rewards.

Works like *Civilization* and *The Swerve* both exemplify and complicate Dyer's discussion of white enterprise and embodiment. Dyer associates white affect with the thrills that attend a colonizing and agential spirit of enterprise, witnessed in cultural forms like Victorian adventure stories and Westerns. Burckhardt's and Greenblatt's works are "imaginative form[s]," akin to the tales of cowboy and Victorian adventurers analyzed by Dyer, that provide "the experience, the thrill and exhilaration, of the exercise of enterprise."[24] However, when linked with the advent of modernity, the white thrills offered by Burckhardt and Greenblatt become arguably more thrilling; each scholar describes not just enterprise but also the dazzling recognition of its very existence as a human activity after, moreover, a long period of medieval blindness.

The Good, the Bad, and the In-Between: Scholarly Sentiment on Modernity from Marx to Jameson

The three remaining white Anglo-European critics of modernity covered in this chapter exemplify how a Burckhardtian idea of medieval Europe can coincide with a range of affective stances toward modernity. This section traces an increasingly pessimistic emotional path, from Marx's optimism that the bourgeoisie will finally undo themselves and enable revolution, to Berman's emotion-drenched dialectic of hope and despair over modern life, and finally to Jameson's coldly Hegelian delivery of the bad news that the totality of modern society is shaped by the oppressive demands of capital.

As we shall see, while all three affirm a hard break between the medieval and the modern, they also engage the medieval in ways that impact their respective affective historicisms. In the case of Marx and his admirer Berman, the medieval proves to be more than just an irrational other. Rather, it is a key means of confronting the complex and contradictory workings of modernity. The medieval brings to light both the tirelessly bracing historicism of the bourgeoisie and their astounding acts of creative destruction. Turning to Jameson, I then examine how his renowned *The Political Unconscious* introduces a ray of hope—and, moreover, cross-temporal white male fellow feeling—into its otherwise dark take on modernity, through Augustine of Hippo. Jameson discovers in the four-fold Christian interpretive system generated by Augustine a means of combating the totality that is late capitalism. Thus, even as both Marx and Jameson affirm the broad alterity of the years in Europe before 1500 CE, they also render certain kinds of medievalness (in Marx's case, the outworn, the magical, and irrational; and in Jameson's case, a totalizing Christian hermeneutic) relevant to their modern moment.

If Burckhardt's account of the medieval-modern divide has proven "decisive," Marx offers, to cite Berman's important discussion of modernism, "probably the definitive vision of the modern environment."[25] Published more than a decade before *Civilization* by a man born the same year as Burckhardt, Marx's colossally influential political tract *The Communist Manifesto* (1848), like *Civilization*, represents the Middle Ages as an irrational and backward epoch. But unlike Burckhardt (or Greenblatt), Marx primarily calls up the stereotype of medieval primitivism not to denigrate the past but rather to clarify the complexities of his current moment. As we shall see, the medieval is not so much a long-gone historical phenomenon for Marx as a problem that resurfaces in multiple guises in modernity.[26]

In the *Manifesto*, Marx opposes the medieval and the modern in a way that resonates closely with Burckhardt's work, down to the metaphor of the veil.[27] But while Burckhardt, an aristocratic liberal who feared socialism, celebrates the momentous Renaissance emergence of a multidimensional and autonomous self, Marx the radical articulates the stakes of the medieval-modern divide in terms of the profit-minded dynamics of a nineteenth-century bourgeoisie who

> has pitilessly torn asunder the motley feudal ties that bound man to his "natural superiors," and has left remaining no other nexus between

man and man than naked self-interest.... It has drowned the most heavenly ecstasies of religious fervour, of chivalrous enthusiasm, of philistine sentimentalism, in the icy water of egotistical calculation ... for exploitation, veiled by religious and political illusions, it has substituted naked, shameless, direct, brutal exploitation.... The bourgeoisie has torn away from the family its sentimental veil, and has reduced the family relation to a mere money relation. The bourgeoisie has disclosed how it came to pass that the brutal display of vigour in the Middle Ages, which reactionaries so much admire, found its fitting complement in the most slothful indolence. It has been the first to show what man's activity can bring about.[28]

Marx stresses in this passage the affective dimensions of the shift from medieval to modern. The move to capitalism from medieval group structures such as the family, feudalism, and Christianity entails discarding a cluster of deeply felt passions: the "drown[ing]" of "heavenly ecstasies of religious fervour, of chivalrous enthusiasm, of philistine sentimentalism, in the icy water of egotistical calculation." In place of "sentimental" family ties and loyalty to "natural superiors," the bourgeoisie substitute "self-interest" based on "money relation[s]."

But such renunciations are not conclusive. As it turns out, for Marx, the bourgeoisie's fierce cathexis to profit and capital ironically reproduces the medieval in their modern world. The bourgeoisie don't simply break from backward "medieval" ways but rather repeatedly encounter in the present a kind of medieval primitivism:

> All fixed, fast-frozen relations, with their train of ancient and venerable prejudices and opinions, are swept away, all new-formed ones become antiquated before they can ossify. All that is solid melts into air, all that is holy is profaned, and man is at last compelled to face with sober senses his real conditions of life, and his relations with his kind. (476)

In this famous account of a creative destruction in which "all that is solid melts into air," Marx imbues the bourgeoisie with a historical and periodizing sensibility that discovers and discards the medieval, over and over, within their modern world. Marx identifies in the bourgeoisie a kind of repetition compulsion vis-à-vis the medieval. In their commitment to progress, the bourgeoisie discern in extant forms—not just in "fixed, fast-frozen relations" but even newly created modern forms that haven't had a chance to "ossify"—remainders of the medieval irrationality, sentimentality, and superstitiousness that have prevented humans from making the most of themselves and their world. Having perceived those new creations as atavistic and "antiquated," the bourgeoisie destroy them and generate still newer formations in their stead. Yet the medieval returns once more. Almost immediately after its fashioning, the new form that replaces a disavowed old form itself takes on the character of the old and is draped in the veil of superstitious and medieval sentiments.

Marx's account indicates the contradictory emotions entailed by the creative destruction and destructive creativity of modernity. His bourgeoisie might seem entirely "sober" and "icy" in their profit-minded calculations; they might appear to lack anything approaching the variety of sentiments in which their medieval predecessors are awash. But, thanks to its entanglement in a fraught dynamic where, as David Harvey puts it, "a new world" can't "be created, after all, without destroying much that had gone before," bourgeois practice is in fact deeply emotional and involves a series of bracing reveals, horrifying and anxious acknowledgments, and hopeful makings.[29] The identification of the medieval in the new isn't just a matter of pitiless rejection but also a cathartic, exhilarating, and anxious identification, stripping away, and replacement of old by new formations—as well as the anxiety and fear of what might happen if the compulsion to make new is ignored. "Man's activity" under capital demands repeatedly identifying and eradicating the medieval in the barely "ossified"—otherwise, as Marx puts it elsewhere, "the tradition of all the dead generations weighs like a nightmare on the brain of the living."[30] Thanks to the obligation to "constantly revolutioniz[e] the instruments of production" in accord with the "need of a constantly expanding market" and thus destroy every trace of the medieval, an "everlasting uncertainty and agitation . . . distinguish the bourgeois epoch from all earlier ones" (476). The medieval—and its rejection—are central to the Sisyphean assertion of a modernity that always slips away.

Even more than the bourgeoisie he portrays, Marx engages in a historicism whose affective components are complex and multiple. Marx situates bourgeois actions broadly in a bona fide progressive trajectory in which he and his communist comrades can invest feelings of optimism. Despite themselves and their avowed self-interest, the bourgeoisie creates "its own grave-diggers. Its fall and the victory of the proletariat are equally inevitable" (483). When the revolution occurs, "man is at last compelled to face with sober senses his real conditions of life, and his relations with his kind" (476). Marx's teleology thus links the revolution of the proletariat to the decline of the bourgeoisie's medieval repetition compulsion complex. The reveals entailed by creative destruction have an end point, when no veil remains to be stripped away and laborers discover, with clear and sober eyes, their alienation and commodification under capital.

Concomitant with Marx's optimistic progressivism is his own disdain for an irrational, superstitious, and backward Middle Ages. Marx's rejection of the medieval and his attending embrace of modernity emerge in his celebration of how "the modern proletarian, thanks to railways, achieve in a few years" the class unification that "the burghers of the Middle Ages, with their miserable highways, required centuries" to attain (481). Their industrial-age counterparts leave medieval technologies of travel in the dust. Medieval roads are contemptible, pathetic, and wretched when compared to railways.

But the relationship of the medieval to the sentiment in Marx's writing is more complex than his dismissal of "miserable" medieval roads would suggest. Consider Marx's characterization above of bourgeois modernization as a ruthless tearing "asunder" and "reduc[tion]" of medieval feelings and formations. That passage from the *Manifesto* connotes a kind of sadness at how medieval Europe, however superstitious and backward, nevertheless enjoyed a certain sociocultural abundance and depth that have no place in a streamlined modern world order. Such moments hint at a certain nostalgia for a lost medieval richness.

Far more important, however, is Marx's deployment of the medieval as a rhetorical tool that produces perhaps the most emotionally charged moments of the *Communist Manifesto*. A key instance emerges in Marx's claim that "modern bourgeois society, a society that has conjured up such gigantic means of production and exchange, is *like the sorcerer* who is no longer able to control the powers of the underworld that he has called up by his spells" (478, my emphasis). Through the medieval image of the "sorcerer," Marx suggests how, as the first class to fully realize "what man's activity can bring about," the bourgeoisie achieve acts of creative destruction on an impressive, unprecedentedly grand scale and with a heretofore unseen and dizzying rapidity. Calling up the awe that accompanied medieval peoples' belief in sorcery, the German philosopher, as Berman puts it (in a reading of Marx's medievalism to which I'm indebted), "projects . . . a sense of wonder over the modern world" and its "vital" and "dazzling" powers (101). Thus, to return to Dyer's account of white "enterprise," in Marx the thrill of white modern achievement might be best conveyed, paradoxically, through medieval metaphors.

But the "wonder" that Marx instills in his readers over the seemingly magical powers wielded in modernity comprises one side of his dialectical citation of the medieval in this important passage from the *Manifesto*. For the precise nature of bourgeois wizardry is "like the sorcerer who is *no longer able to control* the powers of the underworld that he has called up by his spells" (my emphasis). Marx employs the medieval to ask his readers to contemplate what the members of the bourgeoisie cannot face: their own irrational and catastrophically destructive capacities. For, paradoxically, in their very effort to discard those outworn "medieval" elements of modernity that compulsively return and haunt them, the bourgeoisie are themselves medieval. The bourgeoisie understand themselves as rational engineers who make a better world. But the awful truth is that their revolutions unleash unruly forces that do just the opposite. While the fact that, as Berman puts it, "these solid citizens" are so irrationally possessed by capital that they "would tear down the world if it paid" is too contradictory and destabilizing a truism for the bourgeoisie to consciously acknowledge, Marx brings it to horrifying life for the reader through what Berman describes as "vivid and striking images" of medieval sorcery, devilishness, and apocalypse (100–101). As Berman observes, "This image evokes the spirits of that dark medieval past that our modern bourgeoisie is supposed to have buried" (101). Thanks to its construction as all that is other to the cold and calculated march of progress, the medieval serves as an ideal means of exposing the ironies of the bourgeoisie or, to put it another way, of evoking both "a sense of wonder" and "a sense of dread" with respect to the workings of capital. While Burckhardt exhilarates readers with the melting away of a medieval veil to reveal "many-sided men," Marx awes and horrifies by describing how the bourgeoisie, in their assiduous stripping away of one veil of medieval superstition after another, paradoxically foster wondrously yet ultimately unruly creative-destructive "medieval" forces.

In his widely cited and now canonical "masterpiece" *All That Is Solid Melts into Air: The Experience of Modernity* (1981), Marshall Berman celebrates Marx's capacity to confront and ponder such apocalyptic "medieval" horrors in the modern world and then somehow find the means to press on and seek to overcome those dark elements.[31] As Berman's use of Marx's famous quote in his title demonstrates, *All That Is Solid* aims to capture and appreciate how Marx, as well as other nineteenth-century intellectuals, responded to modernity. Berman's avowed aim is to enrich and enliven his own current moment in the long history of modern life, which he diagnoses as a time of despair, by recalling the magnificent expansiveness of thinkers like Marx who hail from an earlier stage of modernity. Affect is central to Berman's project, which is shot through with critical sentiment. Berman wrote *All That Is Solid* during the 1970s, when, he stresses, "so many of us" scholars and intellectuals were "gripped" by a "sense of passivity and helplessness" in the wake of the failures of the "generous" "modernisms and anti-modernisms of the 1960s" (35, 33). Berman's exemplar of the "bleak context" he seeks to change is Michel Foucault (1926–84) and his "endless, excruciating series of variations" on Weber's oppressive "iron cage" (34–35). For Berman, reading Foucault is a feel-bad—indeed, torturous—experience in which oppressive "totalities swallow up every facet of modern life"; Berman's Foucault "chokes" the reader, "clamping his ideas down on [them] like iron bars, twisting each dialectic into our flesh like a new turn of the screw" (34–35).

In lieu of Foucault's utterly "bleak" stance toward modernity, Berman aims to recover contemporary society's "modern roots" in Marx and other nineteenth-century thinkers who responded to modernity with a marvelously rich, nuanced, and complex set of sentiments and ideas (35). While in Berman's current historical moment humans seem to "have stagnated and regressed" so that they can only understand modernity as an oppressive space from which there is no escape, during the nineteenth century, intellectuals like Marx, Nietzsche, Baudelaire, and Goethe exemplify a fuller and richer response to modernity (24). Namely, they engage in a "dynamic and dialectical modernism" whose "voice" is "distinctive and remarkable" in its

> fast and drastic shifts in tone and inflection, its readiness to turn on itself, to question and negate all it has said, to transform itself into a great range of harmonic or dissonant voices, and to stretch itself beyond its capacities into an endlessly wider range, to express and grasp a world where everything is pregnant with its contrary and "all that is solid melts into air." (23)

For Berman, modernity has always confronted humans with immense and overwhelming problems and crises. But if modernity is a far from feel-good era, Berman insists, its great nineteenth-century critics merit the highest praise. For unlike, say Foucault, whose negative dialectic can only recognize the deleterious effects of modernity and occludes alternate possibilities, thinkers like Marx adopt a wider perspective that, Berman hopes, will remind his depressed readers how they have the means within themselves to acknowledge all the horrific forces of modernity *and* heroically be "undeterred in our determination to face these forces, to fight to change their world and make it our own" (13). *All That Is Solid* thus shifts from Marx's stress on class to what is in many respects a version of Burckhardt's "many-sided men," though Berman disavows the presence of a stable self in the maelstrom that is modern existence (110). While Marx directs attention to groups like the bourgeoisie and the proletariat, Berman makes his subject Marx and other exceptional "modern individuals" who perform ever more astounding and expansive mental feats as they take in and comprehend immense—including hugely disturbing—modern phenomena (27).

As I indicate previously, Berman's celebration of Marx showcases an unexpected aspect of the German philosopher's work: the figure famed for his interest in class struggle also enacts a kind of medievalism. Berman deeply admires

Marx's deployment of the medieval to spur his readers' imaginations and assist them in contemplating the horrors wrought by the bourgeoisie. Indeed, Berman not only devotes several key paragraphs to Marx's medievalism but also uses Marx's line regarding "the sorcerer who is no longer able to control the powers of the underworld that he has called up by his spells" as the epigraph to his first chapter (101–2, 37). To be sure, the Marxian medievalism Berman so admires—like the medievalism of all the writers covered in this section—relies on ideas of a "stagnant and closed" "medieval organicism" that restrains and suppresses the full "range and depth of human desires and dreams" (43, 73). Berman (like Marx, Greenblatt, and Burckhardt) endorses a "modern transformation, beginning in the age of the Renaissance and Reformation," when humans reject the "false [spiritualizing] world" of the medieval past in favor of the "newly discovered and experienced" true world situated on "earth, in space and time, filled with human beings" (106).

The opposition between an irrational, dark Middle Ages and a rational, enlightened modernity is integral to Berman's overall celebration of Marx's dialectical and expansive response to modernity. As a result, for Berman, as for Marx, while the medieval might persist or dramatically appear in modern life, the line dividing the two periods stays in place. In other words, medieval always signifies the binary opposite of modern, one side of a bourgeois dialectic that will, at least for Marx, vanish with the advent of revolution. For Berman, the medieval and modern can appear simultaneously but contiguously, like pieces in a mosaic that never intersect, mix, or dissolve into one another. An example of the mosaic-like contiguity of the medieval and the modern appears in Berman's account of Goethe's *Faust*. Faust the character is a modernizing force living in a "Gothic world," but those forces don't mix or cross-pollinate. Instead, a "split" exists between an "independent" cohort of progressive "producers of culture and ideas" and the medieval "feudal enclaves" that define public life overall, so that the "new discoveries and perspectives" of the former group are "locked away" from the latter group (56, 43, 58). Similarly, Berman appreciates Marx's keen comprehension of how a seemingly rational and eminently modern class flips and, surprisingly and paradoxically, becomes its irrational medieval other—that is, the conjurers of dark and unmanageably massive magical forces.

Taken together, Marx and Berman, like Burckhardt and Greenblatt, make clear how the discourse of modernity is charged with sentiment. But while the Renaissance scholars relegate the medieval to what moderns leave behind, Marx and Berman embrace it as a means of clarifying, in strongly affective terms, the contradictions, ambiguities, and precarity of European modernity. To the horror of a profit-driven bourgeoisie, their newly wrought creations become old—become atavistic and medieval—no sooner than they are completed. Moreover, those very acts of creative destruction, performed as a means of banishing the medieval, paradoxically render the bourgeoisie themselves medieval, akin to out-of-control sorcerers. If the story of modernity, as told by Burckhardt and Greenblatt, offers the thrill of the reveal of an enterprising humanity after a long medieval somnolence, Marx and Berman relate an emotional roller-coaster of a narrative in which modernity's lows are rendered viscerally fearsome precisely because of their resonance with the medieval.

The medieval seems to serve a more laudatory role in the final account of modernity covered in this survey, penned by "North America's leading Marxist cultural theorist and critic," Fredric Jameson.[32] His most influential work, *The Political Unconscious: Narrative as a Socially Symbolic Act*, appeared in 1981, the same year as *All That Is Solid*. Like Berman, Jameson is both a Marxist who wrote his book during the seventies, in the wake of failed sixties radicalisms, and a scholar who addressed what he deemed to be lacking in his current U.S. moment. But Berman and Jameson differ starkly in their respective diagnoses of the contemporary crisis. Berman the humanist addresses an attitude problem that can be resolved by revisiting the expansive mentalities of nineteenth-century white male thinkers. Jameson alternatively sees the tendrils of late capitalism appearing in every part of the post-industrial world (and beyond) and lays out an elaborate blueprint for sociopolitical revolution. A structuralist for whom all real events and facts—that is, history—can only be grasped via language and stories, Jameson models a theory of textual analysis to support the collective action that constitutes "the only realistic perspective in which a genuine Left could come to being in this country."[33] Certainly, for all their differences, Jameson is, like Berman, a humanist who finds assistance in a white, male, and all-encompassing vision from the past. But while Berman cathects to modern philosophers like Marx and Nietzsche, Jameson embraces the expansive mentality of medieval Bible interpreters—that is, Augustine of Hippo and other patristic thinkers.

Jameson's modernity is a far more disturbing affair than that of Burckhardt, Berman, or Marx. One of those intellectuals who, in Berman's words, "says a decisive 'No!' to modern life" (27), Jameson understands his contemporary world as utterly and nightmarishly shaped by capitalism. As Jameson describes in a later essay, "The reification and privatization of contemporary life" is inescapably totalizing: "The profit motive and the logic of capital accumulation" determine "fundamental laws of this world" that "set absolute barriers and limits to social changes and transformations undertaken in it."[34] Indeed, the "intensity of social fragmentation" under Jameson's current (that is, 1980s) economic regime is so thoroughgoing that it encompasses the contemporary proliferation of independent left-leaning cohorts (39). "Ethnic groups, neighborhood movements, feminism, various 'countercultural' or alternative life-style groups, rank-and-file labor dissidence, student movements, single-issue movements" don't constitute sites of "any durable and effective" resistance but rather are "a symptom and a reinforcement" of the problems created under "the tendential law of social life under capitalism" (39, 4). Pluralism results from the creation under capital of a "structural, experiential, and conceptual gap between the public and the private, between the social and the psychological, or the political and the poetic, between history or society and the 'individual'" such that it "maims our existence as individual subjects" (4).

Jameson's modernity, far from witnessing the kind of lucidity celebrated by Burckhardt, thus involves its own acts of veiling. While the medieval period entailed a veil of religious symbolism, modernity doesn't witness the falling of the scales from the eyes of the human subject. Rather, in Jameson's view, modernity substitutes the old veil for a new one, woven by the secularizing prime mover of capital. The modern individualism so hailed by Burckhardt figures in Jameson's work as an ideology of selfhood that blinds persons to their ties to larger sociopolitical and economic forms and forces. A version of the ideological veil of individualism even blinds liberal special-interest groups—however left-leaning they might be—to their relation to capital and commodification. The only way to cast that modern veil asunder, for Jameson, is to counter its totalizing form with an equally totalizing—yet ultimately liberating—system. Because capital is a "certain unifying and totalizing force," it can be unveiled (or to use Jameson's preferred idiom, *unmasked*) only by confrontation with the "ideal of totality which they at once imply and repress."[35] Similarly, capital can only be resisted via a socialist perspective that offers an alternate "conception of the social totality" and "the unity of a single great collective story."[36]

With respect to Jameson's scholarly affect, *The Political Unconscious* marries a bleak take on contemporary life with quasi-hopeful consideration of a utopian (albeit impossible) future of real freedom and equality. But Jameson is no man of feeling. *The Political Unconscious* largely eschews sentiment in lieu of the self-avowed and "unavoidably Hegelian tone" Jameson adopts for his serious, careful, and often brilliant scrutiny of works by novelists including Balzac and Conrad (xii). Yet, if Jameson's mood is largely detached, he does warm to patristic authorities and their "striking and elaborate"—attractive and eye-catching—approach (13). He locates an affinity between the "vulgar Marxist theory of levels" and the medieval "allegorical systems" with which it has a "deeper kinship." Augustine and other church fathers are Jameson's kindred spirits, "medieval theorists" to whom "it was clear" back then—just as it is for Jameson in 1981—what sorts of semantic levels "constituted a methodological upper limit and a virtual exhaustion of interpretive possibilities" (17). Thus, just as Berman turns to Marx and other nineteenth-century thinkers to discover an admirably expansive approach to modernity's successes and failures, Jameson seizes upon the all-encompassing intellect of the medieval church fathers.

To formulate his literary critical analysis of "the social totality," Jameson turns to the totalizing reading of the Hebrew Bible generated via medieval allegory, whose four-part method links multiple scales of interpretation (69). Keenly attending to the sophistication and complexity of medieval literary criticism, Jameson describes how patristic interpreters of the Bible begin with readings that inform the life of a single individual (Christ), and then jump scales to ever wider semantic "rewritings and overwritings" that culminate in the widest, most totalizing, and encompassing view possible, the anagogic vision of "the destiny of the human race as a whole" at "the Last Judgment" (57). Jameson appropriates that medieval interpretive model to perform a Marxist analysis that charts the "ultimate determination by the mode of production" within "three concentric frameworks, which mark a widening out of the sense of the social ground of a text" from "political history" to "the struggle between social classes" and, "ultimately, of history now conceived in its vastest sense of the sequence of modes of production and the succession and destiny of the various human social formations" (52, 60).

Jameson, even more than Marx and Berman, would seem to offer the most consequential and feel-good account of how the medieval matters to modernity. However, Jameson's affinity with the church fathers doesn't cancel out the received idea of the alterity of the medieval era to modernity. For all their congeniality, Jameson and his patristic forebears operate "under wholly altered historical circumstances" (117). While the veil generated by capital circulates in Jameson's milieu, the prior medieval veil no longer has any hold on moderns. "The Christian scheme" appeals to Jameson because of its totalizing approach, but "the relationship" it "projects," for example, "between anagogical and moral is not available to us today" (16). The belief in or enchantment with a divine power that undergirded Christian ideas of moral action and salvation history is forever absent from a modern life defined by "rationalizing desacralization in the Umwelt or world of daily life" (27). Endorsing received ideas of medieval superstition and modern rationality, Jameson understands the first stage of capitalism as coinciding with "the desacralization of the world, the decoding and secularization of the older forms of the sacred or the transcendent, . . . the 'realistic' demystification of the older kinds of transcendent narratives."[37] Jameson's idea of periodic division ultimately supports the received Burckhardtian formula. Augustine is no modern avant la lettre.

The Death of "a Perfectly Pictured World": Huizinga's Nostalgic Middle Ages

> Academic medievalists are never dispassionate interpreters of historical phenomena.
>
> —JONATHAN HSY, ANTIRACIST MEDIEVALISMS

As the foregoing discussion of Burckhardt, Greenblatt, Marx, Berman, and Jameson suggests, regardless of their divergent sentiments toward modernity, those scholars all see their object of study as resolutely sundered from and opposed to a superstitious and irrational European era that they term "medieval." And, to this day, medievalist Lee Patterson's 1990 claim still rings true regarding "the pervasive and apparently ineradicable *grand récit* that organizes western cultural history, the gigantic master narrative by which modernity ... rejects the Middle Ages as by definition premodern."[38] The remainder of this chapter turns to major scholarly accounts of the medieval by white European and U.S. critics and engages the profound way in which modern scholars' claims about periodization shape and limit medievalist scholarship. As we shall see, regardless of how much medievalists might reject modernists' construction of the Middle Ages as backward, many medievalists are still bound to the tropes and conventions by which those same modernist scholars construct modernity. Medievalists from Huizinga to Haskins to Bynum remain driven by the identical issues that occupy modernist scholarship; indeed, they make the problem of modernity central to their take on the medieval. As well they should: insofar as the medieval period came into being to assist in the conceptualization of the modern, medievalists cannot ignore modernity. However, medievalists' keen attention and investment in the terms of analysis laid out by modernists comes at an intellectual cost. Namely, medievalists tend to limit their engagement with their own era to a strategy of rebutting its feel-bad rejection by modernists. Modernists' constant relegation of the medieval to a backward and superstitious past usually prompts medievalists to always—to only—invert the received negative associations of their field, and counter modernist rejection with some kind of feel-good affirmation. By allowing the terms of modernist periodization to dictate the scope of their analysis, medievalists often fail to adopt a wider and more critical account of their object of study. Medievalists prove so focused on critiquing modern dismissals of the medieval past that they fail to critique their own era.

While they tend toward good feelings about their area of study, medievalists' positive sentiments about the medieval are by no means homogeneous. Rather, those scholars adopt positive sentiments whose specifics depend upon a scholar's particular take on modernity. An important case in point is "the most influential cultural historian of the later Middle Ages in the twentieth century": Johan Huizinga.[39] *The Autumn of the Middle Ages* (1919), the Dutch scholar's landmark account of late medieval French "forms of thought and life," remains "the most widely read treatment of the medieval period on earth," in large part because of its remarkable emotionality.[40] Deploying "an impressionistic, sensory barrage that has no equivalent in historical literature," Huizinga's visualization of fifteenth-century France and Burgundy hooks the reader like no other scholarly account of the medieval past.[41]

Huizinga's renowned sentimentality has everything to do with his take on modernity, which some might label "anti-modern," but I call "modernist" insofar as modernism (for instance, Eliot's *Waste Land*) responds to not just the successes but also the failures of modernity. *Autumn* voices a white, high modernist critique of progress that bespeaks Huizinga's dismay over multiple aspects of his contemporary world, and especially the losses wrought by the Great War.[42] Huizinga composed *Autumn* during and published it shortly after World War I, when, as Carol Symes puts it, "the lands of which he wrote became the bloody frontier of the Western Front."[43] Huizinga's work is peppered with laments over his modern world. Not unlike Marx, Huizinga understands modernity in terms of the loss of certain affects.[44] But while Marx stresses the replacement of medieval group feeling with the cold profit-mindedness of the bourgeoisie, Huizinga highlights how "progress" reduces lived experience to a numbing and bleary common denominator. While Marx describes how the bourgeoisie "has drowned the most heavenly ecstasies of religious fervour, of chivalrous enthusiasm, of philistine sentimentalism, in the icy water of egotistical calculation," Huizinga decries how mechanization, capitalism, secularism, and science blur what formerly were distinct aesthetic, emotional, sensual, and moral categories.

Huizinga's modernity, in effect, has barred humans from any of the vibrant contrasts that imbue existence with richness and drama. Cognition of visual and aural oppositions diminishes in the "modern city [that] hardly knows pure darkness or true silence anymore" or "the effect . . . of a lonely distant shout" (2). The difference between good and evil disappears as an "ethical value" is attributed to "greed" (26). And the highs and lows of lived experience erode as a result of the "checks and obstacles" placed on passion, rendering humans "hesitant," "cautious," and "tentative" (15, 22). The various forms of everyday life have lost their beauty, meaning, and purpose with the rise of "causal-scientific" or "causal-genetic" thought and the logic of the market (238, 247). Gorgeous cathedrals give way to "carelessly fashioned, ugly factories and monotonous country homes" (2).

Huizinga's feel-bad modernism stands in dynamic relation to a feel-good and even joyously mystical approach to his object of inquiry. Driving Huizinga's medievalist practice is an emotion-soaked and imagination-driven methodology. He believed in the capacity of historians to escape their current moment and time-travel by enlisting all of their senses in a "total engagement" and "complete immersion" in source materials, especially medieval visual artifacts. An abashed Huizinga described the effect of his sensory immersion in a primary source, which he claimed produced "an almost (do not laugh) ecstatic sensation of no longer being myself, of overflowing into the world around me, of touching the very essence of things, the experience of Truth through history."[45] Thanks to his purported capacity to inhabit the positioning of a medieval person by generating "living pictures in the theatre of [his] mind," Huizinga could, he believed, make clear to readers the contrast between their own dulled modern senses and the markedly stronger passions of his medieval subjects.[46]

Autumn's emotional force relies on the divide between an enchanted "then" and disenchanted "now," as its famous opening makes clear:

> When the world was half a thousand years younger, all events had much sharper outlines than now. The distance between sadness and joy, between good and bad fortune, seemed to be much greater than for us; every experience had that degree of directness and absoluteness that joy and sadness still have in the mind of a child. (1)

Like Burckhardt, Huizinga draws the reader's interest by stressing the difference between the medieval and modern worlds. But Huizinga's nostalgic account of medieval personhood reverses the emotional terms of Burckhardt's historicism. In *Civilization*, Burckhardt opposes a lively "many-sided" modern man to a medieval predecessor rendered pathetically comatose and undeveloped due to the nefarious influence of religion and superstition. *Autumn* retains the notion that the medieval is childlike and primitive, as its opening displays. But Huizinga, in the spirit of modernists such as Joseph Conrad and D. H. Lawrence or romanticists like William Wordsworth and Percy Shelley, celebrates the childlike and the primitive aspects of medieval man as embodying a vitality lost to moderns. For the Dutch historian, it is medieval people who truly lived, while modern persons' sensibilities are deadened and dull.

Huizinga attributed medieval Europeans' special aliveness to the same Christian worldview that Burckhardt decried. Like Burckhardt, Huizinga defines the medieval mentality in terms of an "all-encompassing" Christian symbolism that infused and connected all objects, people, locations, and events (235). Yet what Burckhardt decries Huizinga celebrates. Indeed, his "loving attention" to the medieval Christian worldview is unmatched.[47] Medieval

Christianity attracts Huizinga—like Jameson—because of its totalizing perspective. Both critics appreciate a worldview that links individuals and the particulars of their existence to a larger collective whole, or what Jameson describes as the "organic identity of associative or collective life" (60). But while Jameson's admiration extends only to the all-encompassing form of the medieval Christian worldview, Huizinga loves the whole package—that is, both the totalizing form and divine symbolic content of Christian discourse.[48] Thanks both to his belief in a higher power (though not so much his advocacy of a particular religious denomination) and his attachment to a contemporary literary movement, the French symbolist school, Huizinga embraced medieval Christian symbolism in terms that Willem Otterspeer rightly characterizes as "a personal creed."[49] Since Huizinga's student days in the 1890s, the emotion-charged symbolism of Paul Valéry, Arthur Rimbaud, and other French symbolists exerted an "literary influence" that "determined" his "idiosyncratic relationship to reality."[50] Namely, Huizinga believed in the symbolic capacity of all elements of the material world to affirm the mystical reality of "a well-ordered cosmos in which contradictions blend harmoniously and everything is related."[51] For Huizinga, starting in the twelfth-century "spring" of the Middle Ages, medieval Christians happily discovered a means of "keep[ing] the mystical sense of life burning constantly" in each and every component of an organically related universe.[52] By "embrac[ing] in its strong arms all of nature and all of history" as essential partakers in "God's plan," medieval Christian symbolism generated for believers a "perfectly pictured" world with "an indissoluble order of rank, an architectural structure, a hierarchical subordination" (238–40).[53]

The emotional force of that Christian worldview emerges, for Burckhardt, partly from its organization of life according to a system of sharp binary contrasts, such as good vs. evil, heaven vs. earth, joy vs. sorrow, and pity vs. anger. Thus the "passionate and violent mind of the" Middle Ages was "hardened and at the same time prone to tears; on the one side despairing of the world, yet on the other reveling in its colorful beauty" (53). Along with its binary contrasts, the medieval worldview also, in the manner of the French symbolist "literature that was so dear to" Huizinga, provoked powerful sentiments through equivalences that stretched horizontally, along one side or another of its oppositions, linking physical characteristics to their symbolic import.[54] As Huizinga explains, "This connectedness is only truly meaningful and full of mystic significance if the linkage, the quality, the essence between the two constituents of the particular symbolism are shared by each of them" (237). Thus, in the example of the color white, the hue doesn't serve as a "mere label" for the Christian believer but rather a "real entit[y]" in and of itself: "Everything white is beautiful, tender, and everything that is white has to be connected, has to have the same basis to its existence, has to have the same importance before God" (237).

The historian's unmistakable love of the medieval underlies—and casts in dramatic relief—the dominant mood of depression and melancholia for which *Autumn* is famous. For it is precisely the disintegration of that vital and organic medieval symbolizing system—the end of an era when lived experience throbbed with Christian valences—that comprises Huizinga's dark and nostalgic vision. His focus is on the fifteenth century, which for him witnessed the demise—the *herfsttij*, Dutch for "waning," "decline," "evening," or "autumn"—of the medieval Christian worldview. The late medieval people he examines live at the close of a period; for them, "form has lost its power as an instrument of passion" and "the symbolizing function has . . . become merely mechanical" (249). As a result, the people who inhabit Huizinga's fifteenth-century northern Europe are "overburdened, disappointed, and fatigued individuals" who suffer from a "basic mood of discouraged failure," "bitter despondency," "thorough pessimism," and "great emotional depression" (34, 303, 30).

With its stress on the "merely mechanical" and disenchanted stance adopted by late medieval people toward Christian symbolism, *Autumn* suggests a medieval adumbration of high modernist malaise and discontent. Huizinga ascribes to late medieval people a perspective on their world that one might call Eliotic or Yeatsian. For them, "the grand edifice of God-willed dependencies becomes a necropolis"; "individual symbols tur[n] into petrified flowers"; things fall apart as an "exhausted aristocracy laughs at its own ideal" viewing it as "only a vain illusion . . . only style and ceremony, a beautiful and insincere play!" (86, 249, 240, 103). The failed forms and seasonal decomposition that Huizinga locates in the medieval era look toward the "decayed hole" and "dead tree" of *The Waste Land*.[55]

It's no surprise, then, that a modernist Huizinga identifies so fiercely with the depression of the late medieval people whom he studies. Employing his characteristically painterly manner, Huizinga describes in the preface to the original Dutch edition how, "in writing this text," he looked away from any happy and hopeful signs of new life and instead gazed unflinchingly and depressingly at medieval death and decay. Not unlike Eliot's vision of a "heap of broken images" and "black clouds," Huizinga describes how his "eye was trained on the depth of the evening sky, a sky steeped blood red, desolate with threatening leaden clouds, full of the false glow of copper."[56] The depressive tone for which *Autumn* is notorious—its bleak, empty, and dark vision—speaks just as much, if not more, to Huizinga's own dark modernism as it does to anything taking place in a "dark" medieval age. To a great extent Huizinga projects the modern onto the past, where it can be pondered and interrogated at a temporal remove.⁵⁷ All of which is to say, *Autumn* evinces a medievalism that is inseparable from modernity, and above all the losses associated with the Great War.

"The First Sprouts": Medievalists on the Salutary Modernity of Their Period

While Huizinga mourns the "end of an era," many of his fellow medievalists assert a different take on their period.⁵⁸ As he observes in the preface to *Autumn*, "How eagerly the Middle Ages have been scrutinized for evidence of the first sprouts of modern culture." Admitting that even he himself partook in the search for a medieval modernity, he continues: "Did we not see everywhere in this age . . . new growths that all seemed to point to future perfection?" (xix). Huizinga's interest in the demise of a vital and organic medieval European Christian sensibility contrasts with a larger scholarly trend involving a search for new life and fresh beginnings—in other words, signs of modernity. For that latter group of medievalists, modernity isn't a problem—it's not lacking, for example, the medieval Christian vitality described by Huizinga—but rather it's a salutary event worth claiming as their object of study.

Thus, in lieu of Huizinga's modernist nostalgia for the premodern, those scholars join Burckhardt in celebrating modernity, even as they qualify or reject outright his notion that the Renaissance was "the birth hour of the modern world."⁵⁹ In what Ferguson calls "the revolt of the medievalists," these scholars assert the medieval roots of such hallmarks of the modern as individualism, reason, innovation, and progress.⁶⁰

An important post-*Autumn* example is Charles Homer Haskins's "anti-Burckhardt project," *The Renaissance of the Twelfth Century* (1927).⁶¹ A cofounder of the Medieval Academy of America, Haskins was "the first true professional medieval historian in" the U.S., where he "dominated medieval history . . . until the late 1960s."⁶² Like Huizinga, Haskins published *Renaissance* between the wars; Haskins also mirrors his Dutch counterpart in singling out the twelfth century for praise. Yet Haskins has none of Huizinga's modernist malaise. Rather, in keeping with his strong links to Woodrow Wilson (1856–1924), and especially his allegiance to that U.S. president's "Calvinist" faith in societal advance, Haskins embraces his current moment and modern values such as innovation, reason, and civilization.⁶³ Indeed, Haskins's investment in modernity is such that he even enlists "modern research" to support his claims. His preface to *Renaissance* begins by rejecting the contrast of a medieval "epoch of ignorance, stagnation and gloom" with "the light and progress and freedom of the Italian Renaissance" as itself backward and ignorant: "Modern research shows us the Middle Ages less dark and less static, the Renaissance less bright and less sudden, than once was supposed."[64] Modernity, for Haskins, involves a progressive movement toward ever superior understandings of history, moving humans from an ignorant Burckhardtian rejection of the years before 1500 CE to a clearer comprehension of the medieval. And that latest and more "accurate" view of the Middle Ages, according to Haskins, involves not the perfectly pictured symbolic world hailed by Huizinga but rather one of classical revival and unprecedented invention. Indeed, for Haskins, a more enlightened assessment of the past reveals that the "European Middle Ages . . . contain[s]" so many "origins of many phases of modern civilization" that he can't cover them all in a single book and instead must confine himself "to the Latin side" of the twelfth-century Renaissance and its "eager search after knowledge" and "creative accomplishment" (3, xviii, vii).

The contrast between Huizinga's affective historicism and the seeming absence of feeling in Haskins's book is stark. While Huizinga wears his heart on his sleeve, Haskins, in keeping with his endorsement of modern rationality, presents himself as a disinterested and clear-eyed evaluator of the evidence before him. For example, he immediately qualifies a claim about the "great steps forward" made in science during the Middle Ages by recognizing how "they do not bring us fully into the modern spirit" (308). Haskins similarly signposts his measured approach by highlighting how a proto-modern realism can mingle with medieval superstition in a single work: "What most shocks the modern mind" about the Franciscan monk and encyclopedist Bartholomeus Anglicus (d. 1272) is his ability to both endorse the existence of griffins and provide a "description of the domestic cat which, so far as it goes, can hardly be improved upon" (335–36). In such moments, Haskins signals his coolness and lack of bias regarding his medieval object of study.

But undergirding Haskins's calm objectivity is, as Paul Freedman and Gabrielle Spiegel put it, an "optimistic belief in a progressive Middle Ages."[65] *Renaissance* is Haskins's "enduring tribute" to his object of study, an upbeat effort to prove how the Middle Ages, far from a dead and stagnant era, is instead vitally alive with modern activity.[66] Haskins's happy title about a medieval "renaissance" suggests as much, as does his vocabulary. The word "revival" appears over sixty times, and the words "new" and "life," respectively, appear on no less than one hundred occasions in *Renaissance*. That celebratory stance peaks in Haskins's culminating chapter on medieval universities. Haskins locates in the medieval university clear evidence that troubles any hard-and-fast divide between the twelfth century and his current moment:

> These [universities] arise first in the twelfth century, and the modern university is derived in its fundamental features from them, from

Salerno, Bologna, Paris, Montpellier, and Oxford. From these the continuity is direct to our own day, and there was no other source. The university is a mediaeval contribution to civilization, and more specifically a contribution of the twelfth century. (369)

In none other than his own professional arena, academia, Haskins discovers an utterly medieval source for contemporary society. If, well before the Renaissance, medieval people rediscovered *ancient* texts, the built environments and attending corporations and practices associated with that rediscovery—universities—are themselves inexorably medieval. In what might be called an institutional version of the comforting and/or triumphant racial narratives of a "pure" line linking Europeans to their medieval ancestors, Haskins charts an unbroken "continuity" from the medieval university "direct to our own day." Periodization vanishes, in a sense, with respect to the history of higher education in the West. The contemporary university is one and the same as its twelfth-century counterpart. Nothing has changed since the medieval period when it comes to sites of learning.

Haskins's university revises many of the accounts of history put forth by major theorists of periodization. It pushes Burckhardt's timeline back, replaces Huizinga's view of a dying medieval culture with a scene of continuity, and, perhaps most strikingly, reverses the take on modernity put forth by Marx. Marx deploys the idea of a recursive medieval to stress the precarity of modernity—that is, how, no sooner than they appear on the scene, bourgeois creations become outworn and medieval. Haskins, on the other hand, finds in medieval students and their material environment—gargoyles, fortified walls, quadrangles, and all—a stable and unchanging modern entity. Far from a "tradition" that nightmarishly weighs "on the brain of the living," the constancy of academic life asserts a certain reassuring continuity and transcendence, at least for Haskins.

Most encouraging for Haskins are medieval students. "Some" of them, he assures his readers, in a comment that presumably calls on norms of white masculinity, "are full-blooded enough to satisfy any tests" (394). Haskins especially warms to his topic when he considers a 1220 letter from an Oxford clerk to his father. In the missive, the broke son asks his parent for money, thus evincing the poverty—and possibly the prodigality—associated with student life to this day. With palpable affection for his scholarly forebear, and even with a note of triumph at what seems to be iron-clad proof of the medieval roots of modern student life, Haskins proclaims, "The student of all subsequent time is here, sure proof of the existence of the new university life" (395). Haskins implicitly invites his readers—especially his fellow academics—to smile, wryly, at a medieval version of what for many were impoverished graduate student days.

While Haskins often tempers his laudatory portrayal of twelfth-century northern Europe by adopting a neutral tone, his fellow U.S. historian Lynn Thorndike (1882–1965) offers a more overtly celebratory take on the medieval. Along with Haskins, Thorndike was a "leading figure in the institutionalization of both medieval studies and the history of science."[67] His magnum opus, *A History of Magic and Experimental Science* (1923), features among the "modern research" marshaled by Haskins. That eight-volume project laid the foundation for subsequent work in astrology, astronomy, alchemy, and other topics pertaining to medieval science. Thorndike's monumental study also constituted a massive rebuttal of Burckhardt, insofar as it charted progress in science over the entire medieval period.

Thorndike well understood the emotive force of periodization. He concludes his final volume by signaling his objective detachment from the fourteenth- and fifteenth-century writings he has examined—"We have taken them as we have found them"—and then nodding at their potential emotional impact: "Read it and smile or read it and weep, as you please."[68] Unquestionably, any medievalist reader of *A History of Magic* occupies the former camp. Not only does "our period of thirteen centuries" exhibit a "marked tendency . . . to rely upon rationalism and experimental method," but also medieval people even "make some inventions and discoveries of use in the future advance of science."[69] Those thinkers even sensed the thrill of their achievements: "They themselves feel that they are making progress. . . . Magic still lingers but the march of modern science has begun."[70] Two decades after *A History of Magic* appeared, Thorndike would assume an even more markedly affective stance in an essay attacking the idea of Renaissance originality. There, he brazenly overturns Burckhardt's opposition of a stagnant Middle Ages to an innovative modernity. Via the counterintuitive example of an icon of medieval fantasy and superstition, the gargoyle, Thorndike contrasts the "imitative" bent of Renaissance "humanist[s]" with medieval invention and discovery:

> The sculptors of gargoyles and chimeras were not content to reproduce existing animals but showed their command of animal anatomy by creating strange compound and hybrid monsters—one might almost say, evolving new species—which nevertheless have all the verisimilitude of copies from living forms. It was these breeders in stone, these Burbanks of the pencil, these Darwins with the chisel, who knew nature and had studied botany and zoology in a way superior to the scholar who simply pored over the works of Aristotle and Pliny.[71]

For Thorndike, by finding in inert stone a version of what U.S. botanist Luther Burbank (1849–1926) found in plants, medieval sculptors evince a keen knowledge of life and reproductive change. Building toward a triumphant riff on medieval sculptors' proto-modern deployment of "stone," "pencil," and "chisel," Thorndike rouses his readers' admiration, approval, and excitement with all the rhetorical force of a stump speech.

Thorndike evinces how a medievalist's investment in modern values can, instead of precluding scholarly feeling, marshal a rousing rebuttal of received wisdom. But, perhaps, of all such academic studies, that which most approaches Huizinga's depth of feeling is British scholar R. W. Southern's *The Making of the Middle Ages* (1953). Southern's first book, written well into his career as an Oxford don, *Making* was during the twentieth century "the single most widely read and influential book written on the Middle Ages" and translated into no fewer than twenty-seven languages.[72] The tremendous success of *Making* may depend on its appeal to readerly sentiment, which exceeds that of any other post-Huizinga account of periodization.

Southern understood feelings as central to his scholarship; as he puts it in his 1970 presidential address to the Royal Historical Society, "The first duty of the historian" is the creation of "works which are emotionally and intellectually satisfying."[73] In *Making*, he grips readers on two levels, one of which involves a medieval version of Burckhardt's reveal and Greenblatt's swerve. Southern describes how a new "freedom and movement which developed in every branch of life during the eleventh and twelfth centuries" allowed individual and exceptionally gifted men to see, explore, and interpret both the world before them and the contemplative world within them.[74] Southern's examples include Bernard of Clairvaux (1090–1153), whose effort "to lay bare the recesses of the Soul" marked "the farthest point which the modern age had yet reached in the knowledge of God" (229). Importantly, Southern's medieval individuals are not just proto-Renaissance men but also proto-Romantics who unite, as Coleridge puts it, "deep feeling with profound thought" (especially Aristotelian logic).[75] Gregory VII (born Hildebrand of Sovana, 1020–85), for example, is a "man, explosive, filled with a dynamic power . . . eaten up with the one burning passion to restore the glory of the Apostles" (139). Southern thus excites readers through his profiles of great medieval men who are liberated to act upon their extraordinary hunger to learn, grow, and achieve.

But Southern's primary means of soliciting readerly affect pertains to a larger—and, for him, fundamentally unknowable—colonial phenomenon of which the individuals he discusses are a part: the "secret revolution" in which, out "of an area of sheer chaos," "Europe" emerged as a global hegemon (13, 15). Modernity, for Southern, primarily involves a drama in which Europeans ascend to developmental heights that set them apart from—and elevate them over—the rest of the world. As he puts it in his introduction, "For a thousand years Europe has been the chief centre of political experiment, economic expansion and intellectual discovery in the world. It gained this position during the period with which we are concerned: it is only losing it in our own day" (12). Ultimately, the emotional pleasures offered by *Making* entail less the bracing clarity of Burckhardt's reveal than the mystery and awe surrounding the slow and secret making of a massively powerful European entity:

> The significant events are often the obscure ones, and the significant utterances are often those of men withdrawn from the world and speaking to a very few. The truly formative work of the period was often hidden from the eyes of contemporaries and it is doubtless often hidden from ours. The stabilization of the boundaries of Europe, the slow recovery of political order, and the unprecedented acceleration of economic activity were not only in themselves silent reversals of previous tendencies: they were the conditions which made possible even more secret and momentous changes in thought and feeling, and in the direction of society for both secular and spiritual ends. (13)

Here and elsewhere in *Making*, Southern imbues his topic with such gravitas and mystery that the formation of Europe accrues a quasi-cosmic or epic significance that is accessible only through sentiment. He opens his final chapter by stating that the "fundamental changes" that *Making* has tracked "are hard to define . . . and the connexion between them cannot be explained" (219). Unlike Haskins, who uses the tools of modernity (that is, a neutral objectivity) to revise the medieval, Southern infuses medieval phenomena with such weight and grandeur that they exceed reason, "defy definition," and "can more readily be *felt* than explained" (219, my emphasis).

While *Making* shares with *Autumn* a deeply emotional bent, Southern's project directly counters that of Huizinga. The Dutch scholar laments the "autumn," "waning," and/or demise of a medieval Christian sensibility, while Southern celebrates the "making" or creation of a medieval European global power that persisted well into the twentieth century. Importantly, *Making* doesn't so much argue for the presence of modern trends in the medieval as make a case for redefining the *medieval itself* as new, contemporary, and tremendously powerful. As far as Southern is concerned, he and his readers are still very much in a medieval era. As a result, while Southern rarely employs the term "modern," he everywhere—well over two hundred times—uses the word "new."

Southern's model of periodization thus resembles that of Haskins. For both scholars, the medieval, far from the "other" to modernity, establishes modern forms that continue, without break, to the present day. But the stakes of Southern's project vastly exceed those of Haskins's *Renaissance*. In what is surely one of the most feel-good moves a medievalist could undertake, Southern rejects any association of the term "medieval" with backwardness and instead redefines the word as itself affiliated with contemporaneity and tremendous power. *Making* cultivates in its readers an admiration for the emergence of a new geopolitical entity possessed of both spatial and temporal greatness, a medieval European formation that would remain in place for some seven centuries and whose "results," he tells his mid-century readers, "are still with us" (11).

Medievalists would continue to claim a feel-good modernity for their period. In particular, and in keeping with Southern's emphasis on twelfth-century male personalities, scholars would assert the medieval roots of a version of Burckhardt's liberated modern self. Undoubtedly such ideologies of western individualism gained new life from the Cold War and its celebration of personal freedoms.[76] It's no accident that this period witnessed a slew of books about medieval selves, often by scholars like Southern, who saw communism as "the greatest practical threat of [his] time."[77] Consider, for example, the prolific doyen of postwar work on medieval political thought, Anglo-Austrian-Jewish scholar Walter Ullmann (1910–83) and his 1966 volume *The Individual and Society in the Middle Ages*. Written in the U.S. while the Cambridge historian had a visiting position at Johns Hopkins University and published in both the U.S. and Britain, *Individual and Society* charts the medieval roots of key components of those beloved American political concepts, democracy and citizenship.[78] Discovering the roots of a free West in, of all things, medieval feudalism, Ullmann celebrates how that political and economic system, and especially its contractual mechanism, liberated "the mere and so much despised *homo*" from his "tutelage" under a top-down Christian social order.[79] Ullmann renders the medieval "release of human forces and faculties which had hitherto lain dormant" as exhilarating (from a white western perspective, that is) as "New World" conquest: "It was," he writes, "as if a new continent had been discovered."[80]

Literary critics have long contributed to such efforts to claim modernity for the Middle Ages. Examples include U.S. critic Robert Hanning, whose *The Individual in Twelfth-Century Romance* (1977) examines the genre of romance as a response to "a new desire on the part of literate men and women to understand themselves as single, unique persons" during the "twelfth-century Renaissance."[81] Like Southern and Burckhardt, Hanning highlights the tensions and contradictions involved when humans wake up to their full potential. The book contrasts the "faith in the primacy and autonomy of individual experience" witnessed in the romances of Chrétien de Troyes's (b. 1135) with the conflict "between the claims of two visions, social and personal" portrayed in the Lancelot-Guinevere-Arthur plot of the anonymous *La Mort le Roi Artu* (c. 1225).[82] Hanning highlights the emotional impact of medieval romances on modern readers, including himself, through his use of the third person and an idiom of injury. The *Mort*, by "impaling us on the horns of this dilemma" regarding the conflict between self-fulfillment and the greater social good, offers a "moving manifestation" of fundamental desires and problems that remain pertinent to contemporary life.[83] Modern sensibilities, for Hanning, are not stunted and sundered from medieval sentiment in the manner described by Huizinga. Rather, "we" readers are struck sharply and deeply by the modernity of an Old French romance. A community of modern subjects feelingly emerges in the act of reading the *Mort*.

U.S. literary critic Lee Patterson (1940–2012) would celebrate a revised version of the "modern" medieval individual in his "important manifesto" on medieval studies, *Negotiating the Past: The Historical Understanding of Medieval Literature* (1987).[84] Published in the same decade in which *All That Is Solid* appeared, *Negotiating the Past* echoes Berman both in Patterson's rejection of the full-throttle negativity of "anti-modernists" like Foucault and his "recuperation of huma[n]" intellectual and emotional depth.[85] But the expansive and oppositional human consciousness that Berman finds in Marx, Nietzsche, and other nineteenth-century thinkers is found by Patterson, of course, in medieval literary texts. For Patterson, like Haskins and so many other medievalists, the twelfth century inaugurated a modernity that Patterson defines primarily in terms of a "crisis of historicism" (157). The medieval literature analyzed by Patterson presents a medieval, literary, and historicist counterpart to the creative destruction celebrated by Berman. As expansive and searching texts that "not only create the past but meditate upon that process, committing themselves to the endless negotiation that constitutes historicism," works such as Chrétien's *Érec et Énide* (c. 1170) and the *Roman d'Enéas* (c. 1160) offer models for a contemporary moment when, for Patterson, medievalists are in search of best practices (210). Thus, in the case of the anonymous alliterative *Morte Arthure* (c. 1400), Patterson cites Marx's *The Eighteenth Brumaire of Louis Bonaparte* (1852) to argue that "the poem's deepest concern" is not (as many critics suggest) the legitimacy of Arthur but rather a "complex and difficult meditation on the meaning of historical action in a world in which history is given and not made" (217). However, Patterson links his citation of *Eighteenth Brumaire* to a claim whose politics diverge markedly from that of Marx or Berman. *Negotiating the Past* asks the reader to sympathize with the tragic historical awareness and impotence of none other than King Arthur as a universal figure for the human condition: "It is less the king whom we are to admire than the man who must be king whom we are to pity" (230).

Distancing the Medieval from a Dark Modernity

Not all post–World War II medievalists embrace modernity and argue for "the essential continuity between the Middle Ages and the modern age" in the manner of Haskins and his inheritors. While these scholars do celebrate the medieval past, their feel-good Middle Ages resemble that of Huizinga insofar as they oppose the period to a modernity they deem problematic. An important example of this trend is Watson's focus in the piece with which this chapter began, Bynum's *Holy Feast and Holy Fast*. Bynum is arguably "the most influential American medievalist of her generation," and *Holy Feast* is her most renowned work.[86] The book evinces an interest in neo-Huizingan "sharp divisions of past and present" that belies her self-avowed "conviction that binaries and dualisms fail fundamentally to capture the basic issues of the Western intellectual tradition."[87] *Holy Feast* employs the word "modern" well over one hundred times, typically to showcase how "the distance created by many centuries" is nothing less than a chasm separating medieval perspectives from "vastly different modern assumptions."[88] The alterity of the medieval to modernity is utter, for Bynum: the "medieval symbols, behaviors, and doctrines" analyzed in *Holy Feast* "were produced by a world that has vanished" (299). No links remain.

That temporal abyss comprises Bynum's hook.[89] Much of the appeal of the medieval in *Holy Feast* is its sheer strangeness and unfamiliarity to "modern eyes" and "modern sensibilities" (46, 234, 235, 149, 451). A "vivid and disturbing" rhetoric of the strange dominates *Holy Feast*.[90] Terms like "abnormal," "strange," and "peculiar" not only appear over three dozen times in the book but also frequently receive added emphasis, so that medieval practices aren't just odd and bizarre but are "decidedly odd" and "of the most bizarre . . . sort" (190, 20). In keeping with Bynum's interest in medieval weirdness, *Holy Feast* centers on upsetting, even revolting, aspects of female Christian piety in late medieval Europe: fasting to the point of death, consuming the scabs of lepers, rubbing one's nose in pus.

Why highlight an abject Middle Ages? Why "reveal the past in its strangeness" (8)? After all, such aspects of the medieval might embarrassingly confirm Burckhardt's account of a superstitious and wrongheaded Middle Ages.[91] Bynum, however, embraces the strange and revolting based on her commitment to a sensational historicism bent on shocking readers. For Bynum, the weirdest aspects of medieval culture don't so much support negative stereotypes as assist her in shaking up the presentism of her contemporary readers. As Bynum puts it in her 1996 presidential address to the American Historical Association, "I was trying . . . to jolt my listeners and readers into encounter with a past that is unexpected and strange, a past whose lineaments are not what we at first assume, whose traces in our sources answer questions we haven't asked and deliver only silence to our initial, self-referential queries."[92] The strange, for Bynum, helpfully jostles moderns into realizing that there is more to history than the meanings generated by a contemporary mindset.

The feel of the medieval described by Bynum involves a kind of reverse swerve or reveal. If Greenblatt and Burckhardt celebrate a dramatic turn from medieval blindness to modern insight and an authentic vision of how earthly existence really works, Bynum celebrates an equally dramatic (if not more so, insofar as "jolt" carries a greater charge than either swerving or unveiling) turn from modern forms of knowledge production to a shocking confrontation with what proves other to a contemporary worldview. While Greenblatt's and Burckhardt's moderns suddenly see and suddenly know, Bynum thrusts modern readers out of any intellectual complacency.

Contemporary readers need Bynum's historicist shock therapy, *Holy Feast* implies, because it alerts them to a medieval richness and complexity sorely lacking in the present. Bynum's bad modernity thus resembles that of Huizinga. Just as Huizinga laments the deadened sensibilities of moderns, Bynum opens her book by noting how modern life numbs humans to the precious food around them: "In our industrialized corner of the globe, where food supplies do not fail, we scarcely notice grain or milk, ever-present supports of life" (1). And just as Huizinga laments how "causal-scientific thought" is incapable of perceiving the rich range of meanings to which medieval Christian symbolism gives rise (238), Bynum contrasts the "narrow and negative" nature of "modern clinical" approaches to food and the body to "the range and richness of medieval symbols" engaged by Christian women (299, 5). The reductive modern view on food and culture "cut[s] . . . off" and renders "one-sided" the "paradoxical" and multidimensional dynamics of food obsession in medieval Christian Europe (207, 298, 5). By "tak[ing] seriously" strange medieval perspectives and modes that moderns ignore or reject, Bynum and her readers discover "a mystical theology of considerable power and beauty" that showcases the "creativity and dignity" of female mystics and other Christian women (189, 152, 299).

Bynum disavows any Huizinga-like nostalgia or romanticization of the medieval on her part, affirming how "the actual lives of some late medieval women must give us pause" and that "no one could wish to return to a society in which the horrors of leprosy, gangrene, or starvation can be mitigated only by symbols that glorify pain and sacrifice" (299). Nevertheless, Bynum opposes an uplifting medieval feminine piety to a depressing modernity. Regardless of their problematic components, "the range and richness of medieval symbols have something to teach us about the impoverishment of our own" (302). Namely, medieval women's "wide range of positive resonances for both physicality and food" clarify the narrowness of contemporary attitudes. Regrettable modern phenomena like anorexia bespeak how "body and food" sadly are conscripted into limited service as "symbols of the failure of our efforts to control our selves" (300).

Bynum's statements regarding her methodological roots clarify her affinity with Huizinga. The historian has linked her embrace of a strange past to her status as "a product of the 60s" who tacked on her "bulletin board a copy of a Paris wall slogan from the student rebellion of 1968: 'Toute vue de choses qui n'est pas étrange est fausse' ('Every view of things that is not strange [that is, bizarre or foreign] is false')."[93] Bynum's self-alignment with the 1960s counterculture might urge the postmodernity of works like *Holy Feast*. But tellingly, the quote on her bulletin board—which she retained at least through the writing of *Holy Feast*—did not originate in the sixties. Rather, the quote was penned during the earlier modernist period of French symbolist Paul Valéry (1871–1945).[94] Valéry was a contemporary of Huizinga and a member of the aesthetic school whose tenets, as we have seen, were adopted by the Dutch historian. In certain respects, *Holy Feast* delineates a woman-oriented version of the contrasting yet "perfectly pictured world" described in *Autumn* (240). Consider, for example, the mineral metaphor Bynum often uses to characterize medieval women's symbolic thinking: "Like outcroppings of rock that may take differing and sometimes twisted forms but are built on the same crystalline structure," the rich and paradoxical meanings attached to body and food by medieval women religious "share a unifying theme behind their flamboyant variety of detail" (135). Like *Autumn*, and like the work of many French symbolists, *Holy Feast* centers on the intense feelings by which persons understood themselves and their existence within a rich, orderly, and interconnected—"crystalline"— symbolic system. Bynum effectively returns to the sensational historicism of Huizinga, but in a gendered register centered on the category of woman.[95]

While Bynum, like Huizinga, opposes a rich medieval Christian symbolism to an anemic modernity, a substantial group of scholars opposes the medieval to the modern in a more theoretical and philosophical vein. Namely, these critics admire their object of study for its affinity with *modern critiques* of modernity.[96] Examples of this trend include recent work by medievalists in English departments who align themselves with major critics of modernity such as Jameson, Foucault, Georges Bataille (1897–1962), and Weber. For example,

U.S. academics including Andrew Cole, Bruce Holsinger, Ethan Knapp, Erin Labbie, and D. Vance Smith have generated, in Louise D'Arcens's words, "important meta-analyses elucidating the under-acknowledged foundational role of medievalist thought in avant-garde, poststructuralist, and postcolonial theory."[97] Leading the charge to uncover the proto-postmodernity of medieval culture is Holsinger. His *The Premodern Condition* (2004) teases out the implications of the fact that many of modernity's fiercest critics—for instance, members of the French avant-garde such as Bataille, Pierre Bourdieu (1930–2002), Michel de Certeau (1925–86), Jacques Derrida (1930–2004), and Jacques Lacan (1901–81)—received training as medievalists. According to Holsinger, the medievalist education of figures like Bataille and Bourdieu signifies as no minor curiosity but rather "one of the most significant epiphenomena accompanying the emergence and consolidation of so-called French theory as a meta-discourse of posthumanistic inquiry."[98] In Holsinger's hands, feeling good about the medieval assumes an exciting new form in which the medievalist discovers in the medieval a salutary post- or anti-modernism. For Holsinger, continental theorists and philosophers "turned to the Middle Ages not in a fit of nostalgic retrospection," akin to Huizinga or other idealizers, "but in a spirit of both interpretive and ideological resistance to the relentless inevitability of modernity."[99] Neither a dark other nor a Huizinga-like lost ideal, the medieval emerges in *The Premodern Condition* as a "vital, dazzling" stimulus that breathes life into critiques of modernity.[100] Holsinger stresses that happily inspiriting relationship by employing words like "inspire" and "inspiring" nearly fifty times in his book. Holsinger thus turns on its head Burckhardt's famous account of the Renaissance rousing of the human from a long medieval slumber. Far from a soporific, the medieval stirred Derrida et al. to powerfully assess their modern moment.

While Holsinger understands the medieval by engaging its relationship with not modernity but a subsequent postmodern period, the final example of feel-good periodization covered in this chapter, Australian-American-British scholar James Simpson's *Reform and Cultural Revolution* (2002), returns to the Burckhardtian question of the medieval-Renaissance divide with which this chapter began, albeit within a strictly "English" purview. Simpson's book is the first installment of a multivolume institutional series touted by Oxford University Press as "the new century's definitive account" of English literary history.[101] A major rethinking of periodization, *Reform* has received wide attention in medieval English studies. Not only have a "swarm of reviewers and commentators" arisen "around it," but a special issue of the leading periodical *Journal of Medieval and Early Modern Studies* is dedicated to Simpson's volume.[102] The issue features responses to Simpson's "exhilarating and brilliant book" by a slew of luminaries in Middle English studies.[103]

Simpson's purview is English writings from 1350 to 1547, a move not unlike that undertaken earlier by medievalists such as A. C. Spearing.[104] But while Spearing and other scholars examined that time span to problematize the idea of a break, Simpson does so to forcefully assert a division between superior medieval and inferior early modern eras. Overturning the received idea (witnessed in Greenblatt's Norton Anthology essay) that the Henrician era saw the release of the English from the oppressive shackles of a corrupt, authoritarian, and superstitious medieval church, Simpson relates "a narrative of diminishing liberties" (1). Simpson portrays the early English Renaissance as a dark era that retains the pejorative and rejects the praiseworthy components of received understandings of that period by Burckhardt and his inheritors. The Italian despotism acknowledged by Burckhardt in *Civilization* reappears in English guise in *Reform* in the figure of a tyrannical Henry VIII. Henry is so successful at garnering absolute authority for himself that the monarch hampers early modern English thinkers from realizing their human agency in the manner of the Italians celebrated by Burckhardt. Far from the moment when men finally discovered their long-hidden potential, Simpson's early modernity is a time when the "totalizing perspective" and "tighter discursive constraints" demanded by a newly centralized state caused English writers a world of pain (31, 127). A good deal of that suffering, according to Simpson's ingenious argument, results from their break with the past. "Historical rupture" creates within early modern writers a kind of psychic gash or mental ripping (127). Thanks to their pained double consciousness of the utter difference between a medieval "then" and an early modern "now," writers such as John Leland (1503–52), John Bale (1495–1563), Thomas Wyatt (1503–42), and Henry Howard, Earl of Surrey (1517–47), endure a "division of self" that leads to "grief" and "melancholy" (127).

Reform thus might prompt in readers sympathy for the torturous constraints endured by early modern writers. But Simpson's take on those writers' late medieval predecessors is entirely another matter. "Redescribing the relation between the 'medieval' in positive, and 'early modern' in rather more negative terms," Simpson claims that while Henry's authoritarianism oppressed early modern writers, the "terrible and violent instability at the centre" of late medieval English politics paradoxically *assisted* figures like John Lydgate (1370–1451), William Langland (1332–86), the alliterative *Morte Arthure* author, Margery Kempe (1373–1438), and Thomas Malory (d. 1471) and empowered the creators of genres such as saints' lives and cycle plays (560). Factors such as civil war and repeated seizures of the crown freed up a space—what Simpson calls a "decentred discursive field"—for the lively flourishing of a heterogeneous medieval culture unburdened by the authoritarianism and historical discontinuities wrought by a sixteenth-century "revolution" (52). The late Middle Ages in England was a time, for Simpson, when "different authors" not only could "posit different arenas" and various "modes" of "constraining the king" but also were "not at all embarrassed" to approach "the past accretively rather than" being burdened to "begin afresh" (197, 229, 64).[105]

Ironically, Simpson himself proves to be somewhat of a rhetorical tyrant. His argument eschews qualifications and counterclaims for what it announces in the book's first sentence as its "very simple, central, and consistent theme: that the institutional simplifications and centralizations of the sixteenth century provoked correlative simplifications and narrowings in literature" (1). Whether intentional or unconscious, this opening sentence foregrounds a central paradox of *Reform*, whose argument regarding "simplifications and centralizations" is itself "very simple" and "central." As Bruce Holsinger and David Wallace note, the entirety of the volume is governed by a single, "uncompromising," and "powerful organizing idea" that Simpson adamantly asserts with vigor and even willfulness.[106] All of which is to say that qualifying the feel-good heterogeneity of the medieval celebrated in *Reform* is the manifest pleasure taken by Simpson in his own rhetorical absolutism. If Simpson makes us feel bad about early modern melancholics like Leland, he also illustrates the bracing "exhilarat[ion]" of the despot (vii).

Central to Simpson's forceful argument is his rehabilitation of the end of the Middle Ages, the very period portrayed as a time of decline by Huizinga, a scholar who inevitably haunts *Reform*. While Simpson defends Huizinga, claiming that his "critics" often occlude "the richness of his argument," his late medieval England couldn't be more different from its Burgundian counterpart in *Autumn* (260). *Autumn* laments a dying Christian society whose "symbolizing function has," in Huizinga's words, "become merely mechanical" (249). Unconcerned with the sort of "rich and comforting consciousness of communal identity" endorsed by Huizinga and other nostalgic anti-modernists (560), Simpson celebrates how political disorder and the presence of multiple "adjacent, overlapping institutions" such as "fraternities, guilds, and parliament" energized a diverse, reformist, and "self-regulating" late medieval English culture (559).

Simpson counterintuitively proves his thesis through artifacts that would seem to support Huizinga's claims about late medieval morbidity. *Reform* thus opens by contrasting the paralyzing mental impasse suffered by Henrician author John Leland with the "energies" of Lydgate and his seemingly morbid *Danse Macabre*, which Simpson views as a telling exemplar of Lydgate's "heterogeneous oeuvre, which is riven in genre, style and semiotic practice" (67). In the surprising example of the death-obsessed *Danse*, "the energy of the whole text" derives from how "authority is translated, represented, and renegotiated between" different "geographical, institutional, and discursive spaces" (62).

Yet, for all their differences, Simpson's and Huizinga's books follow identical affective trajectories. Each thinker discovers in the medieval elements that, in Simpson's words, "win admiration" (560). While Huizinga's work is saturated with nostalgia for lost high medieval "values of coherence and unity" and Simpson's work is "suffused with the values, hopes, and laments of liberal humanism," both scholars render the medieval era an object of positive scholarly sentiment.[107]

Regardless of their variation, all the feelings that medievalists from Huizinga to Simpson bring to bear on their object of study serve the same affective goal: rejecting the idea of the Middle Ages as the feel-bad other of modernity. My discussion of accounts of periodization by major white scholars of modernity confirms that negative view on the years before 1500 CE. Thinkers from Burckhardt to Marx to Jameson all endorse a discourse that draws a hard line dividing a modern now from a medieval then, to the detriment of the latter era. To be sure, as Marx evinces, the *idea* of the medieval (that is, the superstitious, irrational, backward, emotional) proves to be an attractive rhetorical tool that helps unpack the antimonies of the "human condition" in the West. And, as Jameson indicates, a modern scholar might embrace exceptional thinkers from the medieval period for their hermeneutic breadth and ingenuity. But the medieval period itself—the years between roughly 500 and 1500 CE—is an object of dismay, horror, pity, and, worst of all, disregard and dismissal. Taking their cues from the modern discourse of periodization, an outraged and insulted medievalist cohort retaliates via diverse feel-good rehabilitations of the Middle Ages.

Both the modernist discourse of periodization and medieval scholars' resistance to that discourse are problematic. It goes without saying that 500–1500 CE in Europe entailed a messy complexity that the descriptor "medieval" fails miserably to capture. And modernists' disinterest in any careful and substantial consideration of the years before 1500 CE has created a climate that puts medievalists on the defensive, prompting them to somehow rethink periodicity in ways that reverse the idea of a "bad" Middle Ages. In effect, the rhetoric or discourse of modernity has had far too strong a hold on white ideas about European history. Both the medieval-modern divide and the opposition of a suppressed and a liberated human rationality which that binary evokes obstruct a fuller assessment and critique of the years on either side of 1500 CE.

2

"Between Then and Now"

The Veil of Periodization

And then—the Veil. It drops as drops the night on southern seas—vast, sudden, unanswering. There is Hate behind it, and Cruelty and Tears. As one peers through its intricate, unfathomable pattern of ancient, old, old design, one sees blood and guilt and misunderstanding. And yet it hangs there, this Veil, between Then and Now, between Pale and Colored and Black and White—between You and Me. Surely it is a thought-thing, tenuous, intangible; yet just as surely it is it true and terrible and not in our little day may you and I lift it.

—W. E. B. DU BOIS

Periodization has often been a product of white supremacy.
—MARY RAMBARAN-OLM

In his foundational *The Souls of Black Folk* (1903), Black U.S. scholar-activist W. E. B. Du Bois recounts how his childhood rejection by a white girl at school prompted his sudden and heart-wrenching realization that he was "like" white people "in heart and life and longing, but shut out from their world by a vast veil."[1] Introduced in *Souls* and developed elsewhere in his ample scholarly corpus, Du Bois's metaphor of the veil models a richly dialectical, ambivalent, and contradictory approach to the workings of racism. Described by Howard Winant as "the most nuanced and powerful theory of race and racism ever developed," Du Bois's metaphor of a racializing veil has attracted an outpouring of academic commentary.[2] Much scholarship on the Du Boisian veil engages questions of space, thanks partly to Du Bois's provocative mapping of racism onto a triangular dynamic that, in the example of his initial *Souls* anecdote, involves the girl, Du Bois's younger self, and the totalizing curtain between them. Critics including Arnold Rampersad, Robert Stepto, Adolf Reed Jr., and Robert Gooding-Williams explore Du Bois's spatial emphasis by linking the veil's status as a material barrier to a particular place, typically the region of the U.S. South, and the segregation laws that followed the failure of Reconstruction.[3] That pioneering scholarship on Du Bois has been extended in work on Black diasporic subjectivity by Michelle Wright, on the afterlife of segregation by Michelle Alexander, on Black embodiment by George Yancy, and in other studies that address the full range of spatial and geographic rhetorics in the eminent writer's oeuvre.[4]

Yet Du Bois's veil metaphor possesses not only spatial but also temporal dimensions. For example, consider how the *Souls* anecdote marks a rupture in the periodization of Du Bois's biography. Before his encounter with the girl, a young Du Bois enjoyed a certain innocence with respect to racism. The fall of the veil inaugurates a new period shadowed by the mental and societal fragmentations imposed by whiteness. Consider, moreover, my epigraph, taken from Du Bois's bestselling volume *Darkwater: Voices from within the Veil* (1920). There, Du Bois describes how the white rejection of persons of color also entails assessments of time: the veil that "hangs ... between Pale and Colored and Black and White" also "hangs ... *between Then and Now*."[5] Racism, Du Bois's rhetoric of periodicity suggests, involves segregations that are as historicizing as they are geographic. After all, his dialectic of the veil comprises part of a larger revision of Hegel in which Du Bois inserts Black subjects into an account of "the official drama of historical movement" from which Hegel exiles them.[6] As Michelle Wright puts it, for the German philosopher, "Africa remains mired in a primitive past, one lacking an understanding of freedom—that which should ultimately distinguish humans from animals."[7] White supremacy, Du Bois's veil highlights, is of a piece with representations of a modern white "now" versus a backward "then," a relationship highlighted by Mary Rambaran-Olm in my second epigraph.[8]

Scholars including Paul Gilroy and Eric Sundquist highlight the historical dimensions of Du Bois's veil. Both academics stress how, along with Du Bois's searching account of the Black subject's complex and contradictory ontology in a national and segregated context, one must attend to "the novelty and power of his critique of modernity."[9] Du Bois's fullest critique of white modernity appears in "The Souls of White Folk," the second chapter of *Darkwater*. There, in a shattering assessment, he exposes how the modern discovery of an agential, rational, and enterprising human subjectivity is central to the meaning of the veil. Writing from the critical vantage point of one located behind the veil and thus painfully cognizant of its falsity, he exposes the alignment of all modern virtues—progress, reason, civility—with white supremacy. He identifies as a "very modern thing" how "the world in a sudden, emotional conversion has discovered that it is white and by that token, wonderful!" and that "every great thought the world ever knew was a white man's thought; that every great deed the world ever did was a white man's deed; that every great dream the world ever sang was a white man's dream" (30–31). Pondering western modernity through the "world-old eyes" of "the darker world," Du Bois recognizes how ideas of western civilization and progress are not "truths" but rather part and parcel of a racializing veil—that is, a discourse of whiteness that both cloaks and authorizes horrible practices such as settler colonization and chattel slavery (35, 41). Having torn away the veil of a "wonderful" modern West, he proclaims, "I see these souls undressed and from the back and side. I see the working of their entrails. I know their thoughts. . . . I see them ever stripped,—ugly, human" (29). Pushing through the scrim, Du Bois lays bare the naked truth of a sordid and murderous whiteness.

This chapter takes Du Bois's line, "And yet it hangs there, this Veil, between Then and Now," as an invitation to use theories of race to revisit the questions of periodization covered in Chapter 1. In particular, I consider how Du Bois's veil may be put into productive conversation with work on the politics of periodization by scholars including Johannes Fabian and Edward Said. In their celebrated studies, Fabian and Said articulate how white western elites have used periodic division to assert and legitimize social hierarchy, consigning "inferior" humans to older and seemingly more primitive historical epochs, while aligning "superior" humans with new and improved eras. Said's groundbreaking 1978 study describes how British and French scholars working in the academic discipline of Orientalist studies produce "knowledge" about the "'primitive' state" of non-western peoples who are the object of British and French imperial projects.[10] Five years later, in a book centered on the white western politics of his field of specialization, anthropology, Fabian would state that "the history of our discipline . . . is in the end about the relationship between the West and the Rest" and the deployment of ideas of "naturalized spatialized Time . . . for the purpose of distancing those who are observed from the [modern] time of the observer."[11] Both Said and Fabian clarify how a politics of time—charged oppositions of societal stagnation versus human progress—is foundational to the colonial discourses of western modernity.

Bringing Du Bois's work to bear on what Fabian famously calls a western "denial of coevalness" clarifies how the temporal inequities asserted by moderns are as racial as they are colonizing.[12] More precisely, putting Du Bois's dialectics of the veil into conversation with periodization provides a means of confronting it as a multidimensional and contradictory racializing endeavor. Understanding periodization in terms of Du Bois's telling metaphor demands analyzing what discursive categories like "modernity" do *for* and *to* persons positioned on either side of the veil of race. How does periodization connect whites to and bar nonwhites from a modern subjectivity? And how does periodization assume a new guise when viewed from behind the veil, a location that both burdens persons of color with double consciousness and endows them with a "second-sight" that exposes the wrongheadedness and lethal nature of the white discourse of modernity?[13] In asking such questions, I join an expanding cohort of medievalists who consider Du Bois and periodization. Scholars including Matthew Vernon, Cord Whitaker, Seeta Chaganti, Andrea Achi, and Michelle Warren explore Du Bois's complex historical sensibility and his interest in unsettling received ideas of not just modernity but also, and more surprisingly, the medieval.[14] As Vernon shows, Du Bois engages tropes of an idealized medieval past to expose "'whiteness' to be a fiction separate and apart from medieval source material" and to participate in a larger African American project that claims "the Middle Ages as a point of origin or a creative point of departure . . . to articulate" new ideas of identity and belonging.[15]

This chapter, however, is not centered on Du Bois's direct citations of the Middle Ages, European or otherwise. Rather, I reassess the medieval-modern divide via his searching commentary on racism in the form of the dialectics of the veil. Because Du Bois's graphic metaphor crisscrosses problems of whiteness, periodization, and race, it uniquely speaks to how western authorities living on both sides of 1500 CE have understood their historicity.

In what follows, I first expand on the deeply pessimistic assessment of modernity generated by Du Bois and other critics who are complexly positioned both in and outside the West. After unpacking the "feel-bad" modernisms of thinkers who straddle such a difficult yet revelatory liminal location, the remainder of the chapter considers how Du Bois contributes to a critique of not only modernity but also a longer historical trajectory encompassing the years before and after 1500 CE. On one hand, I take seriously Du Bois's claim, which appears in my epigraph from *Darkwater*, that the veil takes its "pattern of ancient, old, old design" (246). I argue that, as a phenomenon of "old design," the veil manifests a temporal continuity—a *longue durée* of racist discourse— that undoes ideas of historical rupture. Elites in Europe spun racializing veils well before 1500 CE. But on the other hand, as Du Bois instructs, the veil also "hangs . . . between Then and Now." My argument places pressure on Du Bois's use of the preposition "between" to connote the time of the veil. As the *OED* indicates, "between" is an "intervening space" that refers, on a double register, "to space as *separating* or *connecting*."[16] Insofar as the veil describes racializing periodizations that also took place before the so-called rupture of modernity, the idea of a "Veil . . . between Then and Now" connotes its function as not just a gap or barrier but also a temporal bridge. Race both undoes claims regarding temporal rupture *and* provides the very grounds for discourses of rupture in the first place. I explore those complex racial and temporal relationships by returning to the question theorized by the western academics covered in Chapter 1: What is the nature of the relationship between the "periods" before and after 1500 CE? Paying special attention to Jacob Burckhardt's groundbreaking and still influential *Civilization of the Renaissance in Italy* (1860), I take several analytic passes backward in a discussion that engages various components of a racializing "Veil . . . between Then and Now." Because of its multidimensionality as a function of the veil, the relationship between "medieval" and "modern" race demands such recursive sweeps.

My first analytic foray employs the work on "man" by Jamaican intellectual Sylvia Wynter (b. 1928) to explore the medieval roots of whiteness. While Du Bois pioneered thought on the existence of a modern veil of false white consciousness, Wynter expands on that groundbreaking work to clarify how western subjectivity remains caught in a closed and racializing medieval episteme. Drawing on Wynter's analysis of an Italian treatise embraced by Burckhardt as preeminently modern—the "Oration on the Dignity of Man" (1486) by Giovanni Pico della Mirandola (1463–94)—I consider how Middle English writers Geoffrey Chaucer (d. 1400) and Thomas Malory (d. 1471) adumbrate the modern white dynamic revealed by Wynter. My second pass at medieval and modern race engages the formative phenomenon of Christian antisemitism. Among the many instantiations of race before 1500 CE, antisemitism has proven notably influential, so much so that, as Kathleen Biddick and Kathleen Davis affirm, it made possible the linkage of a medieval-modern divide to "one of colonialism's most cherished stories."[17] I trace such connections as they appear in the denials of coevalness performed by Burckhardt and Johan Huizinga. Third, and finally, I return once more to Burckhardt and Christian antisemitism, this time using Du Bois to critique the veil metaphors at play in both *Civilization* and the epistle of an early Jewish-Christian thinker with whom Burckhardt was quite familiar, Saul/Paul (c. 5 to 64–65 CE). Comparing Burckhardt's oft-told account of the reveal of modernity with the representation of a Jewish veil of literalism in Saul/Paul's foundational work, his second epistle to the Corinthians, I clarify how the Swiss historian rejected a veil of medieval superstition in terms that paradoxically expose his complicity with the medieval racialized denials of coevalness established by Paul. Through these Du Bois–inspired recursive passes at Wynter and whiteness, medieval antisemitism, and Burckhardt's Pauline debt, I urge jettisoning received and hardened truisms about western periodization in favor of a dynamic encounter with the multiple and dialectical workings of race over a *longue durée*. The chapter concludes by considering the implications of a Pauline foundation for representations of modernity, especially the carryover of ideas of a Christian spirituality into subsequent ideas of a white European spirit.

The Darkest Side of Modernity

The scholarly accounts of periodization covered in Chapter 1 include studies that attach a particular kind of negative feeling to modernity, namely, the "iron cage" outlook of critics who see a host of oppressive totalities consuming all aspects of modern existence. But in fact, their respective critiques could—and, indeed, should—be far bleaker. The "dark side" of modernity entails more than, say, the false consciousness of individualism under capitalism. The situation is more dire. For those very ideologies of modern individualism are centered upon—and thus attach humanity and agency to—certain populations at the expense of other groups. Consider, for example, the vexed and contradictory gender politics of a modern world that often embraces, as Rita Felski points out, "the modern individual" as "an autonomous male free of familial and communal ties."[18] Or consider the modern marginalization of the differently abled white people analyzed by Lennard Davis, the non-normative sexualities analyzed by Foucault, and the nonhuman "natural" entities discussed by Timothy Morton.[19] The concept of white modern personhood occludes in Europe, to varying degrees, anyone who or anything that isn't an elite heterosexual man.

Yet even when they attend to women and other kinds of outsiders, as long as white critiques of modernity remain "internal" or circumscribed by "the history of Europe itself," they are marred by blind spots and repressions that ignore a still "darker"—more depressing, more horrifying—"side of modernity."[20] As Gilroy puts it, "The critique of modernity cannot be satisfactorily completed from within its own philosophical and political norms, that is, imminently."[21] For the bleakest and also the most penetrating critique of modernity, one must shift from a white Eurocentric assessment to one arising from a different vantage point: that of intellectuals "inescapably" positioned, in Gilroy's words, "both inside and outside the dubious protection modernity offers."[22] Precisely because of their alignment with what Walter Mignolo describes as the "non-European histories entangled with Western modernity," figures as early as Olaudah Equiano (c.1745–97) and Frederick Douglass (1818–95), and later thinkers including Richard Wright (1908–60), C. L. R. James (1901–89), and Gerald Vizenor (b. 1934) have manifested a singularly acute, expansive, and withering evaluation of the years after 1500 CE.[23]

Du Bois describes both the unique vantage point on modernity possessed by intellectuals of color and the disturbing vision it makes available in "Souls of White Folk." Elaborating on his theory of double consciousness as a source of both anguish and special powers of perception, Du Bois explains how the same Black Americans covered by the veil of white supremacy are "singularly clairvoyant" about white people and modern life (29). He relates how, thanks to his ability to "view them from unusual points of vantage" from which he can "see in and through" them, whites are "ever stripped" and consequently "ugly" to a degree ignored in Eurocentric accounts of modernity (33). From his location at a critical remove from white society, "high in the tower, where" he "sit[s] above the loud complaining of the human sea," Du Bois generates an astute critique of the ghastly hypocrisies that attend western modernity (29). Examples include Congo, where the supposedly ameliorating acts of "commerce and civilization" lead instead to "rubber and murder, slavery in its worst form"; and the United States, where "in the name of Civilization, Justice, and Motherhood," "all varieties of "orgy, cruelty, barbarism, and murder [are] done to men and women of Negro descent" (38, 33).

Crucially, for Du Bois and other thinkers who "stand simultaneously both inside and outside the western culture which has been their peculiar stepparent," the horrifying acts witnessed in the years after 1500 CE aren't simply coincidental to or coterminous with modernity.[24] Neither do those inhuman acts comprise a mere portion or fraction of modernity. Rather, they are what Gilroy and Mignolo respectively describe as "the premise of modernity" and "its very condition of possibility."[25] In other words, the critique issued from behind the veil strikes at the core of periodization, exposing how claims about what is modern provide the cognitive foundation for a harmful—indeed, a lethal—discourse.

Du Bois's veil metaphor testifies to that problematic. As a man-made artifact (a piece of fabric), a veil embodies the constructed and false nature of the supposedly objective viewpoint on man and the world enabled by modern life.[26] Additionally, as a single "vast" piece of material made of threads interlaced at right angles, a veil indicates how white western epistemologies craft an expansive, totalizing, and grid-like world woven of a large repertoire of binary oppositions. Finally, as a man-made object that conceals what lies beneath it, the veil indicates how western discourse, for all its semantic world-building, never offers any clear vision of an objective reality. Rather, discourses of modernity occlude the personhood of humans whom they misconstrue as quasi- or even nonhuman. The stereotypes conjured by western discourse blind the white subject to the humanity of persons of color.

A keen scholar of periodization, Du Bois shatters the dominant ways that white westerners misrepresent their historicity to themselves and the world, even as he observes the regrettable omnipresence of the dehumanizing pseudologic of white modernity:

> This theory of human culture and its aims has worked itself through the warp and woof of our daily thought with a thoroughness that few realize. Everything great, good, efficient, fair, and honorable is "white"; everything mean, bad, blundering, cheating, and dishonorable is "yellow"; a bad taste is "brown"; and the devil is "black." The changes of this theme are continually rung in picture and story, in newspaper heading and moving-picture, in sermon and school book, until, of course, the King can do no wrong,—a White Man is always right and a Black Man has no rights which a white man is bound to respect. (44)

With his references to such binaries as white vs. black, good vs. bad, efficient vs. lazy, and honor vs. shame, Du Bois indicates how whites aren't advanced thanks to the objectivity of their modern age; rather, they falsely categorize the world via cognitive opposites. Crucial to Du Bois's analysis is the sheer depth and breadth of a white modern "theory of human culture and its aims." If European critics like Foucault and Weber point to the totalizing reach of the state and capital, Du Bois exposes the totalizing reach of white supremacist discourse. The veil is so vast as to appear "in picture and story, in newspaper heading and moving-picture, in sermon and school book." Through his emphasis on the myriad sites where racism circulates, Du Bois revises dominant ideas of periodization. Having "worked itself through the warp and woof of our daily thought with a thoroughness that few realize," the veil persists long after so-called emancipation, thus undermining narratives of temporal development. As Du Bois puts it in my epigraph from *Darkwater*, while the veil "is a thought-thing, tenuous, intangible," its presence in a host of cultural forms paradoxically renders "it true and terrible *and not in our little day may you and I lift it*" (246, my emphasis). In lieu of white mythologies of European change and advance, Du Bois portrays a dismayingly durable racial culture.

The work on modernity by Du Bois and other scholars situated at various removes from white supremacy has significant implications for the scholarship discussed in Chapter 1. Namely, the view from inside the veil reveals how western scholars—figures who include Burckhardt, Karl Marx, and Marshall Berman—are trapped within the very cognitive mode Du Bois scrutinizes.[27] Instead of recognizing modernity, as Du Bois does, as a cognitive construct—"a thought-thing, tenuous, intangible" that misrepresents the world—they inhabit that discourse and abide by its wrongheaded terms. All too often, major assessments of modernity accept as unquestioned universals what instead are white representations whose politics demand investigation. In effect, western academics often sift the world through the (il)logic of the veil, instead of critiquing it and the damage it wreaks.

Scholars of not just modernity but also the medieval period are implicated in this dynamic. As we have seen, western medievalists frequently advance claims about their object of study in conformity with the terms of a white discourse of periodization. In particular, as Chapter 1 highlighted, as a result of western scholars' denigration and othering of the years before 1500 CE, western medievalists often resist a pessimistic view of their period. Yet by approaching periodization as a racializing veil, one can disrupt that methodological pattern. The analysis of race made available by Du Bois provides a means of dislodging medievalists from their reactive relationship to how the West has long (mis)represented itself to itself. A race-oriented view of modernity puts that white discourse in its place as a *particular* way of construing history that is problematically aligned with the elevation of "the West" and the denigration of "the Rest."[28]

Instead of taking their cues from white discourses of modernity, white medievalists might interrogate the history of a racializing veil itself, along with the violence and divisions that discourse supports. Black U.S. historian Jennifer Morgan models such a mode of inquiry in her 2004 book *Laboring Women*. There, Morgan reverses Du Bois's historical purview. That is, while " Souls of White Folk" explains the *ongoing* power of white supremacist discourse after emancipation, Morgan demonstrates how versions of that discourse circulated *earlier*, at the very dawn of the Atlantic slave trade and settler colonialism, and still earlier, during the Middle Ages. In a multidimensional or intersectional analysis attuned to questions of race, gender, and sexuality, she details how white European men during the sixteenth and seventeenth centuries "laid the discursive groundwork" for slavery by constructing the "black woman" as possessed of a "monstrous body" whose "sole utility" was "the ability to produce crops and other laborers."[29] Like Du Bois, Morgan highlights the "thoroughness" with which western discursive oppositions circulated in all sorts of early writings. Texts from "legislative acts, laws, wills, bills of sale, and plantation inventories" to "journals and adventurers' tales of travels" legitimated slavery by activating oppositions such as white vs. black, pure vs. impure, human vs. monstrous, and spirit vs. body.[30] Moreover, those texts take up earlier medieval representations. Citing evidence from medieval texts including the portrayal of shameless Ethiopian women in the colossally popular *Mandeville's Travels* (c. 1357–71), Morgan shows how "the meanings attached to the female African body were inscribed well before the establishment of England's colonial American plantations."[31]

Sylvia Wynter, the *longue durée* of Race, and Middle English Whiteness

Versions of the medieval racializing discourses cited by Morgan, like their modern counterparts, authorized a variety of offensive historical practices that included, but were not limited to, crusader violence, anti-Jewish pogroms, and the colonization of "savage" populations in Ireland and other border sites in Europe. And, as both medievalists such as Geraldine Heng, Lisa Lampert-Weissig, Jacqueline de Weever, and Cord Whitaker and scholars of modernity including Gilroy, Morgan, Winthrop Jordan, and Cedric Robinson affirm, modern phenomena like chattel slavery, genocide, and settler colonialism and their self-authorizing discourses recall and rework medieval systems of representation and historical practices.[32]

To be sure, when viewed from a global or transnational perspective, there is no denying that the modern era marked a massive shift in the scale of the crimes authorized by white discourse. However detestable, the maltreatment during the Middle Ages of the Irish, Jews, Muslims, and other groups hardly approximates the immensity of the atrocities enacted by modern western agents against Jews, Africans, Native Americans, and other populations around the globe. A medieval-modern rupture with respect to the scale of white supremacist violence is undeniable. The idea of some kind of temporal shift around 1500 CE acknowledges this important historical change.

And yet the worldview that mobilized and enabled modern horrors also marks the continuation of medieval ways of seeing. With, to riff on Du Bois's language, "a thoroughness that few realize," modern assertions of "objective" reality promote subjective Euro- and androcentric assumptions drawn from medieval representational systems. As Heng puts it with respect to high and late medieval racial formations, understanding "the unstable entity we call 'The West' and its self-authorizing missions" that center and empower "*homo europaeus*—the European subject—emerges in part through racial grids produced from the twelfth through fifteenth centuries."[33] Heng's comment radically revises the tenor of work on periodization by such academics as Charles Homer Haskins, R. W. Southern, and Walter Ullmann. As Chapter 1 stressed, those white scholars rejected Burckhardtian ideas of medieval chains that prevented the birth of modern man and redefined the medieval as itself marvelously modern. Centering their arguments often on the twelfth century as the beginning of a "medieval modernity," those academics celebrate figures such as

Hildebrand of Sovana, whom Southern praises as a "man, explosive, filled with a dynamic power."[34] Heng joins those scholars in querying the idea of a rupture. Yet the continuity she traces is not celebratory but sobering. The powerful man embraced by Haskins et al. is of a piece with Heng's "homo europaeus"—that is, a damaging white supremacist.

Perhaps the most monumental contribution made to such antiracist contestations of the medieval-modern divide appears in the oeuvre of Jamaican intellectual Sylvia Wynter. As Somalian-German-U.S. scholar Alexander Weheliye puts it, Wynter's "colossal" and "large-scale intellectual project, which she has been pursuing in one form or another for the last thirty years," entails nothing less than "critiquing the current western instantiation of the human as coterminous with the white liberal subject and . . . crafting a new humanism."[35] Weheliye's rhetoric, with its association of Wynter with a "new humanism," highlights her status as a radical reviser of the received western terms of periodization. The Renaissance humanism that someone like Burckhardt viewed as new, as marking a rupture, is, for Wynter, part of an old white order that she seeks to topple. Over the course of her major intellectual interrogation of the category of the human, Wynter has donned a slew of disciplinary hats, including those of philosopher, literary critic, anthropologist, playwright, economist, and medievalist. Engaging the work of not just medievalists such as Jacques Le Goff, Lynn Thorndike, and Ullmann but also the theories of spiritual subjectivity leveled by medieval thinkers like Thomas Aquinas, Wynter tracks the linkages between the "present ethnoclass (western bourgeois) conception of the human, which overrepresents itself as if it were the human itself," and medieval Christian concepts of personhood.[36]

Wynter focuses on high medieval academic discourses (for instance, scholastic binary oppositions of purity vs. contamination, heavenly vs. earthly, piety vs. sin) to track how, following Le Goff, "the Gregorian reform was actually an effort of modernization" that set the terms for subsequent assertions of white supremacy in the form of a western construction of the human that Wynter terms "Man," in a nod to its androcentrism.[37] The modern dynamic in which western "Man" claims dominance over populations of color involves the secularization of politicized assertions by the medieval clergy of their superior spirituality and the laity's "enslavement to the Fallen Flesh."[38] In an interview, Wynter describes this dynamic in the context of a discussion of the contemporary use of whitening creams and the endorsement of "designer babies" by genetic engineers, asserting that "our present episteme . . . functions, with respect to the knowledge of our contemporary world and its systemic reality, *according to the same cognitively closed descriptive statement . . . as that of the theo-Scholastic knowledge system of the medieval order of Latin-Christian*

Europe."³⁹ Wynter similarly contends in her wide-ranging essay "1492: A New World View" that the western Christian "encoding cosmogonic schema" was "transumed" or "retroped" on behalf of the modern *"civitas saecularis."*⁴⁰ In other words, for Wynter, modernity maintained, albeit in secular terms, the very veil through which Christians, from the high Middle Ages onward, understood and hierarchized social life. Wynter's work effectively elaborates the implications of Du Bois's claim that the veil, a white western "knowledge system," bridges or "hangs . . . between" the supposed rupturing of a medieval "then" from a modern "now." While the veil proclaims whiteness as a "very modern thing" and denies coevality to non-whites, such representations aren't new but rather take their "pattern of ancient, old, old design."

In her mammoth eighty-page essay "Unsettling the Coloniality of Being/Power/Truth/Freedom: Towards the Human, After Man, Its Overrepresentation—An Argument," (2003), Wynter devotes several pages to analyzing Pico della Mirandola's "Oration on the Dignity of Man" as a pivotal event in the transition to modernity and thus whiteness.⁴¹ Burckhardt also singles out Pico's "Oration," claiming that it articulates "the loftiest conceptions" of the "one single result of the Renaissance [that] is enough to fill us with everlasting thankfulness"—that is, how "men and mankind were [in Italy] first thoroughly and profoundly understood."⁴² But what Burckhardt celebrates as "one of the noblest bequests of that great age" (185), Wynter pessimistically links to an epochal shift with potentially apocalyptic ramifications in the new millennium. The relevant moment in Pico's "Oration" serves as an epigraph for Wynter's piece:

> Now the highest Father, God the master-builder, . . . took up man . . . and placing him at the midpoint of the world . . . spoke to him as follows: "We have given to thee, Adam, no fixed seat, no form of thy very own, no gift peculiarly thine, that thou mayest feel as thine own, have as thine own, possess as thine own the seat, the form, the gifts which thou thyself shalt desire. A limited nature in other creatures is confined within the laws written down by Us. In conformity with thy free judgment, in whose hands I have placed thee, thou art confined by no bounds; and thou wilt fix limits of nature for thyself. . . . Neither heavenly nor earthly, neither mortal nor immortal have We made thee. Thou, like a judge appointed for being honorable art the molder and maker of thyself; thou mayest sculpt thyself into whatever shape thou dost prefer. Thou canst grow downward into the lower natures which are brutes. Thou canst again grow upward from thy soul's reason into the higher natures which are divine."⁴³

As Wynter explains, Pico's "manifesto" helped usher in the "new epoch that would become that of the modern world" by rewriting "the Judeo-Christian origin narrative of Genesis" as a tale of the centering of "Man" by God within creation. Instead of the familiar story of a sinful Adam and Eve's exile from Eden, Pico spins a tale in which God

> had created Man on a model unique to him, then placed him at the center/midpoint of the hierarchy of this creation, commanding him to 'make of himself' what he willed to be—to decide for himself whether to fall to the level of the beasts by giving into his passions, or, through the use of his reason, to rise to the level of the angels.[44]

Highlighting how Pico constructs "Man" as a figure divinely situated at the center of the world and whose continuum of behaviors, from animal to angelic, are options laid out solely for him, available for his self-fashioning, Wynter's discussion of Pico, which occupies just a few pages in her massive article, articulates possibly the most brilliantly concise account of whiteness ever penned.

Pico's early modern reimagining of Genesis marks a crucial moment in the articulation of whiteness. His deployment of Christian dualisms for a man-centered universe upends the seemingly objective idea of a medieval-modern divide. And yet, I suggest, Wynter's analysis enables an even deeper unsettling of periodization, in which the links between "then" and "now" encompass medieval articulations of whiteness itself. Consider works by two canonical late medieval writers: Geoffrey Chaucer and Thomas Malory. James Simpson, whose revision of the medieval-modern divide was discussed in Chapter 1, sees both writers as examples of a "heterogeneous," "decentred," and "diverse" Middle Ages that ended during the absolutist clampdown of Henry VIII.[45] Simpson's vocabulary might indicate that Chaucer and Malory are somehow multiculturalists avant la lettre. And yet Wynter's take on Pico clarifies how the kind of diversity indicated by both Chaucer's and Malory's respective literary works can redound to the complex workings of a specifically white male subjectivity. Many of the "discursive freedoms" and "discursive variety" Simpson discovers in those authors' works demonstrate how what Gilroy calls "the dislocating dazzle of 'whiteness'" circulated during the late Middle Ages.[46] Both Chaucer's magnum opus the *Canterbury Tales* (c. 1392) and Malory's prose romance compendium *Le Morte Darthur* (c. 1469–70) generate worlds whose diversity, twists, and turns don't so much provide the reader with a wealth of empowering cultural and identificatory options but rather support a specifically white, Christian, androcentric, and English construction of humanity. Like Pico's version of God and Adam, Chaucer and Malory create a world and situate "Man . . . at the center/midpoint of the hierarchy of this creation."

In the case of the *Canterbury Tales*, despite its famed fragmentary and unfinished form, Chaucer's work exhibits an allegorical totality. Starting with the opening lines of the General Prologue, Chaucer's poem offers an early example of what Stuart Hall, following Louis Althusser, describes as a "field which is 'structured in dominance.'"[47] In other words, Chaucer's work centers and empowers a white, patriarchal, Christian, and English brand of human identity. Starting with the active-male and passive-female binary with which Chaucer opens his text via the piercing of a feminine March by a masculine April, Chaucer activates a richly complex white masculine agency that informs the entirety of his text. Whatever nuances, contradictions, exceptions, or heterogeneity might seem to circulate in the *Canterbury Tales* function within that larger totality centered on white male Christian dominance.

In particular, the *Canterbury Tales* indicate the human complexity, strengths, and foibles of what Anne Middleton has called Chaucer's "New Men," a grouping that centers, as Robert Meyer-Lee demonstrates, on Chaucer himself.[48] Individual pilgrims like the Squire, the Clerk, the Man of Law, the Merchant, the Franklin, and even a woman like the enterprising Wife of Bath bespeak the various and multiple components—and thus the richness, depth, and range—of their white, male, and English creator.[49] Chaucer, in turn, writes for fellow New Men, such as John Gower, intended readers who can identify and mull over their multiplicity as they enter the world created by Chaucer. As an early example of white discourse, the *Canterbury Tales* weaves a world of particularities whose diversity and multiplicity contribute to the representation of the dazzling humanity of the white Christian men who can identify and engage those particulars from an unrecognized and universal location.

Completed nearly a century after the *Canterbury Tales*, Malory's *Le Morte Darthur* might present an even more striking medieval adumbration of modern discourses of whiteness. Malory's importance is unsurprising, given his choice of genre. As Heng makes clear in a withering assessment, Arthurian lore comprises a key literary branch of a medieval chivalric "institution constituted by an elite, exclusive, self-serving, privileged, male fraternity of knights imagined as White-Caucasian and Christian, and closing its ranks to racial and religious others."[50] To the extent that, as Heng stresses, medieval Arthuriana serves ideological ends that support white supremacy, the *Morte* might well present as the most egregious example of that unsettling dynamic. Written by "Sir Thomas Malory," a knight whose "fundamental concern is to transmit his enthusiasm for knightliness" as connoted by the English Arthurian brotherhood, *Le Morte Darthur*—far more blatantly than the *Canterbury Tales*—is oriented toward a white, male, Christian, aristocratic, and English reader.[51] The proto-modern novelistic form of the *Morte* so hailed by critics supports that orientation. By gathering the multiple strands of Arthurian lore together in a text whose organization is unprecedentedly unified, Malory engages in an act of world-building on behalf of a select fully human few, Arthur and his knights.

The world of the *Morte* unfolds, centripetally, around those aristocratic men who sit, in comfort, in chairs around the Round Table, offering an early instance of what Sara Ahmed identifies as the deployment of furniture to connote the comfort and effortlessness of whiteness.[52] Following Fanon, Ahmed describes "whiteness ... as an ongoing and unfinished history, which orientates bodies in specific directions, affecting how they 'take up' space."[53] While whiteness restricts the mobility of racialized bodies, it centers white bodies and empowers them to move through space with facility. In the *Morte*, the white world conjured by Malory is so easy and so available that, as Donald Hoffman, Colin Richmond, and Eugène Vinaver respectively observe, it assumes "vaguely British" or even "Little Englander" contours where even the mythical Muslim city of Sarras seems to lie not near Jerusalem but "within the boundaries of Arthur's kingdoms."[54]

Malory's foremost exemplar of whiteness is his beloved sinner-saint Lancelot. Lone quester, solitary adventurer, and individual achiever, Lancelot models an early version of the enterprising autonomous white English masculinity celebrated in the boy adventure novels that were first issued in the Victorian period.[55] The "contradiction and paradox" that Jill Mann identifies "as fundamental to his being" renders the exceptional Lancelot the most human of humans.[56] As the knight most invested in worldly glory and as the royal fornicator, but also as the father of the holy Galahad and as the quasi-saintly healer of Sir Urry, Lancelot is the figure who most approximates the model of humanity Richard Dyer describes in his 1997 volume *White*. That is, Lancelot "encompasses all the possibilities for human existence, the darkness and the light" (28).

While presented as universals, "all the possibilities" that Lancelot epitomizes are options that function in relation to the white western signifying system laid out in the *Morte*. Comprised of binary oppositions that merge chivalric and Christian discourses, Malory's discourse follows a racial logic that is especially evident in its grail sequence. There, the moral purity of persons, animals, and objects—from knights to horses to ships to shields—is externalized via a notably intense whiteness; for example, during the grail book Gawain has a vision of bulls "so fair and so white, that they couldn't be whiter."[57] That whiteness contrasts an equally intense blackness; thus at one point in the grail book Bors comes upon a man riding a "black horse blacker than a berry."[58] Blackness in turn externalizes moral turpitude; for instance, during his explication of

Gawain's vision, a hermit states that "blackness is the same as saying without good qualities or works."[59] That semantic system works in tandem with an obsession with lineage to connote a white supremacy that is materialized by Galahad's shield, which portrays a background that is "as white as any snow," in whose "midst was a red cross" inscribed via the blood of his ancestor, Joseph of Arimathea.[60]

My discussion of Chaucer and Malory isn't intended to reduce their works to the status of reprehensible white supremacist documents. Rather, I've called attention to their centering of the multidimensional and agential humanity of elite Christian English men to highlight the groundbreaking implications of Wynter's work. Wynter, an acute revisionary historicist, doesn't just clarify how "epochal" moments like 1492 functioned via "a transumed this-worldly variant of the original feudal-Christian goal, as well as of its encoding cosmogonic schema," but also blazes the path connecting Du Bois's veil to the man-centered system of thought outlined by Chaucer and Malory.[61] To return to the language of Burckhardt and Marx, both Chaucer and Malory evince how representations of what a "many-sided" white humanity "can bring about" circulated prior to 1500 CE.[62] Their Middle English texts encourage a revision of periodization that charts medieval adumbrations of modern whiteness.

Medieval Denials of Coevalness: Antisemitism and Periodization

While the last section engaged with Wynter to consider the presence of whiteness before 1500 CE, this next section turns to the other side of the coin—that is, from medieval representations of white people to medieval portrayals of racialized others.[63] Above all, I'm concerned with the question of the relationship between medieval racism and Du Bois's veil of periodization. Did medieval Europeans, that is, assert racializing denials of coevalness, claims that are as much about temporal as they are about geographic alterity? And what relationship do pre-1500 CE denials of coevalness have to the rhetorics circulating later, in so-called modernity?

Among the multiple racializing discourses and practices witnessed in Europe in the years between 500 and 1500 CE, especially germane to this project is antisemitism. Antisemitism was an early instance of medieval Christian othering whose dynamics proved influential to subsequent racisms. Suzanne Conklin Akbari, in her scholarship on medieval Christian ideas of Islam and the Orient, has argued that "understanding medieval constructions of the Jewish body is a necessary first step in the effort to comprehend medieval constructions of the Saracen [a medieval Christian slur for Muslim] body."[64]

M. Lindsay Kaplan has demonstrated how the medieval Christian idea of a "figural slavery" that "renders all Jews, as long as they remain Jews, permanently and innately subordinated" was a "particular articulation" of racism "that powerfully influences the subsequent history of race."[65] Most crucially for the purposes of this chapter, scholars including Kathleen Biddick have shown how medieval Christian ideas of time and Jewish alterity adumbrated and indeed shaped modern racializing claims about the medieval-modern divide.[66] That is, medieval Christian images of Jews didn't just adumbrate modern antisemitisms and provide a template for subsequent ideas about racialized others such as Muslims and the African subjects of slavery. Christian ideas about Jews also played a foundational role in the generation of white supremacist models of periodization. The western denial of coevalness owes much to medieval Christian antisemitism.

The theological basis for medieval Christian denials of coevalness with Jews was the doctrine of supersession. According to this typological schema, a person's habitation of a superior present hinges on their cognitive apprehension of a Christian *modus operandi* that is spiritual and figurative. Jews who reject Christianity, the logic of supersession maintains, adhere to a materialism and literal-mindedness that renders them hopelessly and inherently atavistic. Biddick terms this dynamic "the Christian typological imaginary" and describes it as a means by which "Christian-ness" "was ... affirmed by the repetitive cutting off of the old Jewish time from the new Christian time," thus reducing "temporality into a binary of past and present."[67] An instance of the temporal politics of supersession appears in the writings of the North African church father Augustine of Hippo (354–430). As Jeremy Cohen has shown, Augustine represents contemporary Jews as "fossilized relic[s]" who are stuck "in useless antiquity" and thus embody living historical illustrations of a prior stage in the development of God's people.[68]

Christian claims about Jewish outmodedness supported a slew of offensive dispossessions, both discursive and historical. Discursive examples include cartographic works like the Hereford *mappa mundi* (world map), which portrays a Europe devoid of Jewish people; Petrus Alphonsi's *Dialogue against the Jews* (1108–10), "the most widely disseminated of medieval anti-Jewish polemics," which claims that Jews lack any scientific knowledge and other forms of know-how; writings by religious authorities such as Augustine, Isidore of Seville (d. 636), and Bernard of Clairvaux (1090–1153), who dispossess Jews of their rational faculties, so much so, at times, that they query the very humanity of Jews and reduce them to beasts; and literary works like *The Siege of Jerusalem* (c. 1370–90), which deprive Jews of life altogether and imagine full-blown "extermination."[69] The links between such negative representations and historical acts of anti-Jewish violence are complex; they include resonances between imagined geographic dispossessions and real spatial dispossessions, such as laws forbidding Jews to own property and state-sponsored exiles like the 1290 forced expulsion in England.[70]

The persistence of Christian cognitive modes in modernity is well attested. Critics including Talal Asad and Charles Taylor have demonstrated how Christianity isn't so much the obverse of Euro-American modernity but rather serves as an important source for distinctively western values and beliefs.[71] Moreover, scholars, especially Karl Löwith, have pinpointed the central role of Christian supersession in shaping subsequent western rhetorics of historical progress and societal advance.[72] But while scholars have long discerned how Christianity somehow persists in an ostensibly secular modernity, they don't always tease out the full implications of that phenomenon. Those occlusions often are a function of the fact that many of the scholars who track the modern afterlife of Christianity—for example, Löwith and Taylor—are post-secularists who write from a position of faith that precludes anything approximating a full critique of Christianity. As a result, work on the entanglement of Christian doctrine and western discourse often ignores the feel-bad ways in which damaging aspects of the former carry over into the latter.[73] In particular, that scholarship turns a blind eye to how the modern denigration of certain groups as inherently primitive or medieval grounds itself in the medieval embrace of a new (or modern) Christian *modus operandi* and a concomitant rejection of old, outworn Jews. Biddick is exceptional in her attention to this relationship. In her words, "when early Christians cut off Jews and their Hebrew scriptures from the 'now' and placed them in a past superseded by the New Testament, they inaugurated the denial of coevalness" that was elaborated during the medieval period and persisted in a secular modernity on behalf of white European men.[74] Medieval efforts to dispossess Jews based on claims about Jewish outmodedness set patterns that reappear in colonizing and racializing constructions of non-western peoples as mired in a primitive (that is, medieval) temporality.

Indeed, those offensive denials of coevalness circulate in many of the works covered in Chapter 1, starting with Burckhardt. *Civilization* imbues its Renaissance man with versions of the same virtues that medieval authorities attributed to "modern" Christians—a rational capacity, clear-sightedness, a transcendent "spiritedness"—and bars other humans from achieving a "thoroughly developed nature" (174). The "many-sided" and "complete" humans featured in *Civilization*, figures capable of the most admirable and despicable forms of individualism, are all white Italian men like Leon Battista Alberti, Lorenzo de' Medici, and Ludovico Ariosto (72–73). But other humans are exiled by Burckhardt from the history of human development and advance witnessed by his Italian men. European women enjoy no autonomous trajectory of perfection; rather, "their function was to influence distinguished men, and to moderate male impulse and caprice" (205). Spanish men, "in whom perhaps a touch of Oriental blood, perhaps familiarity with the spectacles of the Inquisition, had unloosed the devilish element of human nature," far from approaching "warlike affairs" in the advanced manner of the Italians—that is, "as a work of art"—instead commit unmatched atrocities (54–55). Above all, the non-western and often non-Christian humans portrayed in *Civilization*, like the constructions of "Orientals" analyzed by Said, are not agential subjects of history but rather timeless objects and "Platonic essence[s]."[75] For example, in Burckhardt's chapter on "Natural Science," Africans, Indians, Muslims, Mongols, and Turks appear not as agential humans but rather as specimens that Italian scientists collect, study, and categorize (150–52).[76]

Medieval antisemitism thus transmutes, in Burckhardt's modernity, into a multiplicity of ethno-racial biases. That temporal practice of othering first emerges in Burckhardt's famous account of the birth of modern man when he states that, "in the same way" the Italian became modern in the thirteenth century, "the Greek had once distinguished himself from the barbarian, and the Arab had felt himself an individual at a time when other Asiatics knew themselves only as members of a race" (70). Burckhardt might seem to evince a kind of objectivity here with his acknowledgment of the human awakening of "the Greek" and "the Arab." But instead, this passage engages in an Orientalist assertion of knowledge regarding (and thus intellectual domination over) Greeks and Arabs as groups who *once*—but no longer—enjoyed a version of what Italian men experienced during the Renaissance. Implicit here is the pastness of Greek and Arab civilization and their subsequent decline and demise. Long gone, their achievements—and indeed their entire way of life—are not active but rather the object of Italian proto-Orientalist academic study (89–145).

Moreover, even Burckhardt's Italy—for all its many-sided men—"forms the superseded grounds of the modern present" in *Civilization*, whose final allegiance is to not Italians but Burckhardt's fellow northern Europeans.[77] As Julia Reinhard Lupton has shown, Burckhardt engages in a version of the fraternal analogy by which medieval people frequently articulated the replacement of an inferior Jewish "then" with a superior Christian "now."[78] Supersession proves so expansive in *Civilization* as to double back on the Italians themselves. As inhabitants of what Burckhardt elsewhere calls the "beautiful, lazy South," the Italians are dispossessed of the ultimate humanity enjoyed by northern Europeans, such as the Swiss historian himself.[79]

A still more stark example of the continuity between medieval antisemitic temporalities and western theories of periodization appears in Burckhardt's medievalist counterpart, Huizinga. In other words, if we shift from an inaugurator of "modern" Renaissance historiography to a founder of "modern" medieval historiography, paradoxically, it is the latter figure, Huizinga, famed as a nostalgic defender of a lost medieval Christian era, who most overtly denies coevalness to persons situated at various removes from a white subjectivity. Tracking the white politics of time in *Autumn of the Middle Ages* (1919), however, demands disentangling Huizinga's complex and even convoluted investment in rationality and progress. *Autumn* in certain respects seems to counter the "modern" values espoused by Burckhardt. In his study, Huizinga pines for a medieval past where everything had its secure place in a world understood via Christian dualisms and hierarchies, such as spirit over the letter, heaven over earth, good over evil, and white over black. Not only did Huizinga at some level admire the medieval worldview; he also rejected a purely rational and coldly objective approach to historiography, embracing instead imagination and the body. Endorsing, as William Bouwsma puts it, "a far more dynamic, creative, and personally responsible conception of the historian's task than a 'scientific' idea of history had permitted," Huizinga believed that the historian could generate, through an intensely sensorial and imaginative identification with the past, what he called "living pictures in the theatre of the mind."[80] Huizinga ascribed to a version of Johann Gottfried Herder's idea of *Einfühlung* (empathy or "in-feeling"), a historiographic mode through which the historian could, in Herder's words, "feel yourself into everything."[81]

Yet both Huizinga's subjective methodology and his nostalgia for a medieval perspective ultimately conform to a larger and highly idiosyncratic ethnocentric project that embraces progress and rationality. As Graeme Small explains, Huizinga strangely maintained that, at its "point of deepest subjectivity," the historical imagination he advocated would reverse itself and obtain, in Huizinga's words, "the highest attainable objectivity."[82] Despite his investments in subjectivity and imagination, Huizinga understood his claims as "based on objective data critically scrutinized."[83] As a result, along with, and indeed in tension with, Huizinga's admiration for the medieval is his construal of that era as a primitive object of rational analysis. Huizinga's modernism is thus complex and contradictory. At the same time as, as Chapter 1 discussed, *Autumn* exhibits Huizinga's modernist discontent for the atrophied aesthetic and emotional capacity of contemporary people, it also embraces an ideology of modern white rationality and advance. *Autumn* thus at once evinces a nostalgia for the Middle Ages and performs a version of a dynamic, described by Ananya Jahanara Kabir and Deanne Williams, whereby moderns "bracket off the

Middle Ages, and keep it as exotic and foreign—and also as domitable—as any orientalist fantasy."[84]

Huizinga's confident endorsement of a superior Orientalist "knowledge" bespeaks his intellectual origins.[85] He did graduate work at the University of Leipzig not in medieval studies but in Sanskrit, where the scholarship of German Orientalist Max Müller (1823–1900) loomed large, and where another Orientalist, Hendrik Kern (1833–1917), directed Huizinga's 1897 dissertation on the *vidushaka* (court jester) in Indian drama.[86] Huizinga would publish on Indian literature and culture and hold university positions as an Orientalist until the early 1900s, when his research began to include Dutch history and eventually shifted to northern Europe during the Middle Ages.

Autumn affirms the pseudo-information gleaned by the Orientalist and applies it to Huizinga's own northern European predecessors. Alongside nostalgia, Huizinga treats medieval northern Europeans with a version of the knowing superiority assumed by Arthur James Balfour and the other Orientalists analyzed by Said. Just as Balfour asserts the "facts" about "Orientals," Huizinga, early on in *Autumn*, calmly lays out the "facts" about late medieval European people:

> Between hellish fears and the most childish jokes, between cruel harshness and sentimental sympathy the people stagger—like a giant with the head of a child, hither and thither. Between the absolute denial of all worldly joys and a frantic yearning for wealth and pleasure, between dark hatred and merry conviviality, they live in extremes.[87]

This passage showcases Huizinga's own creative powers. His striking image of tottering baby-headed medieval giants evinces his habitation of the role of a medievalist who is, as Stephanie Trigg and Thomas Prendergast put it, "powered by a modern imagination that is able to observe and describe without limits both the medieval and its afterlife, as opposed to the medieval past which cannot see its own future."[88] But the passage also stages a version of the superior rationality assumed by the Orientalist. Assuming toward his own medieval predecessors the cool confidence of the Orientalist "that knows [Orientals] . . . better than they could possibly know themselves," he neutrally puts forth their determining characteristics.[89] Huizinga and his reader enjoy a calmly critical distance on their lurching, conflicted, and bewildered object of study. Far from exemplars of an emotional depth lost to modernity, medieval people serve here as historical others or specimens—stressed via the third-person perspective connoted by "they" and "the people"—whom moderns scrutinize, analyze, and assess.

But what Huizinga's negative assessment of the extremes of medieval life puts forth as indicators of objectivity and universality are instead based on a western-oriented cognitive system that involved, in Willem Otterspeer's words, "contrasts" that Huizinga believed "were embedded in . . . reality itself."[90] As with Orientalist scholarship, what passes in *Autumn* as the discernment of universal and objective truths are distortions based on long-standing western oppositions such as new vs. old, west vs. east, present vs. past, civilized vs. primitive, and adult vs. childlike.[91] And his colorful image of a staggering medieval "giant with the head of a child" follows versions of the same Romantic racialism that obtains in Orientalist ideas of a childish and primitive East. The primitive vs. advanced, child vs. adult, and other dualities shaping Huizinga's commentary reveal how his "objectivity" is articulated via the internal logic of a western discourse—Du Bois's veil—that represents the world and humans along white, Christian, masculinist, and northern European lines.

Such moments in *Autumn* comprise part of a larger Orientalist dynamic akin to that analyzed by Tara Fickle in her important reading of Huizinga's later work *Homo Ludens* (1938). Fickle demonstrates how *Homo Ludens* asserts "Orientalist stereotypes . . . as evidence of play's universality" and then uses "this seemingly objective ludic claim, in the style of a feedback loop, to 'discover' evidence of China's particular hyper-formality."[92] A similar circling back occurs in *Autumn*, where Huizinga affirms a kind of shared human behavior only to loop back and matter-of-factly particularize certain human populations according to stereotypes. Huizinga asserts his supposed objectivity and rationality—and thus white superiority—most clearly in those moments in *Autumn* when he assumes a comparative turn. Comments like "there is an astonishing similarity between the ancient Indian, that is the Buddhist, and the medieval Christian . . . exaggerated depiction of putrefaction" might seem to imply an unbiased assessment of a universal humanity and shared cross-cultural human attributes (159). Central to such comparisons is Huizinga's objectification of northern European medieval people as the objects of a kind of Orientalist study. But Huizinga, like Burckhardt, endorsed a white Eurocentric notion of progress in which only he and his own fellow northern Europeans have what it takes to ascend from primitive superstitions to a superior and more rational outlook.[93] *Autumn* situates medieval northern Europeans in a larger history where they "necessarily" advance to humanity's "'superior' stage, to civilized (cultured) western-man," as Jacques Ehrmann puts it in his discussion of *Homo Ludens*.[94] To put it differently, while Huizinga's ancestors were primitive, this was just a stage in their history; they have now moved forward and progressed.

In contrast, certain non–northern European and non-western groups lack that historical trajectory. And, paradoxically, it is precisely in the denials of coevalness that accompany Huizinga's embrace of white progress that his retention and elaboration of medieval dehumanizing practices come to the fore. Alongside its nostalgia for a *lost* medieval world, *Autumn* supports a notion of modernity and progress whose othering of non-European peoples *echoes* medieval supersession and its ideas of enlightened Christians and backward Jews. In the manner of medieval antisemitic ideas of Jewish atavism, Huizinga asserts the unchanging primitivism of virtually any group outside of its white northern European subjects, whose own childlike and "medieval" state is temporary, a stage in a longer journey of development. Not unlike the backward and literal-minded Jews demonized by medieval Christians, certain persons remain caught up or stuck in primitive symbolizations and unities that the Dutch, the English, and other northern Europeans have left behind. For example, in his discussion of medieval mourning, Huizinga observes that "in a primitive culture—I have, for example, the Irish in mind—mourning customs and funeral poetry are still an unbroken whole" (56). The same chapter states that the "formal sense of honor" circulating in the medieval Burgundian court, where "an affront against etiquette" causes a keenly felt social death, "is still the case among many Oriental people" (50). And Huizinga's chapter on piety opens by describing how "a formal separation" of spirituality "from secular life never occurred" in southern Europe and how in "our own time the same difference in temperament separates the Latin peoples from their northern neighbors" (203). Versions of the essentializing medieval temporalities exemplified by ideas of Jews as living relics of ancient ways are rewoven in the discourse—or Du Boisian veil—by which Huizinga associates the Irish, southern Europeans, and "Oriental people" with primitive beliefs and practices.

Paul, Supersession, and the "Spirit" of Modernity

> The West saw itself as a spiritual adventure. It is in the name of the spirit, in the name of the spirit of Europe, that Europe has made her encroachments, that she has justified her crimes and legitimized the slavery in which she holds four-fifths of humanity. Yes, the European spirit has strange roots.
>
> —FRANTZ FANON, *THE WRETCHED OF THE EARTH*

I end this chapter by returning to where I began—the figure of the veil. Veil metaphors, of course, feature in some of the key works covered in Chapter 1. As Berman avers, the idea of a veil distinguishing "between a 'real' world and an illusory one" is "perennial in Eastern as well as Western thought."[95] But that metaphor gained special affective purchase for scholars of Euro-American modernity.[96] Burkhardt describes how a medieval "veil . . . woven of faith, illusion, and childish prepossession . . . first melted into air" before the eyes of men of Renaissance Italy (70). Marx's nightmarish vision of capitalist exploitation describes a bourgeoisie bent on tearing "away" all medieval "sentimental veil[s]" that formerly "bound men."[97] Both writers use the metaphor of a veil to define modernity as a breaking away from medieval superstition to a clear-eyed rational perspective. But, as we have seen, contrary to the received idea that modern people finally witnessed the naked truth of the real workings of the world, modern assertions of "objective" and rational truths embody wrong-headed and subjective claims about who is truly human and who thus enjoys a trajectory of development from primitive "medieval" modes to more advanced modern subjectivities. Burckhardt's and Marx's very trope of unveiling—their narrative of white western man's liberation from his medieval shackles—participates in the racialized veiling described by Du Bois. To put it another way, the unveiling that marks the shift from premodern to modern is itself a dehumanizing veil, a discourse that misrepresents a particular construction of the human as universal. Far from relinquishing an irrationality that blinded their medieval predecessors, Eurocentric theories of modernity are themselves marred by ideas of white subjectivity that occlude the humanity of others.[98]

A final look at Burckhardt's colossally influential trope of unveiling demonstrates how it not only is complicit with the veil critiqued by Du Bois but also participates in the trend covered in the last section, that is, the carryover of Christian antisemitism into modern racism. Perhaps more than any other component of medieval antisemitism, its basis in a "reveal" clarifies just how intimately modern and medieval racisms are entangled.

Striking evidence of those continuities of Burckhardtian and antisemitic practices of veiling appears when one compares the Swiss historian's foundational representation of modern man's birth to an equally influential source for the medieval doctrine of supersession: the writings of Saul of Tarsus/Paul of Rome. A figure whose epistles evolved from his political effort to negotiate, as Lupton explains, "multiple memberships in . . . the Hellenistic city-state, the nation of Israel, and the Roman Empire," Paul proved foundational to Christian theology up to the time of church fathers like Augustine and into the Middle Ages.[99] As Cohen puts it, "The teaching of Paul, as it translated the historical reality of Christianity's Jewish origins into a theology of salvation history, defined the basic parameters for subsequent Christian reflection on the Jews."[100] Although Paul's biblical corpus, in the words of Daniel Boyarin, "is not anti-Semitic (or even anti-Judaic) in intent, it nevertheless has the effect of depriving continued Jewish existence of any reality or significance in the Christian economies of history."[101]

A Pauline text that served as a key source for medieval Christian ideas of a Jewish-Christian periodic divide is his second letter to the Corinthians (c. 52–56 CE).[102] At the time Paul wrote the epistle, the Corinthians consisted of around fifty members of the church the apostle had founded in the seaport of Corinth.[103] Corinth was Rome's third-wealthiest city after Alexandria and a "pluralistic melting pot" whose inhabitants included native Greeks, manumitted Romans, and Jewish aliens.[104] Paul's church seems to have been composed largely of gentiles of the "lower or middle socioeconomic class"; 2 Corinthians responds, in part, to challenges Paul faced from opponents whose elevation of spirituality attracted many Corinthians, thanks to their investment in Hellenistic idea of a "body/soul or material/immaterial dualism."[105]

In his epistle, Paul engages the Corinthians' spiritual leanings via a rhetoric of unveiling. Specifically, in 2 Corinthians 3, he describes the spiritual thrust of a superior new Christian order in reference to the veil worn by Moses in Exodus 34 to shield the Israelites from his shining face after he had spoken with God. "We" Christians, he asserts, are

> not like Moses, who would put a veil over his face to prevent the Israelites from seeing the end of what was passing away. But their minds were made dull, for to this day the same veil remains when the old covenant is read. It has not been removed, because only in Christ is it taken away. Even to this day when Moses is read, a veil covers their hearts. But whenever anyone turns to the Lord, the veil is taken away. Now the Lord is the Spirit, and where the Spirit of the Lord is, there is freedom. And we all, who with unveiled faces contemplate the Lord's glory, are being transformed into his image with ever-increasing glory, which comes from the Lord, who is the Spirit. (2 Cor. 3:13–18 [NIV])

Thanks to the new covenant of the "spirit" made possible by Christ, Paul states, "whenever anyone turns to the Lord, the veil" of an old Jewish covenant of the letter "is taken away." While under Judaism the "minds" of believers were—and remain—"dull" or hardened, veiled, and (as he later puts it) "blinded," God "made his light shine in [Christian] hearts to give [them] the light of the knowledge of God's glory" and the "freedom" of his "Spirit" (2 Cor. 4:4). As a result of the new Christian dispensation, Paul claims, humans are freed from an older and darker age, a time when Jews could only see literal meanings, to envision a new, brighter, and fuller relation to God grounded in spirituality. In his feel-good periodization of soteriological history, Paul charts the wondrous progress humans have made as they shift from the qualified glory of the veiled

Jews to Christians "who with unveiled faces contemplate the Lord's glory" and are "transformed into his image with ever-increasing glory."

Paul served as the primary source for subsequent patristic and medieval ideas of a "new" and improved faith under Christianity, an old and inferior Jewish religiosity, and the veil trope upon which those medieval Christian assertions often drew. In claims that adumbrated post–1500 CE colonizing and racializing constructions of non-western peoples as stuck in a backward medieval temporality, early and medieval Christians used the idea of the veiled Jew to fix Jewish people in an old, outmoded, and irrational past. Pauline-inspired veil metaphors are ubiquitous in medieval supersessionism. As Lampert-Weissig puts it, the "accusation" that a

> veil covers the eyes of Jews, hardening their hearts and leaving them blind to the true word of God . . . echoes through countless permutations in patristic and medieval Christian texts. The veil also appears in figurations of the relationship between the Old dispensation and the New. The time of the Old dispensation is figured as veiled, and the coming of the New is represented by a lifting of that veil, which acts as a kind of curtain between an epoch of blindness and one of understanding.[106]

Bernard of Clairvaux offers one instance of this widespread patristic and medieval trope in a letter about the Second Crusade, where he claims that Christians pray "that the Lord God take the veil from" the hearts of "the perfidious Jews . . . so that they may be led from their darkness to the light of truth."[107] Similarly, the allegorical figure of *Synagoga*—analyzed in detail by Lampert-Weissig—typically appears as veiled in sculpture, texts, and visual arts.[108] Still another instance emerges in the rationale for the burning of the Talmud provided by University of Paris chancellor Odo of Châteauroux (d. 1273), who claimed that the "errors" in that Rabbinic text evince how "a veil has been placed over the heart of these people to such an extent that they [the books] turn the Jews away from not only from a spiritual understanding [of the law] but even from a literal understanding, and they incline them to fantasies and lies."[109] Odo's words reflect how ideas of veiled and atavistic Jews at times supported material acts of dispossession, in this case the incineration of Jewish books.

The son of a clergyman, Burckhardt was steeped in Christian theology and would have been familiar with the rhetoric of supersession. From 1837 to 1839, during his time as an undergraduate at the University of Basel, he took extensive coursework with theology chair Wilhelm de Wette (1780–1849). The fact that those studies with de Wette included none other than a semester dedicated to I and II Corinthians may explain the resemblances between Paul's veil rhetoric and Burckhardt's famous portrayal of the awakening of modern man.[110] Of course, Burckhardt, whose tutelage by de Wette ultimately prompted the Swiss thinker to reject Christianity, deploys Paul's religious metaphor for secular ends. For him, Christianity—or any belief in an enchanted and divinely ordered world of the spirit—was itself a veil of illusion. Far from a means by which Christians gained a spiritual grace denied Jews, Christianity, for Burckhardt, was part of the medieval veil of superstition that modernity swept away, revealing a more scientific and accurate vision of both the world and man's place in it.

But by shifting perspective from one that identifies *with* the terms of Burckhardt's account of modernity to the kind of critical vantage point on those terms offered by Du Bois, the Swiss historian's retention of a veil metaphor to describe historical change reveals how little his epistemic categories have really shifted. Just like the Pauline historical paradigm, Burckhardt's modern historical schema articulates a new and improved human freedom, spirituality, and mental acuity. In the same way that Paul explains how the new Christian ministry is "even more glorious" because "the Spirit of the living God" now writes "on tablets of human hearts" (2 Cor. 3:7–8, 3), Burckhardt's "many-sided" men supersede their medieval predecessors because Renaissance men discover and manifest the spirit of a potent humanity within themselves. Both Paul's opposition of Christian to Jew and the medieval elaboration of that opposition in a wide array of medieval texts and cultural forms call up virtually all the major semantic components of Burckhardt's medieval-modern rupture: the movement from old to new, darkness to light, restriction to freedom, blindness to vision, ignorance to enlightenment, superstition to reason. Burckhardt exemplifies how Christian supersession, in Lupton's words, is "one of the foundational principles of modern periodization per se," with secular thinkers only "rais[ing] Christian patterns of time to a new level of authority and explanatory power by purging them of any specifically religious content or transcendental reference."[111] The continuities between Burckhardt and Paul reflect how, far from having broken from the medieval, Burckhardt remains trapped in a version of the Christian dualisms and hierarchies—such as new vs. old, rational vs. irrational, better vs. outworn, vision vs. blindness, human vs. nonhuman, man vs. woman, Christian vs. Jew—used to center and exalt certain humans and dehumanize and oppress other human populations during the years prior to 1500 CE.

Burckhardt's attribution to medieval Christians of a version of the very "backwardness" that they assigned to Jews hardly means that the medieval period (or medievalists) "suffer" in the manner of historically marginalized groups. Rather, Burckhardt's reveal, when assessed from a Du Boisian vantage point, shows how the very mode by which Burckhardt others the medieval paradoxically does the opposite: evince the dehumanizing "modern" worldview that the modern Swiss historian shares with pre–1500 CE discourses. When Burckhardt hails a modernity that, in Lupton's words, "cancels" the "fossilized spirituality of the Middle Ages," he ironically exposes just how closely his modernity conforms to an antisemitic Christian temporalization in which Jews function as "fossilized relics."[112] Burckhardt evinces how the othering central to modern periodization has everything to do with the othering integral to medieval white Christian supremacy.

What might one make, race-wise, of the Pauline roots of a periodizing veil? Is it possible to push the *longue durée* of whiteness for which I am arguing back still further to Paul and the earliest days of Christianity? Do Burckhardt's Pauline ties indicate the whiteness of Christianity? Certainly not. The diverse persons linked to Christianity over time and in various places (to name a few, the North African Augustine, the Middle Eastern Jew Paul, the African Americans Frederick Douglass and Olaudah Equiano) affirm how, in Dyer's words, "it is by no means clear that whiteness is constitutive of" that religion (17). Moreover, many racial formations, both then and now, have circulated independently of Christianity. Racism need not engage Christianity to operate. But one can identify *certain* historical continuities that involve *particular* and *contingent* occasions when Christianity's doctrine of supersession subtended modern racializing discourses. The existence of multiple Christianities and multiple racializations doesn't mitigate the integral role of that religious doctrine in the making of white supremacy.

In his study of whiteness, Dyer identifies Christianity, along with "'race' and enterprise/imperialism," as the primary "three elements" involved in the "constitution" of white European embodiment (14). Although modernity understands itself as secular and, Dyer stresses, "Christianity as observance and belief has been in decline in Europe over the past half century, its ways of thinking and feeling are none the less still constitutive of both European culture and consciousness and the colonies and ex-colonies (notably the USA) that it has spawned" (15). Among the ongoing influences of Christianity on modern life, Dyer highlights "the distinctive inflection that Christianity gives to Western dualistic philosophy"—namely, its "compelling and fascinating" conceptualization of the relationship of body and spirit. Building on philosopher John Hodge, Dyer points out how, unlike "the two other major world monotheistic religions, Judaism and Islam," Christianity propounds "the mystery ... that somehow there is in the body something that is not of the body which may be variously termed spirit, mind, soul or God" (16).[113] The figure of Jesus both exhibits this mysterious phenomenon of a spirit that is "in the body" yet "not of the body" and establishes a "dynamic of aspiration, of striving ... in the face of the impossibility of transcendence," which, Dyer states, offers "something of a thumbnail sketch of the white ideal" (17). Whiteness thus draws on the singular, miraculous, and unattainable example of how, through Christ, "the Word became flesh" (John 1:14 [NIV]).

It is precisely this mysterious blending of embodiment and spirituality that Paul delineates in his epistle to distinguish Christians from Jews. Paul asserts how Christ, an all-too-corporeal mortal who died on a cross, is also "the Lord," "the Spirit," and, as Paul puts it elsewhere, the "Son of God" (Rom 1:4 [NIV]). Christians "who with unveiled faces contemplate the Lord's glory" are asked to strive for an unattainable *imitatio Christi*, to follow the miraculous example of an embodied yet spiritual Christ, with all the sacrifice, suffering, aspiration, and achievement it entails. The temporal rupture Paul represents involves a move from a time of Jewish literalism to a mysterious Christian embodiment of a spirit not in (yet also somehow in) the body.

The relationship between Christianity, race, and whiteness is not inevitable. But that religion's unique blend of body and soul did assist, in Dyer's words, a "conceptual leap" that informs modern claims about "bodies containing different spiritual qualities, or of some having such qualities and others not having them (a trope of white racism), of bodies containing that which controls them and then extends beyond them to the control of others and the environment (a trope of enterprise and imperialism)" (17–18). Dyer specifies how the Christian body-spirit paradox functions in an imperial context: the mysterious relationship Christianity posits between the body and the spirit helps naturalize western elites as inherently superior, spirited, and self-possessed, worthy colonizers of sites populated by persons who are inherently inferior, body-bound, and needful of control. As the Algerian-French philosopher Jacques Derrida (1930–2004) suggests in his analysis of *Geist* in the work of white German philosopher Martin Heidegger (1889–1976), ideas of a modern "spirit" possessed by certain groups don't transcend problems of biological racism but shift them to a spiritual register.[114] Similarly, Asad describes how a belief in a certain "civilizational essence" demarcates those "inhabitants of the European continent" who are and who are not "'really' or 'fully' European."[115]

Such invocations of the superior "spirit" of white western elites have had everything to do with their modernity. While in Paul, only Christians move from an older Jewish order into a new spiritual order under Christ, in works by many western intellectuals, it is only Europeans—and, above all, northern European elite men—who have the "spirit" that allows them to be modern. To return to the example of Burckhardt, while he might renounce as superstitious the Christian belief that all of creation and its workings refer to God's divine hand, he nevertheless retains Paul's idea that only certain persons are fully human in their possession of an ambitious, striving, and complexly embodied spirit. It is no accident that *Civilization* mentions words like "spirituality," "spirited," and "spirit" over 150 times. Those citations include Burckhardt's famed account of the birth of the modern individual, which describes how in Renaissance Europe "man became a spirited individual and recognized himself as such" (70). *Civilization* refers to the "spirit of Europe," the "modern European spirit," and especially the "modern spirit," a cluster of phrases that imply the interchangeability of modernity, Europe, and spirit (2, 48, 174, 209, 260, 286, 292). To be modern, for Burckhardt, is to be European, and to be European is to possess the spirit of the white subject. The deployment of "spirit" in major works such as *The Spirit of the Laws* (1748) by Montesquieu, *The Phenomenology of the Spirit* (1807) by Georg Hegel, and *The Protestant Ethic and the Spirit of Capitalism* (1904) by Max Weber perform much the same work. Whatever its definition—liveliness, industry, rationality, consciousness, logos, a higher calling, divinity—"spirit" always redounds to the uniquely modern humanity of occidental whites.

Du Bois's periodizing veil "between Then and Now" unsettles ideologies of a modern white spirit. Upending modern riffs on Pauline periodization and their constructions of a primitive and stagnant Black embodiment, he exposes how "the might and energy"—that is, the soul or spirit—of white "modern humanity has really gone" into "dark and awful depths and not the shining and ineffable heights of which it boasted."[116] Conversely, Du Bois showcases the spirit and humanity of Black people. Book and chapter titles such as *The Souls of Black Folk* and "Our Spiritual Strivings" foreground a Black spiritedness. Above all, Du Bois's romance *Dark Princess* (1928) exemplifies his effort to upend understandings of the spirit of modernity as the provenance of whites, via protagonist Matthew Townes's comment that "Black blood with us in America is a matter of spirit and not simply of flesh."[117] Most importantly, Du Bois's dialectics of the veil intimate a more truthful model of human identity untethered to fantasies about discrete and monolithic historical periods. Black double consciousness both reveals white supremacist modernity as a damaging falsehood *and* models an alternate subjectivity, one positioned in shifting relation to "historically specific and unavoidably complex configurations" aligned with the transnational culture of the Black Atlantic.[118]

PART II
Tolkien vs. Hall
White Heritage Fantasy and Diasporic Critique

3
Whiteness, Medievalism, Immigration
Rethinking Tolkien through Stuart Hall

For at least half a century, a significant—maybe even the primary—source of a feel-good medievalism has been J. R. R. Tolkien (1892–1973). And for good reason. Most medievalists occupy the margins of academia, never mind mainstream cultural life. But the popularity of Tolkien—a University of Oxford medievalist from 1925 to 1959—is such that his name has long been a household word within and without the Anglophone world. Of course, Tolkien is renowned not so much as a medievalist but as the founder of the literary genre of epic fantasy; he is widely beloved not for his scholarly publications but for his fiction. *The Lord of the Rings* trilogy, for example, sold an estimated 150 million copies in the twentieth century, and Peter Jackson's *Lord of the Rings* and *Hobbit* films are among the highest-grossing films of all time.[1] But even though it is Tolkien's epic fantasies that enjoy mass consumption, medievalists can nevertheless take pride in Tolkien's acclaim as a writer; for works like *The Lord of the Rings* trilogy are closely tied both to the medieval past and medievalism. Not only does the Shire exhibit an organicism, agrarian organization, and other characteristics that render it a version of medieval England but also, as scholars including Tom Shippey and Jane Chance have demonstrated, virtually all of Tolkien's fiction contains a wealth of medieval lore that medievalists are best positioned to identify and gloss.[2]

Perhaps most importantly, Tolkien's epic fantasies exalt being a medievalist. Nearly all the key figures in his fiction are versions of the Oxford don: they are, with rare exceptions, writers, translators, and researchers who have studied languages, legends, and the deep past. For example, the hobbit Merry has published a treatise on herblore, words, and names of the Shire; Bilbo is a "mighty book-learned" hobbit who wrote a Breton lay that he translated "from its original ancient tongue"; and Aragorn is an expert philologist who "was learned in old lore" and "knew many histories and legends of long ago."[3] The wizards Gandalf and Saruman are aged white men educated in linguistics, folklore, and history. And our hero, the "youthful" Frodo, is a fifty-year-old "scholar in the Ancient Tongue" who can communicate in "high-elven speech" when the occasion arises.[4] *The Lord of the Rings*, in effect, offers the medievalist a fantasy world where, alongside magic and warfare, a bookish historicism proves essential to the rescue of Middle-earth itself.

However, while the medievalism of Tolkien's widely admired epic fantasies has cheered many a medievalist, the reception and especially the political leanings of his readers complicate any easy embrace of Tolkien and his works. For Tolkien's literary and cultural legacy is decidedly mixed. Famously, many counter-cultural, marginalized, and left-leaning readers—especially in the U.S.—have embraced his fiction.[5] While hardly all disenfranchised readers are drawn to Tolkien, at least since the 1960s' hippie rallying cry "Frodo Lives!," certain outsiders have felt his allure for varying reasons. For some of those readers, the agrarian and pastoral dimensions of *The Hobbit* and other works by Tolkien offer primary appeal.[6] Others have been drawn to the alterity of Tolkien's protagonists. Like the mutant comic heroes analyzed by Ramzi Fawaz, Tolkien's elves, dwarves, and hobbits are heroic freaks with whom alienated readers can identify.[7] In particular, the hobbits at the core of Tolkien's fiction prove inspiring because of their unusual size. In the words of Jamaican writer Marlon James with regard to his aims as a novelist, "I want to find what Tolkien found, when he knew that the smallest people can make the biggest difference. Because if there was one thing I knew growing up, [it] is a sense of insignificance."[8] As James indicates, because the diminutive can often serve as a metaphor for powerlessness, some disenfranchised readers find Tolkien's capable little hobbits attractive.

But this is hardly the whole story of Tolkien's legacy, whose heterogeneous fan base also encompasses members of the far-right from western Europe to the U.S.[9] For example, neo-fascist Italian youths—among them, the current ultraconservative Italian prime minister Giorgia Meloni—attended *Campo Hobbit* summer festivals during the 1970s and '80s.[10] Participants gathered at various rural locations in the southern Italian region of Abruzzo, where they lived in tents and engaged in far-right versions of hippie festivals, including performances by the band *Compagnia dell'Anello* (Fellowship of the Ring).[11] During the 1980s, members of the British National Front embraced elements in Tolkien's fiction they understood as racist, going so far as to call a typesetting and page make-up company they had created "Gandalf Graphics."[12] In the U.S., Stormfront, the first white supremacist website of its kind, created a forum devoted to *The Lord of the Rings*.[13] Echoing earlier American neo-Nazi celebrations of *The Lord of the Rings* as "an Aryan work of art," a contributor to a thread about a study guide for home schoolers claims that "*LOTR* would be a great way to teach our children what is truly ARYAN."[14]

The basis for such right-extremist love of Tolkien's epic fantasies varies. Some extremists are drawn to the same elements embraced by left-leaning readers, such as Tolkien's depiction of an impossible quest and his endorsement of a back-to-basics communal life.[15] At the same time, however, Tolkien's fascist fan base responds to some of the most disturbing aspects of his fiction, especially its racial elevation of white northern Europeans.[16] Consider, for example, how Tolkien sets "the White Council" of Middle-earth (that is, Europe) against the "evil power" affiliated with the "Dark Tower" of Mordor.[17] In an early 1969 critique of Tolkien, Catharine Stimpson confronts such white supremacist components of *The Lord of the Rings*, asking "why Tolkien so blandly, so complacently, so consistently, uses the symbol of light and of white to signify the good and the symbol of dark and of black to signify evil?"[18] Assessing a work in terms of its reception is always a tricky matter. However, Leila Norako is correct when she states that one can "see in Middle-Earth a space in which an 'inherent' white superiority is assumed and eventually realized."[19]

Thanks partly to Tolkien's embrace by white supremacists, race figures prominently in Tolkien scholarship, as the presence of entries on "Race and Ethnicity in Tolkien's Writings" and "Racism, Charges of" in the *J. R. R. Tolkien Encyclopedia* attests.[20] Indeed, so many publications address race and Tolkien that Robin Reid could devote over forty pages to them in a recent bibliographic essay.[21] But writing on Tolkien, even by academics, often is itself problematic. With few exceptions, work on Tolkien is penned by devotees who position the epic fantasy founder as untouchable and assume an evasive or defensive stance toward the charges of racism leveled at Tolkien and/or his epic fantasies. Moreover, much of that scholarship is authored by medievalists whose cathexis to Tolkien might hamper a full critique.

In this chapter, I advance a critical assessment of Tolkien's academic medievalism and the epic fantasies with which that scholarly work is closely bound. I argue that a crucial means of understanding both kinds of writing—and indeed, Tolkien himself—emerges in the essentialist beliefs that underwrote his approach to identity, history, and periodicity. As we shall see, Tolkien's blood-and-soil idea of Englishness prompted historical claims that diverge in many respects from the theories of periodization covered in Chapters 1 and 2. Like critics including Jacob Burckhardt and Johan Huizinga, Tolkien's historicism intersects with a white supremacist embrace of northern Europeans. But unlike those scholars, Tolkien doesn't bind his sense of history to modern models of white progress. While Burckhardt and Huizinga identify northern Europeans with a trajectory of advancement that only their supremely human "spirit" can enact, Tolkien imbues even the most ancient northern peoples with a racial essence that entails, from the start, the full package of advanced human traits, such as rationality. To be sure, Tolkien did identify a host of problems pertaining to his modern age. But he also endorsed certain modern white "virtues" and identified that "good modernity" with his early northern European ancestors. Periodization was in key respects irrelevant to Tolkien's idea of an innate and timeless whiteness.

That faith in the transhistorical value of whiteness underwrote a disinterest in progress and periodization by Tolkien that extended to literary history. Tolkien's essentializing impulses encompassed inherent links tying medieval texts to his contemporary novels. English language and literature of all periods serve for Tolkien as privileged sites for the representation of an exalted white northern European essence. *The Lord of the Rings* series and other pieces penned by Tolkien not only participate in this transhistorical manifestation of whiteness but represent in the hobbits and other characters an innate feel for early (that is, medieval) white words and texts.

Of course, *The Lord of the Rings* would attain—even during Tolkien's life—a massive, heterogeneous, and global readership that includes non-English and non-white readers. As scholars including Mariana Rios Maldonado stress, those readers suggest how one might distill and reframe "affordances and nuances" of Tolkien's fiction in a manner that is worth "celebrating," even as one must enact a "transparent discussion of how" Tolkien's fiction "reflects systemic issues."[22] But Tolkien didn't desire that diverse audience. Rather, he believed that his books, like the medieval English poetry he loved, carry what Maria Sachiko Cecire aptly describes as "the inner Englishness that only literature can fully convey."[23] While readers who embrace the diversity and multiplicity of identity and history have crafted liberatory riffs on Tolkien's novels, the don jettisoned challenges of difference as they pertained both to English identity and English temporality.

My starting point for a critical inquiry into whiteness, periodization, and Tolkien is an indirect reference to Tolkien in the memoir of Stuart Hall (1932–2014), the Jamaican-British scholar who was one of the first critics to call for a critical analysis of whiteness and race.[24] As I discuss in the introduction, after receiving his BA in English at Oxford, Hall considered becoming a medievalist. Hall relates in his posthumous memoir, *Familiar Stranger: A Life Between Two Islands* (2017), how "at one point I planned to do graduate work on [William] Langland's *Piers Plowman*," the great fourteenth-century narrative allegory about Christianity and English social ills.[25] But, as Hall relates, "when I tried to apply contemporary literary criticism to [medieval] texts, my ascetic South African language professor told me in a pained tone that this was not the point of the exercise" (156). A chastened Hall abandoned his plan to work on *Piers*. Hall shared the anecdote with his friend and amanuensis Bill Schwarz, who did not press for more information, but it is easy enough to identify Hall's advisor as Tolkien.[26] Of the three early English professors at Merton during that period, only Tolkien hailed from South Africa, having been born in Bloemfontein, capital of the Boer-controlled Orange Free State.[27]

With its unexpected yoking of the future critic Hall and the medievalist-cum-fantasist Tolkien, this autobiographical anecdote provides a valuable hermeneutic for the role of race in Tolkien's life and work. For one thing, the clash confirms the need to extend the scope of analysis beyond Tolkien's fiction to the white privilege he enjoyed as a medievalist at Oxford. At the time of his encounter with Hall, Tolkien was no underdog but rather a white don possessed of ample authority at Oxford. Tolkien and his colleague C. S. Lewis "were major political forces in the English School."[28] Indeed, insofar as Oxford was, as Hall observes elsewhere in his memoir, "the summit of the higher education system" in England (157), Tolkien occupied its pinnacle, thanks to the Merton chair he held at the time of their confrontation. Tolkien famously self-identified with Frodo, but that diminutive alter ego, at least in certain respects, was a scrim masking the Oxford don's white privilege.

Sara Ahmed's work on the phenomenology of whiteness, a project inspired by Frantz Fanon's similar engagement with blackness, helps clarify the racializing aspects of Tolkien's privilege.[29] If we can broadly define whiteness as the ethnicity on behalf of which western civil society (mis)represents the world, Ahmed teases out the roles played by questions of space and comfort in that dynamic. Whiteness, for Ahmed, entails the wide spatial "reach" of "white bodies" who are "so at ease with [their] environment that it is hard to distinguish where one's body ends and the world begins."[30] Tolkien's whiteness underwrote his capacity at Oxford to move "at ease" and ascend to the status of a named professorship. "It is no accident," as Ahmed points out, that academic power is "symbolically given through an item of furniture" like Tolkien's Merton chair; whiteness concerns a privileged orientation to space and "to take up space is to be given an object, which allows the body to be occupied in a certain way."[31] Conversely, Tolkien created for Hall a version of what Ahmed describes as the "blockage" persons of color experience because of whiteness.[32] During the 1950s, "non-white bodies"—and especially persons interested, as Hall was, in decolonizing Oxford and shifting it from its nationalizing and colonizing conservatism—faced considerable obstacles.[33] Evincing the real-world stakes and systemic entanglements of institutional racism, those blockages are unfortunately ongoing, as Anuradha Henriques and Lina Abushouk indicate in a recent essay on student life at Oxford.[34]

Moreover, the anecdote, with its alignment of Tolkien and Hall, shores up the latter figure's important critical legacy, which offers invaluable tools for analyzing and de-centering Tolkien's white modernism and medievalism. The very terms in which Hall characterizes his encounter with Tolkien offer an incisive critique of the beliefs behind the medievalist's gatekeeping. For one thing, Hall characterizes his academic method as a confrontation between periods. Rejecting Tolkien's investment in a transhistorical Englishness, Hall puts medieval texts into conversation with contemporary critical theories. Along with its critical return to questions of historical difference, Hall's anecdote performs the crucial analytical work of dislodging Tolkien's whiteness "from its centrality" and "putting into question its universalist character."[35] By referring to Tolkien not by name but in terms of his South African roots, Hall exposes the medievalist's white particularity, which encompassed the immigrant status that Tolkien shared with Hall.

In what follows, I first explain my methodology, emphasizing whiteness as a necessary category of analysis for a full inquiry into race and Tolkien. I then investigate the workings of the clash between Hall and Tolkien, highlighting the entanglement of methodology and identity politics. In the case of Hall, his interest in "contemporary literary criticism" comprised part of his diasporic cooptation of the historical sensibility denied him as a colonial subject. Turning to Tolkien, I build on the work of Cecire, Dimitra Fimi, Michael Saler, Helen Young, and others to explore how his "pained" rebuff of Hall hinged on the don's closely held essentialist beliefs about the relationship of medieval study to English identity.[36] I then consider the idiosyncratic historicism that informed Tolkien's medievalism, paying special attention to the don's famed lecture on the Old English poem *Beowulf*. Rejecting any idea of a hard medieval-modern divide, the don celebrated the medieval as a portal to a rational and heroic Nordic white supremacy, thanks to the inborn linguistic and literary acumen of not just medieval English poets but also subsequent English readers, including—or especially—Tolkien himself. Exemplifying how English whites understand themselves as both medieval and modern, Tolkien attributed his skills as philologist and fiction writer to his own racial inheritance, which included memories of an Atlantis-like disaster befalling ancient English people.

Returning to Hall's anecdote, I then place Tolkien's medievalism in the context of his institutional affiliation with Oxford, whose relationship to Englishness Hall highlights in his account of his early days at the university. I draw upon Hall's conjunctural methodology to consider how Tolkien's actions not only reflect the don's particularly charged brand of white medievalism but also speak to British immigration and its intersection with Tolkien's essentialist beliefs. In particular, I argue that the don's nativism and Atlantis nightmare may have reinforced each other insofar as media outlets construed non-white migrants through metaphors of hydrospheric engulfment. I conclude by embracing Hall's diasporic approach to identity, which reveals the heterogeneities and ruptures that have always defined individual and collective identities. Pushing past the veil of race that shapes Tolkien's and related western ideas of periodization and English heritage, Hall identifies the negotiations around difference that have informed social life on the English archipelago from the start.

Whiteness and Tolkien's Epic Fantasies

> The "English eye" sees everything else but is not so good at recognizing that it is itself actually looking at something. It becomes coterminous with sight itself.
> —STUART HALL, "THE LOCAL AND THE GLOBAL"

For many readers and critics, the clearest sign of racism at work in *The Lord of the Rings* is its morally charged color binaries.[37] Criticism of Tolkien's black-and-white dualisms was immediate, if a 1955 review by his white colleague, friend, and rival Lewis is any indication. In his assessment of the final two books of the trilogy, Lewis refers to "the complaint," made after the publication of the first book, "that the characters are all either black or white" and surmises that such "readers, seeing (and disliking) demarcations of black and white," will identify "a rigid demarcation between black and white people in the novel."[38] Lewis rejected the idea that Tolkien's writings are racist. But at least as early as Stimpson's essay and continuing up to recent works by Fimi, Young, and others, white scholars have highlighted how, in Young's words, "racialized taxonomies shape the cultures of Middle Earth," where "the Good peoples" are "marked White" and Sauron's troops "are effectively undifferentiated under the one—tellingly black—banner of evil."[39] Creative writers also have pointed to the offensive color coding of the medievalist's epic fantasies. Muslim-American fantasy writer Saladin Ahmed, for example, points to an "irreducible ugliness" at work in the fact that "to be dark-skinned in Middle Earth is to be part of a savage horde—whether orcish or human—rather than to be a true individual."[40] Similarly, Black U.S. science fiction and fantasy writer N. K. Jemisin rejects Tolkien's logics in statements such as, "The Dark Lord is really bad, we know this. Because he's dark. Well, did you do something to him? Doesn't matter, he's dark. That's why he's bad and that's why you've got to go kill him."[41] And James, in his 2019 Pembroke lecture, describes his effort to invert the dark-light imagery presented by Tolkien and other western Anglophone writers in his own fiction.[42]

The essentializing binary oppositions circulating in *the Lord of the Rings* trilogy are crucial factors in any interrogation of its racializing thrust. But, as I discuss in greater length in the introduction, a full analysis of race requires analyzing the totalizing white western discourse to which such dualisms contribute. As Young asserts, attention to whiteness is crucial to any comprehensive assessment of Tolkien's epic fantasies.[43] Hall himself laid the groundwork for such an analysis in his influential writings on whiteness as the particular ethnic identity on behalf of which western civil society has long organized itself and (mis)represented itself to itself. To be sure, discerning whiteness as an ethnicity has its challenges. Precisely because of the claims of western discourse regarding the omnipresence, normativity, and centrality of whiteness (claims that mask the epistemic violence performed by western discourse on alternate meaning systems), whiteness is difficult to locate and analyze.[44] As Hall puts it with respect to English whiteness in the epigraph at the beginning of this section, the "'English eye'" masks its particularity and situatedness as a white ethnicity by passing itself off as "coterminous with sight itself."[45] Thus the "invisibility of whiteness as a racial position in white (which is to say dominant) discourse," in Richard Dyer's words, "is of a piece with its ubiquity."[46] Whiteness disappears into western discourse when it becomes, as Hazel Carby clarifies, "the (white) point in space from which we tend to identify difference" or, to put it another way, when the "whole world" is produced discursively by and for whites.[47] If western discourse is constituted by many particulars—and especially charged and offensive racist dichotomies of color—it produces whiteness as both the basis for those particulars and the unrecognized location from which they are identified and manipulated.

Key to the whiteness of *The Lord of the Rings* is the way those seemingly other and freakish figures, the hobbits—and especially Frodo, Tolkien's alter ego—represent English agency, "spirit," comfort, and drive. The hobbits' homeland (and England's double), the Shire, enjoys a privileged orientation as the base from which Tolkien's elaborate secondary world unfolds. The hobbits' cozy, little-Englander domesticity affirms the "comfort" that Sara Ahmed links to a privileged white orientation.[48] Upon leaving the Shire, Frodo and the members of his hobbit cohort continue to live in a world oriented around them. Consider, for instance, the many passages detailing the expansive views captured by a hobbit's point of view. The world of *The Lord of the Rings* isn't just centered on but exists for the hobbits: Tolkien offers multiple and lengthy descriptions of Frodo, Merry, Pippin, and Sam's extensive movements over the land and the pluck and bravery that hobbit (read:

English) exploration manifests.⁴⁹ A version of the white Victorian adventure story, Tolkien's fiction focuses on the hobbits' initiative, courage, and daring, virtues that evince their possession of the white ennobling human spirit analyzed by Dyer, that ineffable enterprise that transcends the body, allowing the hobbits to rise to challenges, despite their physical size.⁵⁰ Insofar as, in Ahmed's words, "whiteness is an orientation that puts certain things within reach," nearly everything, ultimately, is "in reach" of those can-do explorers, the hobbits.⁵¹

Examining the relationship of Tolkien's fiction to whiteness helps demonstrate how not only its stark color-coded patterns but also its complexity and contradictions contribute to a totalizing western discourse of northern European privilege, or what Hall would call, following Louis Althusser, a society structured in dominance.⁵² For example, the failings of Tolkien's white heroes—that is, their possession of negative traits aligned with "darkness"—don't so much problematize his color dualisms but denote how, as Dyer explains, "the presence of the dark within the white man . . . enables him to assume the position as the universal signifier for humanity. He encompasses all the possibilities for human existence, the darkness and the light."⁵³ Conversely, the few dark-hued yet rounded-out and even celebratory figures in Tolkien's epic fantasies don't so much challenge the racist impulses of those texts but rather testify to Tolkien's and his readers' white "knowledge" and "mastery" of a world where exceptions to the racist rule exist.⁵⁴ And finally, what Tolkien's readers have identified as multiculturalism and cosmopolitanism in his epic fantasies instead contribute—as Tolkien himself pointed out—to his attachment to whiteness. In a letter, Tolkien explains how the diverse creatures who populate his novels portray "certain aspects of Men and their talents and desires."⁵⁵ In other words, *The Lord of the Rings* doesn't celebrate ethnic diversity but rather understands elves, dwarves, etc. as partial humans that *together* bespeak the complexity of an ostensibly universal—but, upon closer examination, distinctly white, English, and masculine—subjectivity.⁵⁶

"The Point of the Exercise"

What does the whiteness of *The Lord of the Rings* have to do with Tolkien's medievalism and, more precisely, his encounter with Stuart Hall? Some readers may contend that, however much Tolkien's epic fantasies might denote white privilege, his relation to Hall was an entirely different matter. One might specifically claim that Hall's rejection by Tolkien pertained not to the racism of the don's fiction but rather his academic practice and related methodological alignments. In other words, Tolkien didn't so much reject the idea of a West

Indian immigrant of color becoming a medievalist but rather queried his student's particular approach to Middle English texts.

To be sure, Hall's methodology did clash with that of Tolkien. The young student subscribed not to the methods of his highly traditional home institution, Oxford, but to more current literary critical practices. As Hall explains in *Familiar Stranger*, the "contemporary literary criticism" he embraced in the 1950s involved "arguments between the Leavisites, the American New Critics like Cleanth Brooks, R. P. Blackmur, Yvor Winters, and the more socially oriented critics." Hall describes how especially, "in the early days," he and the members of his undergraduate intellectual cohort at Oxford "were Leavisites of a kind" (222). Hall certainly rejected the "elitism" of F. R. Leavis (1895–1978), but he appreciated the social and historical questions engaged by the Cambridge critic. Hall especially admired the "more militantly historical view" advocated by such contributors to the Leavisite journal *Scrutiny* as Denys Thompson, L. C. Knights, and Q. D. Leavis (222–23). In his memoir, Hall describes how certain "writers associated with" the "larger intellectual axis" of *Scrutiny* and Leavis "took the broader social perspective seriously and nourished my continuing concern with cultural, rather than exclusively literary, issues" (222–23). Included among the scholarship Hall singles out for praise is medievalist John Speirs's scholarship "on Chaucer's World" (223). Speirs was, as Ethan Knapp puts it, "the house Chaucerian for *Scrutiny*," and Speirs's 1951 volume *Chaucer the Maker* opens by stressing the socio-historical import of Chaucer's poetry.[57] In his notes for *Familiar Stranger*, Hall elaborates on his attraction to Speirs and other medievalists interested in context:

> I liked John Spiers' book on Chaucer because it explored Chaucer and his world. I even got into the Catholic critics who uncovered the medieval world. I got hooked into what you might call the social and historical context of literature.[58]

Work like that of Speirs and the unnamed "Catholic critics" offered a bridge between contemporary methodologies and the medieval texts that dominated the Oxford curriculum Hall encountered as an English student. One could, those critics argued, read medieval texts in a modern way, as gateways to "the medieval world," to the "social and historical context" out of which those early texts emerged.

Hall's investment in contemporary literary criticism contributed to what he describes in his memoir as "a lifelong intellectual disengagement from Oxford and all it stood for" (223). As he puts it in his notes for *Familiar Stranger*, "We were Leavisites—so in any case we were sort of emigres from and critics of the Oxford curriculum."[59] Oxford English had, for decades, diverged radically from the Cambridge- and Leavis-affiliated approach embraced by Hall. In his memoir Hall describes how, in reference to his college community, "our self-conscious identities as critics already marked us out, in relation to Oxford, as outsiders" and how "Oxford literary people . . . despised [Leavis's] Cambridge 'seriousness,' his Puritanism, his belief that literature, language and ideas mattered" (223). Hall's agon with the dominant scholarly ethos at Oxford suggests another sentimental component of his methodology: the thrill of academic trench warfare. Hall's cohort's self-understanding as "embattled" members of a "counter tradition" was such that, "rather like critical renegades or members of an underground movement," they "used to troop off to Blackwell's to buy those uncut issues of *Scrutiny* in a spirit of defiance every time it came out."[60] Hall's account suggests how his academic interests offered him the affective pleasures of rebellion and mutiny against Oxford traditionalism and conservatism.

But how, in particular, did Hall defy a Tolkienian medievalism? For one thing, the very historical and contextual information that "hooked" Hall supported a methodology that the Oxford don stridently rejected. Tolkien, for example, opens his renowned 1936 lecture "*Beowulf*: The Monsters and the Critics" by bemoaning how "*Beowulf* has been used as a quarry of fact and fancy far more assiduously than it has been studied as a work of art."[61] Tolkien's rhetoric—his likening of socio-historical readings of *Beowulf* to mining (and, later, dissection)—makes clear his view that critics such as Speirs inflict a kind of violence on medieval literature.[62] For another, Tolkien's rejection of modern historicizing "dissections" of medieval texts participated in his overall rejection of his contemporary moment. As I describe in detail later, Tolkien viewed modernity as the nadir of human history. He thus rejected the idea of the "plots, motives, symbols" of a great medieval poem, like *Sir Gawain and the Green Knight*, being "handled and pressed into the service of the changed minds of a later time" that is inferior to the superior historical moment of the medieval text.[63]

There's no question that the methodologies of Hall and Tolkien conflicted. However, medievalist methodological friction was tightly bound up with a clash of identities understood in relation to modernity. In his memoir, Hall directly connects his intellectual pursuits to his identity as a West Indian "brought up in a provincial colonial city in the tropics where I was a conscript to their modernity and who had no claim to be a modern person in my own right" (222). Elsewhere in *Familiar Stranger* Hall explains, "I was inserted into history (or in this case, History) by negation, backwards and upside down—like all Caribbean peoples, dispossessed and disinherited from a past which was never properly ours" (61). According to an affective academic formation closely related to his embrace of contemporary criticism, Hall was "excited" by the "historical break" with received ideas of representation enacted by modernists like T. S. Eliot, whom Hall first discovered and loved as a teen in Jamaica (222). Modernism offered "alternate realities" that, as Hall puts it, "allowed me to assemble another life, at one remove from the immediate diktats of the colonial order" (121). "Criticism, the literary theory of its day," was "one route" by which Hall could critically engage modernism, modernity, and—more broadly—the history long denied him, and thus redefine himself in new ways that defied white supremacist English ideas of colonials (222).

The diasporic perspective on identity that activated Hall's effort to put medieval literature into conversation with contemporary theory deeply unsettled Tolkien's white heritage medievalism. Unpacking the whiteness of the don's medieval practice requires a look into its academic roots, starting with comparative philology, "a kind of master discipline for theorizing about human origins in general and human races in particular."[64] An academic field that yoked the racial orientation of German Romanticism (espoused by figures like Johann Herder [1744–1803]) to positivist analysis of the grammatical laws of different languages, comparative philology supported the idea that literature, in Stephen Harris's words, "if properly interpreted . . . reveal[ed] transhistorical racial or cultural characteristics."[65] As Geoffrey Harpham explains, philology became "modern when it found a way to conjoin" its "limited empiricism to a speculative practice" with limitless application.[66] On the basis of a narrow, dry, and erudite scrutiny of language, comparative philologists claimed for themselves a thrilling and expansive "critical power" whose "defining feature" during the nineteenth century wasn't so much scientific as racial.[67] Examples include "the embryo divinity" that French Orientalist Ernest Renan (d. 1892) discovered in Aryan Indo-European languages and contrasted with the inferior, "inorganic," and sterile roots of Semitic languages.[68] European comparative philologists like Renan deployed modern advances—techniques of scientific linguistic analysis—to point to transhistorical racial continuities that old languages manifest, thus evincing the origins of modern Europe's superiority among world peoples.

Especially pertinent to Tolkien's formation as a scholar and writer was the merging of comparative philology with earlier academic celebrations of pagan Icelandic culture and language by Danish language historians Grímur Thorkelin (1752–1829) and N. F. S. Grundtvig (1783–1872). Grundtvig, for example, studied *Beowulf* and other early English texts for their capacity to exhibit a white heroic *Nordens Aand* or "Spirit of the North."[69] Subsequent German and Danish comparative philologists would find in their analyses of language "facts" about the superiority of Scandinavian peoples. The brothers Jacob

Grimm (1785–1863) and Wilhelm Grimm (1786–1859), for example, edited poems taken from the Norse *Edda*, and Danish comparative philologist Rasmus Rask (1787–1832) hailed the "intrinsic excellence, . . . interest and importance" of ancient Scandinavian language and literature "to the inhabitants of the North" in the preface to his *Anglo-Saxon Grammar*.[70] The study of Old Norse formed one strand of European philology's overall project of yoking linguistic history to hierarchizing racial claims about northern European greatness and non-European deficiency.

Tolkien's more immediate predecessors, founding figures of "Anglo-Saxon" studies, looked to those Danish and German scholars for academic inspiration: Benjamin Thorpe (1781/2–1870) studied in Copenhagen with Rask and translated his *Anglo-Saxon Grammar* into English, and John Mitchell Kemble (1807–57) studied in Germany with Jacob Grimm and dedicated his 1833 edition of *Beowulf* to him.[71] In their publications, Thorpe and Kemble celebrated the shared northern identity of ancient England and other locales such as Iceland.[72] Thus, in *The Saxons in England* (1849), Kemble celebrates "the identity of our own heroic story and that of Scandinavia and the continent" and links those groups to a pagan Germanic people whom he celebrates in terms that conjure a flamboyantly racial image of white dominance and power. Evoking sentiments of white awe and pride, Kemble describes how "first, dimly through the twilight in which the sun of Rome was to set for ever, loomed the Colossus of the German race, gigantic, terrible, inexplicable."[73] Versions of that racist attitude persisted in the writings of Tolkien's Scottish tutor, Rawlinson and Bosworth Professor of Anglo-Saxon at Oxford William Craigie (1867–1957), and Tolkien's collaborator, Canadian philologist E. V. Gordon (1896–1938). For example, in the preface to his *Introduction to Old Norse* (1927)—which Oxford University Press retained up to their 1981 edition—Gordon writes,

> [In] Old Norse literature the tastes and ideals of the Germanic race found their most vital expression and . . . the tastes and ideals embodied in it are still part of our [English] racial heritage. We have still, fortunately, some part of the cool rationalism and heroic obstinacy which the sagas prove to be characteristic of our Germanic forefathers.[74]

Reflecting how the white hero, as Dyer has observed, "encompasses all the possibilities for human existence," Gordon's Germanic man is a contradictory and unstable figure, at once thoughtful and stubborn.[75] That blend of qualities also evinces how certain early English scholars like Gordon didn't endorse a Burckhardtian shift from medieval superstition to modern rationality but instead located a rational capacity in early Germanic peoples. Gordon's medievalism is thus feel-good on many fronts: the English now, like their medieval ancestors, have always been innately heroic and clear-headed.

Tolkien adopted versions of the white philological practices outlined earlier, even as he exceeded them in the idiosyncratic brand of essentialism he embraced. An apt starting point for understanding Tolkien's approach to white philology is his take on modernity. On one level, Tolkien fully endorsed ideas of cultural and societal advance and related "modern" virtues such as reason, science, technology, and individualism, with the caveat that such traits must support all that is beautiful and good for humans and nonhumans alike. He even wished he were "rich enough" for an electric typewriter tailored to his own "specifications" to ease his work.[76] Tolkien's affirmation of modernity aligned with his work as both a medievalist and epic-fantasy author. A self-described "professional philologist," he adhered to the positivism of comparative philology as a scientific study of language.[77] And as Saler stresses, Tolkien's rational bent deeply shaped his fiction. Tolkien stated that through his literary works he aimed to "modernize . . . myths and make them credible."[78] Believing that "the keener and the clearer is the reason, the better fantasy it will make," he included in his fiction, as Saler relates, "genealogical charts, detailed chronologies and appendices, and scholarly discussions about nomenclature, geography, history and languages [to] encourage the reader to approach Middle-earth analytically as well as imaginatively."[79]

But even as Tolkien embraced individualism, reason, and other human traits and practices associated with modernity, his view of "our present situation" was immensely negative.[80] Tolkien's rejection of "the cruel modern world" assumed a level of pessimism and disdain that bordered on the internal critiques expressed by European thinkers like Marx, Weber, Horkheimer, and Adorno.[81] Lamenting, in a quasi-Marxian manner, the destructions that modern progress irrationally enacts, Tolkien understood his moment as "indeed an age of 'improved means to deteriorated ends.'"[82] Those "deteriorated ends" included for Tolkien—not unlike Huizinga—a regrettable decline in aesthetics. He described himself as living in a mechanized "Robot Age, that combines elaboration and ingenuity of means with ugliness," as witnessed by "slums and gas-works, and shabby garages, and long arc-lit suburbs."[83] His epic fantasies portrayed the negative effects of modern life; for example, in *The Lord of the Rings*, as Charles Huttar notes, "the desolation of Isengard, 'once . . . green and fair' but 'now filled with pits and forges,' shows how far the landscape had fallen from a [prior and superior] state of nature."[84] Echoing Weber's "iron cage" rhetoric, Tolkien found modernity to be a dehumanizing "prison" that confronted him with "jailers and prison-walls.[85] He rejected, like so many members of his generation, the deleterious effects of both world wars. Moreover, he decried modern globalism and expansions in favor of an insular Englishness; as he put it to his son, "I love England (not Great Britain, and certainly not the British Commonwealth (grr!))."[86]

Tolkien's deep disdain for modernity and global empire comprised part of a larger interpretation of history in which the current moment was the nadir of a longer pattern of decline that began, for the Catholic man of letters, with the expulsion from Eden.[87] Christianity merged, in a contradictory manner, with myth and whiteness in Tolkien's historicism. Thus, regarding the northern Europeans he cherished, Tolkien affirmed Thorkelin's, Grundtvig's, and their academic inheritors' belief that the English were at their prime during ancient times, when northern European men resembled the heroes of Scandinavian myths.[88] In an unfinished 1920s essay on the Norse *Edda* and in "*Beowulf*: The Monsters and the Critics," Tolkien celebrates Icelandic heroes in a German Romantic vein, where the whiteness of the heroes resides in their fierce individualism in the face of insuperable limitations. For Tolkien, as he puts it in his *Beowulf* lecture, all humans are "mortal[s] hemmed in a hostile world" where "man, each man and all men, and all their works shall die" (22–23). But the mythic white masculinity of the Nordic hero entails resisting that "final" and inevitable "defeat of the humane" through an "almost demonic" and godless "reliance upon self and upon indominable will."[89] Tolkien argued that precisely because it is "without hope," the "absolute resistance" of the Norse gods is "perfect."[90] Tolkien's sentiments both mirror Gordon's admiration for the "heroic obstinacy" of Scandinavian protagonists and resonate with Craigie's celebration, in works such as his *Icelandic Sagas* (1913), of a Viking "spirit of independence."[91] Both Gordon and Craigie, like their academic predecessors, esteemed the pagan English and their fellow northerners' shared possession of a fierce individualism rendered all the more heroic—all the more "perfect," all the more white—because of its doomed and tragic nature. In other words, while their white medievalism entailed bad feelings—melancholy, loss—those emotions supported an ultimately pleasurable embrace of persons whose exalted, heroic, and supreme status hinges on their hopeless yet determined self-assertiveness.

Tolkien's white historicism thus departs from the received Burckhardtian take on a medieval-modern divide. Not unlike modern celebrations of the ancient Greeks and Romans, he attributed to ancient Nordic people versions of the individualism, societal and cultural development, and rational capacity Burckhardt associated with modernity. But Tolkien also located in the Middle Ages degrading and disenchanting modernizing forces that pushed his heroic white ancestors toward a more diminutive and mundane experience. The northern European temporal trajectory he traces begins with an initial, ancient period of fiery Nordic male greatness followed by, in his words, "the dying down of the flame, into the gentle smoulder of the Middle Ages, taxes and trade-regulations, and the jog-trot of pigs and herrings."[92] In this account of modernity as a bourgeois phenomenon that tames a passionate white male individualism, the French prominently—and misogynistically—feature; "the gods and heroes" of early northern myths "go down into their Ragnarök, vanquished, not by the World-girdling serpent . . . but by Marie de France, and sermons, medieval Latin and useful information, and the small change of French courtesy."[93] Tolkien sees in England's medieval era a modern domesticating process in which the Normans turn the English away from the public spaces of warfare toward a feminized court.

But Tolkien's Middle Ages aren't utterly diminished; far from it. Because of its relative contiguity to the ancient past, the medieval period proved far more attractive to him than his current, all-time-low modern moment.[94] Tolkien also embraced the medieval period as a gateway to the older heroic northern manhood he extolled. This was "the point of the exercise," to return to Hall's anecdote: to discover in medieval English texts a bridge to the past and witness what Tolkien calls in his *Beowulf* lecture a "supreme expression" of ancient English courage and "unyielding will" (21).[95] Rather than interpret texts in a Leavisite vein as incisive commentaries on social and moral issues pertaining to the moment of their production, English medieval studies should recover and appreciate the ancient pagan English valor evinced in texts like *Beowulf*. Thus understood as a rediscovery of noble white origins, medieval study offered Tolkien and other English readers a way to combat their regrettable modern degradation.[96]

Tolkien premised his embrace of medieval English texts as portals to Nordic greatness on a binding of language, myth, and identity that echoed and expanded the racialism of German Romanticism. He claimed that medieval texts like *Beowulf* manifested northern whiteness, thanks both to the special knowledge Tolkien associated with myth and the innate linguistic and philological sensibilities he attributed to English people, including the *Beowulf* poet and himself. For Tolkien, myths and related literary texts that represented the white masculinity he cherished weren't fictions but "were essentially True" and indeed even more revelatory and significant than historical information.[97] Thus, even as Tolkien adhered to the positivism of the philologist, he embraced a literary sensibility whose value exceeded modern rational assessments of worth. To recall Cecire's insight, when Tolkien arrived at Oxford in the mid-1920s, he "brought a Victorian and Edwardian confidence" in "the inner Englishness that only English literature"—and, especially, medieval English literature—"can fully convey."[98] Tolkien articulates that theory in his *Beowulf* lecture, where he describes how "in places" he finds its "poetry so powerful, that this quite overshadows the historical content" (7). Similarly, in *The Notion Club Papers*, an unfinished novel about a fictionalized version of the Inklings, English professor Wilfrid Jeremy states, "'I have a queer feeling that, if one could go back [in time], one would find not myth dissolving into history, but rather the reverse: real history becoming more mythical.'"[99]

Tolkien not only believed that a people lives on through its literature but also maintained that ancient language and myths live on in a people.[100] In his 1955 lecture "English and Welsh," composed around the time of his encounter with Hall, Tolkien posits two kinds of language acquisition, the language(s) a person learns (which he calls a "cradle tongue") and a "native language," which involves "inherent linguist predilections" that travel over "indefinite generations" and are "never wholly extinguished."[101] An essay that repeatedly refers to blood when describing "native language," "English and Welsh" evinces Tolkien's white essentialist approach to linguistics.[102] For Tolkien, medieval English texts were valuable precisely because of an inherited linguistic acumen that allowed their creators to represent older and mythical—yet somehow real—white heroic identities.

All of Tolkien's beliefs about a diminished modernity, the "truths" found in myth, and inherited white language skills inform his *Beowulf* lecture. There, he stresses the historical sensibility of *Beowulf*: it is "an historical poem about the pagan past"; its author was "learned in old tales" and a figure possessed of "an antiquarian curiosity" (26, 23, 22). However, at the same time the poet senses what is past and gone, the writer is drawn to and succeeds in portraying his white history due to its intimacy and even persistence into his early medieval present. While Christianity has arrived and catalyzed a degrading modernity in England, "that shift is not complete in *Beowulf*"; the poet's very interest in pagan men results from "the nearness of a pagan time. The shadow of its despair, if only as a mood, as an intense emotion of regret, is still there" (23). Along with the poet's temporal intimacy with the heroic pagan era, he brings to his art a mixture of "learning and training" in "native lays and traditions" *and* innate racial-linguistic know-how (27). The *Beowulf*-poet possesses "an instinctive historical sense—a part indeed of the ancient English temper . . . of which *Beowulf* is a supreme expression, but he has used it with a poetical and not an historical object" (7).[103] Thanks to all these factors—historical contiguity, erudition through toil, and inborn knowledge—*Beowulf* portrays a "fusion" or "contact between old and new" whose "most potent elements" are "the theory of courage which is the great contribution of early Northern literature" (20). With a "lofty tone and high seriousness," the poem relates a tragic tale of Nordic whiteness: the "central position the creed of unyielding will holds in the North," whose "old heroes" were "men caught in the chains of circumstance or of their own character, torn between duties equally sacred, dying with their backs to the wall" (19, 21, 17).

Tolkien's claims regarding innate linguistic abilities went far beyond the genetic know-how of medieval northern writers. According to the don, the same inborn propensity for language that enabled the *Beowulf* poet to create his poem allowed contemporary readers to appreciate early English texts. Addressing himself to an intended white English audience in his *Beowulf* lecture, Tolkien states that the Old English poem "is in fact, written in a language that after many centuries has still essential kinship with our own, it was made in this land, and moves in our northern world beneath our northern sky, and for those who are native to that tongue and land, it must ever call with a profound appeal" (33–34).[104] Tolkien's diction indicates the fundamental place of white affect in his medievalism. Comprehending the white content of *Beowulf* requires an approach that goes beyond the rational in the manner of the poet himself, "who feels rather than makes explicit what his theme portends" (15). Tolkien—somewhat like Richard Southern in the account of Europe's emergence in the *Making of the Middle Ages* discussed in Chapter 1—imbues his topic with a significance that lies beyond the "merely" rational and requires a specifically national and racial affect for apprehension. For Tolkien and his readers, the "profound appeal" of *Beowulf* is a matter of sweeping blood-and-soil feelings, of "essential kinship," of how the medieval poet shares "our northern world beneath our northern sky." The English are thus singularly equipped to undertake an affective recovery of both medieval texts and their racial content.

The "profound" attachments Tolkien posits between the English and medieval English texts produce an exceedingly feel-good and almost mystical medievalism. In lieu of the received idea of a modern break that renders the medieval irrevocably other and lost, Tolkien asserts a reassuring racial continuity. Tolkien's medievalism entails the kind of temporal transcendence he imputes, in his essay "On Fairy Stories" (1947) to the otherworldly truths encoded in myths. Such "narratives . . . open a door on Other Time, and if we pass through, though only for a moment, we stand outside our own Time, outside Time itself, maybe."[105] In his *Beowulf* lecture, Tolkien therefore calls up not just the "profound appeal" of the poem for English readers but also the comforting "truth" which that deep attraction manifests: that the past is never lost because the English carry within them the means of overcoming temporal upheavals, including the singular rupture of modernity. The fervency of Tolkien's magical thinking about an innate Englishness emerges in the hallowed tone of such moments in *The Lord of the Rings* as when Frodo, early on in his quest, experiences his literary inheritance. Standing with Sam before an endless road, "suddenly, [Frodo] spoke aloud but as if to himself, saying slowly" a poem that, as he explains later to Sam, "'came to me'" as he recited it "'as if I was making it up; but I may have heard it long ago.'"[106] Such charged, mysterious, and hushed moments signal the affective intensity of Tolkien's investment in an inborn Englishness that eclipsed all sorts of heterogeneities and ruptures.

Tolkien often referred to his inborn knowledge about his "native language" and early English texts and linked those white "predilections" for "old Germanic languages" to his fiction.[107] He saw himself as not just performing a role akin to that of the *Beowulf* poet but also expanding on that linguistic-racial function in a much-needed national direction. For while Tolkien celebrated individual medieval works like *Beowulf* for their manifestation of English identity, he also bemoaned how the English lacked a full-blown national mythology "bound up with its tongue and soil." He acknowledged how "there was and is all the Arthurian world" but discounted Celtic lore in distinctly ethnocentric terms. Arthurian mythology is "imperfectly naturalized, associated with the soil of Britain but not with English." Opposing a mature English rationality to a childish and "wild, incalculable poetic Celt, full of vague and misty imaginations," he claimed that the "'faerie'" of the Britons "is too lavish, and fantastical, incoherent and repetitive."[108] Tolkien echoes the kind of northern European bias evinced in Johan Huizinga's comments about Irish backwardness in *Autumn of the Middle Ages* (discussed in Chapter 2), but with an intensified racial twist: while Huizinga views his contemporary northern European cohort as advanced from a medieval primitivism beyond which the Irish can't move, Tolkien understands his pagan ancestors as already intellectually mature, in the manner of the "cool" Germanic "rationalism" hailed by his colleague E. V. Gordon.

Tolkien thus drew on his imagined racial inheritance to build upon and extend the national essence—"cool and clear, redolent of our 'air,'" heroic, and "high, purged of the gross"—that works like *Beowulf* only partly manifest, and create large-scale epic fantasies "fit for the more adult mind of" an English "land long now steeped in poetry."[109] In *The Lord of the Rings*, Tolkien deployed what he viewed as his innate linguistic knowledge to create a mythology that, in the manner of *Beowulf* but more so, "was imbued with an essential Englishness" so that "individual words, no less than themes and symbols, conveyed a national outlook."[110] Tolkien describes the role of his genetic inheritance in the creation of his epic fantasies in a c. 1951 letter, where he describes how his fictions about Middle-earth "arose in [his] mind as 'given' things," and how he "always . . . had the sense [while writing] of recording what was already 'there,' somewhere: not of 'inventing.'"¹¹¹ Tolkien's reference to not "inventing" indicates how he not only accorded himself the same innate literary skills of medieval writers like the *Beowulf* poet but also understood himself as biologically partaking in the early medieval writers' very linguistic-racial project. As he put it in a 1938 letter, any echo of *Beowulf* in *The Hobbit* "arose naturally (and almost inevitably)."¹¹² To be sure, Tolkien also linked his own philological training to his epic fantasies; but he fundamentally believed that his innate racial-linguistic acumen played a key role in generating those fictions, through which he sought to provide his beloved England with its own white northern mythology.¹¹³

Hall and Whiteness at Oxford

> What would "England" mean without its cathedrals, churches, castles?
> —STUART HALL, "WHOSE HERITAGE"

> Césaire said . . . "I know only one France, the France of the revolution, the France of Toussaint L'Ouverture. So much for Gothic cathedrals." Well, so much indeed for Gothic cathedrals.
> —STUART HALL, "NEGOTIATING CARIBBEAN IDENTITIES"

To return to the Hall-Tolkien encounter, clearly, for the don, the problems posed by Hall's plan of study exceeded his adoption of the "wrong"—that is, modern, Leavisite, and socio-historical—approach to England's literary heritage. Even were Hall to attempt a more philological analysis, he lacked what Tolkien understood as the inborn skills necessary for such work. Tolkien believed that the English were, as Saler puts it, "predisposed by environment, and perhaps by heredity, to grasp" the "mystical significance" of English literary texts.¹¹⁴ According to Tolkien's blood-and-soil beliefs, while the Jamaican Hall—who has described himself as "part Scottish" and thus northern but also part "African, East Indian, Portuguese, Jewish"—could learn certain languages, he did not possess the "inherent linguist predilections" that Tolkien describes in "English and Welsh."¹¹⁵

Hall would go on to generate powerful critiques of the insular, essentialist, and mythic notions of English heritage that Tolkien's medievalism exemplifies. For example, in a keynote address delivered at a 1999 conference on heritage and diversity in Britain, Hall discusses how received ideas of heritage tend toward "a retrospective, nation-alised and tradition-alised conception of culture" whose "double inscription" involves both an "essential meaning" that "appears to have emerged at the very moment of its origin—a moment always lost in the myths, as well as the mists, of time" and "a distilled essence in the various arts and artefacts of the nation."[116] Hall goes on to ask, "Who is the heritage *for?*" and with dismay affirms how "[in] the British case the answer is clear: it is intended for those who 'belong.' A society which is imagined as, in broad terms, culturally homogeneous and unified."[117] Ideas of national heritage, Hall avers, are all too often tied to essentializing myths that reject human diversity and difference.

Nearly half a century before he delivered that address, Hall's experience as a Rhodes Scholar at Oxford confronted him with an early instance of the national problematic he describes. Tolkien's nationalizing exclusions, importantly, comprised part of a larger dynamic at the university. In his memoir and elsewhere, Hall recounts how his arrival at Oxford entailed a fraught encounter with peak Englishness. "It took quite a while," he has stated, "to come to terms with Britain, especially with Oxford, because Oxford is the pinnacle of Englishness, it's the hub, the motor, that creates Englishness."[118] The manner in which "Oxford itself—as place, institution and above all as signifier—came to symbolize for" Hall to national discourses of English identity and hierarchy bespeaks long-standing associations of Oxford with England, links that extend at least as far back as William Camden's 1586 description of it as "the prop and pillar, nay the sun, the eye, the very soul of the nation."[119]

Medieval "heritage" played a key role in the "retrospective, nation-alised and tradition-alised" meaning of Oxford experienced by a young Hall. Renowned for its gothic built environments, Oxford is, in Matthew Arnold's well-known tributes, a "city of dreaming spires," "whispering from her towers the last enchantments of the Middle Age."[120] Long before and well after Arnold's commentaries, the medieval "spires of Oxford! domes and towers!" were admired by writers from Camden to early gothic revivalists such as Thomas Warton and Horace Walpole; Romantics including John Keats, Percy Shelley, and William Wordsworth; Arnold's contemporaries John Ruskin and William Morris; and up to the post–World War II novelists studied by Ian Carter.[121] Hall, who lived "round the corner from Mob Quad, the oldest actual quadrangle in Oxford," was keenly attuned to the medieval character of Oxford—one of "the only two universities" in Britain, as a 1951 popular guide emphasized— that maintained "the medieval college system" of autonomous fortresses.[122] In his memoir, Hall both stresses the medieval roots of his college and indicates his complex response to its gothic architecture: "Merton, founded in the fourteenth century, is one of the oldest Oxford colleges, resplendent in its classic Oxford architecture, a place of medieval seriousness, solidity and gloom" (155). While white English men like Arnold or Morris might gush rhapsodically over

Oxford's medieval built environments, Hall found those structures beautiful yet also gloomy and unwelcoming.

Hall's ambivalent account of Oxford's gothic structures suggests that they contributed to how he generally "felt out of place in Merton College."[123] "Often the only black person in the room," Hall encountered not just off-putting buildings but an overall forbidding and cold environment involving what he describes in his memoir as "a plunge into the icy depths and arcane complexities of Englishness, unexpected even by someone who thought they knew England well" (156–57). Hall's discomfort speaks to the manner in which, as he puts it in the aforementioned address, because "heritage is a powerful source" of "cultural meanings which bind each member individually into the larger national story," it necessarily "follows that those who cannot see themselves reflected in its mirror cannot properly belong."[124] Oxford's function as a "distillation" of Englishness rendered Hall an outsider to the university, including Oxford medieval studies. It was the "site," as he relates in *Familiar Stranger*, where he first came "to terms with being 'other'" (157).

It is precisely in the context of his account of the off-putting white environment at Oxford, and especially the medieval "heritage" of Oxford, that Hall's Tolkien anecdote appears, which I cite in full:

> Oxford was my first close encounter with the British governing classes "at home," and with the institutions by which a hegemonic culture is manufactured. Merton, founded in the fourteenth century, is one of the oldest Oxford colleges, resplendent in its classic Oxford architecture, a place of medieval seriousness, solidity and gloom. I read Chaucer in the Old Library sitting beside books still chained to the wooden desks. College was a plunge into the icy depths and arcane complexities of Englishness, unexpected even by someone who thought they knew England well. A quarter of my course was in languages like Anglo-Saxon and Middle English, which I couldn't understand. High German and Old Norse, other early roots of the English language, seemed impossibly foreign. Actually, I loved some of the poetry—*Beowulf, Sir Gawain and the Green Knight, The Wanderer, The Seafarer*—and at one point I planned to do graduate work on Langland's *Piers Plowman*. But when I tried to apply contemporary literary criticism to these texts, my ascetic South African language professor told me in a pained tone that this was not the point of the exercise. (156)

Hall's portrayal of his relationship to medieval texts may appear contradictory. He states that he "couldn't understand" early English languages, and yet he obviously did. Hall had mastered Old English and Middle English well enough to arrive at a "love" for "some of the poetry." That expertise in early English literature doubtless underwrote Hall's plan to do graduate work on *Piers*. Crucial to understanding this seeming contradiction is Hall's linkage of medievalism to Oxford and ideologies of white Englishness. The medieval thrust of its English curriculum spoke to the overall identity of Oxford as a medieval site, a relation literalized in its material culture through books "still chained to the wooden desks." Hall addresses the offensive discourse of belonging and estrangement that attended such a binding of the medieval to white Englishness when he writes that the "early roots of the English language ... seemed impossibly foreign," a passage that clarifies how the challenge or barrier Hall faced wasn't a matter of his learning ability but of the white insular production of the medieval as "foreign" to him.[125] The challenges that Hall faced in his studies involved not his skillset but rather a version of the racist blockages described by critics including Sara Ahmed and Hall.[126] Tolkien's white discourse of insularity, along with the overall racializing medieval thrust of Oxford, evince how, as Hall would put it in his 1991 essay "The Local and the Global," Englishness is "the ethnicity which places all the other ethnicities."[127] The whiteness of Tolkien and Oxford "placed" Hall in his "otherness, in [his]marginality," beyond the reach of the Oxford English course.[128]

"Beating the Bounds" of Oxford

While Tolkien may have dissuaded his Jamaican-British student from becoming a medievalist, Hall went on to generate a substantial, wide-ranging, and diaspora-inflected body of scholarship, much of which offers powerful tools for analyzing the don's essentializing medievalism, his historical sensibility, and his fiction. Hall may be best known for his conjunctural approach, which attends carefully to the distinct components of a charged societal moment. As Hall puts it, "A conjuncture is a period during which the different social, political, economic and ideological contradictions that are at work in society come together to give it a specific and distinctive shape."[129] In his influential essay "Gramsci's Relevance for the Study of Race and Ethnicity" (1986), Hall draws on Italian Marxist philosopher Antonio Gramsci (1891–1937) to identify the multiple determinants involved in social formations and their racial elements, stressing how "*periodization* is a key aspect of the analysis."[130] Thus, unlike Tolkien, Hall embraces periodization as a tool for analyzing race. But crucially, Hall invokes periodization by stressing contingency and multiplicity, thus radically diverging from the western Eurocentric models of a medieval-modern divide discussed in Chapters 1 and 2. White western discourse endorses identifiable, orderly, and predictable notions of development on the part of particular social groups; above all, it charts northern Europeans' inevitable movement from primitive to advanced modes. Hall's periodization instead identifies moments of crisis between multiple and diverse social groups and highlights how those periods of conflict are contingent and "cannot be mechanically predicted."[131] Instead of focusing on the singular break when an equally singular northern European modernity tore free from the medieval chains that bound whites, Hall's conjunctural analysis carefully attends to how all sorts of different crises "move between periods of relative 'stabilization' and periods of rapid and convulsive change."[132] In lieu of the eternally noble and rational white men hailed by Tolkien, and instead of the modern destiny embraced by whites, "there is no preordained result" to the manifold and multi-determinant crises analyzed by Hall.[133]

Hall's methodology raises the question of the nature of the multiple forces tied to both Tolkien's white beliefs and his ability to enforce those beliefs by dissuading the young Hall from pursuing his plan of medieval study. I suggest that central to a conjunctural interpretation of the Hall-Tolkien encounter are two phenomena that fostered in many white British persons a "little-Englander" insularism and a concomitant ambivalence over empire: world war and immigration. Up to the end of World War II, most of the people who migrated to Britain were Jews, Irish, Italians, Poles, and other Europeans. After the war, though, a new group of migrants, traveling from former British imperial holdings in the West Indies and South Asia, began moving to the metropole. Hall, as a Jamaican and thus West Indian, hailed from one the groups tied to new postwar immigration patterns. Hall arrived in England in 1951, three years after 492 Jamaicans, traveling aboard the SS *Empire Windrush*, inaugurated the new immigration in Britain. Most of that Caribbean migration occurred between 1950 and 1962, when immigration policy was tightened along racial lines.[134] Those immigrants were motivated by a host of reasons, among them disadvantages resulting from the enslavement of members of their community in the past, the failure of the plantation economy, an investment in imperial ideology (or, conversely, a strategic retaliation), a desire to take advantage of labor needs arising partly from the need to rebuild the postwar nation, and, in 1952, the elimination of the U.S. as a destination per the McCarran-Walter Act.[135] As a scholarship student at an elite university, Hall was in a rarified category of West Indian immigrant; most West Indians were "quite prepared to undertake the dirty, dangerous, and poorly paid jobs that white workers no longer wanted."[136] During Hall's time at Oxford, which extended from 1951 to 1957, West Indians, who comprised most of the five hundred immigrants who lived there in 1959, worked in transportation, construction, hospitals, laundries, bakeries, and other businesses.[137] Indians in Oxford during the 1950s lived in the inner city (where

Tolkien also lived from 1950 to 1953) and in southeast Oxford, where a portion of the community inhabited a public housing project.[138]

Immigrants from the West Indies, like their South Indian counterparts, were placed by the English in a separate category from other Commonwealth immigrants. White immigrants, such as those who came from Australia, were viewed as internal, or sharing with the English membership in a single racial collective. Immigrants of color, on the other hand—despite the fact that they were, as Catherine Hall and Sonya Rose put it, "imperial subjects with a long history connecting them to Britain"—were viewed wholly as outsiders, "postwar migrants," and strangers situated outside the sort of history Tolkien so cherished.[139] Representations of West Indians arriving in Britain, as Bill Schwarz observes, rendered them mere "immigrants" of unknown past and origin: "Immigrants, it seemed, had no past, coming into life only at that moment when they entered the line of vision of the native, 'host' population."[140] As Hall relates in *Familiar Stranger* regarding the identity foisted on him by whites in Britain, "We were condemned to be out of place or displaced, transported to a phantasmatic zone of the globe where history never happened as it should" (61).

Tolkien's writings, with their insistently regional focus on England and English (or, at most, northern European) history, reflect the overall disinterest of the British in the particulars of the lives of travelers from elsewhere in the former empire.[141] Moreover, Tolkien's letters and fiction speak to his fervent little-Englander nationalism. Tolkien's insularity emerges in the aforementioned 1944 letter to his son, where he grumbles about "the British Commonwealth," laments how global forces may not leave "any niche . . . for reactionary back numbers like me," and worries that the "bigger things get the smaller and duller or flatter the globe gets."[142] Tolkien's viewpoint echoes the rejection of internationalism throughout the West during the 1940s by conservatives like U.S. poet Allen Tate, who, writing a year after Tolkien, similarly stresses how "the big community . . . is not necessarily bigger spiritually or culturally than the little community."[143] As Saler relates, Tolkien's "essentialist vision of Little England" also reflected specifically national trends that originated, in part, from white ambivalence over "empire," global warfare, and a "growing cosmopolitanism." No colonialist, Tolkien cherished England as a latter-day version of Shakespeare's "sceptred isle," a site set apart from the world and populated by versions of the English "'Little Man,' a figure not dissimilar in character to a hobbit."[144]

That insular nativism informs *The Lord of the Rings*, which thematizes the problem of outsider incursions threatening hobbit enclaves.[145] Its preface recounts how law officers "beat the bounds" of the Shire to "see that Outsiders of any kind, great or small, did not make themselves a nuisance" and relates how, "at the time when this story begins," the number of Bounders "greatly increased" based on reports of "strange persons and creatures prowling about the borders, or over them."[146] Later, the hobbits of Bree encounter people escaping "trouble away in the South" who are "looking for lands where they could find some peace":

> The Bree-folk were sympathetic, but plainly not very ready to take a large number of strangers into their little land. One of the travelers, a squint-eyed ill-favoured fellow, was foretelling that more and more people would be coming north in the near future. "If room isn't found for them, they'll find it for themselves. They've a right to live, same as other folk," he said loudly. The local inhabitants did not look pleased at the prospect.[147]

"Squint-eyed" strangers from "the South" with suspicious looks (and criminal inclinations—the speaker turns out to be a thief) heading north for a better life: this narrative element suggests racialized undesirables immigrating to England's avatar, the Shire. Near the end of the series, it is members of this group—described not just as "squint-eyed" but also "sallow-faced"—whom the hobbits "scour" from the Shire, reestablishing its white insularity.[148]

The insularity and xenophobia in Tolkien's fiction intersected with his own academic practice, as his rebuff of Hall highlights. When Tolkien denigrated Hall's effort to use contemporary criticism to unpack medieval texts, claiming "in a pained tone that this was not the point of the exercise," we might speculate that the don perceived Hall not only as a trespasser into his "Shire" but also as a figure who aimed to go further, taking and misusing its books and stories.[149]

A "Great Dark Wave": Insularity, Atlantis, and Post-Windrush Migration

Tolkien may especially have perceived Hall as threatening because of his student's possible resonances with what is arguably the most fanciful element of the medievalist's essentialism: his "Atlantis complex" or "haunting."[150] Tolkien portrayed in his works—and claimed to witness in dreams—a tragic episode in the ancient past of the mythic peoples called the Númenoreans. As the descendents of elves, the most exalted of all Tolkien's creatures, the Númenoreans are the highest-born humans on Middle-earth. Their habitation is Númenor, an island situated west of Middle-earth and a home gifted them by the gods. The Númenoreans develop an exceptional civilization, until Sauron convinces the current Númenorean king to defy the divine limit placed on his people:

to never, as the appendices to *The Lord of the Rings* relate, "sail west out of sight of their own shores or to attempt to set foot on" a realm called "the Undying Lands."[151] The Númenoreans' rebellion prompts the gods to destroy Númenor through a watery, Atlantis-like, and horrifying apocalypse. Mirroring the fate of Plato's legendary island, "Númenor was thrown down and swallowed in the Sea," thus ending one of the distinct epochs—the "Second Age"—of Tolkien's mythic history of Middle-earth.[152]

Tolkien's portrayal of the disaster was not confined to his appendices; it appeared repeatedly—obsessively, even—in his letters, unfinished works (including two novels), and the fantasy series itself in the portrayal of the dreams of Frodo and the human character of Faramir. For example, in a passage that encapsulates key elements of the mythic disaster, Faramir describes how he "often dream[s] of" the fall of Númenor "and of the great dark wave climbing over the green lands and above the hills, and, coming on, darkness unescapable."[153]

In a remarkable move that reflects how, as he put it to his son Christopher, "it is things of racial and linguistic significance that attract me and stick in my memory," Tolkien believed in this "great dark wave" of his own invention as if it were a memory.[154] Just one indicator of the essentialism surrounding Tolkien's "Atlantis haunting" is an account of his creative process. In a letter to W. H. Auden, Tolkien describes how he "consult[ed]" his "roots" not only via "legends" that possess "the North-western temper and temperature," but also through what his

> heart may remember, even if he has been cut off from all oral tradition, the rumour all along the coasts of the Men out of the Sea.
> I say this about the "heart," for I have what some might call an Atlantis complex. Possibly inherited though my parents. . . . Inherited from me (I suppose) by one only of my children. . . . I mean the terrible recurrent dream (beginning with memory) of the Great Wave, towering up, and coming in ineluctably over the trees and green fields. (I bequeathed it to Faramir.)[155]

As a nightmarish trauma whose inherited character renders it, to cite Verlyn Flieger, a "racial" memory, Tolkien's "Atlantis complex" apparently was as historical as it was mythic.[156] The fabulist thought that, thanks to his own imagined connection to a Númenorean ancestral line, he possessed a genetic memory of that ancient flood.

Tolkien's "Atlantis haunting" performs the dream-like work of condensation described by Freud, bundling together the contradictory affects that inform his approach to periodization, insularity, and race. Because the Númenoreans' catastrophic rupture is as temporal as it is spatial, both the repeated portrayal of that cataclysm in Tolkien's works and its frequent haunting of his dreams suggest the writer's "terrible" fascination with periodization—in fact, with temporal rupture of the most extreme variety.[157] At the same time, though, the dream epitomizes Tolkien's investment in transcending history, by dint of racial continuities. However disastrous, the rupture imagined by Tolkien isn't final. His appendices describe how a small band of Númenoreans manage to escape to Middle-earth, led by the heroic chieftain Elendil and his sons. The appendices go on to affirm Númenorean racial continuity over time: "It was the pride and wonder of the Northern Line that, though their power departed and their people dwindled, through all the many generations the succession was unbroken from father to son."[158]

Tolkien believed that he and his son Christopher partook—as evinced by their genetic memories of the Atlantis-like disaster—in that very exalted white line. His memory thus recalls the experience of the earliest mythic progenitors of the English; he sees what they saw, inhabiting their vantage point. As Flieger puts it, instead of a "Wellsian time-machine," Tolkien and his autobiographical avatars journey to an ancient past via "ancestrally transmitted memories of a past they could not have experienced in their own personae."[159]

Hall, thanks to his ties to the British empire and its aftermath, may have intersected with and even triggered Tolkien's Atlantis complex. The mythic memory concerns territorial boundaries and the dangers of expansion and colonization: the gods forbid the Númenoreans from moving beyond their island. The punishment for expansion in the "Atlantis haunting" departs from the colonial dynamics of 1950s' England. While the mythic narrative involves the actions of the gods and an oceanic engulfment, the contemporary dynamic entails the movement of members of colonial and postcolonial sites to the "motherland." Yet contemporary migration was portrayed by white politicians and in the white mass media via metaphors that resonate with the terrible "dark wave" that destroyed the Númenoreans. The percentage of colonial immigrants of color in England, who hailed from not only the West Indies but also South Asia, was tiny during the mid-1950s. For example, the total number of Commonwealth immigrants in 1956 comprised .09 percent of the total population of the UK.[160] Nevertheless, media outlets and institutions like Parliament construed these recent arrivals as a threatening mass via, as Andy Brown puts it, an "anti-diluvian imagery of flood and disaster."[161] English fears about a cataclysmic "flood" of immigrants transformed individuals whose actions stemmed from a variety of contingencies into a single and unstoppable natural disaster. For example, a 1955 *Times* editorial stated that the "present West Indian and West African invasion is a mere trickle of what we must expect" and cited statistics giving "some idea of the pressure of population and poverty that may soon result in a flood we may well find to be uncontrollable."[162] That hydrospheric rhetoric would persist for decades, most notoriously in the "Rivers of Blood" speech delivered by British MP Enoch Powell (1912–98) in April 1968 and the reference by Prime Minister Margaret Thatcher (1925–2013) to being "swamped" with immigrants on television in 1978.[163]

Tolkien's Atlantis dream was centered on a vulnerable island under threat. With its stress on a bounded land mass engulfed by water, Tolkien's memory resonated with white accounts of the immigration pattern of which Hall was a part. Hall thus may have represented for Tolkien not just an outsider deficient in racial know-how but also a metonym for a disaster of ruinous proportions. The young Jamaican-British student may have prompted Tolkien to "beat the bounds" of medieval study at Oxford—not just because he represented for the don a stranger who practiced different methodologies and lacked an inborn English medieval sensibility, but also because his relation to a "wave" of Black immigration triggered a terrifying nightmare about a "great dark wave" and "darkness unescapable" engulfing Tolkien's mythic ancestors on their island in the West.

Multiplicity, Contingency, and Difference: Hall on Identity Formation

The utility of Hall's critical oeuvre is two-fold. On one hand, Hall's work enables a contextualization of Tolkien's gatekeeping as a function of a slew of "linkages" that include, but are not limited to, the don's insular and blood-and-soil idea of identity, as well as Commonwealth immigration and its [mis]representation by whites. On the other hand, Hall's writings also offer alternate, diasporic approaches to identity and history. In lieu of white fantasies of homogeneity and continuity, Hall's work engages realities of difference, multiplicity, and contingency. In 1970, Hall's scholarship began to turn explicitly to questions of race, diaspora, and identity in essays such as "Black Men, White Media." The article, which appeared in 1974 in the Caribbean journal *Savacou*, analyzes postwar Black immigration and British broadcasting, a topic showcased by Hall through his titular riff on Fanon's important critique of whiteness.[164] There, Hall attacks little-Englander notions of a beleaguered "sceptred isle" by stressing how Black immigrants are merely making visible a long-standing if repressed colonial relation. Rejecting national fantasies about the historical continuity of an essential Englishness, he stresses that "black people," far from disrupting the insular cohesion of Britain, "have had an invisible presence for centuries in British history." The identity treasured by the English isn't racially singular; colonies and their inhabitants have long functioned as a "hidden component" of British identity.[165] The model of history put forth by Hall concerns a kind of temporal continuity, but one that diverges starkly from that of Tolkien. While the don affirmed an unchanging racial essence, Hall asserts a continuously global relation and ongoing heterogeneity.

Hall would develop his diasporic analysis on behalf of a searing critique of "Englishness" in later pieces such as "The Local and the Global." Affirming that "it is almost impossible to think about the formation of English society ... outside of the processes that we identify with globalization," he highlights in that essay how imperialism made the English archipelago, at the very emergence of dominant nationalizing narratives, a heterogeneous site tied to persons and places around the globe.[166] Hall's comments in "The Local and the Global" and other writings radically undo Tolkien's little-Englander investments, such as the cherished tea times and the love of a good smoke that he relates in his letters and bestows on his alter ego, Frodo.[167] For centuries, much of the English lifestyle that Tolkien embraced—versions of white, homey hobbit comforts such as tobacco and sugary treats—relied on the colonies. As Hall puts it in a 2007 interview, "Little Englander nationalism," the white racial formation of which Tolkien was a part "could hardly survive if people understood whose sugar flowed through English blood and rotted English teeth."[168] Hall's rhetoric, with its stress not just on white national consumption habits but on their relation to an embodiment that borders on the abject, eviscerates Tolkien and other white figures' feel-good representations of a unitary and cozily English identity. Coursing "through [the] blood" of people like Tolkien isn't an exalted language and a heroic ethos but rather commodities extracted from colonies on behalf of debilitating white consumption habits.

Hall confronts how, even when one removes a colonizing history from the story of the English archipelago, forms of difference prove definitive to identity formation. He stresses in "The Local and the Global" how not only is the fiction of a "condensed, homogen[e]ous, unitary" Englishness undermined by England's relationship "to those societies with which it was deeply connected, both as a commercial and global political power overseas," but also, in "one of the best-kept secrets of the world," neither do England's fantasies of national essence hold up "in relation to its own territory either."[169] Multiplicity, contingency, and dynamism have always defined the English archipelago. Any claim about England "was always negotiated against difference." The very idea, codified in the Act of Union (1707), "that Englishness could stand for everybody in the British Isles," hinged on "absorbing ... all the differences of class, of region, of gender, in order to present itself as a homogen[e]ous entity."[170] Tolkien exemplifies all those forms of local and global diversity. For example, he was a practicing Catholic in a Protestant country, and, about a century before the medievalist's birth, the Tolkien family, which had been living in modern-day Germany and Poland, emigrated to the UK. Above all, as Hall cannily stresses when he refers to the don not by name but as his "South African language professor," Tolkien was not native to his beloved "mother" country. Indeed, Tolkien, in certain respects, was Hall's double. Like Hall, who was born in Jamaica and had African roots, the don not only was connected to Africa but also had traveled from the periphery of the British Empire to its English center. Hall thus in a sense talks back in his memoir to Tolkien in ways that resonate with his diasporic analysis of identity. Undermining the essentialism that underwrote the don's gatekeeping, Hall highlights Tolkien's African connections. Paradoxically, the writer of racializing fantasies illustrates the status of England as a heterogeneous site crosscut by differences.

Hall's keen attention to difference and identity formation sheds light on the motivation for Tolkien's white investments. The don exemplifies, in Hall's words in "The Local and the Global," the allure of identities as "some stable points of reference which were like that in the past, are now and ever shall be, still points in a turning world."[171] Tolkien only invoked his heterogeneity to dismiss it as irrelevant to his Englishness: he called his South African and German origins "fallacious fact[s]"; he asserted that he was a Suffield (his British mother's maiden name) "by tastes, talents, and upbringing"; and he claimed that "any corner of that county [Worcestershire] (however fair or squalid) is in an indefinable way 'home' to me, as no other part of the world is."[172] Through his fantastical ideas of a timeless and inherited northern European identity, whose encoding in medieval literary texts was heritable, Tolkien sought to transcend and overcome the differences and dislocations of the world of which he was a part.

In his "Whose Heritage?" address, Hall engages the national claims underwriting practices like Tolkien's white English philology and exposes the actual workings of that discourse. Received thinking might identify a "distilled essence" of Englishness

> in the various arts and artefacts of the nation for which the Heritage provides the archive. In fact, what the nation "means" is an on-going project, under constant reconstruction. We come to know its meaning partly through the objects and artefacts which have been made to stand for and symbolise its essential values. Its meaning is constructed within, not above or outside representation.[173]

Hall's structuralist stress on the location of identity "within, not above or outside representation" in certain respects echoes Tolkien's emphasis on language as the source of English identity. Both figures emphasize the primary importance of representation and language. But crucially, as I have discussed, Tolkien stresses language because the don believed that medieval English texts and his own epic fantasies "incorporated an essential Englishness, that existed at a metaphysical level."[174] Hall does the opposite, stressing representation to expose identity as an ever-changing and historically contingent construction or fabrication.

With respect to periodization, Hall's account of identity formation upends the logic of Tolkien's belief in blood-and-soil historical transcendence. Identity for Hall is never singular, and it never rises above time. Tethered to a variety of changing historical forces, identity is in process, always changing, always dependent on negotiations with difference. The very shift in Tolkien's ideas of Englishness, after World War I, from a heroic to a cozy little Englander ethos, exposes that contingency. Instead of anything "real," Tolkien's essentialisms are constructs—representations, versions of Du Bois's veil—that offer discursive legitimation for actual discrepancies of power, inequities that structured everything from global patterns of colonization and migration to the dissertation topics approved or dismissed at Oxford.

4
Stuart Hall's *Piers Plowman*

Stuart Hall, medievalist? For anyone familiar with the humanities, Hall's name calls up a cluster of associations, such as his inexhaustible generosity and critical ferocity, his membership in the British New Left, and his founding role in the fields of cultural studies and multiculturalism. But among Hall's many characteristics and affiliations, an interest in the European Middle Ages, let alone a Middle English text like *Piers Plowman*, is decidedly absent. We associate Hall with the analysis of contemporary political practices like Thatcherism and contemporary cultural forms such as cinema. Medieval study is among the last pursuits one might associate with that influential Jamaican-British intellectual.

And yet, if one looks for it, evidence of a historicizing and, yes, even a medievalizing Hall emerges in his oeuvre. As Chapter 3 discusses, Hall possessed a temporal sensibility that encompassed both his interrogations of modernity and his conjunctural analysis of the array of historical forces that shape different societal articulations at distinctive periods and in certain locations. Moreover, his works evince an interest in the medieval. His 1997 textbook chapter "The Spectacle of the 'Other'" discusses the medieval "European image of Africa" and the legend of Prester John.[1] Hall's 2002 essay "'In but Not Of Europe': Europe and Its Myths" discusses medieval discourses of alterity, going so far as to cite medievalist John Block Friedman's 1981 book *The Monstrous Races in Medieval Art and Thought*, which is a scholarly work familiar only to specialists.[2] Both his oft-cited "The West and the Rest: Discourse and Power" (1992) and "The Spectacle of the Other" substantially concern premodern Europe, especially medieval forms of alterity.[3] Finally, Hall's papers include both teaching notes that adopt a historical perspective that encompasses the years before

1500 CE and notebooks that contain detailed information about medieval travel, cartography, legendary lore, and travel writing. That archive urges a new understanding of Hall as a figure whose interest in modernity required attention to earlier periods, including the years before 1500 CE.

To be sure, if we turn from Hall's overall interest in the Middle Ages to his clash with Tolkien over medieval study, that element of his biography seems all but invisible. Hall's account of his aborted dissertation on William Langland's *Piers Plowman* consists of a slim anecdote in his memoir *Familiar Stranger: A Life Between Two Islands* (2017). And there, Hall even refrains from naming Tolkien, instead calling him his "South African language professor."[4] Furthermore, *Piers* appears just once in Hall's scholarship, in the voice of not Hall but another scholar, sociologist Michael Mann, cited in "The West and the Rest" (323). Similarly, on those occasions when Hall's comments on his literary training, he barely registers his medievalism. When Hall recounts his literary roots, he typically describes his attraction to modernist poets like T. S. Eliot, his love of nineteenth- and twentieth-century novelists, and the dissertation that he actually undertook (only to abandon), on Henry James's novels.[5]

But could Langland and Tolkien have functioned as tellingly absent presences? That is, if one considers Hall's aforementioned medieval investments (registered, as we have seen earlier, in his published and unpublished writings), the near erasure of that gatekeeping episode imbues it with new relevance. Perhaps *Piers* and the don disappear from Hall's biography not because they are inconsequential but because of their significance. Could the experience of professional rejection at the hands of an influential don have rendered Hall's particular medieval avenue of inquiry—the *Piers* dissertation—a fraught, even traumatic, subject for him? I'm opining, in other words, that the rejection of Hall's Langland plans may have been so significant as to demand its suppression, if not repression. Perhaps not despite but because of the scant evidence available, one should take seriously Hall's interest in *Piers Plowman*.

This chapter, then, considers the other side of the coin addressed in the previous chapter. While J. R. R. Tolkien's encounter with Stuart Hall prompted in Chapter 3 a conjunctural and discursive reassessment of the Oxford don, here it inspires a deeper inquiry into Hall's medieval study and its intersection with the diasporic critical practice for which he is renowned. While in the previous chapter Hall assisted my analysis of Tolkien's feel-good yet deleterious white medievalism, this chapter turns to Hall for an alternate, antiracist, medievalism reflective of the sorts of feel-bad historicisms generated by W. E. B. Du Bois, Jennifer Morgan, and other theorists covered in Chapter 2.

Reading Against the Grain for the Medieval Hall

My analysis of Hall's abortive project employs a version of what Edward Said calls a contrapuntal hermeneutical practice. Said advocates a contrapuntal mode of reading that rethinks "the cultural archive" (in his case, the nineteenth-century English novel) by attending to "those other [marginal] histories against which (and together with which) the dominating discourse acts."[6] I repurpose Said to reassess Hall's intellectual biography, considering the Langland-Tolkien anecdote as grounds for reading against the grain of the reigning narrative of Hall's intellectual trajectory. Countering the usual stress on the contemporary thrust of Hall's work, I consider how Hall's abandoned Langland thesis might offer a fresh vantage point on his analysis of history, modernity, race, and national identity.

This chapter thus offers a thought experiment or speculation that takes as its starting point questions like: Why might Langland have attracted Hall as a scholarly object? What were the stakes of Hall's medievalism? How might a Hall-esque analysis of *Piers* have manifested? In other words, my aims overlap with those of thinkers who have variously engaged in acts of, as Catherine Gallagher puts it, "telling it like it wasn't."[7]

To be sure, my project diverges in important ways from similar imaginative inquiries. For one thing, "critical fabulation[s]," counter-histories, and alternate histories are often generated by writers whose identities coincide with their topic.[8] While I am a medievalist by training, my stake in this project isn't personal in the manner of Saidiya Hartman's "Venus in Two Acts."[9] In addition, although this chapter enacts a creative scholarly practice, my speculations regarding Hall's medievalism aren't grounded in the life of an otherwise silenced person, such as the Black women featured in Hartman's critical fabulations, Michel Foucault's "infamous man," or even E. P. Thompson's workers.[10] Rather, this chapter more closely approximates critics' and fiction writers' crafting of counterfactual, alternate, and speculative histories based on imagined premises. I'm interested in what Gallagher and Stephen Greenblatt describe as "possibilities cut short, imaginings left unrealized, projects half formulated, ambitions squelched, doubts, dissatisfactions, and longings half felt."[11]

The blockage performed by Tolkien can't be undone. Hall's Langland dissertation can never be written, and Hall can't be made retroactively into a medievalist. Nevertheless, benefits accrue to serious consideration of Hall's unrealized path. In a recent essay, Mary Rambaran-Olm observes how "the story of Hall's removal from the field prompts a haunting reflection: how might the field have developed differently if intellectuals like him, and perspectives like his, were not discouraged or dismissed outright?"[12] I expand Rambaran-Olm's inquiry beyond the impact Hall may have had on medieval studies to consider how his abandoned project sheds light on his biography, the stakes of his work, and his understandings of race, discourse, and periodization. Just as the anecdote complicates received ideas about Tolkien, it also opens new ways of assessing the place of the medieval—especially Langland and *Piers Plowman*—in Hall's influential scholarly oeuvre.

A contrapuntal reading might assume a host of forms, thanks to the rich complexity of Hall's life and work, not to mention Langland's poem. Among those potential avenues of inquiry, I focus on Hall's meditations on identity as they pertain to race, diaspora, Eurocentric mythologies, and the antinomy of the global and the local. Some might consider Hall first and foremost a neo-Marxist. But, as scholars including Claire Alexander note, Hall's interest in West Indian rights and problems of racialization in England pre-date his engagement with a British Left at Oxford, and his "significance ... in shaping the field of racial and ethnic studies ... is almost impossible to overestimate."[13] Central to Hall's life and influential writings are pieces such as those deployed in the previous chapter, publications that critique white discourses of national and racial belonging in the West and theorize alternate identity formations.

In what follows, I first consider the diasporic stakes of Hall's abandoned dissertation. I suggest that, by writing about *Piers*, Hall was poised to unsettle the medievalism of the left cohort with which he was beginning to ally. As we shall see, the unitary and racialized medievalism that conservatives like Tolkien espoused extended to left-leaning intellectuals, whose assertions about an authentically English populist tradition had long engaged *Piers*. I then consider the alternate view on tradition and identity put forth in Hall's publications, starting with his first essay. Penned at Oxford in the mid-1950s, "Our Literary Heritage" offers a revealing look at a young Hall's diasporic critique of Eurocentrism, modernity, literary history, and medieval literature. I then turn to Hall's subsequent work to both recover its medievalism and explore what the mature Stuart Hall—for instance, the intellectual who discovered Antonio Gramsci, embraced post-structuralism, and pioneered whiteness studies—might have made of medieval European culture and especially *Piers*. The chapter concludes with a dialectical reconsideration of *Piers* in the spirit of Hall's oeuvre. On one hand, I speculate that Langland may have attracted a young Hall due to factors such as the medieval poet's multidimensional methodology and his destabilizing take on English identity. On the other hand, I suggest, a mature Hall may have critiqued Langland as an early instance of how English cultural forms remain within the discursive parameters of whiteness.

Challenging Tolkien's Hegemonic Medievalism

Hall's encounter with Tolkien, when viewed from one angle, both affirms the don's institutional authority in Oxford during the 1950s and reflects the oppressive white climate that confronted a young Hall. Tolkien's capacity to deter his student from graduate medieval study resonates with Hall's account in *Familiar Stranger* of how he had a "sense of always being 'in place'" at Oxford (157). "Always being 'in place'" suggests both the epistemic fixing performed by the stereotype and the institutional fixing it authorizes. In the case of Tolkien, the don denied his student a certain form of academic mobility: pursuing a path to a medieval studies DPhil. A 1989 essay in which Hall writes, "I still experience that indefinable sense of being absolutely placed and put down even today, whenever I cross the threshold between Oxford railway station and Broad Street, gateway to the 'dreaming spires,'" indicates the lingering affective toll of his confrontation with whiteness at Oxford.[14]

However, the anecdote reveals much more than an offensive and harmful instance of white supremacy. It also, I would argue, showcases diasporic insurgency: Hall's interest in challenging entrenched assumptions about the uses and meanings of literary elements of the so-called English heritage. After all, Hall, like the other Windrush generation students whom he befriended at Oxford, hardly inhabited the role of the subordinate colonial. Rather, Hall and his fellow West Indians planned independence and—in a move that seems to resonate with Hall's abortive Langland dissertation—asserted their charged relationship to the nation they had been taught to admire.[15] Inhabiting a diasporic identity "between two islands," Hall cultivated identifications and asserted rights that situated him between the West Indies and the UK.

Hall's interest in becoming a medievalist, I would argue, indicates the specifically cultural dimensions of the diasporic identity he asserted at Oxford shortly after his arrival in England. Hall's very project of working on *Piers* challenged the don's blood-and-soil understanding of inherently English medieval literary forms intended solely for white English readers. Hall would later insist in his 1999 publication, "Whose Heritage? Un-settling 'the Heritage,' Re-imagining the Post-Nation," that English culture should not be understood in culturally racist terms as a matter of inherently English artifacts. Yet this indictment of white Englishness, characteristic of his later career, can be traced back to Hall's early effort to claim his right to study medieval literature, an act that rebelled against "a retrospective, nation-alised and tradition-alised conception of culture."[16]

To begin to explore why Hall desired to write specifically about *Piers Plowman*, I consider two related comments Hall made about his literary studies as a student at Oxford: his claim in an interview that he was "interested in medieval literature . . . in a critical way, not in a scholarly way"; and his assertion in *Familiar Stranger* that he desired to not only work on Langland but also "apply contemporary literary criticism" to medieval texts.[17] As Chapter 3 discusses, Hall had a passion for "contemporary literary criticism" that directly opposed the "scholarly" (or philological) thrust of Tolkien's medievalism. Like other postwar thinkers, Hall looked to what he has termed "the literary theory of its day" for the nuance and seriousness lacking in "the alternative Marxist models [which for him] were far too mechanical and reductive."[18] Above all, Hall was an avid reader of F. R. Leavis and Leavisite productions, who would "go down to the bookstore and buy the next uncut copy of" *Scrutiny* "like it was chapters from the bible."[19]

His devotion to Leavis readily explains Hall's eventual decision to write on Henry James, one of the three writer-thinkers whose keen meditations on English social tensions and contradictions feature in Leavis's *The Great Tradition* (1948). Langland, however, connected Hall's Leavisite leanings to his emerging left politics. In *Familiar Stranger*, Hall describes his time at Oxford and relates how he would only become "deeply involved" in the British Left in 1954, after beginning graduate work (241). But even as an undergraduate, "a broader critical Left, or democratic socialist, outlook" would accompany the anti-imperialism Hall readily espoused as a West Indian colonial rebel (234). He became close friends with "Christian Marxist" (and fellow Rhodes Scholar) Charles Taylor and other members of "the small Communist group" at Oxford, twelve students who also included Hall's future *Universities and Left Review* cofounders Raphael Samuel and Gabriel Pearson (234–35). Leavis, of course, was no Marxist. Langland makes no appearance in *The Great Tradition*. But *Piers Plowman was* embraced by the wider Leavisite orbit. A 1936 issue of *Scrutiny* dedicated to "Revaluations" of English literary texts celebrates *Piers* for its formal sophistication and socio-political acuity.[20] A difficult, complex, and, in Larry Scanlon's Leavis-esque formulation, "profound argument with his own time," *Piers* sensitively responds to English social tensions and contradictions.[21]

Thus, in many respects Langland suited Hall's left interests far more than Henry James. As Hall has acknowledged, James took as his primary focus the "unpromising material" of "rich people."[22] In contrast, Langland's (to trope on Leavis) "very intelligent and serious" study of his "contemporary civilization" takes place in a social register that, as his titular plowman indicates, extended far beyond the upper-class milieu featured in James novels to the lived experience of ordinary people, especially the poor.[23] *Piers* gazes unflinchingly at the corruption of authorities and the suffering wrought by poverty; moreover, it reconceives the terms of Christian salvation via the ordinary figure of a laborer—that is, a fourteenth-century English plowman. While Hall's left colleagues wondered over his official dissertation topic—Hall's memoir recounts E. P. Thompson asking him, "How can you be interested in Henry James?" (217)—they would have readily understood his early interest in Langland, given the medieval poet's relation to labor and social justice.

Piers Plowman and Left Medievalism in Britain

White liberal and left-leaning English writers had long turned to Langland's poem, and for good reason. *Piers* bore associations with workers' rights that went back to Langland's lifetime, when his titular laborer was wrested from his text and deployed by the peasant leaders of the 1381 rebellion.[24] Certainly, as scholars including William Rhodes demonstrate, over the centuries that would follow, and especially after Robert Crowley's sixteenth-century printing of *Piers*, the figures who embraced Langland would hold a spectrum of political stances.[25] Langland's conservative interlocutors in certain ways accord with the politics of the medieval poet, who endorsed traditional social hierarchies, especially in the C-text of *Piers*. But, during the rise of left activism in the nineteenth century, liberals and socialists would praise the poem. Frederick Furnivall (1825–1910), who cofounded the Working Men's College in London, lectured on Langland's poem "because of its sketch of working men in the fourteenth century."[26] And William Morris (1834–96), in an 1887 public lecture on socialism entitled "Feudal England," described *Piers* as "the great example" of proto-Reformation "Lollard poetry."[27]

Perhaps the most consequential of such left-leaning Victorian engagements with Langland was made by the inaugurator in England of a white history from below, John Richard Green (1837–83). A liberal democratic minister and independent scholar, Green affirms the importance of Langland in A *Short History of the English People* (1874), a text that enjoyed considerable popularity during the late nineteenth century and maintained a readership into the twentieth. Green both cites the medieval poet in a prefatory account of his focus on the struggles of ordinary people and devotes several pages to analyzing how *Piers* "throws a flood of light on the social condition of England at the time."[28] Green portrays Langland as an impoverished "silent moody clerk," taken "for a madman" in his own time, who "paint[s] with a terrible fidelity" those "darker and sterner aspects" of late medieval England: "its social revolt, its moral and religious awakening, the misery of the peasant, the protest of the Lollard" (248). Green's influential work contributed to an awareness of Langland as an English social critic and, especially, a writer concerned with labor and the English masses.[29]

A *Short History* even seems to have prompted Karl Marx himself to "grapple ... with Langland's Middle English."[30] Near the end of his life, while convalescing on the Isle of Wight, Marx included *Piers* in the notes he took while reading Green's *Short History* and wrote to his daughter Eleanor, instructing her to obtain a copy of Langland's poem for him.[31]

Langland's appearance in British left politics persisted into the twentieth century. A seven-volume educational series, published during the 1920s and '30s, about "the motives which have swayed or led great masses of plain men" in England from ancient times to the present, bore the name *The Piers Plowman Social and Economic Histories*.[32] In 1938, historian A. L. Morton (1903–87) would cite *Piers* to demonstrate the "background of primitive Communism" behind the 1381 rising in A *People's History of England* (1938), Morton's classic Marxist account of English history written for a popular audience.[33] And, shortly after World War II, a Marxist response to Langland would take musical form in Alan Bush's (1900–1995) symphonic suite *Piers Plowman's Day* (1946/7) and opera *Wat Tyler* (1948–51). Both compositions found inspiration in Langland and presented "radical communist conceptions of English history emerging in the immediate post war period."[34]

Of those twentieth-century left engagements with Langland, the most relevant to Hall was that of Rodney Hilton (1916–2002). A University of Birmingham historian and expert on medieval English peasants, Hilton cofounded in 1946 the Communist Party Historians' Group (CPHG), whose members included such major historians as Eric Hobsbawm (1917–2012) and E. P. Thompson (1924–93).[35] Langland would figure in a CPHG publication project on which Hilton worked with lay writer Hyman Fagan (1903–88); together, the two revised Fagan's 1938 "agitational" history of the revolt, entitled *Nine Days That Shook England*.[36] Fagan's book, which draws heavily on Green's *Short History*, allots several pages to Langland as a writer who "sets forth the whole of English society as seen by an unconscious rebel."[37] For the updated 1950 publication, called *The English Rising of 1381*, Hilton generated a lengthy historical introduction that featured a discussion of Langland. There, Hilton clarified Langland's orthodox approach to medieval social order, affirming how the poet, while "sympathetic to peasant aspirations," also "emphasised the conservative doctrine of each man to his station."[38]

As this overview of the long tradition of white liberal and left-leaning citations of Langland indicates, Hall, by opting to work on *Piers Plowman*, was poised to contribute to an aspect of English heritage that in many ways departed from Tolkien's medievalism. While Tolkien engaged *Beowulf* and other medieval English texts whose depiction of noble warriors spoke to white mythologies of Nordic heroism, left-leaning writers and groups embraced *Piers* for its depiction of ordinary people and fourteenth-century societal problems. The social and historical urgency of the poem may help account for the fact that Tolkien never published on *Piers*.[39]

At the same time, however, the medievalism of the British Left retained key white periodizing components of Tolkien's approach. Namely, far from rejecting the idea of a homogeneous and racially unified England, they embraced a unitary view on national identity, albeit within more liberal, socialist, and communist registers.[40] Figures from Green to Morris and Hilton endorsed an essentialist—but also liberal or left—idea of English identity and heritage. As a result, just as the conservative Tolkien used medieval works like *Beowulf* to endorse a heroic and noble English essence, when left and left-leaning figures cited *Piers*, they typically did so to affirm an inherently British working-class selfhood. To be sure, Tolkien's investment in myth departed from left-leaning thinkers' stress on history. Nevertheless, in much the same way that Tolkien's linguistic essentialism transcended historical ruptures, manifesting an unchanging heroic self, so too did the rebellious English laborer celebrated by left thinkers prove constant over time.

An important case in point is the late-Victorian historian Green. His citations of *Piers* contribute to an unmistakable and at times chilling Saxon-oriented Teutonism.[41] At his most objectionable, Green claimed that the "extermination of the Briton" enabled England to become the "one purely German nation that rose upon the wreck of Rome" (48). *A Short History* opens by locating the "fatherland of the English race" in territories near "the northern seas," where the original English lived as "a race of land-holders and land tillers," "drawn together by the ties of a common blood, common speech, common social and political institutions" (1–3). Green's account of Langland indicates the medieval poet's membership in that kin-group. He identifies "the defiant pride that made [Langland's alter ego Long Will] loth . . . to bow to the gay lords and dames who rode decked in silver and minivere along the Cheap," a characteristic taken from Langland's Teutonic forefather, "'the free-necked man' whose long hair floated over a neck that never bent to a lord" (248, 2). Langland thus contributes to Green's effort in *A Short History* to present the affective pleasures of an inherently Teutonic tradition of "defiant pride" and independence.

Communists and socialists, from at least William Morris onward, also looked to *Piers* for evidence of an essential Englishness, albeit a rural Englishness that existed in dialectical relation to capitalism.[42] Instead of the unbroken historical line from the Teutonic village to contemporary parliamentary democracy posited by liberals, some of the more Marxian intellectuals understood English history in terms of a spiral, marked by the intervening negation of capitalism and evolving toward the "revival, in a higher form, of the liberty, equality and fraternity of the ancient gentes."[43] Most pertinent to Hall's left education were efforts "to create an authentic English Marxism" on the part of the Communist Party Historians' Group.[44] At the core of the CPHG's approach was the idea—reflective of the group's roots in the British Popular Front—that communism crystallizes and improves upon an ancient and pure English tradition of popular rebellion and uplift.[45] Morton, who chaired the CPHG, folded Langland into that project. He cites *Piers* in his *People's History* to demonstrate the "background of primitive Communism" behind the Peasant's Rebellion.[46]

The 1381 rising would figure prominently in the essentialist proletarian nationalism of the CPHG, which embraced the event as the first major English class rebellion. For example, key CPHG member Dona Torr (1883–1957) stressed, echoing the connections drawn by Tolkien between the contemporary English and the *Beowulf*-poet, that "the working-class movement had an organic connection with the past," starting with the Peasant Rising, which she saw as one of two key phases in English history.[47] Similarly, Hilton, in the introduction to *The English Rising of 1381* (1950), and in the 1949 essay "Peasant Movements in England before 1381," incorporates rebel leader John Ball into an ancestral and inherited revolutionary "English tradition as ancient as the more publicized traditions of reverence for old-established institutions."[48] Not unlike Green, Hilton urges pride in a venerable and inherently English rebelliousness.

However dialectical or complex, the thought of intellectuals like Hilton was limited by an essentialism that rendered them blind to the heterogeneity and instability that always inform identity formation. Pertinent to the Jamaican-British Hall is how most English Marxists occluded the intertwining of labor history in the English archipelago with imperial sites and peoples in the colonies. As Paul Gilroy explains, even as British new left intellectuals "reached beyond themselves . . . in the name of discomforting complexity, toward deeply textured accounts of bounded and conflictual consciousness that could illuminate contemporary antagonisms," they also ignored issues of difference and colonization in their analyses of specifically national class dynamics.[49]

A Diasporic Critique of Left Heritage

In her discussion of Hall's oeuvre, Alexander "broadly identif[ies] three phases in Hall's writing on race":

the early engagement with the new immigrant "West Indian" communities and the emerging "second generation"; the turn to theory during his time at the Centre for Contemporary Cultural Studies; and the "cultural turn" from the mid-1980s, which has two distinct, but interconnected themes—the shift in black cultural politics in Britain and debates around "new ethnicities"; and the theorization of postcoloniality and diaspora, in particular in relation to the Caribbean.[50]

In keeping with Alexander's tripartite periodization, Hall's most explicit critiques of white heritage were published during the final, "cultural turn" stage. During that third period Hall would offer a sustained and incisive critique of English essentialisms, left or otherwise. In "Culture, Community, Nation" (1993), he addresses how, according to the "modernizing nation-states of Western modernity," "the secret of [their] success" lies in the "gathering . . . under *one* political roof" of "*one* people, *one* ethnicity" possessed of a "primordial unity" and "an apparently seamless and unbroken continuity towards pure, mythic time."[51] And in "The Local and the Global: Globalization and Ethnicity" (1991), Hall specifies how the English represent themselves "as perfectly natural: born an Englishman, always will be, condensed, homogenous, unitary . . . stable points of reference which were like that in the past, are now and ever shall be, still points in a turning world," a fantasy premised, as Hall puts it elsewhere, on the "selective amnesia and disavowal" of "'Empire.'"[52]

Moreover, during this period Hall also leveled more pointed critiques at the British Left. "Whose Heritage?," for example, confronts how recent efforts to "democratiz[e]" the past nevertheless maintain certain racial occlusions:

> Increasingly, the lives, artefacts, houses, work-places, tools, customs and oral memories of ordinary everyday British folk have slowly taken their subordinate place alongside the hegemonic presence of the great and the good . . . by and large, this process has so far stopped short at the frontier defined by that great unspoken British value—"whiteness." (7)

Written in 1999, this piece at once affirms how versions of the populist British historicism enacted by liberal and left writers like Green, Morris, and Hilton have gained some momentum even as it critiques those efforts for their white orientation. The expansion of heritage to quotidian history and ordinary people occurs within the confines or "frontier" of a white-centered discourse. A still more direct indictment of an essentializing British Left appeared six years earlier in "Culture, Community, Nation." There, Hall cites left intellectual Raymond Williams (1921–88) for his defensive claims about Black immigrants threatening "actual and sustained social relationships" and "whole way[s] of life" in Britain.⁵³ Taking up Gilroy's critique of the "strategic silences" employed by Williams and other white British lefties, Hall affirms that Gilroy "quite correctly fastened on" Williams's comments on British identity

> as representing in its implications a racially exclusive form of social identity, and a sign of the degree to which Williams's work, like so much other thinking on the left, remains both blind to questions of race and framed by certain unexamined 'national' cultural assumptions."⁵⁴

Hall offers here perhaps his most explicit indictment of the British Left. Williams's writings and "so much other thinking on the left" problematically exhibit lacunae pertaining to colonization and race. Members of the British Left possess "unexamined 'national' cultural assumptions" whose implicit support for "racially exclusive" social forms of belonging directly opposes both Hall's early commitment to West Indian identities and his subsequent and extensive effort, in Alexander's words, "to contest, to pry open, essentialized claims of national identity to find a space for the 'others' in the national imaginary."⁵⁵

Hall's aborted medieval dissertation belongs to the early stage tracked by Alexander. In "Life and Times of the First New Left," he recollects that initial period and intimates how the "colonial questions" that so concerned him were ignored by the British radical Left.⁵⁶ He describes how he joined the "independent socialist tradition" at Oxford as a student whose outlook was inflected by his West Indian identity.⁵⁷ He gently acknowledges his divergence from the "communist humanism" of the CPHG, describing it in careful, diplomatic terms as a "unique enclave" whose "reading of British history, and . . . form of Marxist politics" was "in touch with English popular radicalism."⁵⁸ In "Life and Times," Hall also aligns "Reasoners" (writers affiliated with the *New Reasoner*, an antecedent of the *New Left Review*) such as Hilton with the "populism" of "the provincial North."⁵⁹

While Hall makes no mention in "Life and Times" of his medievalism, I suggest that his proposed *Piers Plowman* project might complicate Alexander's periodization. Because Langland had long figured in left-leaning British politics, a Piers dissertation potentially offered a means of asserting the repressed diasporic dimension of received accounts of history and heritage. Even at the start of his academic career, Hall may have found a way to critique not just the national white essentialisms embraced by Tolkien but also those advocated by left scholars from Green to the CPHG and the British New Left.

That Hall, during his early years at Oxford, refused any essentializing notion of medieval English literature is certain. Clear evidence of his diasporic critique of unitary "heritage" cultural forms appears in his first publication.⁶⁰ On

January 3, 1954, about a month shy of Hall's twenty-third birthday, "Our Literary Heritage" appeared in the Sunday edition of the leading Jamaican newspaper, the *Jamaica Gleaner* (Figure 1; Appendix). The piece responds to a two-part essay bearing the same title by J. E. Clare McFarlane (1894–1962), poet laureate of Jamaica and president and founder of the Jamaica Poetry League.[61] The League, a subsidiary of the Empire Poetry League, had long performed a colonial function that, in Derek Walcott's words, "repeatedly draped with fresh shrouds" the "dated body" of works by English poets like Milton, Wordsworth, and Keats.[62] McFarlane's account of why "the relation of the West Indian writer to 'his literary heritage' must be . . . a matter of greatest concern" supports Walcott's withering assessment. In his rebuttal of McFarlane, Hall not only adumbrates the diasporic criticism he would later elaborate but also indicates his keen interest in modern and medieval literary texts.

Hall's editorial performs a multipronged refutation of McFarlane's arguments and especially the poet laureate's "basic allegiances" with Romanticism. While McFarlane the Romantic asserts that "great poetry is always 'the individual

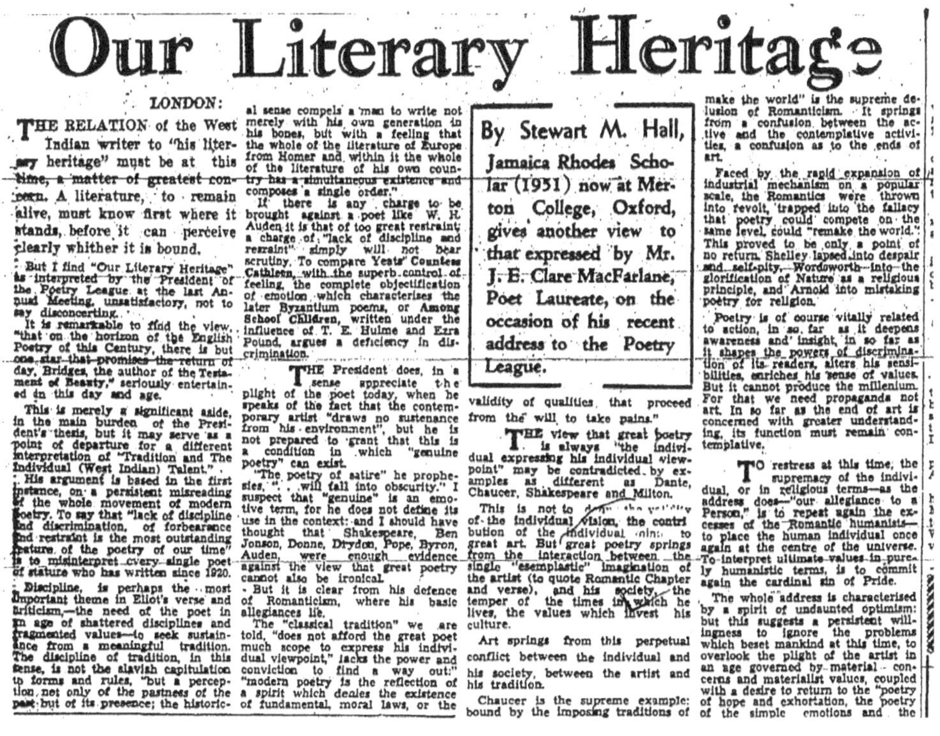

Our Literary Heritage

LONDON:

THE RELATION of the West Indian writer to "his literary heritage" must be at this time, a matter of greatest concern. A literature, to remain alive, must know first where it stands, before it can perceive clearly whither it is bound.

But I find "Our Literary Heritage" as interpreted by the President of the Poetry League at the last Annual Meeting, unsatisfactory, not to say disconcerting.

It is remarkable to find the view, "that on the horizon of the English Poetry of this Century, there is but one star that promises the return of day, Bridges, the author of the Testament of Beauty," seriously entertained in this day and age.

This is merely a significant aside, in the main burden of the President's thesis, but it may serve as a point of departure for a different interpretation of "Tradition and The Individual (West Indian) Talent."

His argument is based in the first instance, on a persistent misreading of the whole movement of modern poetry. To say that "lack of discipline and discrimination, of forbearance and restraint is the most outstanding feature of the poetry of our time" is to misinterpret every single poet of stature who has written since 1920.

Discipline, is perhaps the most important theme in Eliot's verse and criticism,—the need of the poet in an age of shattered disciplines and fragmented values—to seek sustainance from a meaningful tradition. The discipline of tradition, in this sense, is not the slavish capitulation to forms and rules, "but a perception not only of the pastness of the past but of its presence; the historical sense compels a man to write not merely with his own generation in his bones, but with a feeling that the whole of the literature of Europe from Homer and within it the whole of the literature of his own country has a simultaneous existence and composes a single order."

If there is any charge to be brought against a poet like W. H. Auden it is that of too great restraint; a charge of "lack of discipline and restraint" simply will not bear scrutiny. To compare Yeats' Countess Cathleen, with the superb control of feeling, the complete objectification of emotion which characterises the later Byzantium poems, or Among School Children, written under the influence of T. E. Hulme and Ezra Pound, argues a deficiency in discrimination.

THE President does, in a sense appreciate the plight of the poet today, when he speaks of the fact that the contemporary artist "draws no sustenance from his environment", but he is not prepared to grant that this is a condition in which "genuine poetry" can exist.

"The poetry of satire" he prophesies, ". . . will fall into obscurity." I suspect that "genuine" is an emotive term, for he does not define its use in the context: and I should have thought that Shakespeare, Ben Jonson, Donne, Drydon, Pope, Byron, Auden, were enough evidence against the view that great poetry cannot also be ironical.

But it is clear from his defence of Romanticism, where his basic allegiances lie.

The "classical tradition" we are told, "does not afford the great poet much scope to express his individual viewpoint," lacks the power and conviction to find a way out:" "modern poetry is the reflection of a spirit which denies the existence of fundamental, moral laws, or the

By Stewart M. Hall, Jamaica Rhodes Scholar (1951) now at Merton College, Oxford, gives another view to that expressed by Mr. J. E. Clare MacFarlane, Poet Laureate, on the occasion of his recent address to the Poetry League.

validity of qualities that proceed from the will to take pains."

THE view that great poetry is always "the individual expressing his individual viewpoint" may be contradicted by examples as different as Dante, Chaucer, Shakespeare and Milton.

This is not to deny the validity of the individual vision, the contribution of the individual mind to great art. But great poetry springs from the interaction between the single "esemplastic" imagination of the artist (to quote Romantic Chapter and verse), and his society, the temper of the times in which he lives, the values which invest his culture.

Art springs from this perpetual conflict between the individual and his society, between the artist and his tradition.

Chaucer is the supreme example: bound by the imposing traditions of

make the world" is the supreme delusion of Romanticism. It springs from a confusion between the active and the contemplative activities, a confusion as to the ends of art.

Faced by the rapid expansion of industrial mechanism on a popular scale, the Romantics were thrown into revolt, trapped into the fallacy that poetry could compete on the same level, could "remake the world." This proved to be only a point of no return. Shelley lapsed into despair and self-pity, Wordsworth into the glorification of Nature as a religious principle, and Arnold into mistaking poetry for religion.

Poetry is of course vitally related to action, in so far as it deepens awareness and insight, in so far as it shapes the powers of discrimination of its readers, alters his sensibilities, enriches his sense of values. But it cannot produce the millenium. For that we need propaganda not art. In so far as the end of art is concerned with greater understanding, its function must remain contemplative.

TO restress at this time, the supremacy of the individual, or in religious terms—as the address does—"our allegiance to a Person," is to repeat again the excesses of the Romantic humanists—to place the human individual once again at the centre of the universe. To interpret ultimate values in purely humanistic terms, is to commit again the cardinal sin of Pride.

The whole address is characterised by a spirit of undaunted optimism: but this suggests a persistent willingness to ignore the problems which beset mankind at this time, to overlook the plight of the artist in an age governed by material concerns and materialist values, coupled with a desire to return to the "poetry of hope and exhortation, the poetry of the simple emotions and the

Figure 1. Stewart [sic] M. Hall, "Our Literary Heritage," *Sunday Gleaner*, January 3, 1954, 5.
Credit: © The Gleaner Co. (Media) Ltd.

expressing his individual viewpoint'" and thus owes little to tradition, Hall the medievalist counters that

> great poetry springs from the . . . perpetual conflict between the individual and his society, between the artist and his tradition.
>
> Chaucer is the supreme example: bound by the imposing traditions of medieval Europe, circumscribed by the limiting disciplines of sources and literary conventions, Chaucer emerges as a supremely "original" artist.

Hall demonstrates his medievalist bona fides in tandem with a sophisticated diasporic modernism. McFarlane remains attached to a Romantic idea of the autonomous self, but Hall highlights an Eliotic dialectical tension through which an artist negotiates their relation to society and cultural history. Citing "Tradition and the Individual Talent," Hall asserts, contra McFarlane, how the West Indian writer requires "sustanance [sic] from a meaningful tradition," a process that entails not "slavish capitulation to forms and rules" but a hard-won "'perception not only of the pastness of the past but of its presence.'"[63] Eliot's account of great Western authors' complex relation to European literary history cites multiple writers, such as Shakespeare and Dante, but no medieval English poets.[64] Likewise, McFarlane mentions writers no earlier than Romantics such as Wordsworth and Keats. But Hall—in keeping with his interest, as described in his memoir, in "apply[ing] contemporary literary criticism" to medieval texts—claims that Chaucer epitomizes the dynamic Eliot describes. Hall professes in *Familiar Stranger* that he "loved some of the poetry" in Old and Middle English that the Oxford course entailed (156), and that love comes through in this essay, his first work of literary criticism: "Chaucer is the supreme example" of "great poetry"; "Chaucer emerges as the supremely 'original' artist."

Hall's engagement with Eliot complicates and expands the stakes of his editorial. For not only does he use Eliot to critique McFarlane, but he also modifies, in a diasporic manner, the great Anglo-American modernist's unitary idea of heritage and history. At once rejecting McFarlane's Romanticism and challenging Eliot's idea of a homogeneous European literature, Hall theorizes what he calls "Tradition and the (West Indian) Talent." He states of West Indian authors, "We are part of, but different from" the English and European literary traditions. That claim implicitly revises a famous passage from "Tradition" that Hall cites, where Eliot describes the totalizing literary historical sentiment demanded of a great poet:

> The historical sense compels a man to write not merely with his own generation in his bones, but with a feeling that the whole of the

literature of Europe from Homer and within it the whole of the literature of his own country has a simultaneous existence and composes a single order.[65]

Eliot's theory about the poet's affective relation to the collective present and past recalls the essentializing embrace of the medieval by both Tolkien and left intellectuals. Eliot's Eurocentric idea of a self-contained, organic, and unitary literary heritage leaves no room for outsiders. But Hall's idea of "Tradition and the (West Indian) Talent" urges otherwise, charting a specifically literary historical version of what C. L. R. James describes as the diasporic formation of those who are "in western civilization, who have grown up in it but yet are not completely a part" of it.[66] Hall adumbrates work by Amiri Baraka, Houston Baker, and indeed himself on how, as he would put it in a 2005 essay, "culture depends on a knowledge of tradition as 'the changing same' and an effective set of genealogies . . . that enable us, through culture, to produce ourselves anew, as new kinds of subjects."[67]

In his *Gleaner* piece, Hall links West Indian artists to a complex and shifting diasporic vantage point that renders them uniquely, even supremely, well-positioned to perform a searching brand of modernist historicism. In particular, he indicates how the fraught situatedness of West Indians primes them to enact a uniquely complex and mournful version of the relation to the past traditionally tied to white poets like T. S. Eliot or Ezra Pound. In fact, Hall ends the piece with a passage from "Hugh Selwyn Mauberley [Part I]," Pound's ironic and dialectical poem that "feels" the classical past even as it articulates ancient culture's alterity to a mass cultural and capitalistic present. Pound, like Eliot, articulates the tension between the contemporary artist and tradition in Eurocentric or white terms. "It is time we read our Pound again," Hall advises in the closing words of "Our Literary Heritage." But as good as Pound is at representing antinomies of modernity, Hall claims,

> Is the plight of the West Indian artist so different from the European artist in a mass culture? Are we wholly unaffected by the loss of traditions, the loss of fixed conventions, the absence of belief, the decline of values, the fragmentation of a world view?

Hall suggests that West Indian artists are particularly attuned to modern fragmentation: "The West Indian finds himself in his peculiar plight, because . . . he is a man without a history, without a homogen[e]ous culture." Dislocated in a deeper sense than a white poet like Pound or Eliot, the West Indian seizes and transforms "English tradition," rendering it "a reinterpreted tradition, bearing a real relationship to his environment, personality and institutions."

The West Indian poet, who "is in fact in the process of forging his tradition ... based upon a compromise between the heterodox cultures out of which he springs," renders the contradictions portrayed by white modernists in more expansive and multidimensional terms.

While "Our Literary Heritage" never mentions Langland or the British Left, the relationship Hall limns between the West Indian writer and tradition is suggestive. For Hall isn't simply positing a relationship between diasporic writers and European literary history. Through his very penning of "Our Literary Heritage" Hall himself is also enacting—asserting—a relationship between West Indian literary critics and the western canon. Hall demonstrates how the West Indian literary critic, like the West Indian poet, can claim a relation to a long tradition of English literary production *and* critical reception. Hall cites not only Eliot but also Leavis: he invokes Leavis's famous statement that the creative writer is tasked with "show[ing] himself to have been fully alive in his time."[68] "Our Literary Heritage" affirms a young Hall's interest in claiming a relation to—and the authority to critique—both English literary texts and white interpretations of those texts as "heritage." The idea of working on *Piers Plowman* and its reception may have provided Hall a way to perform, in a far more extensive manner, versions of those same interventions. Even better, the diasporic "reinterpreted tradition" Hall might have staged via a Langland thesis might have allowed him to engage problematic components of the very left-leaning milieu with which he was aligned.

Modernity, English Heritage, and National Fantasy

"Our Literary Heritage" looks toward the "between two islands" diasporic perspective for which Hall became renowned. In subsequent essays, such as "Culture, Community, Nation," "Europe and Its Myths," and "Whose Heritage?," Hall develops his early claim in the *Gleaner* editorial that West Indians' complex and shifting situatedness provides a perspective on questions of modernity, tradition, and identity even more searching and disturbing than that of Pound's tortured Mauberley. In those and related publications, Hall—like W. E. B. Du Bois and other theorists of race and colonization—makes explicit the harrowing insights that emerge from the "second sight" possessed by a diasporic subject.

In "Europe and Its Myths," Hall describes how, thanks to their displacement from the West, "we conscripts" inhabit a vantage point from which "we ... view" the West—and, by extension, modernity—"very differently from those who see it from inside" (60). "From within," Hall continues, "Europe has always represented itself as somehow autochthonous—producing itself, by itself, from within itself" (60), in other words, in a manner not unlike the essentializing views of Tolkien, Green, Hilton, Williams, Eliot, and Pound. While white insiders who "see" the West from "within" offer feel-good representations of European civilization, the West takes on a radically changed aspect when perceived from the orientation of a diasporic subject. Those who are "in but not of Europe" offer, as Hall puts it in "Whose Heritage?," "an opportunity to look critically at the whole concept" (3).[69] Unlike those insiders who act according to unquestioned assumptions, "we conscripts," Hall states in "Europe and Its Myths,"

> have always been obliged to ask, "How does Europe imagine its 'unity'? How can it be imagined, in relation to its 'others'? What does Europe look like from its liminal edge, from what Ernesto Laclau or Judith Butler would call, its 'constitutive outside'?" (60)[70]

That critical diasporic view disrupts feel-good white historicism by exposing how the supposedly stable and immutable unity of the West is a fiction. In effect, Hall and other thinkers reject comforting white ideas of identity and history, embracing instead a killjoy diasporic historicism.

As Hall stresses in "Culture, Community, Nation," Britain has long been "diaspora-ized beyond repair."[71] For one thing, Britain is an "ethnic hotchpotch" that "was formed out of a series of earlier invasions, conquests and settlements—Celts, Romans, Saxons, Vikings, Normans, Angevins."[72] No nation has ever been "pure," homogeneous, unified, or eternal. For another, since the advent of imperialism, as Hall puts in in "Whose Heritage?," "the facts of colonisation, slavery and empire" have been "deeply intertwined . . . with the everyday daily life of all classes and conditions of English men and women" (6). English ideas of heritage regularly forget empire and, when they do, they (unsurprisingly) adopt a pleasing internal viewpoint that reinforces ideas of white autonomy and supremacy. English insiders celebrate "*western progress, civilization, rationality and development*" and imagine England as an autonomous and discrete entity "imposing its will, culture and institutions, and inscribing its civilising mission across the world."[73] Hall unsettles such feel-good claims with a biting exposé of how

> the very notion of "greatness" in Great Britain is inextricably bound up with its imperial destiny. For centuries, its wealth was underpinned, its urban development driven, its agriculture and industry revolutionised, its fortunes as a nation settled, its maritime and commercial hegemony secured, its thirst quenched, its teeth sweetened, its cloth spun, its food spiced, its carriages rubber-wheeled, its bodies adorned, through the imperial connection.[74]

Hall dislodges the "Great" or exceptional from "Great Britain." Refusing the English any mythic supremacy, Hall asserts how everything from the Industrial Revolution, the London metropole, and the national economy to the sugar in English tea, the clothes on English backs, and the gems around English necks relied on colonial exploitation.

Beyond such brilliant deconstructions of the ostensible opposition of colonial objects and a "little England" or a supreme and masterful British Empire, Hall engages in an even more disturbing and "necessary work of *deconstruction*" that shores up the darkest or most horrifying aspects of the West.[75] In "Europe and Its Myths," he describes how "Europe's march to modernity," to progress, paradoxically entails a "tortured and violent history," involving "brutal ruptures, grim inequalities" (61). In keeping with Walter Benjamin's *Theses on the Philosophy of History* (1942), Hall affirms how "the values of 'civilisation' and 'barbarism'" are "deeply intertwined" in the West (65). Hall traces that entanglement to the beginning of European modernity:

> The point when we can most confidently say that a European identity exists coincides with the defeat and expulsion of the Muslims from Spain by a militant and purified Catholic monarchy; the expulsion and forced conversion of the Jews; and the launching of the great "experiment" of conquest and exploration down the African coast and into the great unknown across the Green Sea of Darkness. (64)

Insofar as modernity means the so-called "Age of Discovery," the beginning of European "conquest and exploration" was coterminous and mutually constitutive with the horrific abuse of religious others within Europe. Hall turns in that same essay from the initial imbrication of modernity and barbarity to the "current European political trends" of the early 2000s (69). In a piece whose affective import grows increasingly pessimistic, Hall refuses any happy teleology of progress. Instead, he observes how, in contradistinction to whatever "openness" might seem to be signaled by the recently created European Union, "what is 'open' within is increasingly barred without," resulting in still further "historical nightmare[s]" for refugees, exiles, and other expelled and oppressed groups (67–68).

In keeping with its increasingly unhappy thrust, Hall concludes "Europe and Its Myths" with a harrowing consideration of how to best represent Western modernity during his contemporary moment:

> Today, . . . when asked for "a figure for Europe," I cannot help thinking of Paul Klee's . . . Angel of Progress, clanking towards Armageddon, with its face resolutely turned to the past: and of the myopic Walter

Benjamin, peering through glasses as thick as marble, trying to make sense of it all and—failing to do so—taking his own life at some dark, lonely, forsaken European frontier check-point. (69)

Via Benjamin and his beloved *Angelus Novus*, the painting the German Jewish philosopher purchased from the German Expressionist artist Klee in 1921, Hall endorses a consummately negative assessment of modernity. "Progress" in Klee's artwork accomplishes no heaven on earth but rather a catastrophic destruction that leaves in its wake an ever-expanding pile of historical wreckage. Directly countering Burckhardt and other theorists of modernity who celebrate the clear-sighted rationality of the modern individual, Hall highlights how modernity has created a horrific mess that defies efforts "to make sense of it all." Refusing his original auditors at the Myths of Europe conference any consolation whatsoever, Hall ends the piece by recalling Benjamin's self-annihilating despair over the ruinous result of the deeds performed in the name of modernity. Hall's closing words, with their account of Benjamin's suicide at an anonymous "dark, lonely, forsaken European frontier check-point," shatteringly highlights what he describes in "Whose Heritage?" as "the unscripted shadow of the forgotten 'Other,'" the lethal and dehumanizing borders and divisions at the heart of modern western ideas of progress and belonging (28).

Stuart Hall, Medievalist

In essays like "Europe and Its Myths," Hall would not only develop the diasporic claims he first expresses in "Our Literary Heritage" but also return to the medievalism of that early publication. However, while Hall's first essay hails, Eliotically, Chaucer's "individual talent," those later works perform a more ambivalent medievalism. Thanks partly to Hall's post-structuralist destabilization of received modern and western essentialisms, his later work offers a complex dialectical approach to the medieval West as an object of both positive and negative sentiments, of praise and derision.

An important example of Hall's complex relation to the Middle Ages is his single publication that mentions Langland, *Formations of Modernity*, the multi-authored initial volume of a six-part Open University series published in 1992. Langland appears in the final chapter of *Formations*, Hall's "The West and the Rest," where he extensively cites British sociologist Michael Mann's "European Development: Approaching a Historical Explanation" (1988).[76] In the more than two-thousand-word Mann excerpt that appears in the appendix to Hall's chapter, the example of Langland helps explain why the "localized" premodern structures that became "Europe" morphed in the direction of "development" instead of "anarchy or *anomie*." "Europe" as such emerged, for Mann, partly as a result of a medieval version of the "rational restlessness" famously described by Max Weber (322). While Weber's *The Protestant Ethic and the Spirit of Capitalism* (1904) views the Puritans as the first to articulate a modern critical positioning, Mann identifies "a drive for moral and social improvement even against worldly authority" in an "enormous [medieval] literature of social criticism" that includes "some of the greatest works of the age—in English, Langland and Chaucer" (323). The two late medieval English poets precociously adumbrate a "rational restlessness" that worked in tandem with the "common humanity" and "normative regulation" provided by medieval Christianity and its institutions, to make "European development" possible (322–24).

Mann invokes Langland (and Chaucer) on behalf of a model of periodization akin to those of Charles Homer Haskins and his inheritors, as discussed in Chapter 1. As a result of their "currents of dissatisfaction" over the corruption and hypocrisy of Christian society, Langland and Chaucer push the onset of modernity back to the years before 1500 CE (323). The proto-Protestant critical impulses evinced by the two late medieval writers challenge Weber's timeline, but not his European exceptionalism. In that same excerpt, Mann thus cites without critique the German social theorist's claim that "the psychological make-up of Europe [was] the opposite of what he found in the main religions of Asia" (323). Mann tacitly accepts the Weberian idea of a special western "spirit" of development and progress.

But crucially, the Mann citation appears within a larger context provided by *Foundations of Modernity*. And that context challenges ideas of European exceptionalism. Consider the extensive engagement with periodization in Hall's introduction to this volume. Drawing on thinkers including Benjamin, Jacques Derrida, and Hayden White, Hall challenges received white unitary ideas about modernity, both temporal and spatial. Contra Mann's claim that "the date" is "the greatest contribution of the historian to the methodology of the social sciences," Hall stresses how *Formations* will make "no attempt to provide a precise date when modern societies began."[77] While Mann implicitly endorses the idea of Europe's exceptional relation to modernity, Hall rejects "as very Euro-centric stories" representations of modernity as "progress along a single path of development."[78] He explains how formations of modernity have no clear origins, operate in a "slow, uneven way" alongside all sorts of "discontinuities," and depended crucially on "difference."[79] Hall ends his introduction on a decisively feel-bad note that stresses the "Janus-face of modernity": a "dark side," involving "violence, oppression, and exclusion," which "was inscribed in its earliest moments."[80]

Hall expands his introductory critique of white modernity in "The West and the Rest." There, both Hall's global purview and his attention to difference trouble the unitary implications of the medievalism at work in Hall's citation of Mann. Situated in the context of the entire chapter, Langland and Chaucer, however "great," comprise just one element in a larger, contingent, and global medieval history that undermines the notion of a distinctly English or western drive toward modernity. The chapter concerns itself to a substantial extent with the pre-1500 CE "West and the Rest." Embracing a global medievalism, Hall describes how medieval England and other western sites were outpaced by non-western societies. He stresses how, "for much of the Middle Ages, the arts of civilization had been more developed in China and the Islamic world than in Europe" (281). Hall also emphasizes how medieval Europe's shift from disorder into imagined unity was just as much, if not more, a matter of "'the meteoric rise of Islam'" than anything particular to the "West" (287).[81] Whatever unitary message Mann offers is undermined by Hall's stress on the instability of European sites and their contingent and shifting relationship to "others."

Hall's medievalism particularly shines through via his engagement with alterity. Hall exhibits a notable interest in how, as he puts it in "Europe and Its Myths," "constantly, at different times" Europeans have negotiated their identity "in different ways, in relation to different 'others'" (60). That approach to the medieval emerges in not just those two pieces but other publications, including his heritage essay, a textbook chapter on "The Spectacle of 'the Other,'" and unpublished work: two loose-leaf refill pads labeled "Exploration Notebook" and "Age of Exploration Notebook."[82] Taken together, these writings by Hall amass an archive of information about medieval European discourses of self and other. For example, in "Europe and Its Myths," Hall details the "rich medieval mythological and legendary systems which imaginarily peopled the outer perimeters of the European heartland"—that is, "the vast literature devoted to classifying the 'monstrous races of Mankind'" discussed by Friedman (65–66). Hall explains how medieval ideas of the monstrous races "fed" into the "simmering brew," concocted by ancient writers like Pliny and Herodotus, involving the "monsters, hybrids, hermaphrodites and *anthropophagi* of the classical periphery" (66). In "The West and the Rest," Hall also calls attention to medieval Christian "reinterpretation[s]" of "geography in terms of the Bible," which visualized a tripartite, Jerusalem-centered world where "Asia was the home of the Three Wise Kings; Africa that of King Solomon" (298). "The West and the Rest" even reproduces the c. 1260 Psalter *mappa mundi* or world map, whose southern border is populated by so-called "monstrous races" (288). These writings draw on information gathered in Hall's notebooks, which include a page dedicated to the medieval European worldview (Figure 2). Entitled "Medieval World looks out," the page describes the Jerusalem-centered world of medieval *mappae mundi*, whose antipodes (most remote regions) only monsters inhabit. It also lists the "wonders" medieval Europeans linked to Africa and

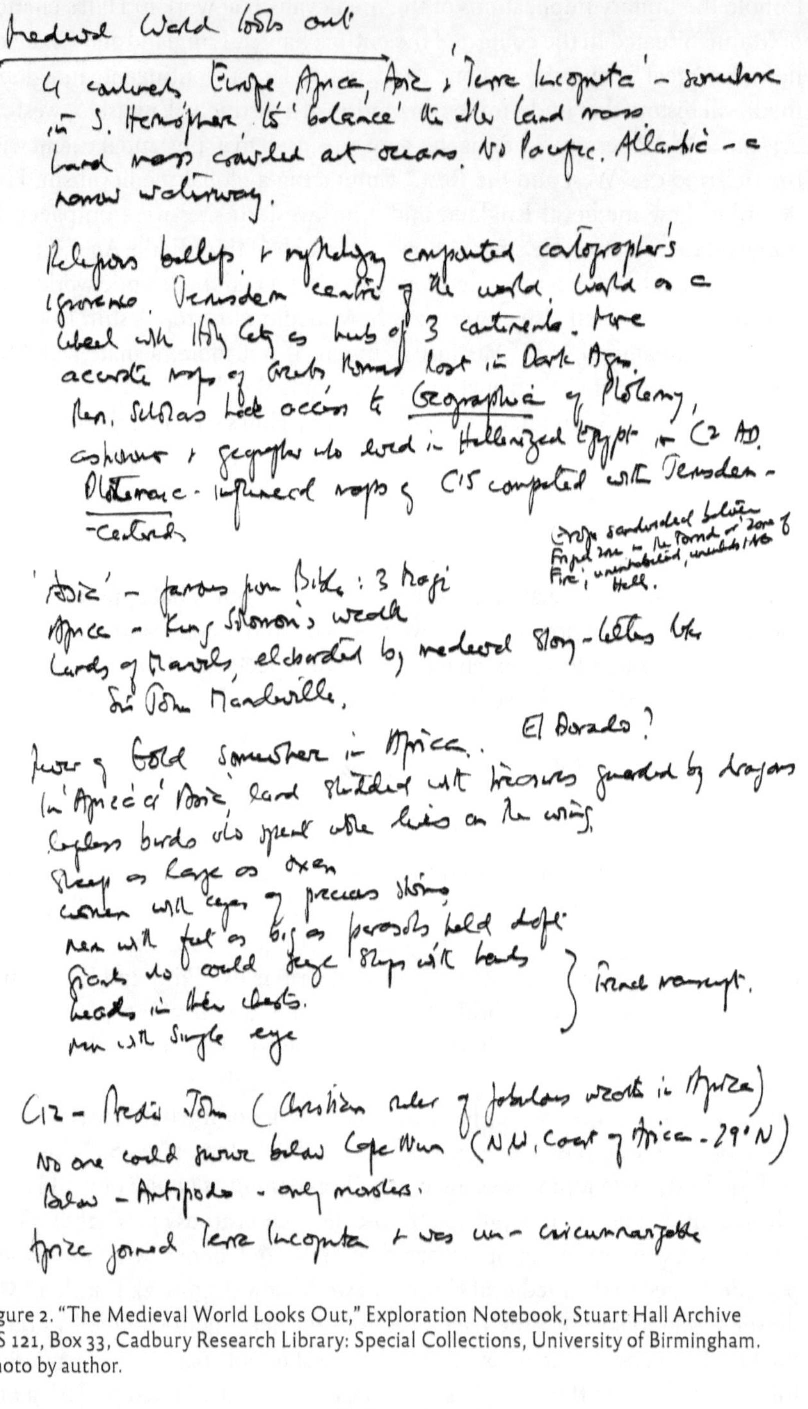

Medieval World looks out

4 continents, Europe Africa, Asia, & 'Terra Incognita' – somewhere in S. Hemisphere, to 'balance' the other land mass. Land mass crowded out oceans. No Pacific. Atlantic – a narrow waterway.

Religious beliefs & mythology compounded cartographer's ignorance. Jerusalem centre of the world. World as a wheel with Holy City as hub of 3 continents. More accurate maps of Greeks, Romans lost in Dark Ages. Ren. scholars look across to Geographia of Ptolemy, astronomer & geographer who lived in Hellenized Egypt in C2 AD. Ptolemaic-influenced maps of C15 competed with Jerusalem-centred.

Europe sandwiched between Frigid zone in the North & Zone of Fire; uninhabited, uninhabitable. Hell.

'Asia' – famous from Bible: 3 Magi
Africa – King Solomon's wealth
Lands of Marvels, elaborated by medieval story-tellers like Sir John Mandeville.

River of Gold somewhere in Africa. El Dorado?
In 'Africa' or 'Asia', land studded with treasures guarded by dragons
Legless birds who spent whole lives on the wing.
Sheep as large as oxen
women with eyes of precious stones
men with feet as big as parasols held aloft
giants who could forge ships with hands
heads in their chests.
men with single eye
} French manuscript.

C12 – Prester John (Christian ruler of fabulous wealth in Africa)
No one could survive below Cape Nun (N.W. Coast of Africa – 29°N)
Below – Antipodes – only monsters.
Africa joined Terra Incognita & was un-circumnavigable

Figure 2. "The Medieval World Looks Out," Exploration Notebook, Stuart Hall Archive US 121, Box 33, Cadbury Research Library: Special Collections, University of Birmingham. Photo by author.

Asia: "sheep as large as oxen," "giants," men with "heads in their chests," and "men with [a] single eye."

Hall's medievalism in "The West and the Rest" emphasizes the richness of travelers' "tall tales," which present "a discourse where description faded imperceptibly into legend" (288). The chapter features a long citation from the Nuremberg Chronicle.[83] With its references to dog-headed Indian men, men "close to Paradise" who "eat nothing," hermaphroditic Libyans, and four-eyed and horned Ethiopians, the citation encapsulates the outlandish nature of medieval representations of persons hailing from India, Africa, and other non-western locales. Hall finds a "particularly rich repository" of medieval pseudo-information about others in "Sir John Mandeville's Travels," which, a scholarly Hall clarifies, constitutes "in fact, a compendium of fanciful stories by different hands." Hall also discusses "Marco Polo's Travels" and—again evincing a medievalist's precision—takes care to explain that the medieval text was "embellished by Rusticello, a romance writer." While Polo-Rusticello's text "was generally more sober and factual" than that of Mandeville, Hall explains, it "nevertheless achieved mythological status" and "was the most widely read of the travellers' accounts" (288).

Hall's interest in medieval alterities encompasses not just external but also internal discourses of difference. "Europe and Its Myths" describes

> the "wild men" and "wild women," and the "wild" armies of the night
> ... who were thought to haunt the woods and wildernesses surrounding the plains and cities and the outer edges of settlement, with their matted hair and naked, hirsute bodies. (66)

On the topic of others internal to Europe, Hall observes, in "The West and the Rest," how medieval "West Europeans often regarded Eastern Europeans as 'barbaric,' and, throughout the West, western women were represented as inferior to western men" (280). Cognizant of the particularly charged alterity of Jews as internal others to the Christian West, Hall stresses in "Europe and Its Myths" how, "across all of" the "categories" of difference connoted by medieval lore, "one could trace the itinerant pathway of that epitome of the internal Other—the wandering Jew" (66).

The medieval discourses of othering delineated by Hall amount to a complex take on identity. By evoking an extensive archive of medieval representations of others within and without Europe, Hall directly opposes the deployment of the medieval on behalf of unitary and heritage historicisms put forth by a wide swathe of intellectuals, from Tolkien to the British Left and the influential sociologist Mann. "These figures" of medieval difference, Hall writes in "Europe and Its Myths," "suspended half-way between fear and fantasy, dream and speculation," worked

to establish, symbolically, the dividing line between "them" and "us,"
... marking out the continent into its different zones, distinguishing
between the "real" European home and the rest, charting the always
porous, always moving frontiers between civilisation and barbarism,
and trying to fix the limit of Europe's internal "others." (66)

From hirsute wild men to Ethiopians who "walk bent down like cattle" and wandering Jews, medieval discourses of external and internal others assisted an ongoing and always shifting process of defining who belongs ("us") and who doesn't ("them").[84]

With respect to periodization, the implications of Hall's unpublished work and pieces like "The Local and the Global" are equally complex. On the one hand, he showcases ongoing discontinuities that are as temporal as they are spatial. Well before and well after 1500 CE, Europeans constructed identities that are not stable and eternal but instead morph and shift over time as they encounter and imagine a variety of alterities. As Hall puts it in "Europe and Its Myths," the "corpus of" medieval "popular and scholarly legend mapped Europe's *shifting* internal borders, and began" a "process" that is "still vigorously alive" in its engagement with difference (66, my emphasis). But, on the other hand, Hall also stresses certain continuities that bind the modern West to medieval culture and society. Above all, Hall's notes and publications highlight how European explorers' "mental picture" of Indigenous peoples "took their form" to a considerable extent from "medieval" "images."[85] His exploration notebooks thus record how Columbus and other explorers were "influenced by the chivalrous epic—knights fighting pagans, monsters and enchanted beings—descendent[s] of medieval crusaders"; were "inspired by "medieval Irish folklore [which] spoke of many Atlantic islands [such as] St. Brendan's island"; and studied the representation of the Far East in the "Travels of Marco Polo" and the "Imago Mundi (c. 15) by Cardinal Pierre d'Ailly."[86] He draws parallels between Columbus's descriptions of Indigenous Americans and passages from a work the Italian explorer knew well, Mandeville's *Travels* (c. 1350–70). His publications highlight such medieval-modern links and their discursive and historical effects. "The West and the Rest" explicates the medievalism of Renaissance explorers as a "regime of truth" that shaped and enforced oppressive and offensive "relations of power" between the "West" and "the Rest" (318). Drawing on Said and Foucault, Hall describes how "the discourse of 'the West and the Rest,'" much like Orientalism, takes up a "library" of fictional "information" that "explained the behaviour" of; provided "a mentality, a genealogy, an atmosphere" for; and identified "regular characteristics" of "the Rest" (329). Starting with their first, early modern assessments upon contact with the "New

World," European writers would draw on an archive of pseudo-knowledge drawn from not just the rediscovered classical texts associated with the Renaissance but also the aforementioned medieval religious, legendary, and exotic travel lore:

> The point of recounting this astonishing mixture of fact and fantasy which constituted late medieval "knowledge" of other worlds is not to poke fun at the ignorance of the Middle Ages. The point is: (a) to bring home how these very different discourses, with variable statuses as "evidence," provided the cultural framework through which the peoples, places, and things of the New World were seen, described, and represented; and (b) to underline the conflation of fact and fantasy that constituted "knowledge." (298–99)

Medieval representations, Hall stresses, aren't something to laugh at—far from it. "Traces of past discourses remain embedded in more recent discourses of 'the West'"; the medieval archive of self and other that Hall delineates, with its binary oppositions, such as civilized vs. barbarous, appear and reappear "in transformed and reworked forms" in modernity (292, 318). In fact, those medieval discourses served as nothing less than the discursive lens "through which" major components of modernity, including the so-called discovery of the "New World," were understood. Not unlike the work by Sylvia Wynter on the pre-modern template for "Man" discussed in Chapter 2, Hall stresses how medieval texts, however fanciful, provide crucial evidence about how modernity skewed reality in ways that supported white identity formations.

As Hall puts it in "Europe and Its Myths," the "New World" encounter, far from a moment of "clear-sightedness," was draped in medieval discourse:

> The gaze which Europe first turned on the "New World" was therefore not an "empty" one. In some ways it was full to overflowing: shaped by a thousand legendary encounters, peopled by tribes of mis-shaped monstrosities, loaded down with the detritus of classical learning and the romance of travellers' tales. These discourses . . . helped form the template within which the New World took shape in the European mind. . . . The New World was produced within the specular gaze of the West, within the conventions of European looking. (66–67)

Hall's stress on vision is instructive, as it recalls and cancels Burckhardt's trope of the modern melting of a veil of superstition. Early modern explorers, conquerors, slaveholders, and colonists viewed the "new world" and its inhabitants via a version of Du Bois's veil, "the specular gaze of the West, within the conventions of [medieval] European looking." Medieval fictions regarding "tribes of mis-shaped monstrosities" and "the romance of travellers' tales" inflected what moderns would claim to know—about "the Rest" of the world.[87]

And what of the affective import of Hall's Middle Ages? His account of discourses of alterity does offer a certain feel-good valuation of difference. In a key moment in "The West and the Rest," for example, Hall alerts his readers to "a surprising twist" in the history of the European Enlightenment:

> In Enlightenment discourse, the West was the model, the prototype and the measure of social progress. It was *western* progress, civilization, rationality and development that were celebrated. And yet, all this depended on the discursive figures of the "noble vs ignoble savage," and of "rude and refined nations" which had been formulated in the discourse of "the West and the Rest." So the Rest was critical for the formation of western Enlightenment—and therefore for modern social science. Without the Rest (or its own internal "others"), the West would not have been able to recognize and represent itself as the summit of human history. (313–14, emphasis original)

Hall invokes in this passage the political utility of post-structuralism. Thanks to the way in which all meanings function in the manner of language, via binary oppositions, identity (as he puts it in "The Local and the Global") "only achieves its positive through the narrow eye of the negative. It has to go through the eye of the needle of the other before it can construct itself. It produces a very Manichean set of opposites."[88] Western identity formations thus expose contingencies—namely, a reliance on difference, on otherness, on a constitutive outside—that undermine claims about their homogeneity, stability, and unity. In Hall's words in "Europe and Its Myths," "in so far as identities depend on what they are *not, they implicitly affirm the importance of what is outside them— which often then returns to trouble and unsettle them from the inside*" (60, emphasis original). The "Rest" (that is, the other), is indispensable to Western modernity, thanks to its basis in a binary discourse.

But this is hardly the whole story. The notions of the other on which the West relies are also, depressingly, *false* representations imbricated in discursive and historical acts of oppression. Thus, in "The West and the Rest," Hall doesn't just happily upend fantasies of western unity and expose the crucial role of "others" in western identity formations. He also, in a feel-bad vein, engages the violence and power asymmetries—both historic and epistemic—that western discourses of self and other enact and make possible. Hall, for example, asserts that "the encounter between the West and the New World" was never "innocent" but instead "was molded and influenced by the play of motives and interests across their language," such as "get[ting] their hands on gold and silver" and "claim[ing] the land for Their Catholic Majesties" (293–94). He stresses how the epistemic violence performed by accounts of Indigenous Americans underwrote genocide, enslavement, and expropriation. Ignoring the heterogeneity and civilizations of Mayan, Incan, and other peoples, Europeans "lump[ed] all distinctions together and suppress[ed] differences in one, inaccurate stereotype" that included horrible claims about the "Indians'" "viciousness and bestiality" (304, 306). And Hall confronts "the horrendous era of New World African slavery," laying bare the dehumanizing practices of which Europeans were guilty. "The charter of the Royal Africa Company, which organized the English slave trade, defined slaves as 'commodities,'" and as "slavery expanded, a series of codes was constructed for the Spanish, French, and English colonies" that defined the slave as a chattel—literally, "'a thing,' not a person" (310).

Ultimately the medievalism at work in "The West and the Rest," like related writings by Hall, destabilizes ideas of a medieval-modern divide in a notably feel-bad manner reminiscent of the end of Hall's introduction to *Formations*. Indeed, in the final section of his chapter, and in a distinctly killjoy academic move, Hall brings his analysis uncomfortably home. Entitled "From 'The West and the Rest' to Modern Sociology," the section opens with Hall correcting those readers who believe that discourses of alterity are long gone. He emphasizes that "discourses don't stop abruptly. They go on unfolding, changing shape, as they make sense of new circumstances" (314). He then describes how a "discourse of 'The West' and 'The Rest'" persists in "the languages of racial inferiority and ethnic superiority which still operate so powerfully across the globe today," even in the "hidden assumptions of modern sociology," the very discipline aligned with Hall and the Open University book series in which *Formations* appeared (292, 318).

Soberingly, Hall describes how two revered figures in sociology—Marx and Weber—endorse ideas of a civilized western self and primitive non-western other that persist in some academic circles. He relates in "the West and the Rest" how, in his *Grundrisse*, Marx associates "countries such as China, India, and those of Islam" with an "(a) stagnation, (b) an absence of dynamic class struggle, and (c) the dominance of a swollen state acting as a sort of universal landlord" that deprives them of "the conditions for capitalist development" (314). Similarly, Weber contended that the "'patrimonial' or 'prebendary'" form of authority in Islamic countries "did not provide the preconditions for capitalist accumulation and growth" (315). Hall concludes with an upsetting truth, evident in Mann's acritical iteration of Weber's opposition of "the psychological make-up of Europe" and Asia: "The discourse of 'the West and the Rest' is still at work in some of the conceptual categories, the stark oppositions and the theoretical dualisms of modern sociology" (315). Hall's very field of sociology is a source of racial capitalist claims about the inherent economic primitivism of non-Western groups.

Open Theorizing/Structuration in Dominance

If essays like "The West and the Rest" deconstruct modernity to reveal a constitutive alterity dependent on false, debilitating, and even lethal medieval representations of self and other, elsewhere Hall would adopt additional strategies for analyzing, critiquing, and resisting western discourse. The sheer voluminousness, depth, and difficulty of Hall's oeuvre—generated over no less than six decades that span the twentieth and twenty-first centuries—precludes me from anything approaching a comprehensive account. But before turning to Langland, I will touch on two elements that potentially bear on speculations regarding what a Hall-esque analysis of *Piers Plowman* might entail. The first pertains to Hall's advocacy of a conjectural and multi-determinant approach to ideological formations and historical practices. In essays that merge Marxism with structural linguistics and the thought of Louis Althusser (1918–90) and Antonio Gramsci (1891–1937), Hall defines "a social formation as 'an ever pre-given structured complex whole,'" devoid of any "simple essence, underlying or pre-dating this structured complexity."[89] Ideology is a highly complex matter whose analysis requires attention to the multiplicities that determine its workings. Hall famously rejects Marx's reduction of bourgeois cultures to a single economic determinant and instead advocates an Althusserian "no guarantees" approach to ideology as "a set of complex practices; each with its own specificity, its own modes of articulation; standing in an 'uneven development' to other, related practices."[90] Instead of the Weberian rational restlessness evoked by Mann, Hall advocates a neo-Marxist (and thus dialectical) restlessness, situated within what Hall calls in his important 1986 piece "The Problem of Ideology—Marxism Without Guarantees" an *"open horizon* of Marxist theorizing—determinacy without guaranteed closures."[91] Hall's work evinces his willingness and ability to press on as a rigorous thinker, modifying and reformulating his analysis, moving in and out of different critical positionings, without ever collapsing into an "easy synthesis" or a belief in "the absolute predictability of particular outcomes."[92] In affective terms, Hall's critical practice affirms the two-sided critical affect famously portrayed by Gramsci:

> I am a pessimist of the intellect and an optimist of the will. I do think you have to analyse the things that are in front of you and try to understand how they really are and not how you would like them to be. And

then try to find out what the possibilities are for change and work with those. Yes, that is my strategy.[93]

In his scholarship, Hall emerges as a thinker who, not unlike (as my introduction discusses) Eve Sedgwick and her complex methodological optimism, is always cognizant of—but never overwhelmed by—the reality of complexity, constraints, and multiple determinants.

At the same time Hall advocated a neo-Marxist analysis alive to the multiple determinants at work during a particular conjuncture, he also was keenly attuned to the false multiplicities that a dominant social formation generates. Following Althusser, Hall used the idea of "societies structured in dominance" to connote the modes of cognition and meaning production that a social formation systematically accepts and rejects.[94] For example, in his groundbreaking 1977 essay "Culture, Media and the 'Ideological Effect,'" Hall analyzes the limits of what counts as a logical representation within "the whole process of argument, exchange, debate, consultation and speculation" in British televised news. Such mass media outlets might seem to portray a rich "interplay of opinions" (342). But instead, they conform to a "field of meanings" that is "structured in dominance"—that is, "a plurality of dominant discourses," all of which support existing white power relations (343). A field "structured in dominance"

> rules certain kinds of interpretation "in" or "out," to effect its systematic inclusions (for example, those "definitions of the situation" which regularly, of necessity and legitimately "have access" to the structuring of any controversial topic) and exclusions (for example, those groups, interpretations, positions, aspects of the reality of the system which are regularly "ruled out of court" as "extremist," "irrational," "meaningless," "utopian," "impractical," etc.). (346)

Critics, especially David Scott, have noted how Hall typically engages in a respectful and considerate "dialogic ethics of generosity" that conveys difficult concepts in an open, reader-friendly manner.[95] But here, Hall's affect toward his object of study entails a withering exposure of how the seemingly multiple options debated within the mass media fail to capture the full range of possibilities available and instead engage only those positions located within a larger "field" or system that supports white elites. These are Hall's "fighting words," as Gayatri Spivak avers in a comment keenly attuned to the fierce sentimental dimensions of this passage.[96]

The tenor of "fighting words" resonates with Hall's diasporic critique of English ideas of belonging and history. To restate a key claim from his heritage essay, ongoing debates about identity and community in Britain have stopped "short at the frontier defined by that great unspoken British value—'whiteness.'" As long as western ideas of identity and heritage remain structured in white dominance, they will fail to engage what Hall identifies in his important 1988 essay "New Ethnicities" as "the extraordinary diversity of subjective positions, social experiences, and cultural identities which compose the category 'black.'"[97]

For instances of that "extraordinary diversity," Hall turns to examples of Black cultural politics that challenge the white "politics of representation itself," that is, unsettle and reject occidental discourses structured in white dominance (442). Hall praises Black cultural producers, such as John Akomfrah and Isaac Julian, who reject the "politics" of white representations—that is, "fixed transcultural or transcendental racial categories" like white vs. black, good vs. bad, beautiful vs. ugly—and instead conceive of identity as having "no guarantees in nature." In lieu of discourses that "classify out the world" in the service of whiteness, the Black artists celebrated by Hall "recogni[ze] . . . the immense diversity and differentiation of the historical and cultural experience of black subjects" (443). That work resonates with Hall's claim in his heritage essay that the English need to reject their "closed . . . 'tight little island'" idea of heritage and "re-imagin[e] 'Britishness' or 'Englishness' itself in a more profoundly inclusive manner" (10).[98]

Stuart Hall's *Piers Plowman*?

How might Hall's complex and substantial intellectual work shed new light on Langland and his poem? This is a challenging proposition. In no way do I claim to speak for Hall and presume to give voice to his approach to *Piers*, whether during his student years or in subsequent decades. And space precludes me from engaging Langland in the extensive manner that his difficult, complex, and rich poetry requires. With those caveats in mind, I suggest that an apt place to begin to *hypothesize* Hall's relation to Langland is at the level of the medieval poet's mode of social analysis. Of course, many aspects of Langland's poem, such as its religious thrust and its conservative aspects (especially in the C-text of *Piers*), diverge from Hall's conception of identity, society, and history. But I would argue that the *methodology* through which Langland imagines a better Christian world in his poem suggests some resonance with Hall.

Consider how medievalist Nicolette Zeeman highlights the multidimensionality and dialectical nature of Langland's meditation on questions of piety, politics, and English society. Zeeman points to such aspects of *Piers* as its episodic nature, multiplicity, and complexity, as well as its many versions—its

A, B, C, and Z texts—as signs of a writer-critic who performs "an ongoing, revisionary, even 'negating,' dialogue with himself . . . a sustained and restless engagement between the many different elements that make up the poet's moral, political, and spiritual landscape."[99] To be sure, Langland's religiosity, conservativism, and largely indignant public voice diverge from the neo-Marxist generosity of Hall. And Zeeman's own approach isn't economic but rather psychoanalytic. But her account of the medieval poet's "sustained and restless engagement between many different elements" in some ways mirrors Hall's own neo-Gramscian methodology. Indeed, as Zeeman stresses, the dialogic restlessness she identifies in Langland is an aspect of *Piers* affirmed by medievalists as diverse as historicist-formalist Anne Middleton, Christian-Marxist David Aers, and theological and philosophical critics D. Vance Smith and Sarah Tolmie.[100] The status of *Piers* as a dialectical and "multimodal" work "rooted in a logic of disputation, of restless argument," suggests how Langland's approach resonates not so much with the Weberian "rational restlessness" cited by Mann but with Hall's aforementioned investment in an "*open horizon* of Marxist theorizing—determinacy without guaranteed closures."[101]

Langland also resembles Hall in the affective intellectual shifts between pessimism and hope that accompany the medieval poet's "sustained and restless engagement between . . . many different elements." Langland's skepticism and negative sensibility on occasion turned the poet away from the world. At his most critical, Langland's view approximates the despairing image with which Hall ends "Europe and Its Myths." Resembling, perhaps, a medieval Christian version of Benjamin "peering through glasses as thick as marble, trying to make sense of it all and—failing to do so," Langland's English vernacular literary enterprise has its all-too-worldly protagonist Will "never soothly" seeing Christ but only as an obscure vision of himself "in a mirour . . . *in enigmate*" (B.15.162–162a).[102]

But Langland's writing—and that of Hall—also testifies to the opposite: an abiding interest in *facing*, carefully, realistically, and critically, not just the dynamics of the world but also the very terms of their respective analytical inquiries. In *Piers*, Langland repeatedly endeavors to imagine how his corrupt and avaricious present should be reformed according to Christian ideals, all the while acknowledging the limits of the inescapably earthly terms of Christian reform. Consider, for example, the proto-deconstructive corruption and destabilization of allegorical figures like Hunger, who shifts in Passus 6 of the B-text from a harsh and capable disciplinarian to a gluttonous figure who "eet in haste and axed after moore" (B.6.296). Langland's keen, extensive, and dialectical engagement with social reform accords with Hall's searching and nuanced methodology, his belief that "you have to analyse the things that are in front of you and try to understand how they really are and not how you would like them to be." Langland's fiercely world-confronting and skeptical methodology resonates, for example, with Hall's important work on the rise of UK prime minister Margaret Thatcher (1925–2013). In *The Hard Road to Renewal: Thatcherism and the Crisis of the Left* (1988), a neo-Gramscian Hall affirms how, as "history shifts gears," the theorist must "attend, 'violently,' with all the 'pessimism of the intellect' at [his] command, to the 'discipline of the conjuncture.'"[103] *Hard Road* confronts the problem at hand from multiple angles: for example, it addresses the multipronged crisis that Thatcherism seemed to resolve; it considers the larger "Great Moving Right Show" of which Thatcher was a part; and it even faces blind spots and weaknesses within the British Left, including the "possibilities and limits" of Hall's own conjunctural approach.[104] Langland similarly refuses easy synthesis in favor of what Middleton calls a "perpetually inadequate yet obsessively necessary 'making.'"[105] One might even go so far as to opine that their methodological and affective affinities suggest a new way of characterizing the medieval poet that riffs on Hall's well-known characterization of his approach. Just as the cultural studies founder famously advocated a "Marxism without guarantees," Langland might be said to lay out in *Piers* a Christianity without guarantees.

Critiquing English Identity in B.15

Turning from the content of the form of *Piers* to the entangled question of its import, many of the issues and topics covered in Langland's expansive poem could be put into productive conversation with Hall's critical corpus, most obviously the medieval poet's concern with economy and a laboring peasantry. But, in keeping with my focus in this chapter on Hall's diasporic approach to identity and how the "unexamined 'national' cultural assumptions" of Hall's left cohort skewed their readings of Langland, I focus on the portrayal of alterity and England in *Piers Plowman*.

Several important studies by medievalists address the national dimensions of Langland's poem, and especially the economic and political registers in which Piers imagines England. For example, Smith examines the Pardon Passus, the figure of Covetous in B.5, and related moments to show how "the economic imaginary of *Piers Plowman* is inseparable from the deep interest Edward took in managing the political economy of England."[106] Smith especially clarifies how the merchants in the margins of the pardon bespeak Langland's support for the deployment of mercantile values on behalf of "the very idea of English *communitas* under Edward III."[107] Shifting from merchants to workers, Larry Scanlon considers how the Prologue of the B-text "has the character of a concise foundation myth" that radically "reconceptualize[es] the estates from the perspective of those who labor."[108] Citing the geographic sweep of *Piers*—its consideration of a corrupt London metropole from the perspective of England's western agrarian border of the Malvern Hills—as an indicator of Langland's "national vision," Scanlon locates "a radically communal notion of political sovereignty" at work in the poem, which "conceives of royal authority as the social concretization of a communal will, responsive to communal counsel."[109]

Hall suggests ways of expanding and complicating critical assessments of Langland and nation through attention to alterity. As we have seen, throughout his career, from his mid-century "Our Literary Heritage" to his new millennium "Europe and Its Myths," Hall's diasporic medievalism critiqued white ideas of stable, homogeneous, and distinct western identities and the discourses of the other on which those national fantasies relied. In the spirit of those Hallian interests, I consider here how the medievalism of essays like "The West and the Rest" might open a linked avenue of inquiry on Englishness and *Piers*, one that examines Langland's representation of England, selfhood, and otherness. I don't mean to suggest that Langland approaches anything like Hall's fierce deconstruction and decentering of English national discourse. Langland maintains throughout *Piers* a national focus on England. What I do intend to claim, though, is that, even as England gains a certain national distinctiveness as the object of Langland's attention, it is also the recipient of feel-bad critiques by the poet that resonate with Hall's work on alterity and the West.

Consider the notably "social and political" Passus 15 of the B text, where a Langlandian discourse of self and other takes place on behalf of an engagement with English national identity.[110] B.15 at once resonates with Hall's work on difference *and* Hall's trenchant diasporic critiques of received ideas of England (along with conceptions of Europe and the West) as "condensed, homogenous, unitary." To be sure, in B.15 Langland does give a kind of pride of place to England, insofar as, to cite Emily Steiner's formulation, "the contours of universal Christian history" traced in the passus "featur[e] an all-star English cast, beginning with the Anglo-Saxon kings Edward and Edmund."[111] However, the England of Passus 15 is far from an object of satisfying national sentiments. Evincing how, as John Burrow bluntly puts it, "Langland is not a patriotic poet," the poem radically unsettles any coherent and celebratory understanding of England.[112] Thus, to return to British left-leaning figures such as Green, Morris, and Morton, the poem that those intellectuals embraced for its proto-proletarian nationalism instead evinces a skeptical attitude toward the very idea of a unitary English nation.

Key to Langland's critical account of Englishness in Passus 15 is his destabilization of a "West and the Rest" discourse, in the form of the opposition of a Christian England to a non-Christian *"surie"* (that is, Syria, understood inconsistently as the Middle Eastern city, the entire eastern Mediterranean, and any Muslim territory).[113] Repeatedly, the passus muddies the line between the English and their ostensible Islamic others. One important example pertains to the account of clerical corruption by the allegorical figure of Anima. Anima relates how, due to their "Coveitise," a greed so thoroughgoing that "no man vseth trouthe," "Englisshe clerkes . . . ben manered after Makometh" and his legendary fraud (B.15.415–16). This passage marks the first time in *Piers* that the national affiliations of the clergy come to the fore. Up until this point, the word "English" appears only to signal when Latin texts are translated to the vernacular. But Langland finally represents Englishness in Passus 15 only to disrupt it, through "Englisshe" clerks' devious and materialist self-fashioning as types of Muhammad. Invoking the myth that Muhammad was "a fals mene" who gained followers through tricks, Langland condemns the English clergy for mimicking Muhammad's treachery, instead of assuming the "charite" or religious integrity of Christ and other holy men (B.15.505). To be sure, Langland reiterates offensively Orientalist pseudo-knowledge about the Prophet. But he also refuses what Hall calls in "Whose Heritage?" a national fantasy of an unchanging "distilled essence" of Englishness (22). Instead of defining England by affirming what it is *not*, Langland weaves what one might speculatively describe, via Hall's work, as a "complex dialectic" between piety and sinfulness, for which England and Syria become "interchangeable signifiers."[114]

The evangelizing thrust of Passus 15 helps account for its stress on *surie*. As global as it is national, this passus faults the contemporary English clergy for failing to venture beyond the borders of England and not following Christ's injunction to go out into the whole world (*universum mundum*) and preach (B.15.489a). During Langland's late medieval era, Muslims were unchecked by crusaders and controlled the *"uncristene"* or non-Christian elements of Langland's imagined world. Langland indicates his cognizance of that global Muslim dominance during the second invocation of Syria in Passus 15, which takes place during Anima's arguments for evangelization. There, Anima enjoins English prelates to bravely travel abroad, regardless of the risks to their physical safety. Anima cites Thomas Becket as an example of the courage English evangelists should assume:

> He is a forbisene to alle bisshopes and a bright myrour,
> And sovereynliche to swiche that of Surrye bereth the name,
> And naught to huppe aboute in Engelond to halwe mennes auteres,

And crepe in amonges curatours and confessen ageyn the lawe.
(B.15.525–28)

Anima celebrates Becket as a shining mirror for English clerics who are "Syrian" because they bear the name of "Surrye." Langland refers here to the papal practice of appointing clerks to sees in former Crusader states.[115] As many critics have observed, Langland the allegorist is everywhere concerned with the instabilities that arise from the gap between a word and its meaning.[116] Here Langland lends a geographic and national charge to the indeterminacy of language. Because English clergy appointed to Syria fail to leave home and take up their Syrian posts, England serves as the setting for the detachment of "Surrye" from its referent in the Outremer and the disgraceful hopping and creeping about of what has become a mere name, word, or image: English clerks who "of Surrye bereth the name" but remain in England. Langland troubles the cohesion of England by paradoxically calling on the English clergy to be *more* Syrian by relocating themselves within the territory to which the "name" of "Surrye" refers.

If Syria is the primary "other" through which Langland destabilizes England in Passus 15, Wales also plays a brief yet telling role in that project. An object of English conquest and colonization not long after 1066, Wales figures at the other end of a long history of English imperialism to which Hall was subject. Insofar as Hall referred to himself—as he puts it in his memoir—as the "last colonial," the first colonials, in a sense, were the Welsh (3). Langland refers to Wales during Anima's discussion of missionary work. At this moment in B.15, Anima praises missionary work by recalling how England—and, oddly, Wales— were first saved thanks to Roman evangelization: "Al was hethynesse som tyme Engelond and Wales / Til Gregory garte clerkes to go here and preche" (B.15.441– 42). On one level, this passage—which blatantly ignores the historical tensions that existed in early England between the Roman emissary Augustine of Canterbury and the Celtic bishops of an already Christian Wales—affirms how, for Langland, in Simon Meecham-Jones's words, "there is no place for Wales to exist, except through its relationship to England."[117] Wales, like Syria, figures in *Piers* only as a means of serving Langland's England-focused project.

And yet those national ends, again, are hardly celebratory. Langland's reference to Wales contributes to his stress in Passus 15 on the discontinuous religious history of England. Instead of the happy and feel-good "consoling circular narrative" of Englishness decried by Hall in "Europe and Its Myths" (61)—and embraced by conservatives like Tolkien and liberal and left-leaning British readers of *Piers*—Langland stresses how, far from always being Christian, England was once just like contemporary Syria—that is, heathen or non-Christian. I would argue that Langland anachronistically links Wales to England to intensify his destabilization of Englishness. In other words, Langland renders England's pagan origins especially troublesome by likening the English to one of the problem populations of his historical moment.[118]

A few lines later in the passus, Langland's destabilization of English identity through the figure of colonial Wales intensifies, so much so that it refuses the national agrarian imagery at the very core of *Piers*, the field of folk first visualized in Passus 1. Wales performs that deeply unsettling function in B.15 when Anima, during his discussion of evangelization, offers the following geographical etymology of the word "hethen" (heathen):

> It is to mene after heeth and untiled erthe
> As in wilde wildernesse wexeth wilde beestes,
> Rude and unresonable, rennyng withouten keperes.
> (B.15.457–59)

For centuries, medieval English colonizers had invoked spatial tropes of wildness and incivility to authorize the subjugation of the Welsh (and other objects of English conquest, like the Irish).[119] In *Piers*, Langland turns that colonizing rhetoric on the English themselves by understanding their pre-Christian state in terms of the uncultivated and wild space of the heath. Langland's alignment of the English with the unruly space of the colonized becomes still more disruptive when we consider it in terms of the overall agricultural thrust of his poem. Langland forces English readers to confront how, prior to its Christian civilizing, England was a site, like the Wales of colonial rhetoric, of "untiled erthe" and "wild wildernesse." Langland thus exposes how England was in a sense other to the very agrarian ideal foregrounded in his poem. Metaphorically, at least, there was a time in England when one couldn't even fathom, let alone put a "feeld ful of folk" to work upon, the half-acre led by Piers (B.P.17).

I've been suggesting that Langland's attention in B.15 to English instabilities—the many troubling ways the English fail to align with Christian virtues—compliments Hall's rejection of any "simple heroic affirmation" of national identity and his emphasis on a discontinuous, heterogeneous, and non-unitary "England."[120] At the same time, however, I would speculate that Hall's work urges a reconsideration of Langland's utility. Namely, I contend, *Piers* is constrained by a "structured ideological field" that supports certain "systematic inclusions . . . and exclusions."[121] Hall's searing critiques of hegemonic discourse reveal the depressing limits of Langland's representation of England and English social problems. Langland's poem, for all its dialogic critical realism and its destabilizing import, takes place within and on behalf of a white, proto-European, and Christian discursive terrain outside of which the medieval poet never travels. Thus Langland's dialectical understanding of England and Syria (and England and Wales) in B.15, takes place within, not outside, what Hall might have called a discursive field structured in Christian dominance.[122] The radical challenge that Islam might pose to Langland's white Christian world—like the systemic challenges a diasporic view might offer to received ideas of English heritage—doesn't figure in *Piers*. Instead, the Muslims, as well as other non-Christians and non-English people (for instance, pagans, Jews, the Welsh) represented in *Piers* "are not so much Jews, Muslims . . . as they are tools" generated to assist Christians in modeling their "soul[s] into a more perfect form of Christ."[123]

I would add, in the spirit of Hall's work, that non-Christians—namely, Muslims—assist a specifically national project of spiritual reform in *Piers*. As the medievalist Hall stresses in "The West and the Rest," making a point that applies as much to England as to Europe, "The challenge from Islam was an important factor in hammering Western Europe and the idea of 'the West' into shape. . . . The word 'Europeans' seems to appear for the first time in an eighth-century reference to Charles Martel's victory [over Islamic forces] at Tours" (289).[124] Hall emphasizes how constructions of a Muslim other were crucial in contributing to western European identity formations. Certainly, it is also the case that Islamic culture and thought crossed into and influenced Christian Europe in manifold and crucial ways.[125] But figures like Langland instead relied on representations of Muslim difference, on Islam as not an interlocutor or an influence but a border, "a physical barrier" (287). Langland is fundamentally uninterested in and closed to Islamic perspectives, to the complexities of Muslim identity.

The foregoing speculative inquiry into the unanswerable question of Stuart Hall's *Piers Plowman* intimates a relationship between the Jamaican-British intellectual and the medieval English poet that entails certain irreconcilable antinomies. Hall the fierce critic of societies structured in dominance might have rejected *Piers Plowman* insofar as Langland's totalizing Christian and national discourse forecloses alternate perspectives, cultures, and identity formations. At the same time, Langland's exposure of English hypocrisy and contradiction, as well as his multimodal realism—his "proto-conjunctural" approach—might have proved generative for Hall. Such aspects of *Piers* may have assisted in the development of Hall's revelatory scholarly oeuvre and especially his rejection of comforting unitary and racializing national mythologies.

Ultimately, then, this chapter ends with no firm answers but only more questions. Could Hall have become a neo-Gramscian without his literary influences, without Langland? Might the story of Hall's conflict with Tolkien, insofar as it enables a renewed awareness of the destabilizing and dialectical elements of *Piers*, intimate not so much a loss to medieval studies but an overall gain for the humanities and social sciences? Is it possible that Langland paradoxically helped Hall achieve a critical vantage point from which he could ultimately reject Eurocentric texts such as *Piers* and espouse alternate, global cultural productions and critiques? We can never fully answer such questions. But, however speculative, they offer new angles on the stakes of both Langland's and Hall's respective writings.

The final chapters of this book consider two works that embody the kind of diasporic artistry Hall celebrates. Both Gloria Naylor and Paule Marshall exemplify a cultural practice that, as Hall puts it in a landmark and oft-cited statement about "black cultural politics" in "New Ethnicities," moves beyond "a struggle over the relations of representation" to contest the "politics of representation itself."[126] As we shall see, both *Bailey's Cafe* and *The Fisher King* reject the essentialisms of a society structured in white dominance, even as they pessimistically affirm the wide reach and ample damage performed on behalf of that hegemonic order. At the same time, they each imagine alternate worlds whose diasporic heterogeneity enacts powerfully counterhegemonic Black feminist medievalisms and modernisms.

PART III
*Black Feminist Modernism,
Black Feminist Medievalism*

5
High Theory, Low Feelings
Gloria Naylor's Bailey's Cafe

> Readers of Naylor have underestimated the depth of her engagement with high theory.
> —ROBERT STEPTO, EMAIL TO AUTHOR, JANUARY 8, 2022

Theory came late to U.S. medieval studies, especially among scholars of early English literature. By "theory," I refer to the turn, by white continental thinkers such as Jacques Derrida, Roland Barthes, and Michel Foucault, to structural linguistics as a key to understanding human subjectivity and social life. The practitioners of theory—aka high theory, structuralism, and, above all in the U.S., post-structuralism—are a heterogeneous lot.[1] But, as Jonathan Culler puts it, "what some regard as the most significant consequence of structuralism" is "its rejection of the notion of the 'subject.'"[2] The death of the subject inaugurated by post-structuralism marks the demise of that entity situated at the core of modern western history, Burckhardt's autonomous individual. In other words, theory carried weighty implications with respect to periodization: a break with modernity and its key player, the white hegemonic individual. Manifold affects accompanied the new era inaugurated by theory, among them the liberation of being "freed . . . from the necessity of 'expression,'" (Foucault); the end of feeling altogether, insofar as feelings are linked to subjectivity (Jameson); and a sorrow or despair over the fragmentation of a self formerly celebrated as stable, whole, and capable of discerning truths about existence.[3]

Medievalists—above all, Swiss medievalist Paul Zumthor—contributed to the burgeoning of theory in Europe.[4] But not until the second half of the 1980s would U.S. scholars of the English Middle Ages ponder in earnest how they might reconceive their object of study in light of the theories advanced by Derrida et al.[5] With respect to Chaucerians, only in 1986 would the annual meeting of the recently formed New Chaucer Society dedicate several panels to theory.[6] Three years later, R. A. Shoaf would launch the first theory-driven medieval journal of its kind, *Exemplaria*. And the following year, *Speculum*, the most traditional of medieval journals, would dedicate a special issue to a theoretically informed "New Philology."[7]

How did the theoretical turn impact medievalists' stance toward both their object of inquiry and questions of periodization? Within Chaucer studies, several scholars located in the medieval writer's corpus an angst-ridden proto-post-structural sensibility. For example, Robert Jordan would contend in 1987 that "Chaucer's poetry" offers "a fragmented and problematic outlook, an uncertainty about fundamental truths, including the truth of poetry—indeed of language—and about the role and status of the poet."[8] A few years later, H. Marshall Leicester, in *The Disenchanted Self: Representing the Subject in the Canterbury Tales* (1990), would argue that the pilgrims, their narratives, and their creator represent an early variation of the secularist disenchantment described by Max Weber, along with "a nostalgia for what it knows has been lost."[9] As the no less than forty-four references in Leicester's book to "despair" indicate, the sensibility he identifies in Chaucer's portrayal of himself and his characters as "sufferers and agents of a culture whose cover is blown" is negative in the extreme.[10] Chaucer, far from a medieval "other" to the time of high theory, evinces a proto-postmodern discontent that accompanies the dissolution of firm truths and essential selves.

Other medievalists responded to the post-structural turn in a more sanguine manner. Discovering in theory some cause for optimism, these scholars reflect the sentiment, iterated by Lee Patterson in his contribution to the *Speculum* "New Philology" issue, that "the crisis of representation can be seen as generating not a paralyzing epistemological sophistication but opportunities for change" and the replacement of "a totalizing metanarrative with a plurality of micronarratives."[11] Peggy Knapp's post-Marxist *Chaucer and the Social Contest* (1990) thus approaches the *Canterbury Tales* as a site of discursive contestation, a work containing multiple and conflicting "patterns of significance," including those "which allow the experience of [reading Chaucer] to challenge received definitions of order."[12] In Knapp's analysis, Chaucer emerges as no hopeless figure but a proto-countercultural artist who helps the reader "throw away despair" by "light[ing]" the poet's "disordered world" with "the warm color of a lover."[13] Similarly, Carolyn Dinshaw's feminist-Lacanian *Chaucer's Sexual Poetics* (1989) contends that "Chaucer's works point to a critique of patriarchal conceptions of language and literary activity" and "suggest alternatives to such misogynistic formulations."[14] Dinshaw's analysis inverts the affective tenor of Leicester's approach, as a comparison of their respective analyses of the *Pardoner's Tale* attests. While Leicester views the Pardoner as "the darkest example and the most trenchant spokesman of an attitude" that Chaucer's narratorial alter ego "comes close to sharing," Dinshaw sees the Pardoner as a category-defying figure who creates possibilities for thinking about a utopian and "radical being in which there is no lack and in which all difference and division are obviated."[15]

For all their divergent readings, however, scholars such as Jordan, Leicester, Knapp, and Dinshaw each align Chaucer with contemporary theory in a manner that renders him newly relevant. Whether they connote an angst-ridden proto-modernist or a socially progressive Chaucer, these studies use theory to appreciate and even love the medieval poet as a resoundingly pertinent figure for the late twentieth century. Academics who identify in Chaucer a depressing cynicism place him—happily—in the company of important modernist and postmodernist theorists such as Weber, Jacques Lacan, and Paul de Man, as well as great modernist authors such as Jorge Luis Borges and Italo Calvino. The members of the more overtly political scholarly camp do affirm how the *Canterbury Tales* participates in more traditional and regressive social formations. Dinshaw, for example, acknowledges how the poem reveals Chaucer's "investment in patriarchal discourse" and the status of the Wife of Bath's performance as "a male fantasy."[16] But such depressing facts are typically eclipsed by the feel-good elements of resistance circulating in the *Canterbury Tales*. For some of the most important Chaucerians of the late twentieth century, the theoretical turn didn't so much challenge as promote a positive identification with their object of study.

While many theory-driven U.S. medievalists in the 1980s and 1990s admired Chaucer as a fellow post-structuralist, this chapter considers a more abidingly critical and feel-bad approach that emerged in not literary criticism but in Black women's fiction: Gloria Naylor's *Bailey's Cafe* (1992).[17] *Bailey's Cafe* (hereafter *Bailey's*) is the final book in a tetralogy that began with Naylor's much-lauded *The Women of Brewster Place* (1982). As its titular citation of Chaucer's innkeeper Harry Bailey suggests, *Bailey's* engages Chaucer's work, and it does so, I argue, via a searing critique that refuses the feel-good historicism that is often so central to the field imaginary of medievalists.[18] If post-structuralist medievalists often viewed Chaucer as alternately rich in disquieting disenchantment or possessed of proto-revolutionary hope, Naylor (1950–2016) uses theory to expose the complicity of the *Canterbury Tales* with oppressive white social formations. As a contemporary work that leverages Naylor's critical distance on the medieval, *Bailey's* may be one of the finest analyses of Chaucer ever written.

My reading of *Bailey's* responds to important work by Black and feminist scholars on Naylor's medievalism. In a 1998 essay, Charles Wilson considers *Bailey's* in terms of both the aftereffects of slavery in the U.S. South and the region's offensive neo-medieval chivalric code to explore how Naylor responds to the "intersection of medievalism and American culture in the nineteenth century."[19] More recently, Matthew Vernon, in *The Black Middle Ages: Race and the Construction of the Middle Ages* (2018), describes how Naylor complexly situates herself within a debate over vernacularity engaged first by Chaucer and later Dryden. Vernon considers how Naylor's was a "soul congenial" to Chaucer, insofar as both writers embraced the "literary plasticity of the vernacular, its ability to emphasize both the individuality and multiplicity of voice."[20] His analysis features an acute reading of the cafe as a metaphor for how the vernacular "morphs through time but maintains its essential character as a refuge for people living in ways that assert their individuality, a place to have a voice."[21] Ultimately, though, as Vernon shows, the "crisis of voice" raised in *Bailey's* poses difficult questions "of vernacular, of communities that become marginalized according to gender, race or space" that loop back to the medieval poet and reveal themselves as "problems that reproduce themselves over time."[22] Suzanne Edwards, in an intersectional reading of *Bailey's*, builds on Vernon's insight regarding Naylor's attunement to the fraught politics of representation in a text like the *Canterbury Tales*. Edwards demonstrates how, thanks to Naylor's acute awareness of how "a desire for Chaucer maintains racist and sexist hierarchies," *Bailey's* "undercuts the allusion to the *Canterbury Tales* in just the moments when a reader would be most inclined to read for Chaucer."[23] Edwards demonstrates how Naylor ingeniously upends the received understanding of literary history by constructing Chaucer as a figure who longs to be a part of the African American female literary tradition.

I complicate these analyses by linking Naylor's critique of Chaucer to her post-structuralist expertise. Naylor is distinguished among contemporary novelists for her academic training in a high-theory milieu. In the early 1980s, Naylor received an MA in African American Studies from Yale, an institution that "you couldn't go through," as Naylor puts it in a 1991 interview, "and not be a structuralist."[24] Moreover, Naylor worked on *Bailey's* during the late '80s as a fellow at the humanities institute of another key U.S. site for theory, Cornell University.[25] The theoretical turn, I contend, comprises an essential context for apprehending both Naylor's achievement in *Bailey's* and her contribution to a productively pessimistic medieval studies.

Naylor was well-versed in both theory and the white western canon. But she does not view Chaucer, as Leicester does, as a fellow post-structuralist critic. Neither does she view the *Canterbury Tales*, as Dinshaw does, as the site of radical liberation. Instead, Naylor enacts via *Bailey's* an acute critique of the *Tales* as a document of whiteness. In an approach that resonates with those of critics discussed in Chapter 2—e.g., W. E. B. Du Bois, Sylvia Wynter, Jennifer Morgan, Cord Whitaker, and Jacqueline de Weever—Naylor critiques Chaucer's work for the white western subject it centers and the manifold others it marginalizes and denigrates. Naylor's Chaucer isn't so much a fellow theorist but rather the object of a fierce post-structuralist commentary directed at white semiotic systems hailing at least as far back as the late medieval world. Naylor's *Canterbury Tales*, far from witnessing Chaucer's existential uncertainty (in the manner of Leicester) or his incipient interest in resisting dominant structures (in the manner of Dinshaw), instead conforms to a white, patriarchal, discursive, and hierarchical "mode, indicative of timeless order."[26] For all its seeming heterogeneity and multiplicity, the *Canterbury Tales* demonstrates how whiteness structures the work of the "father" of English poetry.

Naylor's project resonates with the Black feel-bad approaches to the Middle Ages discussed in earlier chapters, including Sylvia Wynter's account of the scholastic roots of modern "Man" and Stuart Hall's discussion of the modern afterlife of a medieval discourse of the "West and the Rest." But unlike Wynter and Hall, Naylor performs her critique through a novel, a literary form whose generic qualities enable a practice of alternate world making that performs a host of critical functions. *Bailey's* demolishes any white claim to universality on the part of the *Tales* by representing the multiple identities and perspectives of a transnational array of Black subjects. In addition, drawing on an intensely close and acute structuralist reading of Chaucer, Naylor repurposes particulars of the *Canterbury Tales* to both expose Chaucer's complicity in ongoing forms of oppression and reveal the vulnerability of his poem to a literary appropriation centered on the lived experience of Black subjects. Thanks to its binding of post-structuralism to identity politics, the relationship of *Bailey's* to periodization and affect is complex. On one hand, Chaucer's structurality affirms a horrible *longue durée* of racism that erodes notions of periodic break and whose lethal impact on Black humans the novel records. But on the other hand, Naylor also, exhilaratingly, performs her critique via the alternate structurality of her novel. With its portrayal of the heterogeneous subjectivities of a transnational group of Black persons, *Bailey's* wondrously breaks from western periodization altogether.

Critics largely have, in Kathleen Forni's words, viewed Naylor's "invocation of Chaucer" as "more symbolic than substantive."[27] But once one understands Naylor as an acute structuralist, the depth and extensive nature of her critical engagement with Chaucer come to the fore. Contrary to received scholarly opinion, Naylor is a close and combative reader of the *Canterbury Tales*. To be sure, as Edwards demonstrates, at times Naylor practices a "destabilizing evocation and refusal of the *Canterbury Tales*."[28] But elsewhere Naylor—with a precision that often assumes a granular form—excises particulars of Chaucer's work, removing them from the medieval poet's white discursive world and giving them a new and alternate semantic life in the transnational Black feminist world of *Bailey's*. The failure of scholars to recognize the depth and extent of Naylor's response to Chaucer testifies, I would suggest, both to the revolutionary nature of the alternate world she builds and the structuralist precision of her critique of the *Canterbury Tales*.

In *Bailey's*, Naylor draws on her training in theory to demonstrate an extraordinary sensitivity to what Hall calls "a politics of representation."[29] Hall describes a "politics of representation" as a strategy of resistance that involves not "a simple set of reversals, putting in the place of the bad old essential white subject, the new essentially good black subject," but rather a contestation of the discursive terrain of whiteness itself.[30] Multiple, open-ended, and contradictory, *Bailey's* powerfully contests the totalizing heteropatriarchal and Christian discursive terms of the *Canterbury Tales*. Acutely attuned to the semantic codes deployed by Chaucer, Naylor everywhere in her novel disassembles and redirects the medieval poet's discursive codes—for instance, binary oppositions like male vs. female, active vs. passive, spirit vs. matter—on behalf of her poststructuralist Black feminist project. Naylor unmakes Chaucer's allegory and in the process lays claim to the very tradition he embodies. Far from situating Naylor as a worthy inheritor of western discourse, *Bailey's* asserts her authority both as a critic of white semiotics and their harmful notions of progress, primitivism, and heritage and as a diasporic cultural producer who triumphantly imagines alternate identities grounded in difference.

That Black transnational feminist project entails an unflinching exposé of the damage wrought by whiteness. *Bailey's* is a heart-wrenching read, as reviews of the novel affirm. In the words of critics from the *Chicago Tribune* and the *New York Times*, Naylor's affective "address is despair," and the Black "lives" portrayed in *Bailey's* evince a "pain that . . . is seared into" readers' "consciousness."[31] Crucial to Naylor's pessimism is its titular cafe, which caters to a global array of patrons who are on the verge of suicide. Unlike Chaucer's Tabard Inn, the restaurant is a magical realist space. Situated not in but at "the edge of the world," the cafe affirms the absence of any substantial haven for Black persons in a white-dominated world.[32] However, even as Naylor's novel unflinchingly exposes the damage wrought by whiteness, it also triumphantly portrays its characters' ample talents. For all its pessimism, *Bailey's Cafe* brilliantly affirms Black humanity, resilience, agency, and creativity, including the magisterial literary—and literary-critical—abilities of Naylor herself.

In the remainder of this chapter, I first contextualize Naylor's post-structuralist project by recovering how, thanks to her studies at Yale and Cornell, she was intimately tied to the world of high theory and literary criticism and the idea of historical rupture those approaches inaugurated. I then consider how the paratext of *Bailey's*—namely, its acknowledgment page and preparatory poem—signal Naylor's Black feminist post-structural project. The remainder of the chapter then turns to Naylor's contestation and reformulation of Chaucer, focusing on the cafe's two most significant patrons, Sadie and Miss Maple. Their tales—"Mood: Indigo" and "Miss Maple's Blues"—are not only the longest of *Bailey's Cafe*, consuming more than half the text, but also bookend the novel. Naylor's most sustained engagements with the *Canterbury Tales*, the stories of Sadie and Maple particularly respond to the portraits, prologues, and tales associated with Chaucer's key female pilgrims, the Prioress and the Wife of Bath. In the case of Sadie, Naylor "signifies" on Chaucer (to echo Henry Louis Gates Jr.'s formulation) to meet one of her primary Black feminist and structuralist goals in writing the novel: to engage the word "whore" and, as Naylor puts it, "appropriate that word, bleed it of its malignancy and turn it into poetry."[33] I argue that Naylor exalts Sadie—a "twenty-five-cent whore"—via a slew of linguistic transformations of Chaucer's text that, taken together, also critique the medieval Christian antisemitism at work in the Prioress's narrative (40). Naylor's newly sacral figure of the "whore" in "Miss Maple's Blues" both rejects modern stereotypes of Black identity and gestures toward the Jewish humanity occluded in texts like the *Prioress's Tale*.

Sadie's narrative forms an important context for Naylor's final narrative. The only tale centered on a man, "Miss Maple's Blues" resignifies Chaucer to address continuities and differences pertaining to gender and race in the U.S. Miss Maple was raised as a man with the birth name Stanley and continues to identify as male even as he takes to wearing dresses and acquires the feminine moniker "Miss Maple."[34] On one level, the tale of Miss Maple unsettles both the Prioress's and the Wife's narratives to expose how racism overrides sexism in the U.S., foiling the efforts of even the most privileged and talented men to achieve received western notions of success in what is ultimately an all-too-white patriarchy. But on another level, in a move that reflects the relative privileges patriarchy accords Black men, Naylor saves for Miss Maple her most remarkable contestation of Chaucer. Maple's tale ends with a champagne toast that brilliantly deconstructs the *General Prologue* to the *Canterbury Tales*. The fact that Naylor's male character enjoys the most oppositional—indeed, triumphant—relationship to the *Canterbury Tales* speaks to the depressing realism of *Bailey's*, that is, Naylor's acknowledgment of the advantages enjoyed by men in the patriarchal West. At the same time, however, Naylor queries sexism and its relationship to signification. Indeed, the very name "Maple"—bestowed, crucially, by a Black woman named "Eve"—crystallizes Naylor's project of replacing the patriarchal structurality of Chaucer's medieval English text with a new, post-structuralist and nonbinary, signifying system.

Naylor, High-Theory "Hotbeds," and Black Feminism

> When I went to Yale, all of New Haven, so it seemed, was deconstructionist.
> —HENRY LOUIS GATES JR., INTERVIEW BY CHARLES ROWELL

> It would generally be extremely problematic to argue that a literary artist is consciously employing deconstructionist theories either in her own texts or in her interpretations of the works of others. But Naylor did spend two years in New Haven earning an M.A. at Yale, the indisputable hotbed of deconstruction in America, and her comments—and, as I will demonstrate, her first novel—suggest that she absorbed a good deal of its theoretical suppositions.
> —MICHAEL AWKWARD, INSPIRITING INFLUENCES

Michael Awkward, in a footnote in his 1989 monograph *Inspiriting Influences*, "calls for deconstructive exegesis" of Naylor's writing and pedagogy, premised on the implications of her graduate studies at "the indisputable hotbed of deconstruction in America," Yale.[35] As Awkward avers, Naylor stands starkly apart from most female writers of color—or indeed most fiction writers in toto—for her close ties to high theory as it was practiced within the halls of academia during its 1980s heyday. Elaborating on Awkward's note, I suggest we should place Naylor's academic affiliations front and center when assessing *Bailey's Cafe*.

When Naylor embarked in 1981 on a program of graduate work at what was then called the Afro-American Studies Program, she entered an academic milieu in which the tenets promulgated by Yale's deconstructionists reverberated widely across the university.[36] The oft-looming presence of what were alternately labeled the "Yale Critics," "Yale School of Deconstruction," or the Yale "Gang of Four"—that is, J. Hillis Miller, Geoffrey Hartman, Harold Bloom, and de Man, plus the frequent visiting professor Derrida—shook up received ideas and generated heated debates about the methodologies, aims, and stakes of humanities work.[37] Post-structuralism was, in the words of Kimberly Benston, who was an Assistant Professor in English and Afro-American Studies during Naylor's time at Yale, "an important dimension of the air" Naylor "breathed and the discussions she would have had with [Benston] and others" during her graduate studies.³⁸ When, in fall 1988, Naylor spent time as a fellow at Cornell, the novelist's attunement to post-structuralism would only have intensified.³⁹ Along with Johns Hopkins and Yale, Cornell was a primary academic site in the U.S. for high theory.⁴⁰ Naylor arrived at the Society for the Humanities just after Derrida completed a six-year stint there; he would return that October.

For Naylor, theory was always a matter closely intertwined with identity politics. At Yale, the relationship between post-structuralism and Black studies was a major issue. Naylor's most significant encounter with theory took place through her generational peer, Afro-American Studies faculty member Gates.⁴¹ Naylor intensively worked with Gates during a period that coincided with his Black studies–inflected post-structuralist interventions in publications like *The Signifying Monkey* (1988) and the 1985–86 *Critical Inquiry* special issues on "Race, Writing, and Difference." Naylor was Gates's assistant, mentee, and, most importantly, intellectual partner. She served as the teaching assistant for his undergraduate course Black Women and Their Fictions; her MA thesis (her second novel, *Linden Hills* [1985]) was directed by Gates; and she and Gates planned to coauthor a work of criticism on fiction by Black women.⁴² Gates's account of his aborted book project with Naylor reveals how he didn't draw hard lines between the work of the writer and the academic: "We will blend," Gates states, "that which the critic brings to the study of literature and that which the writer brings."⁴³ Such an attitude indicates that Gates brought his post-structuralism to bear on his interactions with Naylor.⁴⁴

If Naylor's time as a graduate student at Yale entailed a confrontation between race and theory, Cornell added gender and sexuality to the mix, precisely during the time of her writing of *Bailey's*. The cohort of fellows gathered under that year's focal theme of "Feminism" counted among its numbers many theory-identified academics. Scholars including Biddy Martin, Molly Hite, Paula Treichler, and Rita Felski shared space with Naylor in the building that housed the Society for the Humanities, the A. D. White House. Theory alone rendered the environment at Cornell highly charged; Felski, for example, recalls the period as marked by "trench warfare between the Lacanians and the sociolinguists."⁴⁵ But debates about race, gender, and sexuality created a particularly fraught milieu.

Indeed, Naylor arrived at Cornell precisely when the idea of a Black woman doing theory became the topic of fierce debate. During the previous year (1987), two key essays arguing against the use of post-structuralism had appeared by Black feminist literary critics. In "The Race for Theory," Barbara Christian denigrated theory as the provenance of white men whose claims regarding the end of the autonomous subject undermined the effort to invest African

Americans and other minority groups with the social agency and rights they had long been denied.[46] And in "The Black Canon: Reconstructing Black American Literary Criticism," Joyce A. Joyce stressed the highly restricted and elitist academic audience to which theoretical work was directed.[47] A version of the charged elitist climate described by Joyce undoubtedly circulated at Cornell in 1988. One of Naylor's co-fellows, Donna Landry, recalls how "every event at Cornell that year . . . produced fierce debates about 'Theory.' Did you talk the talk? Did you know what was at issue? Was Marxism still au courant?"[48] Landry's recollection indicates both the electricity and excitement, as well as the value-laden judgments, that attended discussions of theory at Cornell. While "fierce debates" might be electrifying, questions of what is "au courant" and whether one could "talk the talk" indicate how any academic who resisted the theoretical turn might find themselves subject to a debilitating practice of intellectual periodization. The extent to which a refusal to engage theory rendered a scholar atavistic and irrelevant carried a special weight when that scholar was not just female but also a person of color. Omofolabo Ajayi-Soyinka—a junior member of the fellowship cohort who spent time socializing and sharing work with Naylor and the one other fellow of color, Jane Whitehead—describes the imposing and indeed harmful presence of theory at Cornell: "theory so "dominat[ed] all discussions" that "if you didn't know it, you didn't exist."[49]

Christian's and Joyce's arguments bespeak the complexities and contradictions informing the body of literature and literary criticism generated by Black women in the U.S. On one hand, such factors as the jargon-ridden rhetoric of post-structuralism and its alignment with elite white male scholars made theory problematic for Black writers. But on the other hand, as Christian stresses in "The Race for Theory," "people of color have always theorized."[50] The post-structuralist exposure of the white autonomous subject as contingent and constructed was hardly news to anyone gifted with what Du Bois describes as the second sight afforded by double consciousness.[51] And Black women, possessed of the additional perspective that accrues from "women's insider/outsider status," have been, in many respects, best positioned to critique white masculinist ideas of humanity.[52] Such factors help account for the fact that, even as certain Black female critics rejected theory, others, along with Black male thinkers such as Hall and Gates, considered it a vital means of critiquing and resisting received western ideas of society and identity. In 1988, for example, Hazel Carby published *Reconstructing Womanhood: The Emergence of the Afro-American Woman Novelist*. A work deeply informed by the historicist, neo-Gramscian, and structuralist methodologies of Carby's mentor Hall, *Reconstructing* critiques the essentialisms that have at times informed Black feminism and tracks an "alternate discourse of black womanhood" represented in early African American literary texts.[53] The same year witnessed the publication of Hortense Spillers's "Mama's Baby, Papa's Maybe: An American Grammar Book." Spillers's colossally influential essay dismantles received psychoanalytic models of identity formation and social hierarchy and advocates a critical agenda centered on racial, gendered, and sexual liberation.[54]

Cornell in the late '80s was a key setting for work by Spillers, arguably the most important African American female literary theorist at that time. Naylor arrived at Cornell during Spillers's two-year stint there. And "Mama's Baby" appeared in the Cornell journal *diacritics*. More generally, before, during, and after Naylor's fellowship, Cornell witnessed a slew of public events that featured theory-driven presentations by women of color, such as a spring 1989 conference, Feminisms and Cultural Imperialism: Politics of Difference, in which Rey Chow, Chandra Mohanty, Gayatri Spivak, and other academic heavy hitters affirmed the relevance of female academics of color to theory. Theory-driven presentations by women of color at Cornell were major events that drew crowds of over a hundred people and provoked lively debate long after their conclusion. They suggest how Cornell at times served as a nodal point for the mobilization of post-structuralism to forge notions of agency, activism, and solidarity on the part of feminists and people of color. At Cornell, theory was often viewed as not so much an oppressive enterprise but rather as a powerful catalyst for both contesting western discourse *and* conceptualizing alternate forms of identity and social life.[55]

Culler, Morrison, Chaucer: Naylor's Deconstructive Paratext

Set in 1948, in the wake of the horrors of World War II, *Bailey's* is "a novel of seven songs."[56] Via seven chapters bearing titles signaling its musicality—for instance, one chapter takes the title of Duke Ellington's "Mood: Indigo" and another cites Scott Joplin's "Maple Leaf Rag"—*Bailey's* adapts the lyricism and melancholy of the blues to represent the atrocities endured by Black men and women. The most deconstructive of Naylor's novels, *Bailey's* is intensely intertextual; it features intricate engagements with not just Chaucer but many other texts, among them the Bible and works by Black authors, including Naylor's earlier works.[57]

The novel opens by introducing the proprietors "Bailey" (a figure akin to Chaucer's master of ceremonies Harry Bailey, who never reveals his actual name) and his wife, Nadine, along with some minor characters who frequent the cafe.[58] After telling the story of Eve, the proprietress of a shelter/bordello situated within the magical realist precincts of the cafe, Naylor then recounts the story of Sadie, an aged alcoholic from Chicago's South Side who maintains a feminine grace despite the unspeakable child abuse that has stunted her, scarred her, and forced her into sex work. Sadie's story is followed by that of Esther, who retains her integrity even during her twelve-year imprisonment as a sex worker. Naylor then turns to Peaches, a Kansas City woman at war with her own beauty and the lascivious men it attracts; Peaches forecloses male attention by savagely mutilating her face, yet she nevertheless remains beautiful. Naylor's next tale is that of Jesse Belle, a bisexual ex-junkie from New York who recovers her vitality after her near destruction by a white-identified Uncle Tom figure named Eli. Eli's lethal machinations include killing Jessie's mother, seizing her son, and spreading libels about her lesbian sexuality. Naylor's penultimate tale focuses on Mariam, a mentally challenged girl from a Beta Israel village in Ethiopia whose genital mutilation receives extended, painful, and metaphorical representation via the cutting of a plum by Eve. Finally, Naylor recounts the story of Stanley, a would-be market analyst from California who works at the bordello as a bouncer and housecleaner bearing the name Miss Maple.[59]

Through paratextual elements, Naylor frames her book as a work that puts post-structuralist inquiry in provocative dialogue with literary and cultural traditions. Prefacing the novel is an acknowledgment page that faces a lyrical epigraph by Naylor (Figure 3). In the acknowledgment, Naylor thanks the Guggenheim Foundation and Cornell for their financial support and singles Culler out for "moral support during the writing of this novel." One might dismiss Naylor's gratitude to Culler, the director of the Cornell Society for the Humanities, as pro forma. But Culler was not only Naylor's primary contact but also the foremost elucidator of deconstruction in the world at that time. Culler, that is, was a crucial interlocutor for Naylor regarding matters of theory.[60]

Naylor indicates her links to Culler in a 1991 interview where she describes her "structuralist" bent at Yale.[61] Voicing her admiration for "criticism" as "an art form in itself," Naylor asserts that "it's marvelous what writers" like "Jonathan Culler do with language."[62] Naylor would elaborate even more upon her affiliation with Culler and theory in a Society-sponsored presentation on "The Evolution of a Writer's Voice," which she delivered on November 21, 1988. Naylor begins her talk by stressing her close ties to Culler, as they "have had a chance to really get to know each other." As her talk proceeds, it becomes apparent that their acquaintance involved discussions about theory. For example, during the talk Naylor posits a divide between structuralist Ithaca and her "logocentric" home of Manhattan, which she subsequently undermines. She self-consciously highlights particularities of body, gender, and *parole*, presenting

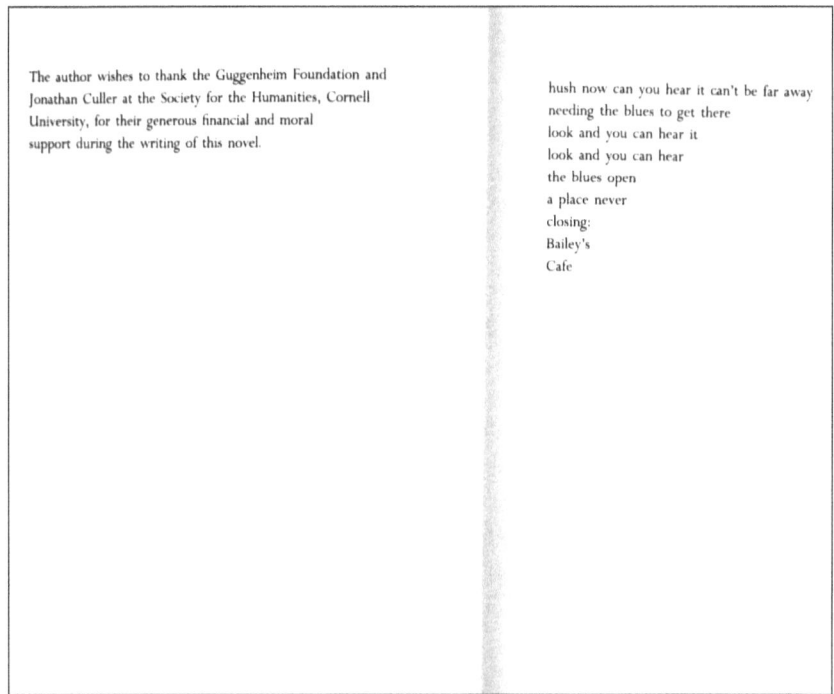

Figure 3. Acknowledgment and Epigraph, Gloria Naylor, *Bailey's Cafe* (New York: Vintage, 1993). Photo by author.

herself to the audience as "the woman in front of you, the woman speaking, the voice in front of you." Naylor also uses a structuralist vocabulary to describe her incipient relation to language from childhood on—that is, the moment when, as she puts it, "I could write my name, when I could begin to understand those codes in that written language," and the journey by which she gained the "authority" as a writer "to speak through the language."[63] Naylor's characterization of language acquisition as a matter of comprehending codes suggests her sensitivity to the constitution of discourse via binary oppositions, as described by linguist Roman Jakobson.[64] Her words also echo closely those of Culler, who asserts, for example, early on in *The Pursuit of Signs* (1981), that "to read is always to read in relation to other texts, in relation to the codes that are the products of these texts and go to make up a culture."[65]

Naylor's citation of Culler in the paratext of *Bailey's* hints at her interest in engaging, via her novel, versions of the theoretical issues she discussed with that explicator of deconstruction. Moreover, the placement of Naylor's acknowledgment of Culler on a page directly opposite her lyrical epigraph confirms the relationship between the novel and post-structuralism. The epigraph, a deconstructive cradle song, tells the reader:

> hush now and you can hear it can't be far away
> needing the blues to get there
> look and you can hear it
> look and you can hear
> the blues open
> a place never
> closing:
> Bailey's
> Cafe

A self-referential lullaby where "look[ing]" leads to "hear[ing]" and a "never closing" site can only be "open[ed]" by the blues, Naylor's lyric exhibits a resistance to closure, reinforced by its stretched-out and attenuated formal organization, culminating in three lines, each of which are dedicated to a single word. As a result of its indeterminacy, the poem indirectly acknowledges Culler, whose account of deconstruction describes "the failure of signifieds to produce closure" and tracks a "structure of repetition and proliferation rather than crystalline closure" in early English poetry.[66] The respective texts on the facing pages speak across to each other, signaling to the reader the post-structuralist hermeneutics Naylor's novel demands.

The lyric also introduces *Bailey's* as a complex hermeneutic project that is as concerned with Black and white traditions of writing as it is with high theory.[67] Among other literary interlocutors, the lyric calls up Naylor's foremother Toni Morrison's adoption of an African American musical aesthetic in *Sula* (1973). At the end of Morrison's novel, Sula's estranged friend Nel recalls and then mourns their special bond, letting out "a fine cry—loud and long—but it had no bottom and it had no top, just circles and circles of sorrow."[68] Taking up where *Sula* left off, Naylor's lyric cites Morrison's deconstructive ending "with a difference," turning the bluesy and open-ended "long and loud" sound emitted by an aged Nel into a whispered nursery rhyme. Citing both the blues and Morrison, Naylor highlights African American cultural forms' resonance with and anticipation of the post-structuralist turn toward indeterminacy, even as she helps generate, through *Bailey's* and its revision of texts like *Sula*, a richly disunified African American narrative tradition.[69]

The final words—"Bailey's Cafe"—of Naylor's lyric signal how her post-structuralist gambit extends to the *Canterbury Tales*. Naylor seems to have been drawn partly to Chaucer's project for its disunity, open-endedness, and heterogeneity—for instance, the motley nature of the pilgrims, their repeated moments of discord, and the fragmentary form of both the poem overall and certain tales. In important respects, as Vernon has demonstrated, Chaucer's was a "soul congenial" to Naylor. Both writers embraced the "literary plasticity of the vernacular, its ability to emphasize both the individuality and multiplicity of voice." Viewed in this way, *Bailey's* defies received notions of periodization; Naylor joins hands across the medieval-modern divide with Chaucer as writers united in their commitment to vernacular "plasticity" and "multiplicity."

But alongside any medieval neighborliness is Naylor's characterization—starting with her lyrical epigraph—of *Bailey's* as an emphatically current text that adopts an irreverent and disparaging stance toward literary history. Even as it might register some points of enabling correspondence between Naylor's and Chaucer's literary projects, *Bailey's* recognizes another, much less congenial and far more pessimistic, temporal continuity: the complicity, as I discuss in Chapter 2, of the *Canterbury Tales* in a *longue durée* of totalizing white western discourses centered on white men like Chaucer. Instead of imagining herself as Chaucer's heir, Naylor positions herself as an anti-Chaucer revolutionary who rejects altogether the *Canterbury Tales'* masculinist, Christian, and white semiotic system.

Naylor's opening epigraph embraces precisely the opposite discursive form of Chaucer's work. Chaucer begins his project with two lines of poetry whose semiotic patterns (that is, the piercing of a feminine March by a masculine April) establish, as structuralist Joel Fineman stressed in a groundbreaking essay, a closed patriarchal Christian discourse that is "repeated with utter systematicity" to organize the entirety of the *Canterbury Tales*.[70] But Naylor instead announces the radical openness and contingency of *Bailey's*. Foregrounding her novel as an act of world-building predicated on the indeterminacies of Black music, Naylor affirms how "the blues open"—render contingent and shifting—her project. Not just Naylor's titular cafe but also *Bailey's Cafe*, the novel, is "a place never closing," a work that challenges the dominant discourse of the "father" of English poetry.

"In laude" of a Twenty-Five-Cent "Whore": The Prioress and "Mood: Indigo"

In interviews and correspondence, Naylor situates her overall aim in writing *Bailey's* at the intersection of post-structuralism, feminism, and antiracism. For example, in a 1992 National Public Radio interview she explains how "what I've tried very subtly to do is to reclaim language" and especially "reclaim the word 'whore.'"[71] Naylor elaborates: "The word 'whore' [has] . . . been used as [a] weapo[n] against women"; "'whore,' [is] a word used to control women's behavior, control their identities."⁷² As critics including Spillers and Jennifer Morgan affirm, representations of Black women as hypersexual were fundamental to the enslavement of Black persons both before and after so-called emancipation. Morgan describes how the "white men who laid the discursive groundwork on which the 'theft of bodies' could be justified relied on mutually constitutive ideologies of race and gender" that made "women's sexual availability the defining metaphor of colonial accessibility and black African savagery."⁷³ Spillers, in her groundbreaking essay published the year of Naylor's fellowship, demonstrates how similar demonizations persist in the form of "nicknames" such as "Brown Sugar" and texts like the Moynihan report (1965), "which borrows its narrative energies from the grid of associations, from the semantic and iconic folds buried deep in the collective past, that come to surround and signify the captive person."⁷⁴

Naylor inaugurates her project through a narrative whose title, "Mood: Indigo," highlights its aching pathos. *Bailey's* first "song," "Mood: Indigo" relates the story of a figure who, on the face of it, exemplifies the sexually available Black woman. Sadie is an unhoused "twenty-five-cent whore" and alcoholic and thus seemingly the lowest of Black sex workers. But Sadie instead merits the deepest awe and highest admiration. Through her moving portrayal of what can only be called the sacred personhood of her protagonist, Naylor generates—to cite Spillers's formulation—"words and deeds that would deny or defy the black woman myth" and thus expose the unspeakable crimes against humanity that have been performed on behalf of modern white supremacy.⁷⁵

Naylor's reclamation, through Sadie, of the word "whore" also entails a medieval-oriented reclamation centered on a Canterbury tale that is as obsessed with Christian purity as it is with Jewish danger: the *Prioress's Tale*. A narrative praising the Virgin Mary told by a fastidious nun, the *Prioress's Tale* is also a *locus classicus* for medieval English antisemitism. As I discuss in Chapter 2, antisemitism not only constituted the most extensive form of racism in the European Middle Ages, but also generated templates on which subsequent racisms drew—including those involved in the Atlantic slave trade. The *Prioress's Tale* enacts the modernizing rhetoric of supersession described in Chapter 2. As Steven Kruger observes, the tale "attempts to cast Judaism into the past"; its Jews are usurers who are "materialistic and not properly spiritual," and its key Christian players—a mother and son—are as pious as they are "newe" or new (VII.584, 627).⁷⁶ Moreover, the *Prioress's Tale* contains the most famous version of a myth used to authorize historic acts of anti-Jewish violence—the boy martyr libel.⁷⁷ In the tale, Jews in an anonymous Asian city have a Christian schoolboy murdered for singing a hymn to the Virgin Mary during his daily walk through their neighborhood. An assassin cuts the boy's throat and hides the body in a latrine. But the Virgin places a mysterious grain ("greyn," VII.662) on the dead boy's tongue that reanimates that organ, enabling the child to resume singing. The song draws the attention of his mother and civic authorities, who violently execute all the Jews involved in the crime. Chaucer wrote the *Prioress's Tale* at the end of the fourteenth century, long after the state-sponsored expulsion of Jews from England in 1290. That tale meets its explicit aim—to "laude" or praise both the Virgin and her equally virginal offspring, "the white lylye flour [lily flower]," Jesus (VII.460–61)—in a narrative whose account of Jewish danger urged England's ongoing national rejection of Jews.

Naylor challenges the politics of Chaucerian representation by resituating elements of the *Prioress's Tale* within an alternate discursive order that rejects white hegemonic norms. A key component of the demonization of Jews in the *Prioress's* performance is its opposition of Christian virginity, purity, and innocence to Jewish carnality, filth, and conspiracy. Contesting that discourse as it appears in the Prioress's portrait, prologue, and tale, Naylor generates in "Mood: Indigo" a new narrative and an alternate structurality that center not on white virginity and Jewish danger but rather on the rich and complex humanity of a Black female character. While the Prioress demonizes the medieval Jewish minority in Europe in her Marian tale, Naylor seizes and repurposes that text to "laude" the wondrous humanity of the aged and alcoholic "whore," Sadie.

Naylor resignifies Chaucer, in effect, to contribute to what she describes, in her one work of literary criticism, as the "unique history and experience" portrayed by Black women writers. The essay, "Love and Sex in the Afro-American Novel," which appeared the year after Naylor's Cornell fellowship, describes how, in a racist U.S., "survival meant that black men and women had to define their roles differently" from white supremacist norms. Thus, in the case of Harriet Jacobs's narrative, white ideas of propriety prove inappropriate; as an enslaved person Jacobs "existed within a different set of moral parameters. And it was within those boundaries that she carved a path of dignity for herself."[78] Naylor similarly imbues Sadie with dignity by repurposing in her narrative representations of Christian refinement and wonder in the *Prioress's Tale*.

Sadie's biography is related by "Bailey," the anonymous host figure known only by the appellation cafe customers mistakenly attribute to him. "Bailey" frames Sadie's life story with scenes set in the otherworldly space of the cafe. A kind of haven for customers on the brink of self-annihilation, the cafe provides a setting where its patrons' human potential and dignity shine forth as they cannot in the outside world. As Maxine Montgomery puts it, the cafe constitutes "an alternate reality" of liberation and transcendence, "where established social hierarchies . . . lose all validity."[79] In the case of Sadie, the cafe stages her enactment of a sacral humanity that belies received ideas of the value of an elderly alcoholic and sex worker.

"Bailey" introduces Sadie as a "lady" whose manners are so refined and dignified that she is "the only customer" whom his wife, Nadine ("Deenie"), "ever served twice in a row":

> It was more than Deenie liking to hear the way she asked [for tea, saying "please"]; it was her bringing the mug and Sadie's fine-boned right hand wrapping itself around the handle with the left one taking the napkin and spoon from her. And somehow, by the time Sadie had made the distance from Deenie's tray to the table, the thick mug had lost its cracks and stains, hitting the tabletop with the ring of china, while the bent tin spoon and paper napkin became monogrammed silver and linen. Kind of an amazing thing to watch. (39–40)

Sadie, as "Bailey" immediately makes clear, is no epitome of aristocratic poise. More often than not, we learn, her alcoholic shakes cause nearly all the tea in her cup to spill. But Naylor also locates a refined beauty, elegance, and grace within the aged woman. In the space of the cafe, we see how a "twenty-five-cent whore" carries within her abilities that exceed those of Chaucer's highest-ranking female pilgrim. Chaucer portrays the Prioress as striving for an aristocratic identity she can't quite achieve: her portrait stresses how the nun "peyned hire to countrefete cheere / Of court" (took pains to imitate the manners of the court; I.139–40), a desire that involves her anxious wiping of her mouth "whan she dronken hadde hir draughte" (when she had drunk her drink, I.135) from "hir coppe" or cup (I.134). While the Prioress's manners are unsatisfactory, Sadie's are nothing less than miraculous. When grasped by Sadie, an old mug becomes "china" and a "bent tin spoon and paper napkin [become] monogrammed silver and linen." While the Prioress decidedly lacks savoir faire—her manners are too forced, too pained—Sadie's manners are elegant and transformative.

Sadie's magical way with a cup engages another element of Chaucer's Prioress: the miraculous and sacred qualities that the nun embraces in her tale. "Hitting the tabletop with the *ring* of china," Sadie's revitalized cup refigures the miracle at the core of the *Prioress's Tale*, in which the Virgin Mary restores a kind of life to the schoolboy whom the Jews of the tale have murdered, allowing the child to resume his Marian hymn "So loude that al the place gan to *rynge*" (So loudly that the entire place began to *ring*, VII.613, my emphasis). While the *Prioress's Tale* highlights the Virgin Mary's ability to overcome an imagined Jewish danger, Naylor seizes and redirects multiple linguistic components of Chaucer's antisemitic program to combat oppressive white stereotypes of the Black woman. The indigent Black sex worker takes on *both* the wondrous abilities linked to the Virgin Mary (she revivifies old and broken tableware) *and* the musical traits aligned with the schoolboy (the "ring" of the china).

After revealing Sadie's wondrously transformative powers in the magical realist space of a cafe "at the edge of the world," Naylor turns to how that white world has prevented the marvelous potential in Sadie from flourishing. As "Bailey" turns to Sadie's heart-wrenching biography, Naylor concentrates attention on her protagonist's childhood development in a manner that resonates with Spillers's work on Black family dynamics. In particular, young Sadie and her mother exemplify how, as Spillers argues, a white supremacist U.S. exiles Black Americans from the western patriarchal symbolic order and the nuclear family with which it is associated. Naylor indicates the role of the state in estranging Sadie's mother—a sex worker—from her, explaining how "mama had just about lost most of her mind" as a result of "four years' worth of drinking pure absinthe when enough corpses hadn't yet piled up on skid row for the government to outlaw the stuff" (42). Governmental neglect contributes to a maternal state of unfreedom that, in turn, puts Sadie into a linguistic, familial, and social crisis. Sadie is so alienated from the symbolic as to not even know her name:

> Sadie heard it so much from her mama that she thought it was her name when she was little: The One the Coat Hanger Missed. Not that the woman ever spoke to her, or hardly ever looked at her, unless she was drinking—and then only to curse her for the daddy's face she wore. But she'd hear it when one of the men her mother brought home for the night would ask about the sleepy child. (42)

This passage revises aspects of the Prioress's schoolboy to represent a host of interlocking oppressions endured by Sadie and her mother. Like the Christian youth, Sadie learns by overhearing. The "litel clergeon" (little schoolboy, VII.503) learned the Marian song he sings in the Jewry by eavesdropping on older children who perform it in a separate classroom at his school. And, like the schoolboy again, Sadie's "education" entails a kind of ignorance. Chaucer's child doesn't understand Latin and thus can't comprehend the words of the hymn, which he memorizes "by rote" (VII.545). But the Prioress ties the boy's ignorance to a youthful innocence the nun prizes. Moreover, the medieval youth has at least some knowledge: he knows that the song concerns the Virgin, about whom his loving mother has instructed him. Sadie's ignorance proves far more extensive and problematic, in ways that bespeak her relation to the horrific child abuse that occurs under the auspices of the white U.S. state.

Sadie's relationship to her parent, to language, and to education is so impaired and fraught that she initially reads as a signifier of herself—that is, the name that situates her within the social order—a phrase that in actuality signals her societal rejection. The One the Coat Hanger Missed, the phrase that the mother uses to refer to Sadie, represents the girl as the unintended outcome of a botched abortion, and thus an object of complete and utter parental rejection. In keeping with Sadie's non-identity as a child whom her mother never intended to bring into the world, the mother deprives the girl of the most basic form of nurturance and familial relation—that is, teaching Sadie her name.

Those deprivations bring forth judgment not on the mother but rather on what Saidiya Hartman calls the "afterlife of slavery" in a U.S. context where unfreedom intertwines with illiteracy.[80] As Robert Stepto affirms in his foundational book *From Behind the Veil*, "The primary pre-generic myth for Afro-America is the quest for freedom and literacy."[81] Naylor foregrounds that dynamic in her *Yale Review* essay. Noting how "eighteenth-century poets" such as Phillis Wheatley "were representative of a people for whom literacy was not just denied but illegal," she stresses:

> I think it is important that we stop a moment and reflect on exactly what this meant.... The laws decreed that there was no place in this society for blacks who could read and write, or who wanted to teach their children to read and write. To attain literacy, then, was actually to attain "being" within the social fabric, and that was an illegal existence until the abolition of slavery.[82]

In the story of Sadie, Naylor develops her critical assessment of the alignment of subjectivity and literacy for Black persons in the U.S. "Mood: Indigo" tracks the ongoing systemic challenges preventing a Black woman from, as Naylor puts it in "Love and Sex," "wresting literacy and [her] very being out of" a white supremacist U.S. society.[83]

At the age of four, Sadie finally learns her name via an excruciating episode that only exacerbates her fraught relation to language and being:

> It took [Sadie] until she was about four years old to ask, Mama, do I have a name? And she learned it was Sadie, because that's what the woman kept screaming each time she brought the leather strap down on her back, shoulders, head—Yes, Sadie. Sadie. (42)

Beating also figures in Chaucer's narrative, where the medieval poet similarly binds violence and childhood education: the boy so loves Mary that he memorizes the Marian song, even though he might be "shent" or beaten for neglecting his official schoolwork (VII.541). The threat of whipping in the *Prioress's*

Tale is realized by Naylor in a horrible scene of domestic pedagogy. The four-year-old girl is literally beaten into a symbolic order as the mother "brought the leather strap down on her back, shoulders, head" while finally imparting knowledge to the child of that most basic and crucial of signifiers, her name.[84] Chaucer's text opposes the violence threatened at the boy's school to the loving maternal lessons imparted at the child's home. Naylor resignifies Chaucer's tale of mother-child love and harsh institutional pedagogy to showcase the pedagogic and parental deficiencies Sadie endures. While in Chaucer's text the boy's literal mother teaches him to love Mother Mary, inspiring him to memorize a hymn to the virgin, an act that in turn prompts Mary's "rescue" of the child, Naylor represents Sadie's traumatic entry into language via maternal violence.

This foundational episode in Sadie's biography teaches her not only the name that refers to her sad identity but also a larger self-canceling lesson: that she must be "very good" (44). Naylor's deployment of the phrase "very good" inverts the piety hailed by the Prioress. The boy signifies his love of the Virgin by loudly singing her song through the Jewry. While the boy's piety thus involves making his presence felt through a Christian refrain, Sadie's "good" behavior means striving for the impossible phenomenological goal of somehow existing and learning "how not to be there," thus accommodating her mother's desire to be childless (51):

> The child discovered ways to make absolutely no noise. Sadie became so good at being quiet in the morning, the woman would have to clear her bleary eyes and open the shutters to find her: under the shelves of the cupboard, a soda cracker softening in her mouth before she dared to chew it; in the middle of her pallet, legs clenched tightly together to hold back her full bladder since a creaky floorboard separated her from the chamber pot. (43)

Naylor conflates and reorganizes key elements of the *Prioress's Tale* to highlight Sadie's abject (non)existence and unfreedom. In Chaucer's text, mobility—what L. O. Aranye Fradenburg describes as "a desire for easy passage"—everywhere informs the portrayal of the youth.[85] Thanks to Mary's miracle, even after the boy's murder and sequestration in the latrine, sound flows out of his throat, allowing for the corpse's discovery and movement, via a procession, to a church. In stark contrast, Sadie's existence is marked by difficult blockages.[86] The basic passages of human survival (movements that even the Jews of the tale possess, with their utilization of the latrine) prove hard for Sadie, as eating and urinating pose marked challenges. The particulars of Naylor's imagery—the saltine on the tongue, her entombment in the cupboard, the clenched bladder, the mother's effort to locate Sadie each morning—brilliantly revise multiple details of Chaucer's narrative. In particular, and in one of Naylor's most inspired responses to Chaucer, the "soda cracker softening in her mouth" engages the "greyn" or grain placed by the Virgin Mary on the dead schoolboy's tongue, but to a very different end. While the grain revives the boy and enables him to resume his Marian song with a bold abandon that fills the Jewry with sound, the cracker dissolving in Sadie's mouth allows her to maintain a radical silence and effectively function as an absent presence in the boardinghouse room. In Chaucer's narrative, the Marian hymn catalyzed by the grain is a function of the tremendous mother love ascribed to Mary. In Naylor's text, the soundlessness perpetuated by the melting cracker reflects the lack of parental affection in Sadie's world.

After describing Sadie's childhood, "Bailey" chronicles the rest of her biography and its multiple and intersecting oppressions. Those traumas include her mother forcing Sadie into prostitution at the age of thirteen, sterilization a year later from a backroom abortion, marriage to an alcoholic veteran, widowhood, alcoholism, indigence, homelessness, and, finally, a return to prostitution to pay for the wine that numbs her pain. Throughout all those many episodes of her life, thanks to her early childhood traumas, Sadie has remained frozen in the subject formation of an abused four-year-old little girl. As her friend Iceman Jones says, Sadie has the "eyes of a four-year-old dreaming to survive" (70). Naylor's emphasis on Sadie's stunted growth reframes the *Prioress's Tale* and its teller's abiding investment in childlike and undeveloped subjectivities. In her prologue, the nun praises infants and compares herself to a pre-verbal baby; the nun's tale reduces the usual age of the schoolboy to seven, highlights the rote nature of his learning, and celebrates how his early martyrdom fixes him in a state of virginal innocence and purity. Naylor repurposes those components of Chaucer's text to radically contest long-standing stereotypes about the licentiousness of Black women. As a sex worker who is also very much a child, Sadie renders wildly inappropriate any effort to fix her within racist ideas of Black female sexuality. At the same time, Jones's reference to Sadie's "dreaming to survive" in and through her stunted subjecthood registers Black female resilience, ambition, and courage.

"Mood: Indigo" concludes by returning to the frame of the cafe and Sadie's miraculous and sacral humanity. There, Iceman Jones takes Sadie "through the sights and sounds and smells of his day, amusing her as you would a child," and coaxes out of her a sound long denied her: laughter (73). Sadie's laughter reprises and expands on the beautiful sound first associated with her skill at courtesy. Alike and yet more wondrous than the "ring of china" made by her transformed mug of tea when it "hit the tabletop," Sadie's "laughter was like music. And the whole cafe stood still. In the presence of something that beautiful and rare, you're afraid to move, afraid to even breathe" (73). By the time the reader witnesses this scene, "Bailey" has described the many abuses that have horribly injured, stunted, and silenced Sadie. Sadie's laughter is thus all the more poignant, all the more wrenching, than the "ring" made by her mug-turned-china, because it reminds the reader of the marvelous possibilities squelched over the course of her life. Sadie's laughter particularly highlights what might have been during her childhood, if she had spent it in a stable and loving home; the "beautiful and rare" sound starkly contrasts the silent terror in which she cowered under the cupboard of a boardinghouse room.

Naylor has described how the end of "Mood: Indigo" "transliterat[es] what you hear the saxophone and the piano keys doing at the end of" Ellington's song: "It's a call and response between the two instruments and they never quite make it. You know, you leave that piece of music feeling every sort of lack, every sort of 'might have been' imaginable."[87] At the same time that Naylor's ending offers a textual version of the open-ended "ending" of Ellington's song, it also reframes the close of the *Prioress's Tale*. The diner's breathless reverence for Sadie resignifies the response of the pilgrims to the *Prioress's Tale*: "whan seyd was al this miracle, every man,/As sobre was that wonder was to se" (When all of this miracle tale was said, every man was so sober that it was wondrous to witness, VII.691–92). The "silent sobriety" of the pilgrims suggests their identification with the antisemitic terms of the tale, whose manifold representations of Christian praise all depend on fantasies about "cursed Jews."[88] If the *Prioress's Tale* occludes the rich humanity of Jews and produces them as carnal, cursed, and murderous others, the critique in "Mood: Indigo" of this viciously dehumanizing discourse culminates in the awe accorded Sadie. The sacral lyricism within Sadie recalls the Jewish sacral humanity denied both in the historical anti-Jewish attacks enacted and antisemitic tales written by medieval Christians. By making Sadie an object of wonder and awe, Naylor saturates the reader with regret and sorrow over the possibilities foreclosed in both contemporary U.S. society and Chaucer's medieval Christian world.

Patriarchy and Racial Capitalism in "Miss Maple's Blues"

If "Mood: Indigo" illustrates the miraculous potential of a woman born into "every sort of lack . . . imaginable," Naylor's final narrative, "Miss Maple's Blues," represents a notably different Black subjectivity and the advantages, however circumscribed, that accrue to it. "Miss Maple's Blues" centers on the sole male protagonist of the "seven songs" told in *Bailey's*, a man whose given name is Stanley, but who assumes the moniker "Miss Maple" after he enters the environs of the cafe. Naylor's shift to a male character enables a complex commentary on Black gender politics that resonates with her lament, in a 1991 letter, that in the U.S., "Black women are nothing. Black men are a little more than nothing."[89] Naylor's comment about the denigration of Black men and women in the U.S.—made in her letter with respect to the 1991 Clarence Thomas–Anita Hill hearings—registers the fact that while Black men (like Justice Thomas) might occupy a higher rung on the social ladder than women, racism radically qualifies those gendered privileges. The "elevation" enjoyed by Black men under patriarchy only renders them "little more" than the "nothing"-ness of Black women. Stanley/Maple's tale exemplifies this dynamic. On one hand, Stanley/Maple possesses far more agency and privilege than Naylor's female characters. On the other hand, for all its benefits, masculinity alone fails to counteract the racism that bars Stanley from the privileges accorded white men in the U.S., a dismaying fact that ultimately leads him to the brink of suicide.

"Miss Maple's Blues" foregrounds the advantages enjoyed by Stanley. In a complete reversal of Sadie's upbringing, Stanley is raised by a doting father in Southern California on a family-run, three thousand–acre Pima cotton farm, where he is largely isolated from mainstream U.S. racism.[90] Epitomizing the difference between Stanley's and Sadie's childhoods are their names. The delayed acquisition of her name, its connection to beatings by her mother, and even the word "sad" that it encloses all bespeak Sadie's status as an unwanted child deprived of any form of parental investment and love. In stark contrast, Stanley's father, a literary man who shares the Wife of Bath's fondness for fine fashion, lavishes his son with, as Vernon puts it, "a superabundance of male names"—Stanley "Beckwourth Booker T. Washington Carver"—that reflect the father's attachment to his progeny as the latest in a long and distinguished line of Black male achievers.[91] Poverty, misogyny, racism, and other oppressions force Sadie's mother to reject her child as "The One the Coat Hanger Missed," a human never meant to exist. Stanley's father, who lives at a remove from white supremacy at the family cotton farm, welcomes his son into a world where he believes the boy's greatness will manifest itself in a manner not unlike the achievements of the many-sided Renaissance men of Jacob Burckhardt's *Civilization*, discussed in Chapters 1 and 2. As Stanley avers, "Papa named me after great men because he expected the same from me" (165).

Naylor folds Chaucer into the father's masculinism by rendering it literary historical. The father amasses a highly curated and utterly patriarchal library. Stanley explains: "Aesop. Aristotle. Aurelius. He kept them in alphabetical order. He'd read almost everything but only chose to bind certain ones. Dante. Donne. Du Bois. Dunbar. I'm leaving you a legacy, he'd say, *a carefully* chosen legacy" (174, emphasis in original).[92] That list of books connotes a notably male western literary line that situates twentieth-century Black authors W. E. B. Du Bois and Paul Laurence Dunbar as the heirs of earlier white writers Dante and John Donne, even as it reverses that inheritance by situating Aesop—a slave said to have been a dark-skinned Ethiopian—at the (alphabetical as well as temporal) start of the line.[93] Chaucer isn't mentioned in this sampling, as it cites the A's and the D's in the father's orderly library, but the implication is that the medieval poet is there, perhaps just ahead of (Countee) Cullen. Implicit as well in the father's library is the idea that gender can supersede race— that is, that great Black men share with great white men a capacity for fine literary achievement. As the father later puts it when Stanley prepares to leave home and attend Stanford University, *"There is no greater love than reaching beyond the boundaries to other men. There is no greater wealth than possessing true peace of mind. When my son left me to go out on his own, I wanted to give him the vision of such a brave new world"* (186, emphasis in original). Fully identified with western European conceptions of the enlightened self, modernity, and progress, the father exalts a community of great male thinkers to which he and his son belong.[94]

Stanley's father's sexism and its literary thrust reiterates the patriarchal linguistics embraced by Stanley's grandfather. The cofounder of the massive family farm where Stanley is raised, his Black grandfather married a Yuma woman who spoke only "some Spanish and her native tongue, Cuchan" (167). "My grandfather," Stanley explains, "set about teaching her the most important phrases in English: *I am the man. You—woman*" (167, emphasis original). The gendered terms of the grandfather's language lesson echo those of both structural linguistics and Chaucer's narrative, as analyzed by Fineman. Fineman demonstrates how the first lines of the *General Prologue* affirm Jakobson's theory regarding the gendered foundation of language acquisition. Following the reasoning of Jakobson and Moris Halle in *Fundamentals of Language* (1956), Fineman describes how Chaucer, in initiating his massive work with an assertion of "the primacy of male April to female March," echoes how the masculine "contrast of consonant and vowel" /pa/ is "the first utterance children learn" and the feminine /ma/ is the sound involved in the second binary a child voices, through which the child is removed forever from the "pure diacriticality" of /pa/ and is launched into a symbolic order.[95] Stanley's grandfather similarly introduces his spouse to the English language via that gendered binary opposition.

But what the sexist men of Stanley's family fail to recognize, and Naylor goes on to reveal, is the fact that western discourse isn't merely sexist but also racist. When Stanley leaves the confines of the quasi-utopian space of the family farm to attend Stanford University, the West Coast equivalent of Ivies like Yale and Cornell, he discovers just how mistaken his father is in believing in a *"brave new world"* of male bonding. Regardless of his many advantages—gender, education, financial—over a figure such as Sadie, Stanley is hardly immune from racism.

Significantly, the prejudice Stanley encounters is linguistic. As he puts it, "Unless I could sit for exams where my use of a given language wasn't open to question, I wouldn't get decent grades" (187). The neutral discipline of math gave Stanley access to A's. But because his "English-literature and philosophy papers were always open as to interpretation, execution of style, compelling ideas," they left him vulnerable to forms of racist gatekeeping (187). In an example that recalls Stuart Hall's encounter with Tolkien, Maple describes the reception of a paper on *Beowulf*:

> My professors never seemed to find the same degree of depth, the same innate understanding, in my treatments of *Beowulf* as they did my peers'. They'd look me straight in the face and say there was something they just couldn't put their finger on—something crude, something lacking in my essays. (187)

In an uncanny echo of the Oxford don's resistance to his Jamaican student's plan of medieval study, the Stanford medievalist endorses a white idea of literary heritage that rejects the transracial literary history embraced by Stanley's father. The father's library reflects his belief that all "great men," regardless of race, partake in a grand literary brotherhood. But Stanley's white professor views his Black student as incapable of Old English literary analysis. Staring Stanley "straight in the face"—visualizing, in other words, his Blackness—the Stanford medievalist constructs his student in terms of racist western binaries that align Blackness with crudeness and insufficiency, violently barring a Black man from interpreting medieval English literary works.

Naylor's portrayal of white racism at Stanford entails not just essentialist ideas of heritage but also an essentializing modernity whose dynamics speak to her own encounters with theory at Yale and Cornell. Stanley describes how he "volunteered as the test subject" for an "experiment" about racism and pedagogy on campus:

> I had a paper due in my theory class, and a group of us sat up all weekend reworking Kant's *Critique of Pure Reason* into contemporary English. We literally stole every one of his concepts and put my name on top of the page. I knew I was risking expulsion, but I took the gamble. I shouldn't have worried; it was the same D. The professor even

took me aside after class to suggest that I attempt another major; please, don't misunderstand; he had agonized greatly over this inevitable conversation, but I just didn't have the necessary equipment for tackling erudite thought. (187)

Naylor's choice to have Stanley study Immanuel Kant allows for a wide-ranging critique of white modernity. While Naylor can't depict Stanley studying Derrida and deconstruction because he attends Stanford during the 1930s, Kant is the closest historical equivalent to contemporary theory. Both the German philosopher's merging of rationalism with skepticism and his revolutionary stress on consciousness in works such as his *Critique of Pure Reason* (1781), in many ways served as the starting point for Derrida's work.[96] Insofar as Kant serves as a kind of stand-in for contemporary post-structuralism, Stanley's plagiarized paper allows Naylor to comment on the gender dynamics of the charged debates about theory, between intellectuals like Christian, Joyce, and Gates, that were taking place during the composition of *Bailey's*. At the time, the primary defenders of theory were men like Gates or Houston Baker; but Naylor here indicates a white resistance to male Black theorists that may reflect the racism that Black male post-structuralists experienced.[97]

In his paper, Stanley delivers verbatim Kant's ideas. In other words, the white professor receives from his student not Stanley's own work but that of Kant, the inaugurator of modern philosophy and theory, and thus a figure who epitomizes white mental prowess. But, ironically, the white professor—in a class centered on reasoning, and while reading a paper iterating Kant's exceptional thought—clings, irrationally, to racist stereotypes about a deficient Black mind. The reception of Stanley's paper demonstrates how racism not only blocks Black men from avenues of advancement in U.S. society but also blinds white racists—in the manner of Du Bois's veil—from anything approaching a rational or clear-sighted assessment. Stanley's repackaging of Kant registers how the ostensible alignment of white academia with modernity, in the form of the cultivation of the mind and powers of reason, is undermined by an irrational racism.

The other side of the coin in this episode pertains to Kant's racism. As philosopher Charles Mills has shown, Kant's theory of the social contract is mutually constitutive with a racial contract. Kant's famed "egalitarianism"—central to his *Critique of Pure Reason*—is premised on the subhuman status of Black persons and Indigenous people and served as a crucial tool for slavery and colonization.[98] Viewed in light of Kant's white supremacy, the ironies and contradictions involved in the Stanford professor's rejection of Stanley's work intensify. For the professor rejects the very philosophical concepts that contribute to his racism and thus render his actions all the more nonsensical. The white professor's stupidity—like Kant's racism—undermines the German philosopher's claims about the superior rationality and full humanity of whites.

With their adherence to racist stereotypes, the Stanford faculty present an elite academic version of the irrational white aggression represented in perhaps the most memorable scene in both "Miss Maple's Blues" and indeed *Bailey's* overall. This episode takes place shortly before Stanley heads to Stanford, when he and his father are attacked by two "illiterate buffoons," the Gatlin brothers (176).[99] "Dickless wonders" whom even the local members of the KKK can barely tolerate, the Gatlins are outraged at how "this country was going to the frigging dogs," because "Real Americans, like them" are poor and Stanley's family are wealthy (176). The Gatlin boys' resentment boils over when they witness Stanley and his father picking up three crates containing the father's deeply literary and patriarchal graduation gift for Stanley, a deluxe thirty-eight-volume set of Shakespeare's complete works. The vision of Stanley and his well-dressed dad collecting the crates—aided, no less, by an appreciative white clerk—prompts the Gatlins to launch an attack in which Stanley and his father eventually overcome their aggressors. First, the Gatlins violently strip the two Black men and lock them in a storage room at the shipping office. Then Stanley and his father hear

> a thud as something was kicked under the door. We smelled it before we saw it. They had gotten to the books. The silk cover was gouged with holes, the spine busted and bent over double. They'd torn out handfuls of pages, crushed what was left between their fists, and then urinated on the whole thing. The stench of *The Tempest* was quickly filling that close room. (183)

By portraying the Gatlins having "torn out handfuls of pages" from books, Naylor cites and revises the central episode of the Wife of Bath's prologue. There, Alisoun's rage over her husband Jankin's nightly readings from his misogynistic *Book of Wicked Wives* leads her to "plight" or tear three pages "out of his book" (VII.790–91). In Chaucer, this charged episode stages a violent if unsuccessful resistance to a patriarchal structurality from which there is no escape or alternative for his female character. When Alisoun physically rips leaves from Jankin's book, she only affirms patriarchal binary oppositions, specifically woman's association with a literal-mindedness and materiality that contrast man's "higher" rationality and spirituality.[100]

Through her citation of Shakespeare, Naylor transforms a Chaucerian scene that foregrounds medieval misogyny into one that showcases modern racism. While in Chaucer's text, a white woman attacks her white husband's misogynistic treatise, in Naylor's text white men attack a Black man's copy of the Bard's colonialist text, *The Tempest*. Naylor's resignification of Chaucer succeeds in performing far more oppositional work than the resistance toward which the Wife can only gesture. While Alisoun ultimately affirms western gendered dualisms, the Gatlins unwittingly undermine the racist idea of white American belonging to which they ascribe. Like the faculty at Stanford, the Gatlins embrace a fantasy of white supremacy and Black inadequacy that their own actions contradict. In the same way that the Stanford professor stupidly rejects Kant's thought, the Gatlins ignorantly destroy a text by a man at the heart of the white western canon. Indeed, the work they use as a urinal—*The Tempest*—like Kant's philosophy, plays a foundational role in racist thinking. *The Tempest* is, of all Shakespeare's works, that which most underwrites the Gatlins' racist thinking, with its depiction of the white European colonist Prospero wisely calling the shots on an island populated by primitives like Caliban.

The name Naylor gives the brothers—"Gatlin"—enriches Naylor's commentary on whiteness and its contradictions. Gatlin suggests the Gatling gun, the iconic technology that epitomizes the lethal effects of modernity, especially for the many non-western and Indigenous populations slaughtered by whites wielding the machine gun. The Gatlin brothers' scene also puts Naylor into conversation with white American medievalisms such as Mark Twain's *A Connecticut Yankee in King Arthur's Court* (1889), where Hank Morgan's introduction of the Gatling gun to medieval England enables the genocide of Arthurian Britain. The Gatlins' destructive actions highlight, in farcical form, both the significance of the Gatling gun as an icon of modern mass destruction and its ties to racist colonial programs.[101]

With its portrayal of a continuum of racist idiocy ranging from the ignorant Gatlin boys to Stanford professors, "Miss Maple's Blues" emphasizes the depressing omnipresence of an irrational and damaging whiteness in U.S. society. That pessimistic view culminates in an event that puts Stanley on the brink of suicide. At Stanford, Stanley circumvents the biases of white discourse by majoring in math, since his facility with numbers can't be suppressed or ignored in the manner of any achievements realized via the English language. Determined to forge his way in the world outside the confines of his family's farm, Stanley travels the country in search of a marketing job. One firm after another rejects him despite his superlative qualifications and talent. The inability of white employers to reckon with the depth and complexity of a Black man persists even when, at his ninety-ninth interview, Stanley finally encounters a company willing to hire him. His interviewer, "the head of domestic marketing," tells Stanley that he "just bet that" Stanley thought that "he wouldn't be able to look past the fact that I was a Negro" (205–6). But as the very phrasing of that comment indicates, with its reference to "the fact" of Stanley's Blackness, the company is aligned with an oppressive whiteness and hires him only as a token, an empty signifier of the progressiveness of a company entrenched in racism.

Naylor represents the oppressive white culture of the company in a scene that resignifies elements of the *Prioress's Tale*. The episode involves Stanley having lunch with the white marketing head and the "second in command at layout and design," who turns out to be the only other Black employee at the company (207). While all three men order, at the white employer's insistence, lobster thermidor in the executive dining room, Stanley witnesses the harsh psychic impact of tokenism on the Black employee:

> The waiter brought our lobsters and a paper bib for each of us. Tie 'em right, said domestic marketing; this stuff is good but it can get pretty messy. Second in command tied his so that the strings dug into his neck. I wondered how he was going to swallow with it so tight. But he took very small bites. . . . My bib was getting splattered and domestic marketing's even more so. . . . But it was the paper bib of the second in command that intrigued me the most; it was remaining perfectly spotless. . . . I was woozy from the rich food and alcohol and probably wouldn't have noticed it if it hadn't been my focal point during the meal, but after the dishes were removed and the third round of martinis arrived, the second in command folded his paper bib into a perfect square in front of him and began shredding it into tiny pieces. . . . The piles of shredded paper were growing in front of his hands. Tiny tiny tiny pieces. He did it without ever looking down. He did it by rote. (208–10)

The Black man's fastidious attention to table manners—his "very small bites" of food and his "perfectly spotless" bib—recall the Prioress and Sadie. In the same way that Sadie uses etiquette to maintain her dignity despite a slew of challenges, the second in command responds to racial capitalism via table manners. By returning the reader to Sadie's tale and the Prioress, Naylor clarifies how well-educated Black male strivers like Stanley and the second in command, for all their seeming advantages over less privileged Black women, aren't immune from white supremacy. Through the second in command's paradoxical actions—first preserving the pristine purity of the paper bib and then shredding it into "tiny tiny tiny pieces"—Naylor refigures elements of the *Prioress's Tale* to elucidate the fraught positioning of Black men in a white supremacist world. The Black man's constriction and discomfort—his bib so tight as to strangle (recalling the schoolboy's severed throat), his ingestion stifled to maintain a pristine demeanor (like Sadie with the cracker)—contrasts with ease of the white employer. Affirming the white orientation of the company, the white man digs into his food without hesitation; he readily dons a bib, so comfortable in his white masculinity as to be immune from its infantilizing valence.

When Naylor goes on to depict the second in command tearing that bib to shreds, she creates a rich image whose multiple meanings repurpose Chaucer's Prioress and Wife of Bath. While the tearing of the bib perhaps suggests a repetition compulsion through which the man manages his tension in a racist workplace, it also might showcase his deep disdain for his company as he destroys a flimsy paper symbol of his coworkers' white privilege. Not unlike the Wife of Bath's violence against Jankin's book, the symbolic destruction of whiteness by the second in command is a far cry from any effort to significantly reform, let alone revolutionize, his oppressive social circumstances. Naylor emphasizes just how depressingly ineffective the bib tearing is by having Stanley, in a revision of the Prioress's little schoolboy's mode of learning, state that the Black man does it "by rote." In Chaucer's text, the boy's rote memorization of a Marian anthem comprises part of the Prioress's overall celebration of an ignorant, childlike, and undeveloped Christianity. A stupid and youthful faith accrues a kind of antisemitic power in the *Prioress's Tale,* where the child's unthinking song resounds through the Jewry, even after his murder. Naylor resignifies "rote" to represent the powerlessness of the second in command. The repetition involved in rote memorization speaks to the ongoing and futile nature of the Black man's position in the company. Management has trotted him out for a lobster luncheon many times before; when the three sit down to order, he "never bothered to open his menu" (208). No substantial changes—no improved conditions—take place in the white workplace. Trapped always as a token employee, the second in command can only resist whiteness at a symbolic level, through the shredded bib.

Stanley recognizes in the second in command's actions the futility of his own capitalist strivings. He leaves the company and seeks out a second-hand gun, with the intention of killing himself. Stanley's suicidality offers perhaps the lowest, most blues-like moment in Naylor's novel. His quest for a firearm reveals how U.S. whiteness produces despair even within a Black person armed with the all the advantages of gender, wealth, class, education, and parental attention. Naylor, however, concludes "Miss Maple's Blues" by radically reversing its ever-despondent emotional momentum. For Stanley is directed away from self-destruction and toward the cafe, where he receives a new name—Miss Maple—and discovers the means to realize his potential and overcome the white blockages he encountered in the U.S. Indeed, it is through the figure of

Miss Maple that Naylor's contestation of the oppressive western binaries at play in the *Canterbury Tales* triumphantly culminates.

Naylor's (Open) Ending and Chaucer's (Closed) Opening

Upon entering the environs of the cafe, Stanley encounters Eve, who renames him Miss Maple and employs him as a housekeeper and sometime bouncer for her bordello-cum-shelter. Eve also gives him the idea of putting his marketing acumen to work by entering jingles in household cleaning supply company ad contests, a plan that marvelously succeeds. But still more remarkably, Miss Maple, far more than any other character in the novel, takes on an identity that resists the western discursive systems of the *Canterbury Tales*, Shakespeare's oeuvre, Kant's thought, and other white texts. Consider how Maple deconstructs white discourse through his troubling of dualities of purity vs. danger, male vs. female, master vs. slave, and virgin vs. whore. Maple is a heterosexual man who shifts in and out of transvestitism depending on the season. Signifying on the facility with "clooth-makyng" or clothmaking highlighted in the Wife's portrait (I.447), Maple "can wear any piece of cloth on his own terms"; he wears "pants and a jacket" in the winter and usually dons "light percale housedresses" in the warmer months (213, 163). Maple is surrounded by women at the contradictory site of Eve's establishment, a "whorehouse convent" (116).[102] There, he works "for free," yet is also "one of the freest men" "Bailey" knows (216).[103]

As Naylor's most destabilizing character, it is fitting that Miss Maple features in the most effective contestation of Chaucer in the novel, the scene of male-male bonding that concludes "Miss Maple's Blues." The date is New Year's Eve, 1949, and the speaker is "Bailey," who describes how Miss Maple

> Takes his full champagne glass to the rear of the cafe. As I watch from the doorway, he steps off boldly into the midst of nothing and is suspended midair by a gentle wind that starts to swirl his cape around his knees. It's a hot, dry wind that could easily have been born in a desert, but it's bringing, of all things, snow. Soft and silent it falls, coating his shoulders, his upturned face. Snow. He holds his glass up and turns to me as a single flake catches on the rim before melting down the side into an amber world where bubbles burst and are born, burst and are born.
>
> —Happy New Year, Bailey.
> —Happy New Year, Miss Maple. (216)

This tour-de-force passage engages in a dizzying destabilization of the totalizing terms of the *Canterbury Tales*. Namely, Naylor resists closure by ending "Miss

Maple's Blues" with a masterful contestation of the beginning of Chaucer's text. If the *General Prologue*, as Fineman stresses, opens by establishing the western semantic system to which the entirety of the *Canterbury Tales* conforms, Naylor concludes her narrative by shattering that white discourse through a battery of inversions and shifts.

Central to Naylor's contestation of the *General Prologue* are temporal and spatial reorientations. For example, while the *General Prologue* situates the national pilgrimage to Becket's shrine in precise seasonal terms, in springtime and, specifically, in April, Naylor sets the scene between Maple and "Bailey" in the dead of winter, on New Year's Eve. Chaucer orients his opening, predictably, in relation to the West and the winds of the classical god "Zephirus" (I.5). Naylor instead describes "a hot dry wind" that, according to medieval climatology, corresponds with the winds of the god Notus, who resided in classical Ethiopia, which during premodernity corresponded to all lands south of the Nile.[104] Naylor's citation of Notus revises received premodern thinking on the effects of the south wind. Medieval western authorities linked Notus with a brutal, scorching heat in Africa. Chaucer, in his translation of Boethius's *Consolation of Philosophy*, describes how "the vyolent wynd Nothus scorklith, and baketh the brennynge sandes by his drye heete" for "al the peples in the south" ("the violent wind Notus scorches and bakes the burning sands with his dry heat" for "all the people in the south").[105] Climate was bound closely to identity in medieval western thought, which understood Notus's scorching heat in terms of its damaging effects on not just the land but the people of Africa, rendering them black-skinned and deficient in a host of ways; in particular, heat was linked with cowardice.[106] Naylor radically reimagines the effects of the south wind. While the south wind was linked with Black insufficiency, Naylor associates it with a gorgeous image of Black culture, sophistication, and bravery. The two men toast the new year with fine Moët champagne, with a wool-cape-bedecked Maple having stepped "boldly" into the void at the back of the cafe.[107]

Naylor's post-structuralist vision both refuses easy inversions and embraces contradiction. While the dry hot wind of this scene "could easily have been born in a desert," it also brings the "snow" of winter. It is a "gentle wind" but so powerful and strong as to keep Maple aloft, "midair." The indeterminacies of this scene mark a radical departure from Chaucer's spatiotemporal specificity. The first sentence of the *General Prologue* grounds us in English soil, indeed takes us underground, inside the roots and veins of flowering plants:

Whan that Aprill with his shoures soote
The droghte of March hath perced to the roote,

And bathed every veyne in swich licour
Of which vertu engendred is the flour. (I.1–4)

(When April with its sweet-smelling showers / has pierced the dryness of March to the root, / and bathed every vein [of the plants] in such liquid / by whose power flowers are engendered.)

Naylor replaces the precision of Chaucer's setting with the geographic indeterminacy of the cafe, which has no permanent location on earth. Maple is suspended in the back of the cafe, in "the midst of nothing," in "midair." Naylor also masterfully refuses Chaucer's gender binaries and hierarchies. In keeping with the traditional medieval alignment of men with action and women with passivity, March in the *General Prologue* is a femininized vessel that is "pierced to the root" by April's masculine, penetrating, even violent showers. In contrast, Naylor binds the utopian no-place of her scene to a certain gender fluidity, in which Maple, a cross-dressing man, holds a glass—that is, a vessel and thus a symbol of womanhood akin to the roots of March. The vessel held by Maple receives a fluid, not in the phallic and violent form of April's "piercing" but rather via the gentle dissolution of a single snowflake.

And yet, in keeping with the destabilizing program of *Bailey's*, those final words through which "Bailey" describes Maple aren't so gentle after all. The image of a single white snowflake "melting . . . into an amber world where bubbles burst and are born, burst and are born" leaves us with a striking metaphor for Naylor's aggressive contestation of Chaucer and white western discourse overall. In *Bailey's*, whiteness dissolves into an "amber" and thus darker "world" that showcases a wrenching oscillation between aspiration and blockage. The bubbles that arise and fall in the "world" of the champagne glass allegorize the infinite cycle of collapsed dreams (a racial sublime) on the part of Black men and women in U.S. society and elsewhere on the globe. As if to stress the sharp turn Naylor takes in her novel away from Chaucerian and other western semiotic forms, the alliteration of this final image, with its stress on the voiced bilabial stop, /b/, suggests a turn from the entry into language toward the preverbal, to babble.[108]

Naylor's granular attention to language continues up to the final word of this final chapter: "Maple." Why have Eve rename Stanley "Miss Maple"? Clearly Naylor is citing Scott Joplin's enormously popular early rag tune. Less obvious, perhaps, is what Naylor might be doing with the language of the *Canterbury Tales*. Maple, I suggest, is a word through which Naylor resists the patriarchal structurality introduced at the start of the *General Prologue*. As we have seen, Chaucer's opposition of an active April and passive March establishes the hierarchy of the paternal /pa/ (signaled via April) over the maternal /ma/

(voiced in March). Naylor undoes that discursive system through "Maple," a word that combines and inverts April and March, along with the phonological sounds /pa/ and /ma/. A name bestowed on Stanley by a woman, Eve, "Maple" suggests a feminist rethinking of patriarchal semantics in which the feminine /ma/ enjoys primacy. Instead of simply inverting the heterosexist politics of white discourse, Naylor envisions an alternate language, an alternate semiotic relation, that is routed through the non-normative relationship between two Black persons.

Centered on the heterogeneity and significance of Black women's and men's lives, *Bailey's Cafe* is a dense, complex, and difficult work that powerfully thinks what has been unthinkable and "give[s] voice to" what has been "voiceless" within the confines of western structures of meaning.[109] Reorienting the reader from the perspective of a white man to that of Naylor, *Bailey's* portrays both the rich potential of its Black characters and the terrible damage wrought on them by a dominant white culture that looks back to Chaucer. Far from a work that presents itself as a worthy successor or homage to the *Canterbury Tales*, *Bailey's* is the locus of a fierce and closely fought literary battle between a writer at the vanguard of a new post-structuralist moment and the Chaucerian originator of a white discourse spanning the medieval and modern periods. Naylor's critique of Chaucer is searing; *Bailey's* exposes how versions of the white discourse circulating in Chaucer's text sadly continue to dominate the globe, supporting social structures that wreak havoc on the lives of Black women and men and push them to the brink of self-annihilation. In contradistinction to medievalists in search of Chaucer's happy resonance with theory, Naylor thus, as Edwards puts it, "lays bare the costs of a desire for Chaucer."[110]

Yet if Naylor opposes Chaucerian desire, she also urges Chaucerian critique. However wrenching that encounter might be, Naylor also clarifies the need to confront the feel-bad components of the medieval. That Naylor diagnoses contemporary sexism and racism through a rich and thoughtful engagement with Chaucer suggests that the *Canterbury Tales* should not be dismissed out of hand for its offensiveness. Rather, Naylor demonstrates how white western canonical texts merit attention as objects not of praise but of a reassessment that both exposes the deep roots and lasting lethal effects of modernity and affirms the vulnerability of white discourse to enabling transformation. Instead of "canceling" the father of English poetry, Naylor indicates, we should scrutinize how his white discourse works, confront its lasting effects, and look to non-western strategies of attacking, disassembling, and repurposing it for more liberating literary ends.

6
Tradition and the Individual Black Talent
Contesting Malory and Modernism in The Fisher King

> Only
> There is shadow under this red rock,
> (Come in under the shadow of this red rock).
>
> —T. S. ELIOT

> How do you really come out from "under the shadow," and I'm quoting T. S. Eliot here, "of that red rock"?
>
> —PAULE MARSHALL

> The mother-poets . . . couldn't take that society didn't even know they existed except as a form of cheap labor. And so they fought back at that verbal level.
>
> —PAULE MARSHALL

That the literary oeuvre of Paule Marshall (1929–2019) radically contests white modernity is indisputable. Celebrated by Hortense Spillers in 2003 as "one of the finest writers in the African Diaspora of the last half century," Marshall generated, via her substantial literary oeuvre, diasporic narratives that powerfully countered western ideologies of progress and liberation.[1] Reflecting how, as Paul Gilroy puts it, "the critique of modernity cannot be satisfactorily completed from within its own philosophical and political norms," Marshall reconstructs history from the transnational perspective of a woman born and raised during the 1930s and '40s in Brooklyn by Barbadian immigrants.[2] Marshall has described how by high school, she had acquired a historical consciousness: "I realized that the history taught me, the little bit of history taught me about black people, was far from the truth. I sensed that early on. Somebody was lying through their teeth to me."³ She would go on to center her literary productions on "the importance of truly confronting the past, both in personal and historical terms, and the necessity of reversing the present order."⁴ Through novels like *Brown Girl, Brownstones* (1959), *Praisesong for the Widow* (1983), and *The Chosen Place, The Timeless People* (1969), Marshall, in Simon Gikandi's words, both "disturbs the dominant version of history and culture" and "promotes an Afro-American modernism that . . . sustain[s] the tension between the persistent ancestral voice in black cultures and imposed European forms."⁵

Critics typically link Marshall's diasporic modernism to her 1969 magnum opus, *Chosen Place*. With its account of a failed U.S. effort to "develop" the fictional Caribbean community of Bournehills, *Chosen Place* is, as Gikandi puts it, "one of the monumental texts on modernization and colonial historiography in the Caribbean."⁶ As Gikandi and Spillers affirm, key to Marshall's achievement in *Chosen Place* is her doubly critical register. First, the novel exposes the colonial and racist underpinnings of a sociologist's efforts during the 1960s to bring progress to part of the "Third World." Second, even as she critiques white modernity, Marshall refuses easy answers to the problem of how a heterogeneous array of West Indian characters might conceive of themselves and their past. As Gikandi puts it, "wholeness and synthesis . . . do not come easily to Marshall or her characters" in *Chosen Place*, thanks to factors including the "historical discontinuity that surrounds them."⁷

Less recognized, however, is how Marshall articulates her critique through a figure located at the heart of high modernism: T. S. Eliot. With striking frequency in interviews, Marshall describes her own literary project in words that engage and contest *The Waste Land* (1922). For example, in a 1991 interview for *Booklist*, Marshall asks her interlocutor, "How do you really come out from 'under the shadow,' and I'm quoting T. S. Eliot here, 'of that red rock'"?⁸ Marshall would allude to that Eliot line again in no less than three more interviews.⁹ Moreover, her first novel, *Brown Girl, Brownstones*, has Clive, the suitor of Marshall's protagonist, cite that same line, when he "draw[s] her close beside him" asking Selina to "'come in under the shadow of this red rock.'"¹⁰

As those multiple references to Eliot's "red rock" indicate, Marshall, like Gloria Naylor and Stuart Hall, claimed for herself a diasporic authority to critique the white canon. Like Naylor and Hall, Marshall knew western literary history quite well. With respect to modernism, in particular, Marshall recounts in interviews her avid consumption during her teens and twenties of works by not just Eliot but other authors, including James Joyce, Thomas Hardy, Thomas Mann, and Joseph Conrad.¹¹ Crucially, for Marshall, as for Naylor, familiarity with white writers hardly meant that her writing constituted merely an addition or reaction to the western canon. Rather, the role of white modernism in Marshall's work functioned in a manner like that outlined in Hall's first publication, "Our Literary Heritage" (1953). As Chapter 4 discusses, Hall's theory of "Tradition and the Individual (West Indian) Talent" describes the diasporic writer's complex relation of familiarity, influence, and rejection vis-à-vis Eliot and other white writers.[12] Namely, Hall describes how the Black diasporic writer replaces Eliotic and related white modernists' fantasies of a unitary cultural heritage with a transnational affirmation of heterogeneity and difference. Equally pertinent to Marshall's modernism are Hall's comments on Eliot during his work on *Universities and Left Review*. During a discussion with fellow *ULR* editors about "historical tradition" and *The Waste Land*, Hall describes how "in order to know" tradition "*differently* one has to know the *Waste Land* as well. . . . this is how one builds, so that it is part of the tradition; even in the act of rejection one is rejecting something which one has known almost too intimately, which has shaped the way in which one has seen the situation."[13] Hall's account of how diasporic writers "almost too intimately" know the white texts they go on to unsettle and critique closely resonates both with Naylor's work with Chaucer in *Bailey's Cafe*, as discussed in Chapter 5, and with Marshall's Black modernist project.

While all of Marshall's works participate in her diasporic revision of the white canon, I argue that her final novel, *The Fisher King*, offers her most pointed contestation of Eliot and his unitary idea of white cultural heritage. Marshall's title might seem to suggest otherwise, with its citation of literary works tied not to modernity but to the Middle Ages and medieval grail mythology. But the grail played a pivotal role in Eliot's modernism and the image of the "red rock" in *The Waste Land* that Marshall repeatedly cites in her writings. Like the white medievalisms that Hall, as Chapter 4 discusses, would critique in so many of his publications, Eliot tied medieval lore—especially Thomas Malory's *Le Morte Darthur* (c. 1469–70)—to a consolingly organic and whole Eurocentric literary tradition. Eliot's modernist nostalgia embraced what he claimed were transcendent white cultural forms that persisted despite historical ruptures. Marshall rejects that white heritage approach to periodization on behalf of her critical vision of transnational complexity and heterogeneity. *The Fisher King* evinces Marshall's intimacy with Arthurian romance even as it affirms her diasporic authority, to cite the modernist slogan popularized by Ezra Pound, to "make it new."[14] Indeed, not only does *The Fisher King* seize elements of a white Arthurian tradition and redeploy them on behalf of her modernist diasporic project, but also the novel includes scenes of Black artistic practice that self-reflexively comment on how Marshall makes white Arthuriana her own.

This chapter specifically examines *The Fisher King* as a radical contestation of the emotional terms and white formations integral to Malory. No other medieval work has figured in white western ideologies in the manner of the *Morte*. As a romance that, from the late nineteenth century on, has functioned "without doubt" as "the central English Arthurian text" and "the default retelling of Arthurian romance in English," the *Morte* has been central to the "red rock" of western tradition that Marshall rejects.¹⁵ Malory's key role in white supremacist discourses is no surprise; as I discuss in Chapter 2, the *Morte* is a key early example of the representation of whiteness during the medieval period. Marshall, like Naylor, understood the complicity of medieval texts in subsequent racializing representations and historical practices, especially the nostalgic white fantasies espoused by Eliot. Thus, while Eliot embraces a *longue durée* of eurocentric organicism, Marshall critiques a *longue durée* of an offensive whiteness. *The Fisher King* reveals Marshall as a writer whose diasporic modernism intertwines with a diasporic medievalism. In what amounts to a major intervention on received ideas of periodization and history, *The Fisher King* resignifies the *Morte* both to critique the long tradition of chivalric whiteness that Malory's work helped inaugurate and to advocate an alternate diasporic modernity that radically breaks from western tradition.

Marshall's radical revision of Malory offers a response to his "Noble Tale of the Sankgreal [Holy Grail]" that especially contests its affective terms. Malory's grail book mourns the loss of an idealized white patriarchal community, a brotherhood whose perfection and wholeness the Round Table materializes. The nostalgic and tearful subjectivity of Arthur and his knights in the "Tale of the Sankgreal" adumbrates and supports the racial nostalgia of white men like Eliot or the U.S. Southerners who mourn their "Lost Cause." In her counternarrative, Marshall resignifies Arthurian lore to ascribe to her Black characters a fraught emotional and communal dynamic, thus shifting attention from whiteness to what Spillers describes as "the rich, moiling interior life" of a Black diasporic community.¹⁶ The Black men and women of *The Fisher King*, in keeping with Marshall's difficult modernist oeuvre, face experiences of loss, difference, and division that remain ongoing and unresolved.¹⁷ Marshall has stressed how her fiction functions as "a political act" precisely because of its "complex and truthful" vision.¹⁸ Thus *The Fisher King* rejects for Marshall's characters the white fantasies of union embraced by Malory and, later, by Eliot—representations that have never had a counterpart in lived experience—and replaces them with a more fraught and thus honest vision.¹⁹ The chapter ends by examining two meta representations of "Tradition and the Individual (Black) Talent" in Marshall's novel. Allegorizing her own creative achievement,

Marshall portrays two artists in *The Fisher King*—the Jazz "king" Sonny-Rett Payne and his grandson Sonny, a visual artist—as Black modernists who seize white European traditions and make them into new Black diasporic forms that mark a triumphant break from a history of white cultural production.

Coming out from under the Shadow of that Red Rock

Marshall's multiple references, in both interviews and her fiction, to the "red rock" of *The Waste Land* indicate her keen attunement to and critical assessment of not only high modernism but also more precisely Eliot's essentializing sense of tradition and poetic identity, particularly as they pertain to medieval Arthurian lore. Eliot's red rock functions as a figure of refuge that gathers within itself multiple western referents. In particular, the rock engages the medieval romances discussed in Jessie Weston's *Ritual to Romance* (1920). Eliot stresses in his notes to *The Waste Land* how Weston's account of "the grail legend" inspired "the plan and a good deal of the incidental symbolism of the poem."[20] The relevant passage from *The Waste Land* appears in the second stanza of its initial section, "The Burial of the Dead":

> What are the roots that clutch, what branches grow
> Out of this stony rubbish? Son of man,
> You cannot say, or guess, for you know only
> A heap of broken images, where the sun beats,
> And the dead tree gives no shelter, the cricket no relief,
> And the dry stone no sound of water. Only
> There is shadow under this red rock,
> (Come in under the shadow of this red rock),
> And I will show you something different from either
> Your shadow at morning striding behind you
> Or your shadow at evening rising to meet you;
> I will show you fear in a handful of dust.[21]

Cleanth Brooks, in an influential essay, links this passage to the description, in Wolfram von Eschenbach's *Parzival* (c. 1225), of the grail as a sheltering stone "'neath its shadow" children "wax and grow."[22] Eliot's reliance on Weston supports Brooks's assertion. *From Ritual to Romance* cites "the Stone" of Wolfram's romance as an example of the material form assumed by the grail as a sacral object with awesome "life-giving potency."[23] To be sure, the red rock, like other western symbols of safety and fertility in *The Waste Land*, exists in tension with the barren landscape of the passage and its emphasis on death, decay, and terror. But however ambivalent, at some level Eliot still views the "red rock" as an ostensible shelter, as a restorative object that one enters and inhabits and whose shadow provides protection and support.

Eliot's idea of the red rock conforms to his celebrated theory of artistic practice and literary history in "Tradition and the Individual Talent" (1919). Critiquing modern values of autonomous individualism, invention, and innovation, "Tradition" defines "great poetry" as a laborious act in which the writer channels a European literary totality:

> The historical sense involves a perception, not only of the pastness of the past, but of its presence; the historical sense compels a man to write not merely with his own generation in his bones, but with a feeling that the whole of the literature of Europe from Homer and within it the whole of the literature of his own country has a simultaneous existence and composes a simultaneous order.

If modernity understands itself as a break from old inferior ways to a superior new temporality, Eliot embraces an idea "of European, of English literature" as an eternal, simultaneous, and "whole" body of art.[24] The shelter provided by the "red rock" in *The Waste Land* entails that of an ongoing white literary tradition that encompasses English medieval grail texts like Wolfram's *Parzival*. Eliot famously rejected modernity for its alienating and destructive effects and felt nostalgic about the loss of older western folkways; but "Tradition" locates a comforting continuity in a venerable and unitary western artistic tradition. Weston's book about grail legends, Eliot's inspiration for *The Waste Land*, affirmed such a continuity. Weston understands the long history of grail lore as "a tradition common to the Aryan race in general, and persisting with extraordinary vitality, and a marked correspondence of characteristic detail, through all migrations and modifications of that race, down to the present day."[25] To that greater white aesthetic good—to "something which is more valuable" than any individual achievement—Eliot happily will engage in "a continual surrender of himself."[26]

Marshall, in *Brown Girl*, has Clive cite Eliot verbatim.[27] But, crucially, in all four of her interviews where she cites the red rock, Marshall silently alters the wording of the lines from *The Waste Land*. Instead of "Come *in* under the shadow of *this* red rock," Marshall asks how one can "come *out* from 'under the shadow' . . . 'of *that* red rock?'" Marshall represents the rock's shadow not as Eliot's shelter but rather as a menace, something to evade and cast off. Marshall also shifts the spatial orientation of Eliot's poetry by substituting singular demonstratives: Eliot's "this" rock becomes Marshall's "that" rock. What in Eliot's work is close at hand and intimate becomes in Marshall's formulation alien, situated at a certain remove.

Marshall's revision of Eliot in her interviews contributes to the critical assessment of western modernity they voice. To an important extent, for Marshall, the very myths and traditions that sustain a despondent Eliot are part of a larger western value system from which she and other non-western subjects seek liberation. Thus, in one interview, Marshall links "getting out from the shadow of that red rock" to moving "out from under the seduction of another's values and the domination of the Herrenvolk (that is, White supremacists)."[28] In another she explicates her citation by observing how "other cultures, especially the dominant culture of the United States, seduce the more fragile ones of the third world, and how hard it is to come out from under that."[29] And in still another interview she uses the rock as a metaphor for "the economic stranglehold of the West" and the "Western cultural values and the sort of neocolonialism that still operates in so many instances." The very western systems of thought that Eliot views as valuable yet potentially lost to modernity Marshall identifies as oppressive and omnipresent. Marshall stresses how getting out from under Eliot's red rock is fundamental to her own artistic project. Resisting the oppressive shadow of western "cultural values," as she puts it in the same interview, "is really at the heart of my work."[30]

Of all Marshall's publications, *The Fisher King* represents her most concerted contestation of Eliot's modernism and its nostalgic heritage medievalism. As its title reflects, *The Fisher King* engages the very medieval grail lore that so attracted Eliot, but it does so in a manner that radically contests his white modernism and advocates an alternate Black diasporic modernity. Eliot incorporated medieval Arthuriana into a national and Eurocentric worldview that centered and exalted white men like himself. *The Fisher King* acknowledges that white signification of medieval romance by, for example, naming two of her key characters Hattie and Sonny-Rett. Those names cite figures, the actress Hattie McDaniel and the character Rhett Butler, associated with the most popular American cinematic representation of slavery and the U.S. South, the historical romance film *Gone with the Wind*.[31] In *The Fisher King*, Marshall acknowledges that offensive white tradition, only to "get out" from under "that red rock" and furthermore attack it, break it up, and repurpose it for a practice of literary world-building oriented toward her own feminist and diasporic perspective.

"Sounds Good, Feels Bad": Contesting Arthurian Wholeness

In *The Fisher King*, Marshall resignifies aspects of the Arthurian lore embraced by white readers like Eliot on behalf of a narrative that, like all her work, defies concise description and summary. Similar to *Bailey's Cafe*, Marshall's novel is in many ways a textual counterpart to the intricacies and shifts of Black music and especially jazz, reflecting how writers of color have, in the words of Barbara Christian, "managed to survive with such spiritedness the assault on our bodies, social institutions, countries, our very humanity," by means of "dynamic rather than fixed ideas."[32] Set largely during a few weeks in the spring of 1984, it centers on eight-year-old Sonny Carmichael Payne and his guardian, Hattie Carmichael. Sonny is a Black Parisian boy who avidly draws versions of the "King Arthur castles" from his medieval picture book.[33] Sonny has never known his biological parents (a runaway Black Parisian mother and a deported Black Cameroonian father) and has been raised in impoverished yet loving circumstances by Hattie. Hattie is an expat from Bedford-Stuyvesant who moved to Paris during the early 1950s to live with the boy's maternal grandparents, jazz legend Sonny-Rett Payne and Cherise Jones, both of whom were childhood friends and eventual lovers of Hattie. Through flashbacks and multiple points of view, *The Fisher King* describes the complex intra-racial dynamics that ensue—and charged memories that erupt—when Sonny and Hattie are lured back to Brooklyn for a memorial concert honoring Sonny's namesake, his deceased grandfather Sonny-Rett. The novel features an account of the fraught relations between and painful recollections of a multigenerational and transnational cast of Black characters that encompasses Sonny, Hattie, Sonny's great uncle Edgar Payne, Sonny's imposing West Indian American great grandmother Ulene Payne, and his equally imposing African American great grandmother Florence Varina McCullum-Jones.

Marshall has emphasized how her sources never function "in any direct way" in her fiction; rather, "it's always in bits and pieces... everything that has happened to me, that I have experienced firsthand or heard about or read about—however it's come to me—it's all stored in the data bank of the mind, this repository, this hopper."[34] Through such comments, Marshall signals how her novels don't offer full-scale revisions of source material on the order of, say, Gloria Naylor's engagements of canonical western authors (e.g., the Dantean *Linden Hills*). But however archived and filtered it may be, Marshall's relationship to sources is worth pursuing. *The Fisher King* constitutes a powerful resource for querying the western values associated with medieval Arthurian lore.

Marshall has made one explicit connection between *The Fisher King* and white canonical sources. During a 2000 reading at Medgar Evers College in Brooklyn, N.Y., she linked the French children's book that inspires Sonny's drawings to an Arthurian volume that she read in elementary school. "The Fisher King," the Brooklynite Marshall explained to her auditors, "is a legend that comes from King Arthur and the Round Table, which was required reading when I went to PS35 here."³⁵ Marshall's youthful encounter with Arthuriana not only mirrors the relation to Arthurian lore of her young protagonist Sonny but also was an experience she shared with Eliot. In a 1934 book review of a new edition of the *Morte*, Eliot describes how a "children's edition" of Malory "was in my hands when I was a child of 11 or 12."³⁶ Marshall doesn't specify that she read Malory. But the late medieval English author's influence was such that, if a young Marshall didn't read Malory's work directly, she would have done so in an indirect manner. More than any other medieval text, the *Morte* has been read by contemporary readers and inspired contemporary adaptations. The children's book assigned at Brooklyn PS35 doubtless comprised part of the "explosion" of "Malory adaptations, especially for children" that occurred after 1860.³⁷ To be sure, an international array of possible sources might have been included in the "hopper" from which Marshall drew for *The Fisher King*.³⁸ At the same time, though, the unique popularity and influence of the *Morte* urge putting Marshall's novel into conversation with Malory.

The *Morte* also offers an important Arthurian entryway into a dynamic at the heart of this book: the relationship of the medieval to modernity. More than any other medieval western romance and perhaps more than any medieval text produced in England or elsewhere, the *Morte* has enjoyed a special perceived relation to literary modernity. As Colin Richmond puts it, the *Morte* has "seem[ed] to so many an exemplary *modern* work, indeed the transitional English text into modern literary culture."³⁹ For academic medievalists, the modernity of the *Morte* has often been a matter of form. Eugène Vinaver famously celebrated "the aesthetic principle involved" in Malory's replacement of "the complex structure of his sources" with "a principle of 'singleness' that underlies the normal structure of a modern work of fiction."⁴⁰ As Dorsey Armstrong puts it, the "belief that Malory's work is a unified one—more akin to the modern novel"—remains "strongly-held" by medievalists.⁴¹

As *The Waste Land* evinces, the *Morte's* relation to modernity emerges in not only the "progressive" formal features celebrated by scholars but also the embrace of Malory's work by an array of modern white male writers. In addition to Eliot, Malory found appreciators and enjoyed influence with many proto- and late modernists—Tennyson, the pre-Raphaelites, Twain, and Steinbeck—whom Marshall mentions in commentaries on her youthful reading habits.⁴² Eliot loved Malory. In the book review of the *Morte* edition he received as a pre-teen, he states, "It was then, and perhaps has always been, my favorite book." Eliot's childhood affection for Malory grew into an adult modernist nostalgia. Later in that same book review, he describes the appeal of Malory in terms that correspond with his larger modernist investment in a time prior to his own industrialized and disenchanted contemporary moment. Putting the *Morte* on a par with the Bible and Greek authors like Aeschylus and Homer (whom he cites in "Tradition"), Eliot describes how the medieval romance offers "a simpler and truer view of life" whose "primitive" morality "belongs to the nature of things as our shallow manners do not."[43] *The Waste Land* in many respects registers a longing to recapture that "simpler and truer" Malorian perspective.

While Eliot nostalgically embraces the older organic white world represented in the *Morte*, Marshall identifies the Arthurian book she read as a girl during the 1930s with white cultural domination—that is, Eliot's "red rock." She explains to her audience at Medgar Evers that the children's book was "required reading" in accordance with "a strictly European agenda": no "Zora Neale Hurston, no Langston Hughes, no James Weldon Johnson."[44] In notes Marshall generated to prepare for interviews and readings, Marshall further observes how, when she attended school, "the cultural revolution of the sixties had yet to come. Only the icons of western literature were considered worthy."[45]

While Arthurian lore comprised part of the "domination of the Herrenvolk" during her childhood, *The Fisher King* reverses that power dynamic. As Marshall puts it in her notes for an interview with *Essence*, "I simply took this icon of western European literature that was required reading when I went to school and altered it to serve my own purposes."[46] If Malory has long been a staple of white mythologies, Marshall appropriates his work on behalf of her vital addition to the Black diasporic canon. An apt starting point for an inquiry into Marshall's contestation of Malory is the Arthurian dynamic her title cites. As Marshall explains in the talking points she prepared for interviews, her title refers to "the tale of the wounded Fisher King holed up in his castle waiting to be healed and reinvigorated."[47] In Malory, the healing by Sir Galahad of an injured king—the ancient, blind, and wounded Sir Evelake—exemplifies how his text folds into its larger narrative of the break-up of a perfect, whole brotherhood discrete episodes when broken individuals regain their former wholeness. Marshall's young protagonist, Sonny, and his grandfather, Sonny-Rett, bear striking resemblances to Galahad and Evelake. Like Malory's old and lame king, Sonny-Rett suffered a devastating injury: he died during a police chase from wounds sustained during a fall down a flight of stairs in a Paris metro. Sonny-Rett also resembles Evelake in his status as both "royalty" (that is, a jazz "king") and the ancestor of the young man who seeks to heal him. Turning to Sonny, the child—like Galahad—bears a relation to purity and chastity, thanks to his own youthful innocence and inexperience. Finally, Sonny's Arthurian drawings are infused with an intentionality that mirrors the relationship of Galahad to Evelake. As Sonny explains to his cousins, his "namesake grandfather lived inside the castles and fortresses" he creates, "placed there by him for safekeeping" (156). Similar to Galahad, who heals Evelake's body "full of grete woundys" (full of great wounds) (701.35–702.1; 156), Sonny imagines that his grandfather, sheltered in the boy's make-believe castles, is "healed as well, all the bloody head wounds he had suffered in the Metro completely healed."[48]

Such parallels between *The Fisher King* and medieval grail texts support radically different notions of identity and social life. To begin with, Sonny emphatically lacks the racial purity or wholeness ascribed to Galahad. As Marshall stresses in her reading at Medgar Evers, Sonny "is African American" (from his grandmother Cherisse), "West Indian" (from his grandfather Sonny-Rett), and "African, because his father . . . was an African vendor" in Paris. She continues, "What I wanted to do with that was have him embody the great wings of the African diaspora, he brings them together."[49] Marshall's conception of Sonny revises the racial approach to identity evident in Malory. Galahad can make the old king whole because he, in Jill Mann's words, "embodies inner wholeness."[50] That "inner wholeness" hinges on an idea of purity that is Christian—Galahad is a saintly virgin—and genealogical. Galahad has an exalted bloodline. As Guinevere puts it:

> He is of all parts come of the best knights of the world and of the highest lineage: for his father, Lancelot, is eight degrees separated from Our Lord Jesus Christ, and this Sir Galahad is nine degrees separated from Our Lord Jesus Christ. Therefore I daresay they are the greatest gentlemen of the world.[51]

This passage demonstrates how, as Martin Shichtman puts it, one of "the consuming obsessions of Malory's 'Tale of the Sankgreal'" is "genealogy," and specifically the ancestry of Galahad "as preeminent grail knight."[52] While Sonny, as "an innocent," does share Galahad's moral purity, he opposes the *Morte's* aristocratic white essentialism. In contrast to Galahad's exalted blood line, which extends back to biblical times, Sonny embodies a diasporic heterogeneity. Moreover, his family ties exceed biology. As Hattie, Sonny's adoptive parent, puts it, " 'There're all kinds of family and blood's got nothing to do with it!' " (16).

If Galahad's racial ties to Evelake prove crucial to his capacity to heal his ancestor, Sonny's diasporic heterogeneity imbues the boy with a far greater healing potential. As Sonny's grandmother Florence puts it in a key passage whose importance Marshall underscores by using it as her epigraph to the book, "'You got some of all of us in you, dontcha? What you gonna do with all that Colored from all over creation you got in you? Better be somethin' good'" (9). Insofar as he embodies the gathering of the "great wings" of the diaspora, Sonny suggests the prospect of a more expansive societal healing. And to be sure, Sonny's relations are sorely in need of such collective restoration.[53] A transnational community created via the violence of western slavery and colonization, the Black persons of *The Fisher King* are, from the opening pages of the novel, a group facing all sorts of intrapersonal tensions. The communal challenges facing Sonny Jr.'s extended family in Brooklyn, a mix of West Indian immigrants and African Americans, exemplify how, as Marshall relates, "the white man had succeeded in dividing our house. Economics, sociology, psychology—and politics."[54] Sonny, then, holds the potential for a contemporary Black inversion of the white chivalric trajectory of the *Morte*. While the Round Table crumbles, Sonny looks toward the reconciliation of Black diasporic divisions.

Sonny's potentially "healing properties," then, are manifold and expansive. But, in keeping with the difficult and complex Black modernism that distinguishes Marshall's body of work, *The Fisher King* ultimately refuses feel-good scenes of healing and reconciliation. Consider, for a start, Sonny's relation to Sonny-Rett. The boy's Arthurian artistry does soothe the child's own psyche, lessening the frequency of his nightmares and troubling thoughts. Sonny also plays a role, as Caroline Rosenthal suggests, in the "restoration" of Sonny-Rett's memory via the memorial concert.[55] But unlike the miraculous mending of the maimed king in Malory and other medieval sources, the healing of jazz "royalty" Sonny-Rett only occurs at an imaginative or symbolic level. The grandfather is long dead; his injuries can never be overcome. In a similar vein, Sonny's potential to ease the woes of his ailing relations and mend their divisions remains decidedly unfulfilled. Sonny does offer minor ameliorations. For example, he provides Ulene what she describes as an "'easement,'" and at one point Florence turns to the child "for comforting" and receives his embrace (175, 166). At such moments, as Marshall has stressed, "the pain of life is softened, tempered."[56] But Sonny's healing powers never come close to approximating the unification he embodies. For example, Sonny attempts to reconcile his warring grandmothers by bringing to Ulene a tree branch from Florence Varina's yard. When Ulene immediately rejects the peace offering, Sonny acquires the sad and resigned "feeling that couldn't be translated into thoughts or words—that he had done his part, he had tried, really tried with them, the two great-grandmother women, his relatives, kin, family, and blood, and nothing more could be done" (176–77).

With respect to Hattie, Sonny's healing capacities tragically recede over the course of the novel. However imperfect, Sonny and Hattie, whom he calls "fathermothersisterbrother" (16), have built a closely knit and loving life together in Paris. Part of that loving relationship involves Sonny's keen attunement to when his adoptive and drug-using parent "was upset or feeling low and didn't have her *médicaments* with her." To "soothe" Hattie "and restore her to herself and to him, he quietly slipped his hand into hers. It always worked" (71). But heart-wrenchingly, in the final pages of the novel, Sonny's healing powers cease. When he sees an agitated Hattie (unbeknownst to Sonny, she has just consented to his great uncle Edgar's demand that the boy live with him in the States), the youth "quietly slipped his hand into hers, as he always did when she was upset" (220). But "for the first time that he could remember, nothing happened. She didn't suddenly rally . . . the hand he held remained slack and unresponsive. A stranger's hand" (221). Sonny, ultimately, is no miracle worker akin to Galahad or his literary predecessor, Percival. Unlike the physical ailments of King Evelake, the multiple forms of injury at play in the world of *The Fisher King*—physical, psychic, and social—remain unresolved. In notable contrast to the healing trajectory of the medieval Fisher King myth, the novel ends, harshly and abruptly, just after Sonny's failed effort to soothe Hattie. The final line describes a confused and fearful Sonny wondering why "Hattie, who had been fathermothersisterbrother and all other kin until now, was for some reason deliberately avoiding the sight of his face" (222).

An indicator of just how far *The Fisher King* is from "feel good" is an anecdote from Marshall about the reception of the novel by "readers [who] got so involved emotionally." During a reading in Berkeley, California, a female reader said to the novelist, "Well, I loved *The Fisher King* but that ending! I can't forgive you for that ending."[57] All of which is to say, and as the title of Lori Leibovich's *New York Times* review indicates, despite its portrayal of "little areas in life that bring a measure of satisfaction," *The Fisher King* "Sounds Good" but "Feels Bad."[58]

"Letting Go" in Malory and "Holding in" in *The Fisher King*

The Fisher King thus confirms how, as her most acute critics contend, Marshall's novels are fundamentally unsettling modernist works that refuse easy answers to Black diasporic problems and deny readers comforting images of transcendence, unity, and healing. Fundamental to the Black modernist pessimism of *The Fisher King* is a radical reformulation of the affective terms of texts like the *Morte*. Malory's work—like that of Eliot and Marshall—is awash with emotion. With his grail sequence, Malory pivots from what had been largely a celebratory narration of the worldly adventures of Arthur's knights to sorrowfully tracking the breakup of the Round Table. With its focus on the failure of Arthurian culture to persist, the *Morte* exemplifies one of the two major historical stances that Caroline Eckhardt identifies in late medieval English Arthurian discourse. One of those positions optimistically maintains faith in a future when Arthur shall return. The other attitude, in which the *Morte* participates, "is primarily one of nostalgia and distance. The Arthurian world represents a glorious British past radically different from the present corrupt world that cannot be expected to return."⁵⁹ Arthur introduces the concept of the utter demise of the Round Table, early in Malory's grail book. As various knights commit to the questing of the grail, the king sadly announces, "'Never shall I see you again whole together'" ("'nevyr shall I se you agayne holé togydirs'" 672.26–27). Such moments adumbrate the melancholic interest in a lost white male ideal witnessed in modernist works like *The Waste Land*. The wholeness and categorial pastness of the Arthurian world articulated here by Arthur—and elsewhere by Malory himself—helps account for its appeal to a nostalgic white male modernist like Eliot.

Malory represents Arthurian melancholia via outpourings of human emotion. Thus Arthur, upon acknowledging the demise of his knightly community, articulates the negative affect that that knowledge produces, telling his men that "'it shall grieve me right sore, the breakup of this fellowship'" and follows up that claim with physical evidence of his anguish: "And immediately the tears fell in his eyes."⁶⁰ Arthur is far from the only figure who displays sadness at this point in the *Morte*. Scenes of weeping dominate the grail book, in which men and women repeatedly speak and act "with weeping cheer," "sore weeping," "making great sorrow," "all weeping," and suffer "marvelous sorrow" and such "heaviness that there might no tongue tell."⁶¹ Like the *Morte* and *The Waste Land*, *The Fisher King* is notably concerned with affect, so much so that the words "felt," "feel," "feeling," and "feelings," appear nearly sixty times in her compact 222-page work. Moreover, she—like Malory and his inheritor Eliot—places special stress on bad feelings. Indeed, in a move that echoes Naylor's naming of her protagonist "Sadie" in *Bailey's Cafe*, Marshall renders suffering so fundamental to her characters as to embed it in the name of Sonny's paternal line, "Payne," a "last name obviously being a homonym of pain."⁶²

But Marshall's depiction of Black sorrow involves no mere transference to Black people of the grief portrayed in works like the *Morte*. As we have seen, Malory repeatedly stages scenes in which men like Arthur readily produce spectacular outpourings of tears, affects that testify to the human richness of those white knights. Marshall shifts attention from those white affects to showcase the deep and intricate emotional life of Black persons or what Jennifer Nash calls the particularity of Black life as "a felt experience."⁶³ Namely, through her repeated portrayal of versions of an emotion I will call, following Marshall's own vocabulary, "holding in," *The Fisher King* precipitates a telling contrast of Malorian and Black feeling (36). The verb "hold" has roots in the Old English verb *haldan* (to hold or keep) and is defined by the *OED* as "to keep, preserve, hold."[64] Marshall conscripts "hold" and its early English valence on behalf of her own Black modernist project via the phrasal verb "hold in." Defined in the *OED* as "to keep in, confine, retain; to restrain, keep in check," "hold in" resonates with the noun "hold" and its harrowing relation to the vestibular and fatal confinement of slaves during the Middle Passage.[65] "Holding in" thus serves in *The Fisher King* as emotion akin to the "ugly feelings" described by Sianne Ngai. Similar to how Ngai "approaches emotions as unusually knotted or condensed interpretations of predicaments," Marshall employs "holding in" to represent her characters' hermeneutical reaction to their fraught positioning. "Holding in," like the "negative affects" Ngai discusses, is a feeling "that read[s] the" political "predicaments posed by a general state of obstructed agency with respect to other human actors or to the social as such."[66] In contradistinction to how Malory's knights, with tears flowing abundantly from their eyes, "let go," Marshall's characters "hold in" or contain their emotion, offering a hermeneutic that responds to the blockages of diasporic persons in the afterlife of colonialism and slavery, or what Marshall calls "the psychological damage brought on by history."[67]

In Chapter 3 of *The Fisher King*, the novel's first sustained representation of Black feeling, Marshall introduces "holding in." In this chapter, shortly after their arrival in Brooklyn, Hattie introduces Sonny to his great grandmother Florence at her brownstone, situated across the street from the home of his other great grandmother, Ulene. Initially upbeat, the tone of the visit alters when Florence considers the man whom Sonny's name memorializes. The boy's grandfather, Sonny-Rett, recalls the long-standing strife between Florence's African American family and the matriarchal Barbadian household where the jazz musician was raised by Florence's arch-enemy, Ulene. "Suddenly, like a citywide power failure, all" of Florence's "brightness and enthusiasm died, her dark, unhappy frown returned and tears—angry ones this time—welled up" (36). A furious Florence asks Hattie why she gave the boy "'that man['s]'" moniker. When Hattie responds by asking whom she should have "'name[d] him after,'" Florence unleashes an attack—laden with anti-Caribbean slang—on "'that W.I. woman across the street'" so violent as to resemble "the sound of a dam bursting." Florence then, in a quasi-apologetic mode, turns to Sonny and tells him to cover his ears, since "'I promised myself I wasn't gonna do or say anything to spoil our first visit, but I can't help it. Been holding in too much too long!'" (36).

This episode represents two interrelated emotions: both Florence's resentful outpouring of tears and the long, painful, and anguished period when she restrained herself from engaging in such displays. The very suddenness of Florence's tears refers to the distressingly excessive—"'too much too long'"—time when she held them back, like a dam holding back a torrent of water. Marshall carefully registers the significance of this charged moment. Like the monumental dam-bursting metaphor, the simile "like a citywide power failure" imbues Florence's affective shift with the expansiveness—the grandeur—of changes occurring over an entire metropolis.

Marshall highlights Florence's affect by making "'been holding in too much too long'" the epigraph for that chapter (29, see also 169). By foregrounding the phrase as an epigraph, Marshall signals how Florence enacts an affective dynamic that serves a broader thematic function. Indeed, the "holding in" that pertains first to Sonny's great grandmother soon extends to Hattie. In Chapter 3, as Florence unshackles her fury on Sonny's guardian, "Hattie's face was a window with the shade drawn all the way down. Nothing to be seen there" (40). Like the "citywide power failure" to which Marshall compares Florence Varina's affective change, Marshall bestows on Hattie's own practice of holding in—her complete shielding of feeling from Florence Varina—a version of the architectural and urban metaphors for which she is famous. By the close of the chapter, which coincides with the end of the visit, the resemblance between Florence's and Hattie's sentiments intensifies, as Hattie—"sounding as if it had been too much too long for her also"—releases her own "suppressed outburst" of anger over the fact that, until that day, she had never before entered Florence's home, despite her long and close friendship with Florence's daughter, Sonny's grandmother Cherisse (41).

Marshall's portrayal of Black feeling performs a complex and multipronged response to literary history that engages much more than white traditions of writing. For example, the periods of painful suppression represented in *The Fisher King* revise not only Malory but also a long-recognized source for Marshall's novel, James Baldwin's short story "Sonny's Blues" (1957). Baldwin's narrative is told in the voice of an anonymous male narrator, an algebra teacher, whose brother Sonny, a talented jazz pianist, is arrested for heroin possession. At the start of the narrative, news of Sonny's arrest produces in the teacher a torturous experience of holding in memories of his brother as he "taught [his] classes algebra":

> I was scared, scared for Sonny. He became real to me again. A great block of ice got settled in my belly and kept melting there slowly all day long. . . . It was a special kind of ice. It kept melting, sending trickles of ice water all up and down my veins, but it never got less. Sometimes it hardened and seemed to expand until I felt my guts were going to come spilling out or that I was going to choke or scream. This would always be at a moment when I was remembering some specific

thing Sonny had once said or done. . . . When the last bell rang, the last class ended, I let out my breath. It seemed I'd been holding it for all that time.[68]

Baldwin brings to life the inner dynamics of the narrator's painful suppression of feelings regarding his brother, representing it via the metaphor of expanding "frozen ice" exerting a pressure within the teacher so great as to "choke" and so painful as to force out a "scream." Marshall expands and modifies Baldwin's portrayal of "holding in" by attributing that affect to an array of Black characters, including women like Florence and Hattie. As Patricia Lespinasse puts it, *The Fisher King* "positions a magnifying lens on the silenced portions of Baldwin's jazz short story," including its "absent black female voice."[69] Marshall's work thus enacts a complex engagement of her "individual Black talent" with both white writers like Malory and Eliot and a Black literary tradition that includes Baldwin.[70]

Both Marshall's and Baldwin's representations of "holding in" suggest sentimental dimensions of the blockages described by Ahmed in her work on the phenomenology of whiteness. Following Fanon, Ahmed describes "whiteness . . . as an ongoing and unfinished history, which orientates bodies in specific directions, affecting how they 'take up' space."[71] While whiteness centers white bodies and empowers them to inhabit and move through space with ease, racialized bodies experience restricted mobility in that white sociodiscursive field.

For example, in *The Fisher King*, Sonny's grandfather Sonny-Rett is so restricted by segregation and other forms of racism in the U.S. that he flees his homeland for Paris. Eventually, however, even Paris becomes a constricting space for the expat musician, who perishes as the object of a police manhunt. Marshall's novel demonstrates how the spatiality of whiteness has its emotional components. Thus, Sonny-Rett, in addition to the spatial blockages he encounters, also "holds in." Namely, "at all times" the musician's "gaze" was "guarded" by a "drawn curtain" (196). In the example of Sonny-Rett, white supremacy—the Du Boisian veil discussed in Chapter 2—prompts a protective act of veiling on the part of the Black person. Unlike the clear-eyed individual of Burckhardt's *Civilization*, the jazz genius guards himself through "the curtain of his gaze" (136), holding in his thoughts and feelings.

Marshall's most sustained treatment of Black sentimental containment pertains to young Sonny, whose "balloon of bad feelings" most closely recalls Baldwin's portrayal of affective confinement (174). Whenever troubling thoughts come to the child's mind—for instance, his "runaway" mother, his deported father, or his long-dead grandfather—"right away he felt the cruel balloon he secretly carried around in his chest begin to inflate, crowding his heart and lungs, his throat, and threatening to reach his eyes and explode in a babyish flood of tears" (78). Sonny's "cruel balloon" of "bad feelings," much like the ice of fear choking the narrator of "Sonny's Blues," clarifies how "holding in" doesn't entail simply the suppression of emotion but also the sentiment that attends that very act of restraint: young Sonny's burning eyes, stifled breath, and so on. These key set pieces in *The Fisher King* pertaining to Sonny's feelings amplify how emotion in Marshall's novel bespeaks the fraught social life of modern Black subjects. *The Fisher King*, in other words, illustrates Ahmed's insight that emotions are a kind of "doing" that pertains to the working of signs in concert with bodies to "materialize the surface and boundaries that are lived as worlds."[72] The painful sensation of "bad feelings" pressing against Sonny's "heart and lungs," "throat," and "eyes" are physical manifestations of the lines drawn by a society that constructs emotions and attaches them to certain bodies. For example, Sonny's fear of seeming "babyish" indicates how the "inflation" of "bad feelings" intersects with dominant twentieth-century understandings of masculinity and human growth; unlike the medieval men of the *Morte*, real men don't cry in Sonny's contemporary world. At the same time that Sonny's feeling of holding in speaks to gender norms, the anguish and fear trapped inside the child point to broader issues of social injustice. The absence of his parents, the death of his grandfather, and the wretched state of his caretaker bespeak the manifold harms done to Black persons through the afterlife of slavery.

Tradition and the Individual Black Talent: Sonny-Rett

Like *Bailey's Cafe*, *The Fisher King* conveys harrowing truths about Black experience and white supremacy through a triumphant contestation of the politics of western discourse. Whether in terms of their critical take on medieval English authors or their heart-wrenching narratives of Black struggle, both works are difficult reads. At the same time, Naylor and Marshall convey their pessimism through wonderfully revolutionary cultural means: the radical transformation of white representations. Marshall self-reflexively comments on her artistic achievement in *The Fisher King* through her portrayal of the jazz modernism of pianist Sonny-Rett and his namesake, Sonny, a visual artist and budding modernist in his own right. In each meta-component of the novel, Marshall revises Eliot's theory of artistry in a manner that expands on Hall's claims about "Tradition and the Individual (West Indian) Talent." In "Our Literary Heritage," Hall contests Eliot's Anglocentric and Eurocentric theory of art, decrying anyone who would "deny Derek Walcott his Dante."[73] Marshall similarly portrays the modern artistry of both Sonny-Rett and Sonny as a matter of critically engaging older white art forms. In both cases those Black modernists not only problematize Eliot's essentialist idea of a unitary western tradition but also reject his theory of artistic "self-sacrifice." In contradistinction to Eliot's notion that "the progress of an artist is a . . . continual extinction of personality" for a greater western aesthetic good, both Sonny-Rett and Sonny (and by implication, Marshall) wondrously make western forms their own.[74]

The given name of Sonny's grandfather is Everett Carlyle. The moniker "Sonny-Rett" is bestowed on Everett to mark the periodization of his biography: the transformative moment when he first makes a splash on the Brooklyn music scene. Importantly, Marshall doesn't simply represent Everett as Sonny-Rett but indicates the training that prepared him for his breakthrough performance and future career. That education presumably began in the same inauspicious manner experienced by young Sonny, when his grandmother (and Everett's mother) Ulene forces Sonny during their first meeting to mimic the movement of the keys of her player piano. As critics including Rosenthal and Jürgen Grandt observe, Ulene's player piano, with its pristine "long roll of white paper" and the European scores imprinted on it, suggests her cathexis to a white version of upward mobility (20).[75] Once Ulene has scraped together cash for lessons, Everett moves from copying the white music that the piano encodes to devoting "years dutifully practicing Bach, Beethoven, Chopin, et al. on the old t'row-off player piano." All the while, however, Everett balances his mastery of white music with an alternate Black education that involves "sneaking into" the local record shop to hear African American greats "Muddy, Basie, Tatum, et al." (137). After exposure to Kansas City blues near the base where he is stationed during World War II, Everett is primed for his "catalytic jazz moment."[76]

Marshall complexly narrates that groundbreaking episode, routing it largely through the memories of Hattie. Importantly, Hattie's recollections of Everett's breakthrough, related both publicly at his memorial and privately to herself, offer verbal riffs on the shifts and intricacies of jazz, and vie with—or, indeed, outshine—that signature event.[77] The formal organization of Marshall's portrayal of Everett's great performance via Hattie's public and private storytelling also signifies the resonances of jazz with Marshall's own narrative project. An initial recollection of Sonny-Rett's performance, in the book's sixth chapter, occurs during a planning meeting for the memorial concert honoring Sonny-Rett. Later, in Chapter 11, during a visit to the venue—now renovated by his brother Edgar—where Everett performed, Edgar and Hattie briefly remember that day, an exchange that prompts a longer, private, and personal reminiscence by Hattie. Finally, in the third- and second-to-last chapters of the novel, during the memorial concert itself, Marshall, in a literary call and response, interweaves the official memory of the event Hattie shares with the audience with the memories Hattie keeps to herself.

Marshall's most detailed representation of Sonny-Rett's achievement appears, appropriately, in Hattie's long private recollection during her initial visit to the renovated music venue. The setting is "Sunday evening," and "Everett Payne, not long out of the army," is "invited to sit in" with the band (134). Everett takes the stage, privately consults with some players, and plays "the opening bars of 'Sonny Boy Blue,'" the sound of which immediately draws scorn from the crowd. "'"Sonny Boy Blue"!' That hokey-doke tune,'" audience members exclaim in "open disgust" (136). As a prior recollection of Sonny-Rett's performance at the planning meeting indicates, "Sonny Boy Blue" is "a Tin Pan Alley tune . . . from a Broadway musical at the time" (80). Everett's performance occurs on a "Sunday in '47" (184), when the mainstream songs and musicals associated with Broadway and Tin Pan Alley testified to a colonizing American whiteness.[78] Hit '40s musicals like *Oklahoma!* (1943), *Bloomer Girl* (1944), and *Finian's Rainbow* (1947) exemplify how Black talent and creativity was, in Richard Dyer's words, "subsumed into white needs, white goals, and white displays."[79] Tin Pan Alley and Broadway were linked popular phenomena that expanded into, incorporated, and took ownership over spirituals, ragtime, jazz, and other instances of Black musical innovation.[80] "Sonny Boy Blue," the name of the tune Everett plays, both pays homage to Baldwin's short story "Sonny's Blues" and reflects the incorporation of Black music into the white musical numbers performed on Broadway and hawked by Tin Pan Alley.

Through Everett's initial pass through "Sonny Boy Blue," Marshall engages in a complex revision of Eliot's idea of tradition and the individual talent. Everett first plays "the song straight through as written . . . with great care, . . . at a slower tempo . . . and with a formality that lent the Tin Pan Alley tune a depth and thoughtfulness no one else would have accorded it"; the bassist and drummer join in, "treating the original as if it were a serious piece of music" (136). Eliot claims that "the historical sense" of the artist "compels" him "to write not merely with his own generation in his bones, but with a feeling that the whole of the literature of Europe from Homer and within it the whole of the literature of his own country has a simultaneous existence and composes a simultaneous order." The history of U.S. popular music to which "Sonny Boy Blue" refers exposes the fault lines of Eliot's theory about a great unitary artistic tradition, at least insofar as it applies to American aesthetics. The song is a "hokey-doke" or simpleminded tune—hardly an example of aesthetic greatness—that moreover involves the appropriation of prior Black musical achievement. But Everett nevertheless plays the song with care, uniquely lending it "a depth and thoughtfulness." On one level, Everett's style suggests a mimetic subversion of Eliot. That is, the excessive nature of Everett's respect for tradition points to the absurdity of the concept of a grand, homogeneous, and white U.S. aesthetic tradition. On another level, though, by slowly moving through the melody—perhaps "feeling in his bones" the sobering seizure of a vital Black blues culture by a crass Tin Pan Alley—Everett reverses the trajectory of American pop music. If a white music industry stole Black music to make merely "hokey-doke" tunes, Everett shows how a Black artist can perform a white song with a masterful skill that imbues it with qualities heretofore unrecognized. As Hattie puts it during the planning meeting, "'From the moment [Everett] put his hands down on that piano, from the very first chord, it was "Sonny Boy Blue" like it had never been played before'" (80). Everett thus contests Eliot's idea of the sacrifice of the individual artist, showing how, even when Black artists play white songs, they don't so much pay homage to a greater American aesthetic good but assert their individual excellence.

Marshall's portrayal of tradition and individual Black artistic excellence gains momentum as Everett's performance continues:

> Everett Payne took his time paying his respects to the tune as written, and once that was done, he hunched closer to the piano, angled his head sharply to the left, completely closed the curtain of his gaze, and with his hands commanding the length and breadth of the keyboard he unleashed a dazzling pyrotechnic of chords (you could almost see their colors), polyrhythms, seemingly unrelated harmonies and ideas—fresh, brash, outrageous ideas. It was an outpouring of ideas and feelings informed by his own brand of lyricism and lit from time to time by flashes of the recognizable melody. He continued to acknowledge the little simpleminded tune, while at the same time furiously recasting and inventing it in an image all his own. (136–37)

Directly countering Eliot's idea of "the continual extinction of personality" on the part of the artist, Everett maintains a connection to the song—"he continued to acknowledge" it—even as he "recast[s] and invent[s] it in an image all his own." To return to Hattie's words at the earlier gathering, "'That tune . . . didn't have *nothing* to do with Tin Pan Alley or Broadway when he laid into it'" (80). If Eliot ascribes to an ongoing "whole" tradition to which the artist contributes, Everett's performance reveals the triumphant severing of ties between the Black artist and white culture. In the Black musician's hands and in accord with "his own brand of lyricism," the ordinary becomes extraordinary, "hokey-doke" becomes "dazzling pyrotechnics."

In lieu of Eliot, Marshall advocates a relation to tradition akin to both Ralph Ellison's account of modern jazz artistry in *Shadow and Act* (1964) and Hall's concept of the modern diasporic writer. As Rosenthal observes, Marshall's account of Everett's performance "reads like a variation of one of Ellison's claims that 'each true jazz moment . . . springs from a contest in which each artist challenges all the rest.'"[81] A bit later in her remembrance, Hattie notes how Everett engages not just the Tin Pan Alley song but also a heterogeneous tradition involving both white European and Black U.S. music: "You heard them, both Bach and the hard, pure lyricism of the blues" in "Muddy, Basie, Tatum, et al." (139). Everett's performance is a battle where instead of Eliotically sacrificing himself, the artist "challenges all the rest." Everett's combination of mastery and innovation illustrates Hall's aforementioned account of how "even in the act of rejection," the diasporic artist "is rejecting something which one has known almost too intimately, which has shaped the way in which one has seen the situation."

Marshall imbues Black artistry with a triumphant agency and expressiveness that challenge the blockages that can inform Black life, including those pertaining to "holding in." Everett is simultaneously "holding in"—he has "completely closed the curtain of his gaze"—and letting go: "unleash[ing]" chords and displaying an "outpouring of ideas and feelings." As Lespinasse puts it in her reading of Hattie's musical abilities, jazz is both a "moment" when "the historical past replays in the mind of the" artist and "a moment of self-assertion . . . an attempt to achieve ultimate freedom."[82] Everett's music at once nods toward all artistic predecessors, prompting "the curtain of his gaze" to close, and spectacularly seizes the now, the new, and the individual: "fresh, brash, outrageous ideas."

Because Everett is a Black artist, Marshall's representation of the musician's relation to western traditions comprises a self-reflexive element of the novel. That is, Everett's music allegorizes the creative achievement that is *The Fisher King*. Everett's remarkable transformation of a Tin Pan Alley tune, playing it "like it had never been played before," speaks to Marshall's project of remaking "in an image all" her "own" prior traditions, including the Arthurian tropes and conventions of works like the *Morte*.[83] In fact, to signpost how her character's achievement reflects on her own literary method, Marshall's response to Arthuriana culminates in her portrayal of Everett's musical triumph. No other aspect of *The Fisher King* approaches the dense contestation of Malory at work in her rendering of the breakthrough.

Consider, for example, how Everett's performance reframes the fundamental role of violence in attaining that all-important knightly attribute, honor, a virtue that pertains to a person's good name or public image. In Malory, as in other Arthurian texts, honor and its opposite, shame, hinge on physical injury and pain, so much so that references to "hurt" outnumber references to "honor" in the *Morte*. When it occurs through chivalrous means, making another knight "sore hurt" produces honor for the injurer and dishonor for the injured. And conversely, when an Arthurian knight causes a wrongful death, that loss, as Lancelot puts it when he learns in the grail book of a king slain by Gawain, "'ys a grete hurte [is a great hurt] unto Kynge Arthurs courte'" (777.27–28). Marshall appropriates that Malorian dynamic on behalf of Everett's art. While the jazz great doesn't engage in literal acts of aggression, his relationship to white culture partakes in the violence and fury witnessed in chivalric combat. For instance, Hattie indicates the rage and ferocity involved in Sonny-Rett's breakthrough when she ponders to herself how he "acknowledge[d] the little simpleminded tune, while at the same time *furiously* recasting and inventing it in an image all his own" (my emphasis).

Even more significant than the aggression signaled in Hattie's private remembrances are Marshall's repeated characterizations of Everett's achievement through a slang phrase for injury. During Hattie's initial memory of the fabled performance during the planning meeting, Shades Bowen, who played with Sonny-Rett and witnessed his breakout performance of "Sonny Boy Blue," interjects and exclaims, "'Cat put a hurtin' on it!'" (80). Hattie takes up Bowen's phrasing a bit later, telling Edgar Payne, "'Your brother took that sappy little tune, put a hurtin' on it like Shades said, and made it his tune, his song'" (81). Later, when Hattie again shares Sonny-Rett's story, this time during the memorial itself, she repeats how the musician was "putting a hurtin' on the hokey-doke tune" (182). A slang phrase for a deliberate physical and/or emotional assault, "put a hurtin' on" indicates how Sonny-Rett's version of "Sonny Boy Blue" appropriates the economy of physical violence and "hurt" at work in medieval romance.[84] While a knight literally triumphs over and injures his opponent, Sonny-Rett engages in an act of cultural aggression toward the Tin Pan Alley tune. And, not unlike the knight who gains honor—a good name—thanks to his capacity to prevail over his foes, Everett Payne is renamed "Sonny-Rett Payne," thanks to his furious transformation of white music.

The violence involved in Sonny-Rett's performance also speaks to the broader—and far from honorable—forms of violence at work in white cultural forms like "Sonny Boy Blue" or Malory's *Morte*. White artifacts like a contemporary Broadway tune or a late medieval English romance discursively excise and cut away alternate subjects, communities, and orientations. And that white discursive violence, in turn, has helped authorize historical acts of aggression that have wreaked havoc on Black bodies and Black minds. We might say, then, that the aggressivity involved in Sonny-Rett's and Marshall's art not only revises medieval rhetorics of violence and honor but also reverses a long-standing trajectory. While the historical "hurts" of the Black community have long been authorized and enabled by cultures of whiteness, Sonny-Rett upends that pattern by "putting a hurtin' on" and "furiously recasting" a white cultural form, just as his creator, Marshall, endeavors not merely to "get out" from the "red rock" of western tradition but also to attack it and demolish it and "furiously recast" it for her literary project.

Marshall doesn't just portray Sonny-Rett as a kind of jazz Lancelot who triumphs gloriously over his (cultural) foe. She also imbues the performer with a version of the sacral and awe-inspiring qualities of the grail. Repeatedly in his grail book Malory inserts moments when the grail is revealed to various groups of knights, always inspiring in them a speechless and even breathless wonder. For example, during the first revelation of the grail, "there was no knight who might speak one word for a great while, and so they looked, every man on the other, as if they had been struck dumb."[85] Only after "the holy vessel" is withdrawn had "they all regained breath to speak."[86] In Malory's text, the awe evoked by the grail reflects the enchanted world that medieval Christians believed they inhabited. The grail draws on transubstantiation, the Catholic belief that the Eucharistic wafer becomes the body of Christ during the consecration at Mass. In Malory, the revelation of the grail culminates in a literal manifestation of that doctrine. Near the end of the grail book, the knights Galahad, Bors, and Percival witness a priest "lifting up" the host, at which point "there came a figure in likeness of a child, and the visage was as red and as bright as any fire, and thrust himself into the bread, that they all saw it that the bread was formed of a fleshly man."[87]

In Marshall's secular modernist vision, it is Sonny-Rett's musical innovation and excellence that produces awe and wonder. In the same way that, according to medieval Christian belief, ordinary bread and wine at mass become extraordinary—the body and blood of Christ—Sonny-Rett's achievement involves a miraculous transformation. As the adjectives used to describe it affirm, "Sonny Boy Blue" is decidedly ordinary; it is "hokey-doke" and "simpleminded." But in Sonny-Rett's hands, what was sentimental fluff becomes a piece so great as to approximate the divine. As Hattie puts it during her initial reminiscence at the preparatory gathering:

> "We couldn't believe what we were hearing. Nobody we knew, certainly nobody from Brooklyn had ever played piano like that. When he was done we all just sat there, dumbstruck. Remember, Shades?"
>
> He nodded solemnly, eyes hidden behind the blindman's glasses.
>
> "Sat there," Hattie went on, "like we were in church and weren't supposed to clap." (80)

Thanks to Sonny-Rett, the Putnam-Royal becomes "like" a "church" (81). Similar to the grail, before which Arthur's knights look as if "they had bene doome" (as if they had been struck dumb) (674.1–2), Sonny-Rett's music fills the concert hall with a holy solemnity, generating a community of "dumb-struck" worshippers: "silence like in church. Everybody blown away" (184).

The transformation into a church-like space of the built environment where Everett triumphs contributes to a larger contestation of Malory—indeed, what is arguably Marshall's most biting contestation of medieval grail lore. Hattie, during her initial public reminiscence at the planning meeting, characterizes the Putnam Royal in language that recalls a primary meaning of the grail. "'I tell you,' she states, 'old bucket-o'-blood Putnam Royal had never seen anything like it!'" (81). Hattie uses the phrase twice again, when she returns to the building and during her official reminiscence during the memorial itself; Marshall revisits it a final time in the last chapter of the book (124, 182, 212). The descriptor "bucket-o'-blood" suggests a slang approximation of the grail as it appears in Malory and other medieval Arthurian texts. A bucket is a vessel; the word "grail" is etymologically rooted in both *gradale*, a medieval Latin word for a large and deep serving dish or vessel, and *graal*, an Old French term for vessel or cup.[88] Eliot's "red rock" (and its possible source, Wolfram's stone) reflect how the grail came to refer to a variety of objects. But the grail's associations with various kinds of vessels remained dominant in medieval texts. In Malory it is precisely the grail's status as a blood-filled "holy vessel" that makes it the ultimate object of knightly questing and the pinnacle of white male wonder. First used by Christ at the Last Supper, it is the chalice used during the "sakerynge" or consecration at Mass. The grail is also used by the gospel figure of Joseph of Arimathea to gather Christ's blood after the crucifixion. Malory even indicates that the grail is a blood relic—that is, a vessel that still contains Christ's blood. A wonder among wonders, the grail not only is the "holy blood" in which the miracle of transubstantiation literally manifests but also is crucial to the *Morte's* racial obsession with white bloodlines. Joseph is Lancelot's ancestor; Galahad heals Evelake by means of the grail; and no other knight encounters the grail in the manner of those high-blooded men, Lancelot and Galahad.

Marshall takes that icon of Christian whiteness, the grail—whose achieving in Malory means witnessing "the grete mervayles that no tunge may telle, and more than ony herte can thynke" (the great marvels of which no tongue may tell and that are beyond what any mind can think)—and radically demystifies it, emptying it of its religious and racial symbolism (775.11–12). American slang terms like "bloody bucket" or "bucket of blood" first appeared in the nineteenth century and describe a rough, violent, and dangerous area or place of business in a town (for instance, a saloon, bar, or speakeasy).[89] The Putnam Royal, during the time Sonny-Rett played there, clearly was such an establishment. Despite its name, which is an aristocratic appellation suggestive of a castle or royal palace, Putnam Royal was nothing more than a "faux medieval façade" fronting a "'dump where,'" as Florence Varina puts it, "'somebody was always getting cut at the rowdy dances held there on Saturday Nights!'" (124, 132). Instead of the mythic Christian means by which a white male aristocratic line is codified and exalted, the bloody vessel of Marshall's text is a metaphor for a place marked by base male behavior, a rough hall. Marshall empties the grail of medieval lore of its mystical powers and transfers those transformative abilities to Black persons. Edgar's renovation of the old building "amaze[s]" Hattie, while Everett renders the place "like a church" during his signal performance.

Sonny and Marshall: Jousting with Tradition

If Marshall reserves her most searing contestation of Malory for Sonny-Rett's performance, she most clearly allegorizes her own literary achievement in the drawings of young Sonny. Marshall embeds her first account of Sonny's visual art near the start of the crucial sixth chapter of *The Fisher King*, which features the first representation in the novel of Sonny-Rett's breakthrough. Their contiguous portrayal in Chapter 6 binds the artistry of the child to that of his grandfather. The chapter opens from the point of view of the boy, whom Hattie has brought to the planning meeting and whose "drawing *bloc*" draws the attention of a "man" who Sonny soon learns is his great uncle Edgar (73). Edgar admires Sonny's drawings and asks, "'Where'd you get the idea to draw all these castles?'" (74). Marshall then provides the reader with a detailed and telling account of both the context in which Sonny's art arose and his artistic process:

> The book, a big colorful picture storybook with page after page of medieval castles and fortresses and armored knights setting forth on their caparisoned horses to slay dragons and gorgons and to find something called the Holy Grail, had been among the secondhand toys, games and books that the church in their *quartier* . . . collected from children elsewhere in the city and then, like a lending library, loaned to those like himself. . . . He had borrowed the one book so often, they finally made him a present of it. Once it was his, he set about drawing the castles and fortresses inside. Using tracing paper, he painstakingly copied each one and afterward retraced it onto a page in the drawing blocs Hattie bought for him. After a while, when

he found he could draw them reasonably well without having to first trace them, he began making up his own. Castles and fortresses of his own invention. (74)

Reorienting the reader from western creative models to a Black diasporic take on tradition and individual talent, Marshall describes how, for Sonny, the goal sought by knightly questers is irrelevant. The "Holy Grail" is just "something" and lacks any lofty, salvific, and miraculous associations. Sonny's demystification of the grail adumbrates that of Marshall, when, a few pages later, she introduces her characterization of the Putnam Royal as a mere "bucket-o'-blood" (81). But while Sonny is disinterested in the grail narrative, he is fascinated by Arthurian imagery.

Marshall details Sonny's artistic process. At first, he devotes time and energy to "painstakingly" scrutinizing and tracing the original western images until he masters them. Sonny's expertise with respect to older European forms echoes that of his grandfather, who spent "years . . . practicing Bach, Beethoven, Chopin." The child's education in western forms even more closely mirrors that of Marshall. Not only did she, like Sonny, read of King Arthur at PS35 in Brooklyn, but also Marshall became a "great reader" who, before she became aware of the Black writers like Paul Laurence Dunbar and Gwendolyn Brooks, familiarized herself with "the great sweeping eighteenth- and nineteenth-century novels" that "came out of the canon of European literature" and white modernists such as Eliot, Joyce, Mann, and Conrad.[90] Marshall went on to study literature at Brooklyn College and Hunter College, where she could have taken a course with a leading authority on the Fisher King legend, medievalist Helaine Newstead.[91]

In her representation of Sonny's artistic practice, Marshall then recounts how he succeeds in making older western forms new and taking ownership over white culture. The images he now generates are no longer bound up with whiteness; they aren't—to riff on Cheryl Harris—the "property" of whites like Malory.[92] Like the music generated by his grandfather, Sonny-Rett, Sonny's art enjoys full liberation from the white original. In language that looks toward Marshall's representation of Sonny-Rett's "invent[ion]" of "Sonny Boy Blue" "in an image all his own," Sonny's drawings are "his own" and "of his own invention." Marshall also endows Sonny's drawings with the sacral qualities of his grandfather's musical artistry. Later in the novel, when Sonny visits his great uncle's home and shows his two young cousins his artwork, their response is sheer wonder. As Sonny "slowly turn[s] the pages," his cousin Benjamin "kept asking in awe" if Sonny did them all by himself (154). Eventually, after Sonny has "reached the last finished drawing" and explained the magical protective properties of the castle, he looked over to find that Benjamin had twisted his baseball cap around to the side of his head so that he could look at him more fully, without the visor getting in the way. Large eyes gazing at him as if he had suddenly grown as tall and important-looking as his uncle.

"You mean you really did all this yourself no kidding."

It was no longer a question.

The awe. (155)

Like his grandfather, Sonny wondrously asserts his individual Black talent. Marshall embeds in the plot of the novel that entanglement of the two artists by having Sonny generate a drawing of the Putnam Royal, the site of the grandfather's triumph, which Edgar plans to frame and hang in his office (141).

Underscoring the relation of Sonny's drawings to radical Black creativity is his signature. "In the bottom right-hand corner of every drawing," where white tradition dictates that the creator signs their name, Sonny "always drew a miniature version of himself in full armor, his visor down. . . . Himself armed with a lance, a wicked-looking halberd, or a Sir Lancelot broadsword" (75). Sonny's self-portrait revises the accoutrements of knightly identity. Repeatedly inscribing himself in different drawings, "in full armor, his visor down," Sonny suggests a complex identity politics that is at once destabilizing and empowering. Unlike the idea of a hereditary white aristocratic line endorsed by Malory's grail book, Sonny's knightly self-fashioning is predicated not on a biological fantasy—on myths about givens and essentials—but on a visual artistry that resonates with the Black expressive culture theorized by Kobena Mercer. Mercer considers such aspects of Black culture as conking, jive talk, and the zoot suit as instances of what he calls a "black style/politics."[93] For Mercer, such practices constitute "dialogic interventions of diasporean, creolizing cultures" that "combin[e] elements from any source black or white, past or present—into new configurations of cultural expression" (51). Sonny's signature exemplifies a similar style/politics. His "new configurations" of Arthurian material deploy creativity and artifice to generate an identity that, as Mercer puts it, "ambushes any attempt to track down fixed meanings or finalized readings and opens out instead on to ambiguous relations" between systems of signification (49).

By encasing his entire body in "full armor, his visor down," Sonny crafts for himself an identity untethered to the public display of physical qualities. The white New World cultures that were built on slavery legitimated themselves via essentializing discourses about the meaning of skin color, hair, and other visible bodily features. Sonny has experienced first-hand the persistence of racist beliefs about Black bodies at his Paris schoolyard, where a boy "mimed a gorilla" and "screamed at" Sonny, "'retourne à la brousse!'" (151). Through his "signature," however, Sonny takes imaginative ownership over his embodiment, making his physicality a secret and private affair. In addition, the suit of armor, along with his medieval weaponry, projects power, strength, and indestructibility, traits that at once acknowledge and defy the vulnerability of Black people in a white dominant society. This latter point receives more support when we consider why Sonny builds his "castles and fortresses" in the first place. Unbeknownst to all but the cousins in whom he confides, Sonny imagines that Sonny-Rett lives within his castles, with Sonny standing as sentinel to safeguard his grandfather from the systemic dangers that led to the musician's fatal encounter with the Parisian police.

The Fisher King signposts how Sonny's visual art allegorizes Marshall's literary creation via its title page, which contains none other than a version of the boy's iconic "signature" (Figure 4). Situated in the bottom right-hand corner of the page—in the very location of Sonny's castle drawings—the image intertwines the boy's visual art with Marshall's literary transformation of Arthurian lore. Importantly, Marshall's identification with Sonny, like her relationship to jazz "king" Sonny-Rett, is cross-gendered: while Sonny—like his grandfather—is a male artist, Marshall is a female author. One might view Marshall's gendering of Black artists within her novel—like Naylor's characterization of Miss Maple— as a mark of her feminist pessimism, that is, as a nod to the existence of certain patriarchal overlaps between western society and Black communities. In a similar vein, one might opine that Marshall made her young visual artist a boy to suggest how medieval Arthurian lore, because of its own stress on a brotherhood, is especially available for appropriation by Black males, just as jazz has been largely a "man's" world.

Marshall has acknowledged how the gender of such knightly healers as Galahad or Percival would have made it "hard to have the image really work" "with a girl."[94] But I would argue that the title page suggests something different: that Marshall advocates cross-gender identification and solidarity. Marshall's early interviews suggest her investment in female empowerment and her desire to show through her writings how women "can as easily embody the power principles as a man."[95] Starting with Silla Boyce's resistance in *Brown Girl, Brownstones* to received modes of Black immigrant belonging in Brooklyn, the most "radical opposition to dominance" leveraged by Marshall's writing has long involved, as Mary Helen Washington contends, "the story of sexual politics, of female resistance to the claims of community, of the emergence of female power."[96] However, Marshall increasingly grew interested in using her writing to address, as she put it in 1991, "the need for black men and women to come together in wholeness and unity."[97] In *The Fisher King*, Marshall

TRADITION AND THE INDIVIDUAL BLACK TALENT 245

The Fisher King

— A NOVEL —

Paule Marshall

Scribner

NEW YORK   LONDON   TORONTO   SYDNEY   SINGAPORE

Figure 4. Title Page, Paule Marshall, *The Fisher King* (New York: Scribner, 2000). Photo by author.

foregrounds her desire to portray in her writing "*some kind* of relationship—Black people, men and women—in a more egalitarian fashion" through its title page.[98] Marshall's wording—"some kind"—is telling and reflects her complication of easy fantasies of "wholeness and unity." In lieu of the perfection of the Round Table, the novel draws more complex and difficult lines of connection. With Sonny situated in its corner, Marshall's name at the center, and just above it, the titular "Fisher King" (who really represents not just Sonny-Rett but the plethora of injured elderly men and women in the novel), the title page visualizes a complex, triangulated approach to Black community that critiques white Arthurian brotherhoods and depends upon a version of the dynamic "theorizing" celebrated by Barbara Christian.[99] Through her rendering of a key means by which Sonny "jousts" with Arthurian tradition, Marshall foregrounds the status of *The Fisher King* as a kind of jousting ground where she contests and furiously recasts Arthuriana on behalf of her own Black modernist project. From this initial paratextual feature onward, *The Fisher King* rejects totalizing ideas of culture and society and instead advocates a triangular and complex take on identities and collectives.

Consider Hattie's relationship with Cherisse and Sonny-Rett. While Hattie's heart breaks when the two fall in love with each other after Everett's groundbreaking performance, she "told herself it might not be as bad as it felt at the moment; that in fact, it might be the way things were meant to be, the three of them like the connected sides of the triangles she used to draw in geometry in high school, with her as the base, joining them to herself" (140–41). "The triangle" that Hattie "had envisioned" comes to fruition when, later, the three live together in France in "sheer euphoria" (189). But after two decades, their arrangement ceases when first Sonny-Rett, then Cherisse, prematurely perish. Hattie, Cherisse, and Sonny-Rett's love triangle might initially suggest a contemporary Black version of the famous Arthurian love triangles.[100] But the public, mutually arranged, and agreed-upon nature of their union, along with Hattie's explicitly mathematical conception of its form and function, urge a comparison with the geometrical shape that symbolizes community in Malory: the Round Table. While, like the Round Table, the triad is a community whose demise causes great mourning and sadness (Hattie is "beyond comforting" when Sonny-Rett dies, and her body "bowed under the stone weight of her grief" after Cherisse dies from cancer [206]), the group departs radically from Malory's communal ideal. No grand and perfect circle, this lovers' community is small-scale, pointy, and angular. They form a nonnormative and temporary triangle of lovers. Their triangularity speaks, metonymically, to Marshall's approach to Black identity.[101]

This book began by tracing the modernity problem at work in white western accounts of history and identity. Relying on the insights of non-western thinkers like W. E. B. Du Bois and Sylvia Wynter, Part I confronted racializing continuities with medieval beliefs that expose how western modernity, far from a time of lucidity and human agency, instead endorses debilitating and irrational ideologies of a white *Geist* or spirit. Part II turned to the historical encounter between Tolkien and Hall described in the latter's memoir. While the Oxford don's rejection of Hall's proposed methodology reflects the intimacy of a bad white medievalism and white modernity problem, Hall's diasporic approach to *Piers Plowman* endorsed alternate ideas of identity and periodicity that adumbrated the brilliant poststructuralist and neo-Gramscian intellectual work he went on to perform. This final chapter on Paule Marshall, along with the previous chapter on Naylor, considered how Black U.S. women's fiction offers a singularly powerful corrective to a bad western medievalism and the white modernity problem it supports. Instead of working inside the discursive terms of western ideas of humanity and history, *Bailey's Cafe* and *The Fisher King* build alternate worlds that make possible critical—indeed, badass—medievalisms and modernisms. For Marshall and Naylor, the medieval serves as no repository for fantasies of a supreme white *Geist*, and modernity doesn't serve as the setting for the realization of white human potential. Instead, both writers make the medieval a newly strange means of unsettling whiteness: just as *Bailey's Cafe* explodes the *Canterbury Tales*, *The Fisher King* shatters white Arthurian lore. Pulling fragments from the ruins, both works brilliantly reconfigure the medieval as a resource for imagining Black selves and collectives not in a totalizing manner but rather in complex and shifting relation to historical multiplicity and heterogeneity.

Acknowledgments

I am delighted to acknowledge the many forms of support I received for this book.

I am very grateful for the financial support provided by the University of Iowa: a Strategic Research Priorities Grant, an Arts and Humanities Initiative Grant, a Career Development Award, and a Stanley International Travel Award.

Several librarians, archivists, scholars, and administrators helped me research the lives and work of J. R. R. Tolkien, Stuart Hall, Gloria Naylor, and Paule Marshall: Suzanne Edwards and Nadia Butler, Gloria Naylor Archive, Lehigh University; Julian Reid, Merton College Library, University of Oxford; Marianne LaBatto, Brooklyn College Archives; Mary Helen Washington, Paule Marshall Papers, Schomburg Center for Research in Black Culture, New York; Jenna Molster, National Public Radio; Nick Beech, Stuart Hall Archive, Cadbury Library, University of Birmingham; Kina Viola, Cornell Society for the Humanities, Cornell University; Eisha Neely, Division of Rare and Manuscript Collections, Cornell University; Adrienne Clay, American Studies Program, Cornell University; Genevieve Coyle, Manuscripts and Archives, Yale University Library; and Jamie Morris, English Department, Yale University.

Current and former students and colleagues at my home institution supported me through their friendship and by serving as generous readers and interlocutors: Bluford Adams, Asha Bhandari, Micah Bateman, Sarah Bond, Lori Branch, Frank Durham, Gigi Durham, Anahita Ghazvinizadeh, Blaine Greteman, Naomi Greyser, Rebekah Kowal, Marie Kruger, Brooks Landon, Tom Lin, Anna Morrison, Beth Oakes, Will Rhodes, Phil Round, Garrett Stewart, Stephen Voyce, Deborah Whaley, Doris Witt, and Nick Yablon. I'm grateful for everything I learned from the students in my fall 2022, spring 2022, and spring 2024 Critical Race Theory classes and the insights on Paule Marshall that my spring 2023 Arthurian romance students shared with me. I'm thankful for what I have learned about intersections of gender, religion, race, and sexuality from Thelma Trujillo. I'm grateful for the difficult but rewarding experience of teaching the Foundations of the English Major class at Iowa in 2018 and 2019 and the support and feedback that I received from students in those classes.

For their tips, willingness to be interviewed, collegiality, hospitality, and other forms of support, I thank Folabo Ajayi-Soyinka, Suzanne Conklin Akbari, Kate Baldwin, Rob Barrett, Dave Bullwinkle, Maria Sachiko Cecire, Lisa Cooper, Taylor Cowdery, Andrea Denny-Brown, Carolyn Dinshaw, Brian Edwards, Ruth Evans, Susanna Fein, Rita Felski, Catherine Hall, Robert Hanning, Eileen Joy, Aranye Fradenburg Joy, Wan-Chuan Kao, Peggy Knapp, Steve Kruger, Missy D. Kubitschek, Rob Latham, Stuart Lee, Emma Lipton, Eric Lott, Evan Marshall, Paul Megna, Jennifer Morgan, Ruth Nisse, R. D. Perry, Susie Phillips, Shyama Rajendran, Sara Ritchey, Jessica Rosenfeld, Bill Schwarz, Stephen Shapiro, R. A. Shoaf, Sandhya Shukla, Robert Stepto, Sylvia Tomasch, Jacqueline de Weever, Cord Whitaker, and Doris Witt.

I benefited from the rich environment for navigating Stuart Hall's oeuvre that was provided by the Stuart Hall Reading Group, organized by Deborah Whaley and hosted by the Obermann Center for Advanced Studies at Iowa: Loren Glass, Naomi Greyser, Chris Henderson, Michael Hill, Meena Khandelwal, Tom Oates, Jacki Rand, Laura Rigal, George Rozsa, Travis Vogan, Darrel Wanzer-Serrano, and Doris Witt.

I'm grateful to all the organizers of the talks and conferences where I presented work related to this book: the 2018 Celebrating Belle da Costa Greene Conference (Tarrell Campbell, Ruth Evans); the 2021 colloquium on Global/Premodern/Race at the University of California, Santa Barbara (Debra Blumenthal, Heather Blurton); the 2021 *Exemplaria* panel at the IMC (Jessica Rosenfeld); the 2021 Gloria Naylor Symposium (Lucia Acosta-Mack, Suzanne Edwards); the 2022 University of Alabama English Department Symposium on Race and American Medievalism in the U.S. South and Beyond (Alexandra Cook, Donna Beth Ellard, Cassander Smith); the 2023 Harvard English Medieval Colloquium at the IMC (Emily Sun, Jason Thames); the 2024 lecture series on Caste, Class, and Race at the Loyola University Medieval Studies Center (Theresa Gross-Diaz). I'm grateful to all who attended and responded to those talks, as well as my book-related conference presentations at: the New Chaucer Society (2018, 2020, 2024); Modern Language Association Convention (2019); International Society for the Study of Narrative Conference (2020);

American Comparative Literature Association (2023); and International Piers Plowman Society (2023).

I got by during the years it took to write this book, which encompassed the pandemic and so many other disasters at so many scales, in no small part through the friendship and neighborliness of Peter Binkow, Ann Connors, Rob Cornell, Tom Fesenmeyer, Brett Lanford, Hélène Lesage, John Murray, Kumar Narayanan, Shanti Roundtree, Valery Sedivy, Susannah Strode, Scott Thomas, Tim Wager, Jan Weissmiller, Stephanie Wells, and Elizabeth Willis.

Certain friends and treasured colleagues merit a special shout-out: Jenny Adams, Paula Amad, Kim Benston, Johanna Blakely, Suzanne Edwards, Laurel Farrin, Michael Flaum, John Ganim, Jennifer Hellwarth, Joann Jacobs, M. Lindsay Kaplan, Steven Kruger, Lisa Lampert-Weissig, and Susie Nakley.

I'm especially beholden to colleagues who read and commented on drafts and chapters: Jonathan Culler, Frank Grady, Geraldine Heng, Bruce Holsinger, Julia Lupton, Julie Orlemanski, Will Rhodes, Caroline Rody, Cathy Sanok, Larry Scanlon, James Simpson, Garrett Stewart, Lawrence Warner, Mary Helen Washington, and my anonymous readers at Fordham. I thank them from the bottom of my heart for their support, suggestions, corrections, and expertise. This book is stronger thanks to their input; all infelicities are my own.

An earlier version of Chapter 3 appeared in *postmedieval* 12, no. 1–4 (2021): 29–51. My editor at *postmedieval*, the phenomenal Julie Orlemanski, gave me exceptional guidance on that article. Elements of both that chapter and Chapter 4 appeared in a dialogue with Mariana Rios Maldonado in *postmedieval* 14, no. 1 (2023): 231–48. I am grateful to Mariana for her contribution to that piece. An earlier version of Chapter 6 appeared in *Women's Restorative Medievalisms: Forgotten Pasts and Unimagined Futures*, edited by Suzanne Edwards and Matthew X. Vernon (Leeds: Arc Humanities Press, 2024). Both Suzanne and Matthew offered extremely helpful input.

My final thanks are to members of my family, especially my mom, Mary, and my beloved and extraordinary daughter, Nina. Lastly, but also firstly and everywhere in between, my incalculable gratitude belongs to my best friend, co-parent, adventure partner, and absolute best reader and interlocutor, Harry Stecopoulos. Harry, who cheered me on from beginning to end and commented on countless drafts, may know this book better than I do. As always, this book could not have been written without the wisdom, guidance, encouragement of, and light that shakes from, Harry.

Stuart Hall's First Publication

Thanks belong to Nick Beech at the University of Birmingham for invaluable assistance in locating this editorial.

Periodical: *The Sunday Gleaner*, the Sunday edition of the *Daily Gleaner*, Kingston, Jamaica.
Date and page: January 3, 1954, 5.
Title: "Our Literary Heritage"
Byline: Stewart [sic] M. Hall,
Dateline: London
Lead: Jamaica Rhodes Scholar (1951) now at Merton College, Oxford, gives another view to that expressed by Mr. J. E. Clare MacFarlane [sic], Poet Laureate, on the occasion of his recent address to the Poetry League.

Body:
The relation of the West Indian writer to "his literary heritage" must be at this time, a matter of greatest concern. A literature, to remain alive, must know first where it stands, before it can perceive clearly whither it is bound.

But I find "Our Literary Heritage" as interpreted by the President of the Poetry League at the last Annual Meeting unsatisfactory, not to say disconcerting.

It is remarkable to find the view "that on the horizon of the English Poetry of this Century, there is but one star that promises the return of day, Bridges, the author of the Testament of Beauty," seriously entertained in this day and age.

This is merely a significant aside, in the main burden of the President's thesis, but it may serve as a point of departure for a different interpretation of "Tradition and The Individual (West Indian) Talent."

His argument is based in the first instance, on a persistent misreading of the whole movement of modern poetry. To say that "lack of discipline and discrimination, of forbearance and restraint is the most outstanding gesture of the poetry of our time" is to misinterpret every single poet of stature who has written since 1920.

Discipline, is perhaps the most important theme in Eliot's verse and criticism,—the need of the poet in an age of shattered disciplines and fragmented values—to seek sustenance [sic] from a meaningful tradition. The discipline of tradition, in this sense, is not the slavish capitulation to forms and rules, "but a perception not only of the pastness of the past but of its presence; the historical sense compels a man to write not merely with his own generation in his bones, but with a feeling that the whole of the literature of Europe from Homer and within it the whole of the literature of his own country has a simultaneous existence and composes a single order."

If there is any charge to be brought against a poet like W. H. Auden it is that of too great restraint, a charge of "lack of discipline and restraint" simply will not bear scrutiny. To compare Yeats' Countess Cathleen, with the superb control of feeling, the complete objectification of emotion which characterises the later Byzantium poems, or Among School Children, written under the influence of T. E. Hulme and Ezra Pound, argues a deficiency in discrimination.

The President does, in a sense appreciate the plight of the poet today, when he speaks of the fact that the contemporary artist "draws no sustenance from his environment," but he is not prepared to grant that this is a condition in which "genuine poetry" can exist.

"The poetry of satire" he prophesies, ". . . will fall into obscurity." I suspect that "genuine" is an emotive term, for he does not define its use in the context: and I should have thought that Shakespeare, Ben Jonson, Donne, Dryden, Pope, Byron, Auden, were enough evidence against the view that great poetry cannot also be ironical.

But it is clear from his defence of Romanticism, where his basic allegiances lie.

The "classical tradition" we are told, "does not afford the great poet much scope to express his individual viewpoint," lacks the power and conviction to find a way out":[1] "modern poetry is the reflection of a spirit which denies the existence of fundamental, moral laws, or the validity of qualities that proceed from the will to take pains."

The view that great poetry is always "the individual expressing his individual viewpoint" may be contradicted by examples as different as Dante, Chaucer, Shakespeare and Milton.

This is not to deny the validity of the individual vision, the contribution of the individual mind to great art. But great poetry springs from the interaction between the single "esemplastic" imagination of the artist (to quote Romantic Chapter and verse), and his society, the temper of the times in which he lives, the values which invest his culture.

Art springs from this perpetual conflict between the individual and his society, between the artist and his tradition.

Chaucer is the supreme example: bound by the imposing traditions of medieval Europe, circumscribed by the limiting disciplines of sources and literary conventions, Chaucer emerges as a supremely "original" artist. To consider Shakespeare merely as an "individual expressing his individual viewpoint," is to appreciate only one facet of his dramatic achievement.

The traditions of medieval folk drama, the hierarchy of medieval values which he asserts in the face of a rapidly emerging capitalist and individualist society, are only to name of two of the multitude of "disciplines" within which the dramatist worked. Even Milton, in some way the greatest of the "individualist" poets, was bound in his execution of Lycidas and Paradise Lost by the conventions of the pastoral and epic kinds. If we are going to consider literature as simply "individual expression" we are left with Shelley and Blake: and they are not enough.

The notion that poetry can "find a way out," "remake the world" is the supreme delusion of Romanticism. It springs from a confusion between the active and the contemplative activities, a confusion as to the ends of art.

Faced by the rapid expansion of industrial mechanism on a popular scale, the Romantics were thrown into revolt, trapped into the fallacy that poetry could compete on the same level, could "remake the world." This proved to be only a point of no return. Shelley lapsed into despair and self-pity, Wordsworth into the glorification of Nature as a religious principle, and Arnold into mistaking poetry for religion.

Poetry is of course vitally related to action, in so far as it deepens awareness and insight, in so far as it shapes the powers of discrimination of its readers, alters his sensibilities, enriches his sense of values. But it cannot produce the millennium. For that we need propaganda not art. In so far as the end of art is concerned with greater understanding, its function must remain contemplative.

To restress at this time, the supremacy of the individual, or in religious terms—as the address does—"our allegiance to a Person," is to repeat again the excesses of the Romantic humanists—to place the human individual once again at the centre of the universe. To interpret ultimate values in purely humanistic terms, is to commit again the cardinal sin of Pride.

The whole address is characterised by a spirit of undaunted optimism: but this suggests a persistent willingness to ignore the problems which beset mankind at this time, to overlook the plight of the artist in an age governed by material concerns and materialist values, coupled with a desire to return to the "poetry of hope and exhortation, the poetry of the simple emotions and the tender human heart."

In the Twentieth Century, that must inevitably be a poetry of release and escape from vital issues, a poetry of simplification and illusion. Can the mature sensibility in our age—be it European or West Indian—find life so simple and assuring to support once again a poetry of pure "hope and exhortation"? Is the plight of the West Indian artist so different from the European artist in a mass culture? Are we wholly unaffected by the loss of traditions, the loss of fixed conventions, the absence of belief, the decline of values, the fragmentation of a world view?

I do not understand what the President means when he suggests that "through an allegiance to . . . a Person, individuals will find themselves part of a community holding in honour a common tradition." It is this tradition which seems to me perilously positioned at this time, and precisely because of this "exaltation of the human personality."

I understand less when he continues, "and here we come face to face with the true nature of the poet's office." For the poet's office is, in these terms, curiously defined. "All we can fairly ask of the poet," writes F. R. Leavis, "is that he shall show himself to have been fully alive in this time." Or, to put it another way, as James did, that he shall be a man "on whom nothing is lost."

Ultimately, we return to the tantalising problem of the relation of the West Indian artist to his tradition, in his struggle to act the role of midwife to the new emerging culture. The argument is too long to be entered on here, but the fundamental point is that the West Indian finds himself in his peculiar plight, because, as Simey and Eric Williams have both pointed out, he is a man without a history, without a homogenous [sic] culture.[2]

He is in fact in the process of forging his tradition; but that tradition will ultimately be created from a synthesis, based upon a compromise between the heterodox cultures out of which he springs. It must begin within the English tradition, because his medium is ultimately determined by language: but it must be a reinterpreted tradition, bearing a real relationship to his environment, personality and institutions.

It is ridiculous to say "we are not part of the English tradition, and are part of it, in so far as we are part of the English tradition, and the English is part of the European."

Would he deny Derek Walcott his Dante and leave him only his Christopher Fry? And which influence has been the more valuable? We are part of, but different from, as the American culture is different, only perhaps more so.

As Ezra Pound says in Hugh Selwyn Moberly:

"The age demanded an image
Of its accelerated grimace
Something for the modern stage
Not, at any rate an Attic grace;

The age demanded chiefly a mould in plaster
Made with no loss of time,
A prose kinema, not, not assuredly, alabaster
Or the 'sculpture' of rhyme."

It is time we read our Pound again.

Notes

Introduction: Race, Affect, Periodization

1. This speculative opening foray in no way claims access to or the right to speak for other persons' affective formations.

2. Rita Felski and Susan Fraiman, introduction to "In the Mood," ed. Rita Felski and Susan Fraiman, special issue, *New Literary History* 43, no. 3 (2012): v–vi.

3. Terms like "the West" and "Europe" are imagined forms that are contingent on global processes and often tied to ideologies of "civilizational essence"; Talal Asad, *Formations of the Secular: Christianity, Islam, Modernity* (Stanford: Stanford University Press, 2003), 168. My use of such terms reflects my pragmatic need for always imperfect and problematic "short-hand generalizations"; Stuart Hall, "The West and the Rest: Discourse and Power," in *Formations of Modernity*, ed. Stuart Hall and Bram Grieben (Cambridge: Polity Press, 1992), 185–86. Recent work on Burton and Kant includes Drew Daniel, *The Melancholy Assemblage: Affect and Epistemology in the English Renaissance* (New York: Fordham University Press, 2013), and Robert Clewis, *The Kantian Sublime and the Revelation of Freedom* (Cambridge: Cambridge University Press, 2009).

4. Lorraine Daston and Peter Galison, *Objectivity* (Brooklyn: Zone, 2007).

5. Felski and Fraiman, introduction, vi.

6. Marshall Brown, "Periods and Resistances," *Modern Language Quarterly* 62, no. 4 (2001): 309.

7. Michel Foucault, "Nietzsche, Genealogy, History," in *Language, Counter-Memory, Practice: Selected Essays and Interviews*, trans. Donald F. Bouchard and Sherry Simon (Ithaca: Cornell University Press, 1977), 154.

8. Fredric Jameson, *A Singular Modernity: Essay on the Ontology of the Present* (London: Verso, 2012), 94.

9. Paul Freedman and Gabrielle Spiegel, "Medievalisms Old and New: The Rediscovery of Alterity in North American Medieval Studies," *American Historical Review* 103, no. 3 (1998): 678.

10. "*Antiquitas* . . . is distinguished from *nostris temporibus* or the *seculis modernis*" as early as Cassiodorus's sixth-century writings and would continue to serve as a touchstone for understandings of modernity—whether as exemplar, double, foil—through the Italian Renaissance and up to the late seventeenth-century *querelle des anciens et des modernes*; Hans Robert Jauss, "Modernity and Literary Tradition," trans. Christian Thorne, *Critical Inquiry* 31, no. 2 (2005): 333, from *Literaturgeschichte als Provokation* (Frankfurt: Suhrkamp Verlag, 1970), 11–66.

11. Jürgen Habermas, "Modernity: An Unfinished Project," in *Habermas and the Unfinished Project of Modernity*, ed. Maurizio Passerin d'Entrèves and Seyla Benhabib (Cambridge, Mass.: MIT Press, 1997), 39.

12. *Oxford English Dictionary*, s.v. "medieval," accessed March 2024, https://doi.org/10.1093/OED/1192845685; *Collins English Dictionary and Thesaurus*, s.v. "medieval," accessed March 2024, https://www.collinsdictionary.com/us/dictionary/english/medieval.

13. Louise Fradenburg, "'So That We May Speak of Them': Enjoying the Middle Ages," *New Literary History* 28, no. 2 (1997): 211.

14. David Harvey, *The Condition of Postmodernity* (Oxford: Blackwell, 1989), 244, 249. Harvey draws on Samuel Edgerton, *The Renaissance Rediscovery of Linear Perspective* (1975), who in turn relies upon Erwin Panofsky's *Perspective as Symbolic Form* (1924–25).

15. Wallace Ferguson, *The Idea of the Renaissance in Historical Thought: Five Centuries of Interpretation* (Boston: Houghton Mifflin, 1948), 329.

16. Margreta de Grazia, "The Modern Divide: From Either Side," *Journal of Medieval and Early Modern Studies* 37, no. 3 (2007): 457.

17. In *The Light Ages: The Surprising Story of Medieval Science* (New York: Norton, 2020), Seb Faulk cites examples of "the irresistible medieval drive to tinker, to redesign, to incrementally improve or upgrade technology" to show how "the medieval reality" is "a Light Age of scientific interest and inquiry" (56, 4). With his use of contemporary technological and late capitalist catchphrases—for instance, Richard of Wallingford's decision to name his "planetary supercomputer" Albion was a "masterstroke" of national "branding"—Faulk suggests how a "line runs from the Middle Ages to the new neoliberal millennium" (151, 292). In *The Bright Ages: A New History of Medieval Europe* (New York: Harper Collins, 2021), Matthew Gabriele and David Perry contend that "everything in the Italian Renaissance . . . finds its foundations literally and figuratively squarely in the Middle Ages" (234). Soliciting readerly affect through abundant exclamations, *Bright Ages* gushes over a past that boasts a wealth of "shimmering," "gleaming," "dawn," "sun-dappled," "golden," "radiant," "glistening," and "brilliant" sights. Mary Rambaran-Olm critiques Gabriele and Perry's Eurocentrism in "Sounds About White," *Medium*, April 27, 2022, https://mrambaranolm.medium.com/sounds-about-white-333docofd201.

Jonathan Hsy discusses how "earnest calls by white medievalists to defend an 'abused' Middle Ages can misleadingly send a message to the public that medieval Europe was somehow 'innocent' of historical forms of racism, xenophobia, or prejudice in its own right" and cites related commentaries on that problematic trend in *Antiracist Medievalisms: From "Yellow Peril" to Black Lives Matter* (Leeds: Arc Humanities Press, 2021), 7.

18. Examples include Hortense Spillers, "Mama's Baby, Papa's Maybe: An American Grammar Book," *Diacritics* 17, no. 2 (1987): 65–81; Sylvia Wynter, "The Ceremony Must Be Found: After Humanism," in "On Humanism and the University I: The Discourses of Humanism," ed. William Spanos, special issue, *boundary 2* 12, no. 3–13, no. 1 (1987): 19–70; Alexander Weheliye, *Habeas Viscus: Racializing Assemblages, Biopolitics, and Black Feminist Theories of the Human* (Durham, N.C.: Duke University Press, 2014); Sara Ahmed, *The Promise of Happiness* (Durham, N.C.: Duke University Press, 2010); Sianne Ngai, *Ugly Feelings* (Cambridge, Mass.: Harvard University Press, 2005); Anne Anlin Cheng, *The Melancholy of Race* (Oxford: Oxford University Press, 2001); Lauren Berlant, *Cruel Optimism* (Durham, N.C.: Duke University Press, 2011); Jennifer C. Nash, *Black Feminism Reimagined: After Intersectionality* (Durham, N.C.: Duke University Press, 2019); and Heather Love, *Feeling Backward: Loss and the Politics of Queer History* (Cambridge, Mass.: Harvard University Press, 2007). Subsequent page citations of Love, *Feeling Backward*, and Ngai, *Ugly Feelings*, appear parenthetically in the text.

19. Wynter, "Ceremony," 22, 63.

20. Stuart Hall with Bill Schwarz, *Familiar Stranger: A Life between Two Islands* (Durham, N.C.: Duke University Press, 2017), 155.

21. Stuart Hall, "Stuart Hall Interview—2 June 2011," interview by Hudson Vincent, *Cultural Studies* 27, no. 5 (2011): 757–58.

22. Hall, *Familiar Stranger*, 156.

23. Cf. J. R. R. Tolkien, *The Monsters and the Critics, and Other Essays* (Boston: Houghton Mifflin, 1984), 33–34.

24. Hall, *Familiar Stranger*, 156.

25. The meanings of "medievalism" and "modernism" are subject to scholarly debate. I follow Hsy and David Matthews in defining medievalism as a phenomenon that encompasses how professionals and non-professionals have made the Middle Ages an object of inquiry and engagement; see Hsy, *Antiracist Medievalisms*; David Matthews, *Medievalism: A Critical History* (Cambridge: Brewer, 2015). While scholars often understand modernism as an embrace of modernity (however defined) and/or an aesthetic movement tied to writing and art produced between the two world wars, I define it as an expansive and flexible phenomenon that exceeds the period of high modernism and responds to not just the successes of modernity but also its failures, or what other critics call "anti-modernism." I understand modernism not just as the productions of a cohort of largely white male artists from 1918 to 1940 but as a wide array of aesthetic,

intellectual, and popular ideas about the promise and the benefits, as well as the shortcomings and dangers, of modernity.

26. Jacqueline de Weever, *Sheba's Daughters: Whitening and Demonizing the Saracen in Medieval French Epic* (New York: Garland, 1998); Geraldine Heng, *The Invention of Race in the European Middle Ages* (Cambridge: Cambridge University Press, 2018); Wan-Chuan Kao, *White before Whiteness in the Late Middle Ages* (Manchester: Manchester University Press, 2024); Cord Whitaker, *Black Metaphors: How Modern Racism Emerged from Medieval Race-Thinking* (Philadelphia: University of Pennsylvania Press, 2019); Wynter, "Ceremony"; see also works cited in note 96.

27. Examples include Lawrence Grossberg, "Postmodernity and Affect: All Dressed Up with No Place to Go," *Communication* 10, no. 3–4 (1988): 271–93; Brian Massumi, *Parables for the Virtual: Movement, Affect, Sensation* (Durham, N.C.: Duke University Press, 2002).

28. Rei Terada, *Feeling in Theory: Emotion after the "Death of the Subject"* (Cambridge, Mass.: Harvard University Press, 2001), 11.

29. Raymond Williams, *Marxism and Literature* (Oxford: Oxford University Press, 1977); Ngai, *Ugly Feelings*; Sara Ahmed, *The Cultural Politics of Emotions* (Edinburgh: Edinburgh University Press, 2014). See also the critics cited in Ahmed, *Cultural Politics*, 9.

30. Sara Ahmed and Sigrid Schmitz, "Affect/Emotion: Orientation Matters; A Conversation between Sigrid Schmitz and Sara Ahmed," *Freiburger Zeitschrift für GeschlechterStudien* 20, no. 2 (2014): 100.

31. Gregory J. Seigworth and Melissa Gregg, "An Inventory of Shimmers," introduction to *The Affect Theory Reader*, ed. Melissa Gregg and Gregory J. Seigworth (Durham, N.C.: Duke University Press, 2010), 1; Williams, *Marxism and Literature*, 132.

32. Ahmed, *Cultural Politics*, 195.

33. Ibid., 191.

34. Ahmed and Schmitz, "Affect/Emotion," 100.

35. Berlant, *Cruel Optimism*, 13.

36. Especially relevant to Stuart Hall is Melissa Gregg, *Cultural Studies' Affective Voices* (New York: Palgrave, 2006).

37. Sara Ahmed, "A Phenomenology of Whiteness," *Feminist Theory* 8, no. 2 (2007): 149–68; Ahmed, *Cultural Politics*, 182.

38. Berlant, *Cruel Optimism*, 121–22.

39. L. O. Aranye Fradenburg, "'Voice Memorial': Loss and Reparation in Chaucer's Poetry," *Exemplaria* 2, no. 1 (1990): 172.

40. Ibid.; Kathleen Biddick, *The Shock of Medievalism* (Durham, N.C.: Duke University Press, 1998); Donna Beth Ellard, *Anglo-Saxon(ist) Pasts, PostSaxon Futures* (New York: Punctum, 2019); Thomas Prendergast and Stephanie Trigg, *Affective Medievalisms: Love, Abjection and Discontent* (Manchester: Manchester University Press, 2019). A striking example of the latter formation (medievalists'

enjoyment of sacrifice) is the charged zero-sum game Fradenburg identifies in Paul Olson's *The Canterbury Tales and the Good Society* (Princeton: Princeton University Press, 1986). Olson's claim that, were Chaucer viewed through a modern lens, contemporary critics would "despise his vision," exposes how, for that Chaucerian, nothing less than "catastrophic rejection and loss" would result from the failure to identify with the medieval poet's "conscious . . . views"; Fradenburg, "'Voice Memorial,'" 174–75; Olson, *Canterbury Tales*, 18.

41. This scholarship includes Fradenburg, "'So That We May Speak of Them'"; Carolyn Dinshaw, *How Soon Is Now? Medieval Texts, Amateur Readers and the Queerness of Time* (Durham, N.C.: Duke University Press, 2012); and Prendergast and Trigg, *Affective Medievalisms*.

42. Lisa Lampert-Weissig, *Gender and Jewish Difference from Paul to Shakespeare* (Philadelphia: University of Pennsylvania Press, 2004), 17–19.

43. Carolyn Dinshaw, "Pale Faces: Race, Religion, and Affect in Chaucer's Texts and Their Readers," *Studies in the Age of Chaucer* 23 (2001): 20, 40.

44. Cord Whitaker, "Race-ing the Dragon: The Middle Ages, Race and Trippin' into the Future," *postmedieval* 6, no. 1 (2015): 3–11; Hsy, *Antiracist Medievalisms*; Shokoofeh Rajabzadeh, "The Depoliticized Saracen and Muslim Erasure," *Literature Compass* 16, no. 9–10 (2019): 1–8; Kao, *White before Whiteness*; Kavita Mudan Finn, "'Many Straunge Sgnes and Tokyns': The Affective Power of Thomas Malory's Palomides," *Arthuriana* 31, no. 2 (2021): 108–23.

45. Finn, "'Many Straunge Sygnes and Tokyns,'" 110–11.

46. Frantz Fanon, *Black Skin, White Masks*, trans. Richard Philcox (New York: Grove, 2008), 109. Fanon inspires much Afropessimism, for instance, Frank Wilderson, *Afropessimism* (New York: Liveright, 2020); and David Marriott, *Lacan Noir: Lacan and Afro-Pessimism* (Cham, Switzerland: Springer, 2021). The expanding recent work on race and affect, which encompasses both assessing how, as Divya P. Tolia-Kelly and Mike Crang put it, "racial categorisation is felt and enacted through a profoundly emotive register" *and* rejecting ideas of emotionality and racial hierarchy, includes Tolia-Kelly and Crang, "Affect, Race, and Identities," *Environment and Planning A* 42 (2010): 2309; and Eduardo Bonilla-Silva, "Feeling Race: Theorizing the Racial Economy of Emotions," *American Sociological Review* 84, no. 1 (2019): 1–25.

47. Rita Felski, *The Gender of Modernity* (Cambridge, Mass.: Harvard University Press, 1996), 11; see also Bruno Latour, *We Have Never Been Modern*, trans. Catherine Porter (Cambridge, Mass.: Harvard University Press, 1993), 10–12. Latour and Felski are just two of the plethora of critics who confront the challenge of defining modernity.

48. Felski, *Gender of Modernity*, 11–13. For definitions of modernism and medievalism, see note 25.

49. Jauss, "Modernity and Literary Tradition," 333.

50. Ibid., 336, 347.

51. Alexander Woodside, *Lost Modernities: China, Vietnam, Korea and the Hazards of World History* (Cambridge, Mass.: Harvard University Press, 2006), 1;

Susan Stanford Friedman, *Planetary Modernisms: Provocations on Modernity across Time* (New York: Columbia University Press, 2015), 105–19; Aaron Gerow, *Visions of Japanese Modernity: Articulations of Cinema, Nation and Spectatorship, 1885–1925* (Berkeley: University of California Press, 2010).

52. Felski, *Gender of Modernity*, 13.
53. Friedman, *Planetary Modernisms*, 7, 318.
54. Ibid., 56, citing Latour, *We Have Never Been Modern*, 10.
55. Jennifer Fleissner, *Maladies of the Will: The American Novel and the Modernity Problem* (Chicago: University of Chicago Press, 2022); Robert Pippin, *Idealism as Modernism: Hegelian Variations* (Cambridge: Cambridge University Press, 1997).
56. Edward Said, *Orientalism: Western Conceptions of the Orient* (New York: Vintage, 1979); Johannes Fabian, *Time and the Other: How Anthropology Makes Its Object* (New York: Columbia University Press, 1983); Dipesh Chakrabarty, *Habitations of Modernity: Essays in the Wake of Subaltern Studies* (Chicago: University of Chicago Press, 2002); Kathleen Davis, *Periodization and Sovereignty: How Ideas of Feudalism and Secularization Govern the Politics of Time* (Philadelphia: University of Pennsylvania Press, 2008).
57. Chakrabarty, *Habitations*, ix.
58. Claire Alexander, "Stuart Hall and 'Race,'" *Cultural Studies* 23, no. 4 (2009): 458.
59. Stuart Hall, *The Fateful Triangle: Race, Ethnicity, Nation*, ed. Kobena Mercer (Cambridge, Mass.: Harvard University Press, 2017), 32. Subsequent page citations appear parenthetically in the text.
60. Noel Ignatiev, *How the Irish Became White* (New York: Routledge, 1995), 76; W. E. B. Du Bois, *Black Reconstruction* (New York: Harcourt, Brace, 1935), 83. See also Eric Goldstein, *The Price of Whiteness: Jews, Race, and American Identity* (Princeton: Princeton University Press, 2006); and David Roediger, *The Wages of Whiteness: Race and the Making of the American Working Class* (London: Verso, 1991).
61. Kobena Mercer, introduction to Hall, *Fateful Triangle*, 15.
62. As the stress on psychological absolutes in antisemitic discourse exemplifies, racism doesn't always entail claims centered on bodily appearance (and especially skin color). See Kathy Lavezzo, *The Accommodated Jew: English Antisemitism from Bede to Milton* (Ithaca: Cornell University Press, 2016); Steven Kruger, "The Bodies of Jews in the Late Middle Ages," in *The Idea of Medieval Literature: New Essays on Chaucer and Medieval Culture in Honor of Donald Howard*, ed. James Dean and Christian Zacher (Newark: University of Delaware Press, 1992), 301–22.
63. Stuart Hall, "New Ethnicities," in *Critical Dialogues in Cultural Studies*, ed. David Morley and Kuan-Hsing Chen (New York: Routledge, 1996), 446.
64. J. J. Chinn, I. K. Martin, and N. Redmond, "Health Equity among Black Women in the United States," *Journal of Women's Health* 30, no. 2 (2021): 212; Michelle Alexander, *The New Jim Crow: Mass Incarceration in the Age of Colorblindness* (New York: New Press, 2010), 1–2.

65. Stuart Hall, "Race, Articulation, and Societies Structured in Dominance," in *Sociological Theories: Race and Colonialism*, ed. Marion O'Callaghan (Paris: UNESCO, 1980), 325.

66. Hall's approach resonates with other work highlighting the "manifold and simultaneous" factors (race and gender, but also sexuality, ability, age, class, and more) that catalyze what Deborah King describes as a "multiple jeopardy, multiple consciousness" in people of color, and especially, as Ahmed puts it, "all those who travel under the sign women"; Deborah King, "Multiple Jeopardy, Multiple Consciousness: The Context of a Black Feminist Ideology," *Signs* 14, no. 1 (1988): 43; Sara Ahmed, *Living a Feminist Life* (Durham, N.C.: Duke University Press, 2017), 14. Examples include the Combahee River Collective's account of how "major systems of oppression are interlocking," Kimberlé Crenshaw's oft-cited intersectional metaphor, and Jasbir Puar's reformulation of Deleuze and Guattari's theory of "assemblage"; Combahee River Collective, "A Black Feminist Statement," *Women's Studies Quarterly* 42, no. 3–4 (2014): 271; Kimberlé Crenshaw, "Mapping the Margins: Intersectionality, Identity Politics, and Violence against Women of Color," *Stanford Law Review* 43, no. 6 (1991): 1241–99; Jasbir K. Puar, "I Would Rather Be a Cyborg Than a Goddess: Becoming-Intersectional in Assemblage Theory," *philoSOPHIA* 2, no. 1 (2012): 49–66. As scholars including Jennifer Nash stress, Black feminist work on the complexities of identity is rich and various and includes but also extends beyond the dynamic Crenshaw famously has described as intersectional; see Nash, *Black Feminism Reimagined*. On Hall's emerging consciousness of gender, see Stuart Hall and bell hooks, *Uncut Funk: A Contemplative Dialogue* (New York: Routledge, 2018).

67. Hall, "Race, Articulation," 338.

68. Examples include Mary Rambaran-Olm, "A Wrinkle in Medieval Time: Ironing Out Issues Regarding Race, Temporality and the Early English," *New Literary History* 52, no. 3 (2021): 385–406; Ellard, *Anglo-Saxon(ist) Pasts*; Joshua Davies, "The Middle Ages as Property: *Beowulf*, Translation and the Ghosts of Nationalism," *postmedieval* 10 (2019): 137–50; Mary Rambaran-Olm, M. Breann Leake, and Micah Goodrich, "Medieval Studies: The Stakes of the Field," introduction to "Race, Revulsion, and Revolution," special issue, *postmedieval* 11, no. 4 (2020): 356–70.

69. Michelle Warren, *Creole Medievalism: Colonial France and Joseph Bédier's Middle Ages* (Minneapolis: University of Minnesota Press, 2011).

70. Adam Miyashiro, "Our Deeper Past: Race, Settler Colonialism, and Medieval Heritage Politics," *Literature Compass* 16, no. 9–10 (2019): 4.

71. Rambaran-Olm, "Wrinkle," 395–97.

72. Miyashiro, "Our Deeper Past," 9. Hsy tracks work by scholars of color on "the coopting of medieval imagery and rhetoric by modern extremist groups for racist, antisemitic, and Islamophobic aims" in *Antiracist Medievalisms*, xi, 1–12. Matthew Vernon unpacks the white U.S. workings of ideas of medieval heritage in *The Black Middle Ages: Race and the Construction of the Middle Ages* (Cham, Switzerland: Palgrave-Macmillan, 2018), 1–43.

73. Those strategies of othering also have aimed at competing groups and competing political, legal, religious, and other structures that are internal to the West, including those Europeans deemed at some level un-European and unmodern; see Davis, *Periodization*; Roberto Dainotto, *Europe (in Theory)* (Durham, N.C.: Duke University Press, 2007); Asad, *Formations of the Secular*; Margaret R. Greer, Walter D. Mignolo, and Maureen Quilligan, eds., *Rereading the Black Legend: The Discourses of Religious and Racial Difference in the Renaissance Empires* (Chicago: University of Chicago Press, 2007).

74. Davis, *Periodization*, 4.

75. Nadia Altschul and Kathleen Davis, eds., *Medievalisms in the Postcolonial World: The Idea of the "Middle Ages" outside Europe* (Baltimore: Johns Hopkins University Press, 2009).

76. Ananya Jahanara Kabir, "Analogy in Translation: Imperial Rome, Medieval England, and British India," in *Postcolonial Approaches to the European Middle Ages*, ed. Ananya Jahanara Kabir and Deanne Williams (Cambridge: Cambridge University Press, 2005), 194–95; see also John Ganim, *Medievalism and Orientalism: Three Essays on Literature, Architecture and Cultural Identity* (New York: Palgrave Macmillan, 2008), 8.

77. Warren, *Creole Medievalism*, xxvii. On medievalism and creole coloniality, see also Nadia Altschul, *Geographies of Philological Knowledge: Postcoloniality and the Transatlantic National Epic* (Chicago: University of Chicago Press, 2012).

78. Simon Gikandi, "Africa and the Signs of Medievalism," in Altschul and Davis, *Medievalisms in the Postcolonial World*, 370.

79. Ibid. Claims about the medieval qualities of Africa are ongoing; see Matthews, *Medievalism*, 88–89.

80. Nancy Leys Stepan and Sander L. Gilman, "Appropriating the Idioms of Science: The Rejection of Scientific Racism," in *The Bounds of Race: Perspectives on Hegemony and Resistance*, ed. Dominick LaCapra (Ithaca: Cornell University Press, 1991), 74.

81. Frederick Douglass, "The Claims of the Negro Ethnologically Considered: An Address Delivered in Hudson, Ohio, on July 12, 1854," in *The Speeches of Frederick Douglass*, ed. John McKivigan, Julie Husband, and Heather Kaufman (New Haven: Yale University Press, 2018), 132; "Statement on Race, Paris, July 1950," *Four Statements on the Race Question* (Paris: UNESCO, 1969), 33.

82. Vernon, *Black Middle Ages*, 18; Frederick Douglass, *My Bondage and My Freedom*, (New York: Miller, Orton and Mulligan, 1855), 61. On Douglass, see Vernon, *Black Middle Ages*, 45–75.

83. Douglass, *My Bondage*, 61.

84. A blog post on the medievalism of the capitol attack containing a helpful bibliography is Richard Fahey, "Marauders in the US Capitol: Alt-right Viking Wannabes and Weaponized Medievalism," *Medieval Studies Research Blog*, University of Notre Dame, January 15, 2021, https://sites.nd.edu/manuscript-studies/tag/insurrection/.

85. Susan Page, "What They Saw: Police Officers Describe the Jan. 6 Capitol Attack Like 'a Medieval Battle,'" *USA Today*, July 27, 2021, https://www.usatoday.com/story/news/politics/2021/07/27/jan-6-assault-capitol-like-a-medieval-battle-police-testify/8001477002/.

86. Amy Wang, "Biden Slams Trump for Watching Jan. 6 Riot as Police Faced 'Medieval Hell,'" *Washington Post*, July 25, 2022, https://www.washingtonpost.com/national-security/2022/07/25/biden-jan6-trump-medieval-hell/. Hsy clarifies how rejecting contemporary racist medievalisms "can create a falsely reassuring sense of progressive collective identity that leaves longstanding racial power structures unchanged"; *Antiracist Medievalisms*, 7. See also Louise D'Arcens, *World Medievalism: The Middle Ages in Modern Textual Culture* (Oxford: Oxford University Press, 2021), ix.

87. Stepan and Gilman, "Appropriating the Idioms," 77.

88. Ibid., 76.

89. Ahmed, "Phenomenology," 161.

90. Hall, "New Ethnicities," 448.

91. Hartman's analysis of fungibility, Harris's analysis of whiteness as property, and Spillers's theorization of "female flesh 'ungendered'" clarify how slavery, in Hartman's words, "has yet to be undone" in the U.S.; Spillers, "Mama's Baby," 68; Saidiya Hartman, *Lose Your Mother: A Journey along the Atlantic Slave Route* (New York: Farrar, Straus, and Giroux, 2008), 6. Examples of the afterlife of slavery include Black persons' "limited access to health and education, premature death, incarceration, and impoverishment," and the function of whiteness as safeguard against the "threat of commodification"; Hartman, *Lose Your Mother*; Cheryl Harris, "Whiteness as Property," *Harvard Law Review* 106, no. 8 (1993): 1721.

92. Simon Gikandi, *Slavery and the Culture of Taste* (Princeton: Princeton University Press, 2011), 41.

93. Unfortunately, however, the association of the medieval with a sundered past has proven hard to reject. As Davis shows, even the most penetrating analyses of Eurocentrism and periodization fail to view the medieval as anything more than modernity's other; *Periodization*, 2–3.

94. Fanon, *Black Skin*, 91; Robert Sturges, "Race, Sex, Slavery: Reading Fanon with *Aucassin et Nicolette*," *postmedieval* 6, no. 1 (2015): 12–22.

95. De Weever, *Sheba's Daughters*, 54.

96. Richard Sévère, "Arthur from the Margins: Race, Equity, and Justice in Arthurian Studies," *Arthuriana* 31, no. 2 (2021): 4. Key studies include Lindsay Kaplan, *Figuring Racism in Medieval Christianity* (New York: Oxford University Press, 2019); Magda Teter, *Christian Supremacy: Reckoning with the Roots of Antisemitism and Racism* (Princeton: Princeton University Press); María Elena Martínez, *Genealogical Fictions: Limpieza de Sangre, Religion, and Gender in Colonial Mexico* (Stanford: Stanford University Press, 2008); Kim Phillips, *Before Orientalism: Asian Peoples and Cultures in European Travel Writing, 1245–1510* (Philadelphia: University of Pennsylvania Press, 2014); Sharon Kinoshita, *Medieval*

Boundaries: Rethinking Difference in Old French Literature (Philadelphia: University of Pennsylvania Press, 2013); de Weever, *Sheba's Daughters*; Whitaker, *Black Metaphors*; Kao, *White before Whiteness*; Alice Rio, *Slavery after Rome, 500–1100* (Oxford: Oxford University Press, 2017); Hannah Barker, *That Most Precious Merchandise: The Mediterranean Trade in Black Sea Slaves* (Philadelphia: University of Pennsylvania Press, 2019); Thomas Hahn, ed., *A Cultural History of Race in the Middle Ages* (London: Bloomsbury, 2022); Kimberly Coles and Dorothy Kim, eds., *A Cultural History of Race in the Renaissance and Early Modern Age* (London: Bloomsbury, 2021); Heng, *Invention*; Lisa Lampert-Weissig, *Medieval Literature and Postcolonial Studies* (Edinburgh: Edinburgh University Press, 2010); Robert Bartlett, *Gerald of Wales: 1146–1223* (Oxford: Clarendon Press, 1982); Sierra Lomuto, ed., "The Medieval 'Undone': Imagining a New Global Past," special issue, *boundary 2* 50, no. 3 (2023); Cord J. Whitaker, Nahir I. Otaño Gracia, and François-Xavier Fauvelle, eds., "Race, Race-Thinking and Identity in the Global Middle Ages," special issue, *Speculum* 99, no. 2 (2024).

97. Heng, *Invention*, 20–21.

98. Heng, *Invention*, 44.

99. I use CE, itself a deeply problematic temporal designation, for pragmatic purposes and not to endorse its Christian bias; see Miriamne Krummel, *The Medieval Postcolonial Jew, In and Out of Time* (Ann Arbor: University of Michigan Press, 2022).

100. Kao, *White before Whiteness*, 11. Kao investigates "what things are recognized or misrecognized as 'white' in late medieval sociality and thought" and contrasts "the broad sense and the capacious constellation of subjectivities enfolded within premodern whiteness" with "the delimiting, homogenizing and singularizing sense of whiteness in modernity" (9–10).

101. Davis suggests how medieval thinkers—namely, the Venerable Bede—provide alternate approaches to time that might assist contemporary thinkers in getting beyond rigid, confining, and misleading temporal binaries in *Periodization*. Adam Miyashiro describes an alternate periodization based on ideas of a global tributary order in "Race, Medieval Studies, and Disciplinary Boundaries," *boundary 2* 50, no. 3 (2023): 107–21. Shirin Khanmohamadi describes ethical interactions with difference on the part of medieval Christians in *In Light of Another's Word: European Ethnography in the Middle Ages* (Philadelphia: University of Pennsylvania Press, 2014). On southern European intellectuals, themselves the object of othering by northern Europeans, who put forth an alternate model of interaction and historical change, see Karla Mallette, *European Modernity and the Arab Mediterranean: Toward a New Philology and a Counter-Orientalism* (Philadelphia: University of Pennsylvania Press, 2010), and Dainotto, *Europe (In Theory)*.

102. Edward Said, "The Clash of Ignorance," *Nation*, October 22, 2000, 11–13. Cf. Said, *Orientalism*, 68–63; Sharon Kinoshita, "Deprovincializing the Middle Ages," in *The Worlding Project: Doing Cultural Studies in the Era of Globalization*, ed. Rob

Wilson (Berkeley, Calif.: North Atlantic, 2007), 61–75; Kathleen Davis, "Time behind the Veil: The Media, the Middle Ages, and Orientalism Now," in *The Postcolonial Middle Ages*, ed. Jeffrey J. Cohen (New York: Palgrave, 2000), 105–22; Kathleen Biddick, "Coming out of Exile: Dante on the Orient Express," in Cohen, *Postcolonial Middle Ages*, 35–52.

103. Robyn Wiegman, "The Ends of New Americanism," *New Literary History* 42, no. 3 (2011): 390.

104. Miri Rubin, *Gentile Tales: The Narrative Assault on Late Medieval Jews* (Philadelphia: University of Pennsylvania Press, 1999), 139; Peter Haidu, *The Subject of Violence: The Song of Roland and the Birth of the State* (Bloomington: Indiana University Press, 1993), 37; Jo Ann McNamara, "The *Herrenfrage*: The Restructuring of the Gender System, 1050–1150," in *Medieval Masculinities: Regarding Men in the Middle Ages*, ed. Clare Lees (Minneapolis: University of Minnesota Press, 1994), 22. This important work includes scholarship on medieval racism and related work generated by the collectives linked with the Medievalists of Color, the BABEL Working Group (2004–17), the journal *postmedieval*, and Punctum Books.

105. Alan Wolfe, "Anti-American Studies: The Difference between Criticism and Hate," *New Republic* 228, no. 5 (2003): 26, 30; Frederick Crews, "Whose American Renaissance?," *New York Review* 16 (1988): 68; Wiegman, "Ends of New Americanism," 389–90.

106. Michael Calabrese, "Performing the Prioress: 'Conscience' and Responsibility in Studies of Chaucer's *Prioress's Tale*," *Texas Studies in Literature and Language* 44, no. 1 (2002): 69; D. Vance Smith, "The Application of Thought to Medieval Studies," *Exemplaria* 22, no. 1 (2010): 87, 85.

107. Tarren Andrews, "Indigenous Futures and Medieval Pasts," *English Language Notes* 58, no. 2 (2020): 6.

108. Calabrese, "Performing," 71.

109. As a white, straight, upper-middle-class woman raised in the U.S. as a Catholic by Italian and Irish parents, I have—and still do—felt and enjoyed many, if not all, of the comforts, possessions, privileges, and powers of white normativity as it manifests in discourse and historical practices. As a white woman embedded in the field formation of my discipline, I am complicit in what George Lipsitz describes as "the impossibility of the anti-racist subject," as well as the "tension between particularity and universality" through which, as Robyn Wiegman stresses, whiteness functions; George Lipsitz, private correspondence with Wiegman, cited in Robyn Wiegman, "Whiteness Studies and the Paradox of Particularity," in *The Futures of American Studies*, ed. Donald Pease and Robyn Wiegman (Durham, N.C.: Duke University Press, 2002), 275; Wiegman, "Whiteness Studies," 270. For example, to the extent that the range of the topics analyzed and the identifications performed in this book produce my rational mobility, I risk contributing to the reification that, in Ahmed's words, "allows whiteness to be done"; "Phenomenology," 150; see also Wiegman, "Whiteness Studies."

110. Barbara Christian, "The Race for Theory," *Cultural Critique* 6 (1987): 52.
111. Weheliye, *Habeas Viscus*, 3.
112. Ibid., 5.
113. Cheng, *Melancholy*, 137.
114. Stuart Hall, "Culture, Media and the 'Ideological Effect,'" in *Mass Communication and Society*, ed. James Curran, Michael Gurevitch, and Janet Woollacott (London: Edward Arnold, 1977), 315–48.
115. Gayatri Spivak, "Thinking Cultural Questions in 'Pure' Literary Terms," in *Without Guarantees: In Honour of Stuart Hall*, ed. Paul Gilroy, Angela McRobbie, and Lawrence Grossberg (London: Verso, 2000), 335. I discuss Hall and affect further in Chapter 4.
116. Frantz Fanon, *The Wretched of the Earth*, trans. Constance Farrington (New York: Grove, 1991), 45.
117. See, for example, Jared Sexton, "The Social Life of Social Death: On Afro-Pessimism and Black Optimism," *InTensions* 5 (2011): 1–47; Calvin Warren, *Ontological Terror: Blackness, Nihilism, and Emancipation* (Durham, N.C.: Duke University Press, 2018); Frank Wilderson, *Red, White and Black: Cinema and the Structure of U.S. Antagonisms* (Durham, N.C.: Duke University Press, 2010); David Marriott, "The X of Representation: Rereading Stuart Hall," *new formations* 96–97 (2019): 177–228; Saidiya Hartman, *Scenes of Subjection: Terror, Slavery, and Self-Making in Nineteenth-Century America* (Oxford: Oxford University Press, 1997); Harris, "Whiteness as Property"; Nash, *Black Feminism Reimagined*; and Spillers, "Mama's Baby."
118. Warren, *Ontological Terror*, 3. Similarly, Love stresses how a critical confrontation with modernity "shows up the inadequacy of . . . narratives of progress"; *Feeling Backward*, 15.
119. Drawing on Hall, Orlando Patterson, and other Black scholars, Afropessimists often view Blackness as the foundational systematic exclusion enacted by the modern world order. In Wilderson's words, modernity understands human identity and life discursively via a "political ontology" premised on the "social death" of racialized "non-beings"; Frank Wilderson, *Red, White and Black: Cinema and the Structure of U.S. Antagonisms (Durham, N.C.: Duke University Press, 2010)*, 22–25. Marriott pursues the consequences of Hall's claims regarding "'the end of innocence,' or the end of the innocent notion of the essential black subject," to confront "an absence that can neither be nor conceived without blackness, and vice versa, a blackness that can neither be nor conceived without . . . confront[ing] the experience of meaninglessness itself"; Hall, "New Ethnicities," 444; Marriott, "X of Representation," 187.
120. Spivak, "Thinking Cultural Questions," 353.
121. Ibid., 335–36.
122. Ibid., 336.
123. Rita Felski, "Context Stinks!," *New Literary History* 42, no. 4 (2011): 590, 580.
124. Ibid., 579.

125. Jennifer Nash, "On the Beginning of the World: Dominance Feminism, Afropessimism, and the Meanings of Gender," *Feminist Theory* 23, no. 4 (2021): 570.

126. Audre Lorde, "The Master's Tools Will Never Dismantle the Master's House," in *Sister Outsider: Essays and Speeches* (Berkeley, Calif.: Crossing Press, 1984), 110–14.

127. Spivak, "Thinking Cultural Questions," 336.

128. De Grazia, "Modern Divide," 453.

129. Toni Morrison, *Playing in the Dark: Whiteness and the Literary Imagination* (Cambridge, Mass.: Harvard University Press, 1992).

130. Warren, *Ontological Terror*, 3; Love, *Feeling Backward*, 15; Cheng, *Melancholy*, 135.

131. Hall, "New Ethnicities," 444.

132. Christian, "Race for Theory," 56.

1. Modernity, the Medieval, and the Feel of Periodization

1. Nicholas Watson, "Desire for the Past," *Studies in the Age of Chaucer* 21 (1999): 93. Subsequent page citations appear parenthetically in the text. Watson's understanding of affect draws on Karl Morrison, *"I Am You": The Hermeneutics of Empathy in Western Literature, Theology, and Art* (Princeton: Princeton University Press, 1988).

2. Ernesto Laclau and Chantal Mouffe, *Hegemony and Socialist Strategy* (London: Verso, 1985).

3. Key studies of medieval and modernist affects include Barbara Rosenwein, *Emotional Communities in the Early Middle Ages* (Ithaca: Cornell University Press, 2006); Rosenwein, *Generation of Feeling: A History of Emotions, 600–1700* (Cambridge; Cambridge University Press, 2016); Glenn Burger and Holly Crocker, eds., *Medieval Affect, Feeling, and Emotion* (Cambridge: Cambridge University Press, 2019); Sanja Bahun, *Modernism and Melancholia: Writing as Countermourning* (Oxford: Oxford University Press, 2014); Jonathan Flatley, *Affective Mapping: Melancholia and the Politics of Modernism* (Cambridge, Mass.: Harvard University Press, 2008); Jennifer Fleissner, *Maladies of the Will: The American Novel and the Modernity Problem* (Chicago: University of Chicago Press, 2022).

4. Important studies of the feelings driving popular, mass cultural, and non-academic medievalisms include Louise D'Arcens and Andrew Lynch, eds., "Feeling for the Premodern," special issue, *Exemplaria* 30, no. 3 (2018).

5. Edward Said, *Orientalism: Western Conceptions of the Orient* (New York: Vintage, 1979); Johannes Fabian, *Time and the Other: How Anthropology Makes Its Object* (New York: Columbia University Press, 1983).

6. See Rita Felski, *Hooked: Art and Attachment* (Chicago: University of Chicago Press, 2020).

7. Mary Rambaran-Olm, "A Wrinkle in Medieval Time: Ironing Out Issues Regarding Race, Temporality, and the Early English," *New Literary History* 52, no.

3–4 (2021): 389, 388. Rambaran-Olm specifically refers to scholars of Early England, but her insight applies broadly to the field of medieval studies. Work stressing the centering of white men in ideas of modernity includes Rita Felski, *The Gender of Modernity* (Cambridge, Mass.: Harvard University Press, 1995); and Alice Jardine, *Gynesis: Configurations of Woman and Modernity* (Ithaca: Cornell University Press, 1985).

8. Richard Dyer, *White* (London: Routledge, 1997), xiii.

9. Ibid., 213.

10. When negative sentiment emerges in work by white medievalists it typically pertains to the modern belief in the utter alterity of the past. That is, white medievalists exhibit pessimism about the prospect of even accessing their period. Stephanie Trigg and Thomas Prendergast exemplify this trend, insofar as they use "abjection" to describe how professionalization prompts the rejection (abjection) of any loving relationship to the medieval "as an embarrassing sign of amateurism"; Trigg and Prendergast, *Affective Medievalisms: Love, Abjection and Discontent* (Manchester: Manchester University Press, 2019), 107. Similarly, for Trigg and Prendergast, "discontent" concerns the awareness that even the most rigorous of methodologies cannot make the past fully known (118–33).

11. Jacob Burckhardt, *The Civilization of the Renaissance in Italy*, trans. S. G. C. Middlemore (New York: Oxford University Press, 1937), 224, hereafter cited parenthetically in the text by page number.

12. Jacob Burckhardt, *Die Kultur der Renaissance in Italien* (Stuttgart: Alfred Kröner, 1922), 99.

13. Julia Reinhard Lupton, *Afterlives of the Saints: Hagiography, Typology and Renaissance Literature* (Stanford: Stanford University Press, 1996), 6.

14. Wallace Ferguson, *The Idea of the Renaissance in Historical Thought: Five Centuries of Interpretation* (Cambridge, Mass.: Houghton Mifflin, 1948), 190, 185.

15. Ibid., 190, 185.

16. Charlton Lewis and Charles Short, *A Latin Dictionary* (London, 1896), s.v. "revelo."

17. Lionel Gossman, *Basel in the Age of Burckhardt: A Study in Unseasonable Ideas* (Chicago: University of Chicago Press, 2000); John Hinde, *Jacob Burckhardt and the Crisis of Modernity* (Montreal: McGill Queen's University Press, 2000); Alan Kahan, *Aristocratic Liberalism: The Social and Political Thought of Jacob Burckhardt, John Stuart Mill, and Alexis de Tocqueville* (Oxford: Oxford University Press, 1992); Richard Sigurdson, *Jacob Burckhardt's Social and Political Thought* (Toronto: University of Toronto Press, 2004); Thomas A. Howard, *Religion and the Rise of Historicism* (Cambridge: Cambridge University Press, 2000). Cf. Hayden White, *Metahistory: The Historical Imagination in Nineteenth-Century Europe* (Baltimore: Johns Hopkins University Press, 1973), 236.

18. Stephen Greenblatt, *Shakespearean Negotiations: The Circulation of Social Energy in Renaissance England* (Berkeley: University of California Press, 1988), 1.

19. Stephen Greenblatt, *The Swerve: How the World Became Modern* (New York: Norton, 2011), 5.

20. Suzanne Conklin Akbari links Greenblatt's "affective historiography" to questions of voice and mortality in "Love for Lucretius: The Perils of Affective Historiography," *Exemplaria* 25, no. 4 (2013): 349–52.

21. "To prize a person for . . . many-sidedness . . . was virtually unheard of" during the Middle Ages; Greenblatt, *Swerve*, 16; cf. Burckhardt, *Civilization*, 70. See also Greenblatt on medieval "constraints . . . around curiosity, desire, individuality" and Burkhardt on medieval man's "slavery to books and tradition" (*Swerve*, 9–10; cf. *Civilization*, 148); and Greenblatt on how medieval "identity came with a precise, well-understood place in a chain of command and obedience" and Burckhardt on medieval men understanding themselves "through some general category" (*Swerve*, 16; cf. *Civilization*, 70).

22. Greenblatt, *Swerve*, 9–10, my emphasis.

23. Ibid., 199. Greenblatt duplicates this affective dynamic in his 2018 introductory essay "The Sixteenth Century" for the single most influential account of English literary history, *The Norton Anthology*. A representative passage describes how English humanists found inspiration in a "brilliant" Italian Renaissance world where the medieval "submission of the human spirit to penitential discipline gave way to unleashed curiosity, individual self-assertion, and a powerful conviction that man was the measure of all things"; Steven Greenblatt, "The Sixteenth Century," in *The Norton Anthology of English Literature: The Major Authors*, gen. ed. Steven Greenblatt, 8th ed. (London: Norton, 2018), 322.

24. Dyer, *White*, 33.

25. Marshall Berman, *All That Is Solid Melts into Air: The Experience of Modernity* (New York: Simon and Schuster, 1981), 21, hereafter cited parenthetically in the text by page number. Berman specifically refers to the first chapter of *The Communist Manifesto*.

26. The patterns I trace are part of Marx's medievalism, which also dialectically embraces the medieval: "The Middle Ages . . . represents in classic Marxism . . . both a prelapsarian pastoral of 'free peasant proprietors . . . farming independently for themselves,' . . . and, simultaneously, a field of production sown with the seeds of capital and promising to yield the worst exploitative tendencies of industrial capitalism"; Bruce Holsinger and Ethan Knapp, "The Marxist Premodern," *Journal of Medieval and Early Modern Studies* 34, no. 3 (2004): 464–65, citing Marx, *Capital*, trans. Ben Fowkes, vol. 1 (New York: Penguin, 1992), 877–78. While aspects of Marx's oeuvre examine economic formations circulating before 1500 CE, my concern is how, elsewhere, Marx fully embraces, and subtly deploys, a definition of the medieval as irrational and backward.

27. If Burckhardt took his veil metaphor from Marx, the Swiss historian adapted it to direct attention away from his own class-obsessed "wretched age" to what Burckhardt claimed was modernity's initial—and superior—period of individualism

and humanism; Jacob Burckhardt, *The Letters of Jacob Burckhardt*, ed. and trans. Alexander Dru (New York: Pantheon, 1955), 97; cf. Kahan, *Aristocratic Liberalism*.

28. Karl Marx, *Manifesto of the Communist Party*, in *The Marx-Engels Reader*, ed. Robert Tucker (New York: Norton, 1978), 476, hereafter cited parenthetically in the text by page number.

29. David Harvey, *The Condition of Postmodernity: An Enquiry into the Origins of Cultural Change* (Oxford: Blackwell, 1989), 16.

30. Karl Marx, *The Eighteenth Brumaire of Louis Bonaparte*, in Tucker, *Marx-Engels Reader*, 595.

31. Andy Merrifield, "Marshall Berman, 1940–2013," *Radical Philosophy* 183 (2014): 67.

32. Sean Homer, "Fredric Jameson," in Oxford Bibliographies Online: Literary and Critical Theory, article last modified March 25, 2020, https://doi.org/10.1093/OBO/9780190221911-0011. One index of Jameson's importance is that *The Political Unconscious* has never gone out of print and has been translated into over twelve languages; see Andrew Cole and Robert Tally, "Fredric Jameson's *The Political Unconscious*, Forty Years On," *PMLA* 137, no. 1 (2022): 405.

33. Fredric Jameson, *The Political Unconscious: Narrative as a Socially Symbolic Act* (London: Routledge, 1983), 39, hereafter cited parenthetically in the text by page number.

34. Fredric Jameson, "Cognitive Mapping," in *Marxism and the Interpretation of Culture*, ed. Cary Nelson and Lawrence Grossberg (Urbana: University of Illinois Press, 1990), 350–51.

35. Jameson, *Political Unconscious*, 38; Jameson, "Cognitive Mapping," 348.

36. Jameson, "Cognitive Mapping," 355; Jameson, *Political Unconscious*, 3.

37. Ibid., 349.

38. Lee Patterson, "On the Margin: Postmodernism, Ironic History, and Medieval Studies," *Speculum* 65, no. 1 (1990): 92.

39. James Simpson, *The Oxford English Literary History, vol. 2, 1350–1547: Reform and Cultural Revolution* (Oxford: Oxford University Press, 2002), 45.

40. Johan Huizinga, *The Autumn of the Middle Ages*, trans. Rodney Payton and Ulrich Mammitzsch (Chicago: University of Chicago Press, 1996), xx, hereafter cited parenthetically in the text by page number; Tracy Adams and Charles-Louis Morand-Métivier, "Introduction: Working with Huizinga's Legacy," in *The Waxing of the Middle Ages: Revisiting Late Medieval France*, ed. Tracy Adams and Charles-Louis Morand-Métivier (Newark: University of Delaware Press, 2023), 1. On the translations and editions of Huizinga's titular *herfsttij* (first rendered in English as "Waning") and his Dutch work overall," see Edward Peters and Walter Simons, "The New Huizinga and the Old Middle Ages," *Speculum* 74 (1999): 587–90.

41. Peters and Simons, "New Huizinga," 608.

42. A recent account of Huizinga and World War I is Thor Rydin, *The Works and Times of Johan Huizinga (1872–1945): Writing History in the Age of Collapse* (Amsterdam: Amsterdam University Press, 2023).

43. Carol Symes, "Harvest of Death: Johan Huizinga's Critique of Medievalism," in *Rereading Huizinga: Autumn of the Middle Ages, A Century Later*, ed. Peter Arnade, Martha Howell, and Anton van der Lem (Amsterdam: Amsterdam University Press, 2019), 237.

44. See Willem Otterspeer, *Reading Huizinga*, trans. Beverly Jackson (Amsterdam: Amsterdam University Press, 2010), 230–34.

45. Graeme Small, "The Making of the Autumn of the Middle Ages I: Narrative Sources and Their Treatment in *Herfsttij*," in Arnade, Howell, and van der Lem, *Rereading Huizinga*, 172.

46. Ibid., 173.

47. Adams and Morand-Métivier, "Introduction," 1; cf. Simpson, *Reform and Cultural Revolution*, 45. Subsequent page citations of Simpson's volume appear in the text.

48. Huizinga's faith was more complex than his Mennonite heritage and service-going suggest. On Huizinga's faith and its relationship to *Autumn*, see Otterspeer, *Reading Huizinga*, 23–26, 33–34, 186–201, and Walter Simons, "Wrestling with Angels," in Arnade, Howell, and van der Lem, *Rereading Huizinga*, 41–64.

49. Otterspeer, *Reading Huizinga*, 197.

50. Ibid., 73. At Groningen University, Huizinga joined a group of aesthetes who avidly read French decadent and symbolist writers including Remy de Gourmont, J.-K. Huysmans, and Paul Verlaine. Huizinga's ongoing interest in French symbolism is reflected in his citation of Huysmans in *Autumn* (363). See Otterspeer, *Reading Huizinga*, and Peters and Simons, "New Huizinga," 607, especially works cited in note 65.

51. Otterspeer, *Reading Huizinga*, 73.

52. Huizinga, *Autumn*, 239; Otterspeer, *Reading Huizinga*, 198.

53. See Peter Arnade, "Huizinga: Anthropologist *Avant la Lettre*?," in Arnade, Howell, and van der Lem, *Rereading Huizinga*, 265.

54. Otterspeer, *Reading Huizinga*, 73.

55. T. S. Eliot, *The Waste Land*, in *The Waste Land: Authoritative Text, Contexts, Criticism*, ed. Michael North (New York: Norton, 2001), 5, lines 25–26.

56. Eliot, *Waste Land*, lines 22, 385, 396, 5, 18; Huizinga, *Autumn*, xix.

57. As Symes observes, "Most of the major sentiments and trends which Huizinga attributes to the 'life-and-thought-forms' of late medieval Burgundian culture are also those of his own generation"; "Harvest of Death," 241.

58. Adams and Morand-Métivier, "Introduction," 17.

59. Ferguson, *Idea of the Renaissance*, 296.

60. Ferguson tracks the earliest of these claims in ibid., 290–328.

61. Norman Cantor, *Inventing the Middle Ages* (New York: William Morrow, 1991), 255.

62. Paul Freedman and Gabrielle Spiegel, "Medievalisms Old and New: The Rediscovery of Alterity in North American Medieval Studies," *American Historical Review* 103, no. 3 (1998): 677–704; Cantor, *Inventing*, 246.

63. On Haskins and Wilson, see Cantor, *Inventing*, 245–57; Heather Blurton, "An American in Paris: Charles Homer Haskins at the Paris Peace Conference," in *Medievalisms in the Postcolonial World: The Idea of "the Middle Ages" Outside Europe*, ed. Nadia Altschul and Kathleen Davis (Baltimore: Johns Hopkins University Press, 2009), 265–85; and Freedman and Spiegel, "Medievalisms," 681–86.

64. Charles Homer Haskins, *The Renaissance of the Twelfth Century* (London: Oxford University Press, 1927), vii, hereafter cited parenthetically in the text by page number.

65. Freedman and Spiegel, "Medievalisms," 693.

66. Ibid., 684.

67. Michael H. Shank and David C. Lindberg, introduction to *The Cambridge History of Medieval Science*, ed. David C. Lindberg and Michael H. Shank, vol. 2 (Cambridge: Cambridge University Press, 2013), 13.

68. Lynn Thorndike, *A History of Magic and Experimental Science*, vol. 4 (New York: Columbia University Press, 1923–58), 615.

69. Thorndike, *History of Magic*, 4:970–71, 979.

70. Thorndike, *History of Magic*, 4:979.

71. Lynn Thorndike, "Renaissance or Prenaissance?," *Journal of the History of Ideas* 4, no. 1 (1943): 73.

72. Cantor, *Inventing*, 338.

73. R. W. Southern, "Presidential Address," *Transactions of the Royal Historical Society* 20 (1971): 175.

74. R. W. Southern, *The Making of the Middle Ages* (New Haven: Yale University Press, 1978), 224, hereafter cited parenthetically in the text by page number.

75. Samuel Taylor Coleridge, *Bibliographia Literaria*, ed. Adam Roberts (Edinburgh: Edinburgh University Press, 2014), 61.

76. On Cold War debates about individualism in a specifically American context, see Eric Foner, *The Story of American Freedom* (New York: Norton, 1998), 249–74.

77. R. W. Southern, *Western Views of Islam in the Middle Ages* (Cambridge, Mass.: Harvard University Press, 1962), 2. An index of the degree to which, by the early 1980s, medievalists had joined Haskins, Ullmann, and Southern in asserting the medieval dawn of the individual is *Renaissance and Renewal in the Twelfth Century* (1982). Based on a conference honoring the fiftieth anniversary of the publication of Haskins's book *Renaissance and Renewal* is a "monumental" 781-page edited volume in which twenty-six scholars develop and modify Haskins's claims; Jacqueline Murray, review of *Renaissance and Renewal in the Twelfth Century*, ed. Robert Benson and Giles Constable, *Renaissance and Reformation* 28, no. 3 (2010): 73.

78. John Watt, "Walter Ullmann, 1910–1983," *Proceedings of the British Academy* 74 (1988): 499.

79. Walter Ullmann, *The Individual and Society in the Middle Ages* (Baltimore: Johns Hopkins University Press, 1966), 128, 6.

80. Ullmann, *Individual*, 109, 128. Ullmann even prompts his readers to feel good about the medieval church's "theocratic-descending" government, insofar as it

preserved the same commitment to justice and the rule of law embraced by Founding Father James Madison (75).

81. Robert Hanning, *The Individual in Twelfth Century Romance* (New Haven: Yale University Press, 1977), 1.

82. Ibid., 242.

83. Ibid.

84. John Ganim, review of *Negotiating the Past*, by Lee Patterson, *Studies in the Age of Chaucer* 11 (1989): 267.

85. Lee Patterson, *Negotiating the Past: The Historical Understanding of Medieval Literature* (Madison: University of Wisconsin Press, 1987), 34, 72, hereafter cited parenthetically in the text by page number.

86. Martha Howell, quoted in Mary Jungeun Lee, "A Southern Medievalist," *Columbia College Today*, November 2001, https://www.college.columbia.edu/cct_archive/nov01/nov01_feature_medievalist.html.

87. Kathleen Biddick, "Genders, Bodies, Borders: Technologies of the Visible," *Speculum* 68, no. 2 (1993): 397; Caroline Walker Bynum, "My Life and Works," in *Medieval Women in the Academy*, ed. Jane Chance (Madison: University of Wisconsin Press, 2005), 999.

88. Caroline Walker Bynum, *Holy Feast and Holy Fast: The Religious Significance of Food to Medieval Women* (Berkeley: University of California Press, 1988), 5, hereafter cited parenthetically by page number.

89. A modern idea of a medieval other also contributes to enjoyment of the medieval (as, for example, the delightfully strange, arcane, and weird; as the object of sacrificial pleasures such as spending long hours mastering dead languages, learning philological techniques, etc.; and as the basis for a certain pride in disciplinary specialization). Important work on academic desire for an "othered" medieval past includes L. O. Aranye Fradenburg, *Sacrifice Your Love* (Minneapolis: University of Minnesota Press, 2002).

90. Freedman and Spiegel, "Medievalisms," 677. Freedman and Spiegel situate Bynum within a larger historiographical interest in the medieval grotesque that began in the late 1970s, after a long Haskins-esque stress on a rational medieval modernity.

91. Cf. Freedman and Spiegel, "Medievalisms," 693.

92. Caroline Walker Bynum, "Wonder," *American Historical Review* 102, no. 1 (1997): 1.

93. Bynum, "Wonder," 1.

94. Paul Valéry, *Oeuvres*, ed. Jean Hytier, vol. 2 (Paris: Gallimard, 1993), 501.

95. In certain respects, Bynum's relationship to Huizinga functions in a manner akin to her relationship to Victor Turner, as Kathleen Biddick describes it; Biddick, "Genders, Bodies, Borders," 396. Bynum cites Huizinga several times in *Holy Feast*; her only criticism of *Autumn* involves an argument about the continued vitality of medieval Christian symbolism for women into the closing centuries of the Middle Ages (451).

96. This work includes U.S. academic Patricia Clare Ingham's discussion of medieval Christian versions of the modern ambivalence toward the new described by T. Jackson Lears; Ingham, *The Medieval New: Ambivalence in an Age of Innovation* (Philadelphia: University of Pennsylvania Press, 2015); T. Jackson Lears, *No Place of Grace: Antimodernism and the Transformation of American Culture, 1880–1920* (New York: Pantheon, 1981).

97. Louise D'Arcens, "Introduction: Medievalism; Scope and Complexity," in *The Cambridge Companion to Medievalism* (Cambridge: Cambridge University Press, 2016), 11. See Andrew Cole, *The Birth of Theory* (Chicago: University of Chicago Press, 2014); Bruce Holsinger, *The Premodern Condition: Medievalism and the Making of Theory* (Chicago: University of Chicago Press, 2005); Holsinger and Knapp, "Marxist Premodern"; Andrew Cole and D. Vance Smith, eds., *The Legitimacy of the Middle Ages: On the Unwritten History of Theory* (Durham, N.C.: Duke University Press, 2010); Erin Labbie, *Lacan's Medievalism* (Minneapolis: University of Minnesota Press, 2006).

98. Holsinger, *Premodern Condition*, 3.

99. Ibid., 17, 15.

100. Ibid., 17.

101. Simpson, *Reform and Cultural Revolution*, back cover. See also https://global.oup.com/academic/content/series/o/oxford-english-literary-history-oelh.

102. Helen Cooper, review of *Reform and Cultural Revolution*, by James Simpson, *Studies in the Age of Chaucer* 29 (2007): 547; David Aers and Sarah Beckwith, eds., "Reform and Cultural Revolution: Writing English Literary History 1350–1547," special issue, *Journal of Medieval and Early Modern Studies* 35, no. 1 (2005).

103. David Aers and Sarah Beckwith, "Reform and Cultural Revolution: Introduction," *Journal of Medieval and Early Modern Studies* 35, no. 1 (2005): 3.

104. A. C. Spearing, *Medieval to Renaissance in English Poetry* (Cambridge: Cambridge University Press, 1985).

105. Simpson's approach to the fifteenth century resembles that of other medievalists such as Eamon Duffy; see Derek Pearsall, "The Apotheosis of John Lydgate," *Journal of Medieval and Early Modern Studies* 35, no. 1 (2005): 27–28.

106. Bruce Holsinger, "Lollard Ekphrasis: Situated Aesthetics and Literary History," *Journal of Medieval and Early Modern Studies* 35, no. 1 (2005): 69; David Wallace, "Oxford English Literary History," *Journal of Medieval and Early Modern Studies* 35, no. 1 (2005): 14.

107. Simpson, *Reform and Cultural Revolution*, 560; Aers and Beckwith, "Introduction," 8.

2. "Between Then and Now": The Veil of Periodization

1. W. E. B. Du Bois, *The Souls of Black Folk*, ed. Brent Hayes Edwards (Oxford: Oxford University Press, 2007), 8.

2. Howard Winant, *The New Politics of Race: Globalism, Difference, Justice* (Minneapolis: University of Minnesota Press, 2004), 25. Work on Du Bois is vast and ongoing. In addition to works cited elsewhere in this chapter, pieces crucial to my thinking include Patricia Wald, *Constituting Americans: Cultural Anxiety and Narrative Form* (Durham, N.C.: Duke University Press, 1995), and Shamoon Zamir, *Dark Voices: W. E. B. Du Bois and American Thought, 1888–1903* (Chicago: University of Chicago Press, 1995).

3. Arnold Rampersad, *The Art and Imagination of W. E. B. Du Bois* (Cambridge, Mass.: Harvard University Press, 1973); Robert Stepto, *From Behind the Veil: A Study of Afro-American Narrative* (Urbana: University of Illinois Press, 1980); Adolph Reed Jr., *W. E. B. Du Bois and American Political Thought: Fabianism and the Color Line* (Oxford: Oxford University Press, 1997); Robert Gooding-Williams, *In the Shadow of Du Bois: Afro-Modern Political Thought in America* (Cambridge, Mass.: Harvard University Press, 2009). Gooding-Williams's book develops claims introduced over a decade in some of his earlier pieces, including "Philosophy of History and Social Critique in *The Souls of Black Folk*," *Social Science Information* 26, no. 1 (1987): 99–114.

4. Michelle Wright, *Becoming Black: Creating Identity in the African Diaspora* (Durham, N.C.: Duke University Press, 2004); Michelle Alexander, *The New Jim Crow: Mass Incarceration in the Age of Colorblindness* (New York: New Press, 2010); George Yancy, *Black Bodies, White Gazes: The Continuing Significance of Race in America*, 2nd ed. (Lanham, Md.: Rowman and Littlefield, 2016).

5. W. E. B. Du Bois, *Darkwater: Voices from within the Veil* (New York: Harcourt, Brace, and Howe, 1920), 246, my emphasis. This work is hereafter cited parenthetically by page number.

6. Paul Gilroy, *The Black Atlantic: Modernity and Double Consciousness* (London: Verso, 1993), 134.

7. Wright, *Becoming Black*, 14.

8. Mary Rambaran-Olm, "A Wrinkle in Medieval Time: Ironing Out Issues Regarding Race, Temporality, and the Early English," *New Literary History* 52, no. 3–4 (2021): 387.

9. Gilroy, *Black Atlantic*, 137; Eric Sundquist, *To Wake the Nations: Race in the Making of American Literature* (Cambridge, Mass.: Harvard University Press, 1993). Both scholars highlight the global, diasporic, and transnational dimensions of the Black experience Du Bois interrogates.

10. Edward Said, *Orientalism: Western Conceptions of the Orient* (New York: Vintage, 1979), 120.

11. Johannes Fabian, *Time and the Other: How Anthropology Makes Its Object* (New York: Columbia University Press, 1983), 28, 25.

12. Ibid., 25–36. Cf. Said's racial turn in *Orientalism* when he describes how Orientalist studies construes non-European backwardness in terms of "genetic universals" (120).

13. Du Bois, *Souls of Black Folk*, 8.

14. Looking at Du Boisian texts including *Darkwater, The Souls of Black Folk, Dark Princess* (1928), and "The Princess Steel" (c.1908–10) and medieval texts such as Julian of Norwich's *Showings*, these critics reveal how a real or imagined Middle Ages—European and African—figures in Du Bois's effort to describe the Black experience in the U.S., challenge received ideas of space and time, and "conceive of alternative possibilities for how the society around" him "might be constructed"; Matthew Vernon, *The Black Middle Ages: Race and the Construction of the Middle Ages* (Cham, Switzerland: Palgrave, 2018), 22; cf. 19–22, 108–11. In addition to Vernon's *The Black Middle Ages*, see also Vernon, "Of Saxons and Spectres," *Journal of Medieval History* 48, no. 2 (2022): 282–87; Cord Whitaker, *Black Metaphors: How Modern Racism Emerged from Medieval Race Thinking* (Philadelphia: University of Pennsylvania Press, 2019), 125–29; Whitaker, "'The Noblest Blood God Ever Made': W. E. B. Du Bois's Medievalism in the Contexts of the World Wars," in *Thinking of the Medieval: Midcentury Intellectuals and the Middle Ages*, ed. R. D. Perry and Benjamin Saltzman (Cambridge: Cambridge University Press, 2022), 68–87; Seeta Chaganti and Andrea Myers Achi, "'Semper Novi Quid ex Africa': Redrawing the Borders of Medieval African Art and Considering Its Implications for Medieval Studies," in *Disturbing Times: Medieval Pasts, Reimagined Futures*, ed. Catherine Karkov, Anna Klosowska, and Vincent van Gerven Oei (Goleta, Calif.: Punctum Books, 2020); and Michelle Warren, "'The Last Syllable of Modernity': Chaucer in the Caribbean," *postmedieval* 6 (2015): 79–93.

15. Vernon, *Black Middle Ages*, 29, my emphasis.

16. *Oxford English Dictionary*, s.v. "between," accessed July 2024, https://doi.org/10.1093/OED/5486910617, my emphasis.

17. Kathleen Davis, *Periodization and Sovereignty: How Ideas of Feudalism and Secularization Govern the Politics of Time* (Philadelphia: University of Pennsylvania Press, 2008), 4. See also Kathleen Biddick, *The Typological Imaginary: Circumcision, Technology, History* (Philadelphia: University of Pennsylvania Press, 2003).

18. Rita Felski, *The Gender of Modernity* (Cambridge, Mass.: Harvard University Press, 1995), 2.

19. Lennard Davis, *Bending Over Backwards: Disability, Dismodernism, and Other Difficult Positions* (New York: New York University Press, 2002); Michel Foucault, *The History of Sexuality*, trans. Robert Hurley, 4 vols. (New York: Pantheon, 1978–2021); Timothy Morton, *The Ecological Thought* (Cambridge, Mass.: Harvard University Press, 2010).

20. Walter Mignolo, *The Darker Side of Western Modernity: Global Futures, Decolonial Options* (Durham, N.C.: Duke University Press, 2011), xii.

21. Gilroy, *Black Atlantic*, 56.

22. Ibid., 58. "The key to comprehending" the western and non-western, or white and non-white, antimonies of modernity, as Gilroy puts it, "lies not in the overhasty separation of the cultural forms particular to both groups into some ethnic typology but in a detailed and comprehensive grasp of their complex interpenetration" (48).

23. Mignolo, *Darker Side*, xi. On Equiano, see Laura Doyle, *Freedom's Empire: Race and the Rise of the Novel in Atlantic Modernity, 1640–1940* (Durham, N.C.: Duke University Press, 2007), 183–214. On Douglass, Wright, and James, see Gilroy, *Black Atlantic*, 58–74, 146–86. On Vizenor and other Indigenous critics, see Matt Hooley, *Against Extraction: Indigenous Modernism in the Twin Cities* (Durham, N.C.: Duke University Press, 2024). This list, of course, represents a small sampling of the critiques leveraged by a host of thinkers situated inside and outside the West.

24. Gilroy, *Black Atlantic*, 49.

25. Ibid., 54; Mignolo, *Darker Side*, 3.

26. As Wynter puts it, "The human is, meta-Darwinianly, a hybrid being, both bios and logos"; Sylvia Wynter and Katherine McKittrick, "Unparalleled Catastrophe for Our Species? Or, to Give Humanness a Different Future: Conversations," in *Sylvia Wynter: On Being Human as Praxis*, ed. Katherine McKittrick (Durham, N.C.: Duke University Press, 2015), 16.

27. On the Eurocentrism or Anglocentrism of the writers covered in Chapter 1, see, for example, Stuart Hall, "The West and the Rest: Discourse and Power," in *Formations of Modernity*, ed. Stuart Hall and Bram Gieben (Cambridge: Polity Press, 1992), 275–332; Gilroy, *Black Atlantic*, 46–48; David Wallace, "Oxford English Literary History," *Journal of Medieval and Early Modern Studies* 35, no. 1 (2005): 13–23; Jeffrey Jerome Cohen, "The Swerve Code," *Exemplaria* 25, no. 4 (2013): 367–70; Kathleen Biddick, "Genders, Bodies, Borders: Technologies of the Visible," *Speculum* 68, no. 2 (1993): 389–418.

28. My phrasing cites Stuart Hall, "The West and the Rest: Discourse and Power," in *Formations of Modernity*, ed. Stuart Hall and Bram Gieben (Cambridge: Polity Press, 1992).

29. Jennifer Morgan, *Laboring Women: Reproduction and Gender in New World Slavery* (Philadelphia: University of Pennsylvania Press, 2004), 12, 14.

30. Ibid., 12.

31. Ibid., 16–17.

32. Geraldine Heng, *The Invention of Race in the European Middle Ages* (Cambridge: Cambridge University Press, 2018); Lisa Lampert-Weissig, *Medieval Literature and Postcolonial Studies* (Edinburgh: Edinburgh University Press, 2010); Jacqueline de Weever, *Sheba's Daughters: Whitening and Demonizing the Saracen Woman in Medieval French Epic* (New York: Garland, 1998); Whitaker, *Black Metaphors*; Gilroy, *Black Atlantic*, 9; Morgan, *Laboring Women*; Winthrop Jordan, *White over Black: American Attitudes toward the Negro, 1550–1812* (Chapel Hill: University of North Carolina Press, 1968); Cedric Robinson, *Black Marxism: The Making of the Black Radical Tradition* (London: Zed, 1983).

33. Heng, *Invention of Race*, 24.

34. R. W. Southern, *The Making of the Middle Ages* (New Haven: Yale University Press, 1978), 139.

35. Alexander Weheliye, *Habeas Viscus: Racializing Assemblages, Biopolitics, and Black Feminist Theories of the Human* (Durham, N.C.: Duke University Press, 2014), 22, 24.

36. Sylvia Wynter, "Unsettling the Coloniality of Being/Power/Truth/Freedom: Towards the Human, After Man, Its Overrepresentation—An Argument," *New Centennial Review* 3, no. 3 (2003): 260.

37. Jacques Le Goff, *The Medieval Imagination*, trans. Arthur Goldhammer (Chicago: University of Chicago Press, 1985), 102, cited in Wynter, "Unsettling," 259.

38. Wynter, "Unsettling," 275.

39. Wynter and McKittrick, "Unparalleled Catastrophe," 20, emphasis original.

40. Sylvia Wynter, "1492: A New World View," in *Race, Discourse, and the Origin of the Americas: A New World View*, ed. Vera Lawrence Hyatt and Rex Nettleford (Washington, D.C.: Smithsonian, 1995), 14.

41. Wynter, "Unsettling," 276–77, 287–88.

42. Jacob Burckhardt, *The Civilization of the Renaissance in Italy*, trans. S. G. C. Middlemore (New York: Oxford University Press, 1937), 184; hereafter cited parenthetically by page number.

43. Giovanni Pico della Mirandola, "Oration on the Dignity of Man," trans. Charles Glen Wallis, in *On the Dignity of Man, On Being and the One, Heptaplus*, ed. Paul Miller (New York: Bobbs-Merrill, 1965), 4–5; cited in Wynter, "Unsettling," 259–60.

44. Wynter, "Unsettling," 276.

45. James Simpson, *The Oxford English Literary History, vol. 2, Reform and Cultural Revolution* (Oxford: Oxford University Press, 2002), 286, 52, 2.

46. Ibid., 2:1, 52.

47. Stuart Hall, "Culture, Media, and the 'Ideological Effect,'" in *Mass Communication and Society*, ed. James Curran, Michael Gurevitch, and Janet Woollacott (London: Arnold, 1977), 346.

48. Anne Middleton, "Chaucer's 'New Men' and the Good of Literature in the 'Canterbury Tales,'" in *Literature and Society: Selected Papers from the English Institute*, ed. Edward Said (Baltimore: Johns Hopkins University Press, 1980), 15–56; Robert Meyer Lee, *Literary Value and Social Identity in "The Canterbury Tales"* (Cambridge: Cambridge University Press, 2019).

49. L. O. Aranye Fradenburg demonstrates how the enterprising Wife of Bath and the proselytizing and magical heroine of her tale serve as placeholders for Chaucer's social ambitions and function as tools by which New Men manage knightly resistance to a new social order in "The Wife of Bath's Passing Fancy," *Studies in the Age of Chaucer* 8 (1986): 31–58.

50. Geraldine Heng, "An Arthurian Empire of Magic, and Its Discontents: An Afterword," *Arthuriana* 31, no. 2 (2021): 130. Heng responds to a special issue on race and Arthurian romance edited by Richard Sévère. See also Vernon's discussion of how, in Du Bois's romance "The Princess Steel," "it is impossible to see any of the modern world without seeing the simultaneous and fundamentally interconnected

systems of white chivalric ideology and racial exploitation in the infrastructure of the modern world"; Vernon, "Of Saxons," 286.

51. P. J. C. Field, *Romance and Chronicle: A Study of Malory's Prose Style* (Bloomington: Indiana University Press, 1971), 157.

52. Sarah Ahmed, "A Phenomenology of Whiteness," *Feminist Theory* 8, no. 2 (2007): 149–68.

53. Ibid., 150.

54. Donald Hoffman, "Assimilating Saracens: The Aliens in Malory's *Morte Darthur*," *Arthuriana* 16, no. 4 (2006): 58; Colin Richmond, "Malory and Modernity: A Qualm about Paradigm Shifts," *Common Knowledge* 14, no. 1 (2008): 36; Thomas Malory, *Malory: Works*, ed. Eugène Vinaver (Oxford: Oxford University Press, 1977), 761n543.

55. Richard Dyer, *White: Essays on Race and Culture* (New York: Routledge, 1997), 31–2; hereafter cited parenthetically by page number.

56. Jill Mann, "Malory and the Grail Legend," in *A Companion to Malory*, ed. Elizabeth Archibald and A. S. G. Edwards (Cambridge: Brewer, 1996), 217.

57. "So fayre and so whyght that they might be no whytter"; Thomas Malory, *Le Morte Darthur*, ed. P. J. C. Field, vol. 1 (Cambridge: Brewer, 2013), 724, lines 6–7. Subsequent citations are by page and line numbers.

58. "Blacke hourse, blacker than a byry"; Malory, *Le Morte Darthur*, 737.30–31.

59. "Blackenes ys as much to sey withoute good vertues or works"; Malory, *Morte*, 728.1.

60. "The shylde hynge as whyght as ony snowe, but in the myddys was a rede crosse"; Malory, *Morte*, 678.26–27; cf. 680–82.

61. Wynter, "1492," 13. Cf. claims by Southern (*Making*) and other post–World War II scholars about medieval individualism. On one level those claims project the politics of those scholars' Cold War moment. Yet writers like Chaucer and Malory may have encouraged such a view, via the "Man"-centered worlds they represent.

62. Burckhardt, *Civilization*, 73; Karl Marx, *Manifesto of the Communist Party*, in *The Marx-Engels Reader*, ed. Robert Tucker (New York: Norton, 1978), 476.

63. I discuss Chaucer and Malory's portrayal of racialized others respectively in Chapters 5 and 6.

64. Suzanne Conklin Akbari, *Idols in the East: European Representations of Islam and the Orient* (Ithaca: Cornell University Press, 2009), 113. Those lines of influence were not one way or straightforward. Cf. Jeremy Cohen, "The Muslim Connection, or On the Changing Role of the Jew in High Medieval Theology," in *From Witness to Witchcraft: Jews and Judaism in Medieval Christian Thought*, ed. Jeremy Cohen (Wiesbaden: Harrassowitz Verlag, 1996), 141–62.

65. M. Lindsay Kaplan, *Figuring Racism in Medieval Christianity* (New York: Oxford University Press, 2019), 55, 14–15.

66. Biddick, *Typological Imaginary*.

67. Ibid., 1–2.

68. Jeremy Cohen, *Living Letters of the Law: Ideas of the Jew in Medieval Christianity* (Los Angeles: University of California Press, 1999), 94.

69. Biddick, *Typological Imaginary*, 23; Akbari, *Idols*, 125. See also David Leshock, "Religious Geography: Designating Jews and Muslims as Foreigners in Medieval England," in *Meeting the Foreign in the Middle Ages*, ed. Albrecht Classen (New York: Routledge, 2002), 202–25; Heng, *Invention of Race*, 55–109; Elisa Narin van Court, "'The Siege of Jerusalem' and Augustinian Historians: Writing about Jews in Fourteenth-Century England," *Chaucer Review* 29, no. 3 (1995): 227–48.

70. Work on antisemitic representations and anti-Jewish practices includes R. I. Moore, *The Formation of a Persecuting Society: Authority and Deviance in Western Europe, 950–1250*, 2nd ed. (Oxford: Blackwell, 2007); David Nirenberg, *Communities of Violence: Persecution of Minorities in the Middle Ages* (Princeton: Princeton University Press, 1998); Anthony Bale, *Feeling Persecuted: Christians, Jews and Images of Violence in the Middle Ages* (London: Reaktion, 2010); Jeremy Cohen, "Christian Theology and Anti-Jewish Violence in the Middle Ages: Connections and Disjunctions," in *Religious Violence between Christians and Jews: Medieval Roots, Modern Perspectives*, ed. Anna Sapir Abulafia (London: Palgrave, 2001), 44–60.

71. Talal Asad, *Formations of the Secular: Christianity, Islam, Modernity* (Stanford: Stanford University Press, 2003), 1–66; Charles Taylor, *A Secular Age* (Cambridge, Mass.: Harvard University Press, 2018).

72. Karl Löwith, *Meaning in History* (Chicago: University of Chicago Press, 1949).

73. Walter Benjamin, as Lupton discusses, intervenes and disrupts dominant models of modernity, Christianity, and Judaism by advocating a counter-periodization or theology of history that "take[s] shape at the site of the breakdown of Christian-secular historiography"; Julia Reinhard Lupton, *Afterlives of the Saints: Hagiography, Typology and Renaissance Literature* (Stanford: Stanford University Press, 1996), 32. The "theology of history" of Benjamin's *Origin of German Tragic Drama* links baroque German modernity to the Middle Ages as a "historicity that falls out from typology as its ruins, taken as the object of a more searching, because less synthesizing, dialectical thought" (Lupton, *Afterlives*, 30). Lupton provocatively sees Benjamin transforming the degraded and ruined "Jewish" object of Christian typology into a site for a "searching" and more "genuinely historical thought" (Lupton, *Afterlives*, 29). See also Lupton on Löwith (3–36).

74. Biddick, *Typological Imaginary*, 22–23.

75. Said, *Orientalism*, 38.

76. See also Burckhardt's account of early modern Italian "Oriental studies" (*Civilization*, 102).

77. Lupton, *Afterlives*, 12.

78. In the same way that medieval Christians, following Romans 9:12, defined themselves as younger brothers who supersede older brothers, Burckhardt represents "the Italian as 'the first-born among the sons of modern Europe'"; Lupton, *Afterlives*, 12. The "implicit argument" of Burckhardt's work is that Italy is barred from the "destiny [that] was reserved for the northern countries which, like [the biblical

younger brother Jacob], inherited the cultural legacy intended for the first-born son. . . . The precocity of the Italian Renaissance made possible the maturity of European modernity, a destiny that the Italians themselves necessarily missed in the very act of founding" (ibid.).

79. Burckhardt to H. Schauenburg, Basle, Feb. 28, 1846, in *The Letters of Jacob Burckhardt*, trans. Alexander Dru (New York: Pantheon, 1955), 96. See also Roberto Dainotto's "genealogy of Eurocentrism" involving the rejection of southern Europeans as internal others in *Europe (in Theory)* (Durham, N.C.: Duke University Press, 2007), 4.

80. William Bouwsma, "'The Waning of the Middle Ages' by Johan Huizinga," *Daedalus* 103, no. 1 (1974): 38; Johan Huizinga, *Dutch Civilisation in the Seventeenth Century and Other Essays*, trans. Arnold Pomerans (London: Collins, 1968), 237, cited in Graeme Small, "The Making of *The Autumn of the Middle Ages* I: Narrative Sources and Their Treatment in Huizinga's *Herfsttij*," in *Rereading Huizinga: "Autumn of the Middle Ages," a Century Later*, ed. Perter Arnade, Martha Howell, and Anton van der Lem (Amsterdam: Amsterdam University Press, 2019), 173.

81. Johann Gottfried Herder, *Herder: Philosophical Writings*, trans. Michael Forster (Cambridge: Cambridge University Press, 2002), 292. Wan-Chuan Kao links Huizinga's empathic and Herderesque mode to structures of empathy in the *Canterbury Tales* in *White before Whiteness in the Late Middle Ages* (Manchester: Manchester University Press, 2024), 311.

82. Small, "Making," 173; J. H. Huizinga, "The Aesthetic Element in Historical Thought," in *Dutch Civilization in the Seventeenth Century, and Other Essays*, trans. Arnold Pomerans (London: Collins, 1968), 237.

83. Bouwsma, "Waning," 38.

84. Ananya Jahanara Kabir and Deanne Williams, "Introduction: A Return to Wonder," in *Postcolonial Approaches to the Middle Ages: Translating Cultures*, ed. Ananya Jahanara Kabir and Deanne Williams (Cambridge: Cambridge University Press, 2005), 2.

85. *Autumn* adumbrates the raced dynamic Tara Fickle identifies in her analysis of Huizinga's influential work on games; my account of Orientalism, whiteness, and race in *Autumn* is indebted to her reading of *Homo Ludens*, in Fickle, *The Race Card: From Gaming Technologies to Model Minorities* (New York: New York University Press, 2019).

86. Ibid., 117; Walter Simons, "Wrestling with the Angel: Huizinga, *Herfsttij*, and Religion," in Arnade, Howell, and van der Lem, *Rereading Huizinga*, 58–60.

87. Johan Huizinga, *The Autumn of the Middle Ages*, trans. Rodney Payton and Ulrich Mammitzsch (Chicago: University of Chicago Press, 1996), 24, hereafter cited parenthetically by page number.

88. Stephanie Trigg and Thomas Prendergast, *Affective Medievalism: Love, Abjection, and Discontent* (Manchester: Manchester University Press, 2018), 24.

89. Said, *Orientalism*, 35.

90. Willem Otterspeer, *Reading Huizinga*, trans. Beverley Jackson (Amsterdam: Amsterdam University Press, 2010), 97.

91. An early and important commentary on Huizinga's ethnocentrism is Jacques Ehrmann, "Homo Ludens Revisited," trans. Cathy Lewis and Phil Lewis, *Yale French Studies* 41 (1968): 31–57; cf. Fickle, *Race Card*, 115–16.

92. Fickle, *Race Card*, 121.

93. Huizinga endorses, in Fickle's words, an ethnocentric understanding of human history as a trajectory that, "starting with primitive man would lead necessarily, in its 'superior' stage, to civilized (cultured) western-man"; Fickle, *Race Card*, 10.

94. Ehrmann, "Homo Ludens Revisited," 48–49.

95. Marshall Berman, *All That Is Solid Melts into Air: The Experience of Modernity* (New York: Simon and Schuster, 1981), 106.

96. A provocative and controversial critique of such modern rhetorics of unmasking is Peter Baehr, *The Unmasking Style in Social Theory* (London: Routledge, 2019).

97. Marx, *Manifesto*, 476.

98. Thus the "unveiling" I perform in this chapter, unlike the unveilings of Burckhardt et al., reveals the impossibility of essentialisms and related hard-and-fast "truths" regarding identity, society, and the world; instead, in the manner of Du Bois's reveal of the veil, I highlight contingencies and multiplicities. As Sara Ahmed puts it with respect to Lukács and the veil of false bourgeois consciousness, "the veil is not unveiled to reveal the truth; the veil is revealed, which is a revelation that must be partial and flawed"; Ahmed, *The Promise of Happiness* (Durham, N.C.: Duke University Press, 2010), 166.

99. Julia Reinhard Lupton, "Citizen Paul," *European Legacy* 9, no. 1 (2004): 68.

100. Cohen, *Living Letters*, 392.

101. Daniel Boyarin, *A Radical Jew: Paul and the Politics of Identity* (Los Angeles: University of California Press, 1994), 32.

102. S. J. Hafemann, "Corinthians, Letters to the," in *Dictionary of Paul and His Letters*, ed. Gerald F. Hawthorne et al. (Downers Grove, Ill.: Intervarsity Press, 1993), 177.

103. Ibid., 164.

104. Ibid., 173.

105. Ibid., 173–74.

106. Lisa Lampert-Weissig, *Gender and Jewish Difference from Paul to Shakespeare* (Philadelphia: University of Pennsylvania Press, 2004), 44.

107. Cohen, *Living Letters*, 234.

108. Lampert-Weissig, *Gender and Jewish Difference*, 44–48.

109. Cohen, *Living Letters*, 324.

110. Thomas Howard, *Religion and the Rise of Historicism: W. M. L. de Wette, Jacob Burckhardt, and the Theological Origins of Nineteenth-Century Historical Consciousness* (Cambridge: Cambridge University Press, 2000), 131.

111. Lupton, *Afterlives*, 4. Cf. Lupton's tracking of how the Swiss historian's idea of the Renaissance emerges via "a dialectic that borrows and renovates the paradigm of

typological transumption provided by the New Testament" (12). In a Hegelian reading, Lupton stresses both the offensive "razings" or cancelations *and* the potentially admirable "raisings" or preservations of medieval typology performed by Burckhardt and other modern writers (4). Following Du Bois's anti-synthesizing dialectic of the veil and its stress on racializing divisions, I highlight the disturbing preservation of medieval Christian forms of dehumanization in Burckhardt's idea of the birth of modern man.

112. Ibid., 11.

113. See John Hodge, "Domination and the Will in Western Thought and Culture," in *Cultural Bases of Racism and Group Oppression*, ed. John Hodge, Donald Struckman, and Lynn Dorland Trost (Berkeley, Calif.: Two Riders Press, 1975), 8–48.

114. Jacques Derrida, *Of Spirit: Heidegger and the Question*, trans. Geoffrey Bennington and Rachel Bowlby (Chicago: University of Chicago Press, 1989), 39–40.

115. Asad, *Formations of the Secular*, 168.

116. Du Bois, *Darkwater*, 39.

117. W. E. B. Du Bois, *Dark Princess: A Romance* (Jackson: University of Mississippi Press, 1995), 19.

118. Gilroy, *Black Atlantic*, 46.

3. Whiteness, Medievalism, Immigration: Rethinking Tolkien through Stuart Hall

1. Mike Collett-White, "Tolkien Novel Published 34 Years after His Death," *Reuters*, August 9, 2007, https://reuters.com/article/us-arts-tolkien-novelidUSL 1626402420070416/; "Top Lifetime Grosses, Worldwide," Box Office Mojo by IMdPro, Data as of May 10, 18:01 PDT, https://www.boxofficemojo.com/chart/ww _top_lifetime_gross/?area=XWW.

2. Tom Shippey, *The Road to Middle Earth: How J. R. R. Tolkien Created a New Mythology* (New York: Houghton Mifflin, 2014); Jane Chance, ed., *Tolkien the Medievalist* (New York: Routledge, 2003).

3. J. R. R. Tolkien, *The Fellowship of the Ring* (New York: Ballantine, 1994), 17, 210, 218, 209, 216.

4. Ibid., 90.

5. On Tolkien's fan base during the 1960s, when at one point U.S. sales of *The Lord of the Rings* outstripped that of the Bible, see Joseph Ripp, "Middle America Meets Middle Earth: American Discussion and Readership of J. R. R. Tolkien's *The Lord of the Rings*, 1965–1969," *Book History* 8 (2005): 245–86; and Mike Foster, "America in the 1960s: Reception of Tolkien," in *J. R. R. Tolkien Encyclopedia*, ed. Michael Drout (New York: Routledge, 2006), 14–15.

6. Stuart Hall, "The Hippies: An American Moment," in *Student Power*, ed. Julian Nagel (London: Merlin, 1969), 179.

7. Ramzi Fawaz, *The New Mutants: Superheroes and the Radical Imagination of American Comics* (New York: New York University Press, 2016); Chris Schulenburg,

"Nerd Nation: *La breve The Lord of the Rings maravillosa vide de Oscar Wao* and Life in Tolkien's Universe," *Modern Language Notes* 131 (2016): 503–16; Garth Sundem, *The Geeks' Guide to World Domination* (New York: Three Rivers, 2009), 98–99.

8. Marlon James, "Our Myths, Our Selves," 7th Annual J. R. R. Tolkien Lecture on Fantasy Literature, Pembroke College, Oxford University, February 29, 2019, https://youtube.com/watch?v=jV2bysurBds&t=18s.

9. Michael Saler, *As If: Modern Enchantment and the Literary Prehistory of Virtual Reality* (Oxford: Oxford University Press, 2012), 162.

10. Jason Horowitz, "Hobbits and the Hard Right: How Fantasy Inspires Italy's Potential New Leader," *New York Times*, September 21, 2022, https://nytimes.com/2022/09/21/world/europe/giorgia-meloni-lord-of-the-rings.html; Kathryn Lavezzo, "Multiculturalism in Middle-Earth: On Amazon's 'The Lord of the Rings: The Rings of Power,'" *Los Angeles Review of Books*, November 7, 2022, https://lareviewofbooks.org/article/multiculturalism-in-middle-earth-on-amazons-the-lord-of-the-rings-the-rings-of-power/.

11. On the *Campi Hobbit*, see Piero Ignazi, *Extreme Right Parties in Western Europe* (Oxford: Oxford University Press, 2002); Marco Tarchi, *La rivoluzione impossibile: Dai Campi Hobbit alla nuova Destra* (Florence: Vallecchi, 2010); and Roger Griffin, "Revolts against the Modern World: The Blend of Literary and Historical Fantasy in the Italian New Right," *Literature and History* 11, no. 1 (1985): 101–23.

12. Graham Macklin, *Failed Führers: A History of Britain's Extreme Right* (Abingdon: Routledge, 2020), 473, 523.

13. Leila Norako, "'And the Walls Became the World All Around': An Introduction," *postmedieval* 9, no. 1 (2018): 9; Helen Young, review of *The Body in Tolkien's Legendarium*, ed. Christopher Vaccaro, *Journal of Tolkien Research* 1, no. 1 (2014): 5, http://scholar.valpo.edu/journaloftolkienresearch/vol1/iss1/5/. The Stormfront website first appeared in 1996.

14. Martin Kerr, "J. R. R. Tolkien and 'That Noble Northern Spirit,'" *White Power* 10 (1979), cited in Saler, *As If*, 162; http://www.stormfront.or/forum/t47250-6.

15. Ignazi, *Extreme Right Parties*, 40.

16. Christine Chism, "Race and Ethnicity in Tolkien's Writings" and "Racism, Charges of," in Drout, *J. R. R. Tolkien Encyclopedia*, 555–56, 558–59.

17. Tolkien, *Fellowship*, 57.

18. Catharine Stimpson, *J. R. R. Tolkien* (New York: Columbia University Press, 1969), 44–45.

19. Norako, "And the Walls," 9.

20. Chism, "Race and Ethnicity"; Chism, "Racism."

21. Robin Reid, "Race in Tolkien Studies: A Bibliographic Essay," in *Tolkien and Alterity*, ed. Christopher Vaccaro and Yvette Kisor (Cham, Switzerland: Palgrave Macmillan, 2017), 33–74.

22. Kathy Lavezzo and Mariana Rios Maldonado, "Tolkien, Fandom, Critique, and 'Critical Joy': A Conversation," *postmedieval* 14, no. 1 (2023): 243–44.

23. Maria Sachiko Cecire, *Re-enchanted: The Rise of Children's Fantasy Literature in the Twentieth Century* (Minneapolis: University of Minnesota Press, 2019), 90.

24. Todd Kuchta, "The Dyer Straits of Whiteness," *Postmodern Culture* 9, no. 1 (1998): n1, http://pomoculture.org/2013/09/19/the-dyer-straits-of-whiteness/; Isaac Julien and Kobena Mercer, "De Margin and De Centre," in *Stuart Hall: Critical Dialogues in Cultural Studies*, ed. Kuan-Hsing Chen and David Morley (London: Routledge, 1996), 458.

25. Stuart Hall with Bill Schwarz, *Familiar Stranger: A Life between Two Islands* (Durham, N.C.: Duke University Press, 2017), 156, hereafter cited parenthetically by page number.

26. Bill Schwarz, email message to author, October 8, 2019.

27. Stuart Lee and Julian Reid, email message to author, December 6, 2018; Humphrey Carpenter, *Tolkien: A Biography* (Boston: Houghton Mifflin, 1977), 7–15.

28. Cecire, *Re-enchanted*, 105.

29. See also Helen Young, *Race and Popular Fantasy Literature: Habits of Whiteness* (New York: Routledge, 2016), which analyzes Tolkien in light of Ahmed's theorization of habits of whiteness.

30. Sara Ahmed, "A Phenomenology of Whiteness," *Feminist Theory* 8, no. 2 (2007): 156, 159, 158.

31. Ahmed, "Phenomenology," 160.

32. Ahmed, "Phenomenology," 161.

33. Ahmed, "Phenomenology," 159. On empire, colonization, and the origins of English as a discipline at Oxford and empire, see Cecire, *Re-enchanted*.

34. Anuradha Henriques and Lina Abushouk, "Decolonising Oxford: The Student Movement from Stuart Hall to Skin Deep," in *Dismantling Race in Higher Education: Racism, Whiteness and Decolonising the Academy*, ed. Jason Arday and Heidi Safia Mirza (New York: Palgrave, 2018), 297–309. The group Medievalists of Color has performed important work addressing how, as Jonathan Hsy puts it, "the overwhelming whiteness of our own institutions and professional structures quietly continue to exclude, alienate, and harm people of color"; Hsy, *Antiracist Medievalisms: From "Yellow Peril" to Black Lives Matter* (Leeds: Arc Humanities Press, 2021), 7.

35. Richard Dyer, *White* (New York: Routledge, 1997), 10; Stuart Hall, "New Ethnicities," in Chen and Morley, *Critical Dialogues*, 446.

36. I am particularly grateful for two important analyses that have emerged since I first shared my findings about Tolkien and Hall in 2018 at the Celebrating Belle da Costa Greene Conference at St. Louis University, St. Louis, Mo.: Mary Rambaran-Olm, "'Houston, We Have a Problem': Erasing Black Scholars in Old English Literature," *Medium*, March 3, 2020, https://medium.com/the-sundial-acmrs/houstonwe-have-a-problem-erasing-black-scholars-in-old-english-821121495dc; and

Dorothy Kim, "The Question of Race in *Beowulf*," JSTOR Daily, September 25, 2019, https://daily.jstor.org/the-question-of-race-in-beowulf/.

37. Tolkien's defenders are many and include those who view him as "a man of his time," an argument that hinges on the idea of a "routine normativeness of whiteness" from which Tolkien could not escape. But an array of perspectives on identity existed in his time, including that of Hall; see Vron Ware and Les Back, *Out of Whiteness: Color, Politics and Culture* (Chicago: University of Chicago Press, 2002), 5.

38. C. S. Lewis, *Image and Imagination: Essays and Reviews* (Cambridge: Cambridge University Press, 2013), 104–5; see also Young, *Race and Popular Fantasy*, 30.

39. Young, *Race and Popular Fantasy*, 23; see also Stimpson, *Tolkien*, 44–45; Dimitra Fimi, *Tolkien, Race, and Cultural History: From Fairies to Hobbits* (Basingstoke: Palgrave, 2009), 145–47.

40. Saladin Ahmed, "Is 'Game of Thrones' Too White?," *Salon*, April 1, 2012, https://salon.com/2012/04/01/is_game_of_thrones_too_white/.

41. Quoted in Laura Miller, "If Tolkien Were Black," *Salon*, November 9, 2011, https://salon.com/2011/11/09/if_tolkien_were_black/.

42. James, "Our Myths, Our Selves."

43. Along with the work of Saler and Cecire, this chapter is indebted to Young, who draws on Ahmed to analyze how Tolkien helped lay the foundation for "Habits of Whiteness in Fantasy" fiction that "simultaneously influence who can be present, and what is seen, thought, and done, by creating patterns of bodies and spaces alike"; Young, *Race and Popular Fantasy*, 11.

44. Julien and Mercer, "De Margin and De Centre," 458.

45. Stuart Hall, "The Local and the Global: Globalization and Ethnicity," in *Culture, Globalization, and the World-System: Contemporary Conditions for the Representation of Identity*, ed. Anthony King (Minneapolis: University of Minnesota Press, 1991), 20–21.

46. Dyer, *White*, 3

47. Hazel Carby, *Cultures in Babylon: Black Britain and African America* (New York: Verso, 1999), 249–50.

48. Ahmed, "Phenomenology," 158. As James Eli Adams observes, Tolkien's "kindly vision of a . . . pre-Norman" England, which masks over "the earlier obliteration of Roman Briton," looks back to "the combination of lurking genocidal thought and openly progressive, well-nigh utopian longing" witnessed in Victorian historians including John Mitchell Kemble; Adams, "Historiography," in *A New Companion to Victorian Literature and Culture*, ed. Herbert Tucker (Chichester: Wiley-Blackwell, 2014), 423.

49. Early examples include Tolkien, *Fellowship*, 81, 85–86, 98–102.

50. Dyer, *White*, 14–18.

51. Ahmed, "Phenomenology," 152.

52. Stuart Hall, "Race, Articulation and Societies Structured in Dominance," in *Sociological Theories: Race and Colonialism*, ed. Marion O'Callaghan (Paris:

UNESCO, 1980), 305–45; Hall, "Culture, the Media and 'the Ideological Effect,'" in *Mass Communication and Society*, ed. James Curran, Michael Gurevitch, and Janet Woollacott (London: Arnold, 1977), 315–48.

53. Dyer, *White*, 29.

54. Critical whiteness studies thus clarifies how the counter examples to the light-dark binaries in *The Lord of the Rings* cited by Curry and other readers do not undermine but contribute to the racist elements of Tolkien's fiction; see Patrick Curry, "Tolkien and His Critics: A Critique," in *Root and Branch: Approaches towards Understanding Tolkien*, ed. Thomas Honegger (Zurich: Walking Tree, 2005), 87–90.

55. Tolkien to Peter Hastings, September 1954, in *The Letters of J. R. R. Tolkien*, ed. Humphrey Carpenter (Boston: Houghton Mifflin, 1981), 189.

56. Readers who stress Tolkien's multiculturalism include Sandra Straubhaar, "Myth, Late Roman History, and Multiculturalism in Tolkien's Middle-earth," in *Tolkien and the Invention of Myth: A Reader*, ed. Jane Chance (Lexington: University Press of Kentucky, 2004), 101–11; Patrick Curry, *Defending Middle-Earth: Tolkien, Myth and Modernity* (Boston: Houghton Mifflin, 2004); and Jane Chance, "Tolkien and the Other: Race and Gender in Middle Earth," in *Tolkien's Modern Middle Ages*, ed. Jane Chance and Alfred Siewers (New York: Palgrave Macmillan, 2005), 173–88.

57. Ethan Knapp, "Chaucer Criticism and Its Legacies," in *The Yale Companion to Chaucer*, ed. Seth Lerer (New Haven: Yale University Press, 2006), 341. "We should not, of course, read Chaucer (or any author) merely to discover what his society was like. The present value is in the poetry, not in the one-time society. Nevertheless, the complexity (and value) of that society is still, if it is anywhere, in the complexity (and value) of the poetry which is our present object"; John Speirs, *Chaucer the Maker* (London: Faber and Faber, 1951), 15.

58. Stuart Hall and Bill Schwarz, "Displacements: Lives and Ideas in Two Black Diasporas," annotated typed draft of *Familiar Stranger*, in Stuart Hall Archive US121, Box 61, Cadbury Research Library: Special Collections, University of Birmingham. The affective formation described by Hall—his account of why he "liked" Spiers's work—offers a historicist riff on the idea of being "hooked," explored recently by Rita Felski in *Hooked: Art and Attachment* (Chicago: University of Chicago Press, 2021). If Felski advocates attention to texts themselves as solicitors of readerly attachment, Hall describes how being "hooked" as a scholar involves the larger contextual issues engaged by literary works.

59. Hall and Schwarz, "Displacements."

60. Stuart Hall, "Stuart Hall Interview—2 June 2011," interview by Hudson Vincent, *Cultural Studies* 27, no. 5 (2011): 757; Hall and Schwarz, "Displacements," 223.

61. J. R. R. Tolkien, "*Beowulf*: The Monsters and the Critics," in *The Monsters and the Critics, and Other Essays* (Boston: Houghton Mifflin, 1984), 5; hereafter citations from Tolkien's lecture appear parenthetically by page number in the text.

62. "It is as an historical document that it [*Beowulf*] has mainly been examined and dissected"; ibid., 6.

63. J. R. R. Tolkien, "Sir Gawain and the Green Knight," in *Monsters*, 72.

64. Geoffrey Harpham, "Roots, Races, and the Return to Philology," *Representations* 106, no. 1 (2009): 44.

65. Stephen Harris, "Race and Ethnicity," in *A Handbook of Anglo-Saxon Studies*, ed. Jacqueline Stodnick and Renée Trilling (Oxford: Wiley-Blackwell, 2012), 166.

66. Harpham, "Roots," 37, 39.

67. Ibid., 40, 41.

68. Ernest Renan, *History of the People of Israel* (Boston, 1892), 40, cited in Harpham, "Roots," 47.

69. Nikolaj Grundtvig, *Bjovulfs Drape eller det Oldnordiske Heltedigt: Brage of Idun* 4 (1841): 524; translation from Tom Shippey and Andreas Haarder, *Beowulf: The Critical Heritage* (London: Routledge, 1998), 244. See also Joshua Davies, "The Middle Ages as Property: *Beowulf*, Translation and the Ghosts of Nationalism," *postmedieval* 10 (2019): 141.

70. Rasmus Rask, *A Grammar of the Anglo-Saxon Tongue*, trans. Benjamin Thorpe (Copenhagen: Moller, 1830), iii.

71. Donna Beth Ellard, *Anglo-Saxon(ist) Pasts, PostSaxon Futures* (Santa Barbara: Punctum, 2019), 59. I place "Anglo-Saxon" in quotes to register the ties of the term, within and without academia, to white supremacy. Recent work on the racist and nationalist ideological investments voiced by practitioners well into the new millennium includes Davies, "Middle Ages as Property"; Adam Miyashiro, "Our Deeper Past: Race, Settler-Colonialism, and Medieval Heritage Politics," *Literature Compass* 16 (2019): 1–11; Mary Rambaran-Olm, M. Breann Leake, and Micah Goodrich, "Medieval Studies: The Stakes of the Field," *postmedieval* 11, no. 3 (2020): 56–370; Rambaran-Olm, "A Wrinkle in Medieval Time: Ironing Out Issues Regarding Race, Temporality and the Early English," *New Literary History* 52, no. 3 (2021): 385–406.

72. See also Young, *Race and Popular Fantasy*, 21. Other nineteenth-century English medievalists singled out the English as supreme within the Germanic tradition; see Reginald Horsman, "Origins of Racial Anglo-Saxonism in Great Britain before 1850," *Journal of the History of Ideas* 37, no. 3 (1976): 387–410.

73. J. M. Kemble, *The Saxons in England* (London: Longman, 1849), 427, 5; see also Michael Banton, *The Idea of Race* (London: Tavistock, 1977), 23.

74. E. V. Gordon, *Introduction to Old Norse* (Oxford: Clarendon, 1927), v.

75. Dyer, *White*, 30.

76. Tolkien to Christopher Bretherton, July 16, 1964, in *Letters*, 344; Charles Huttar, "Tolkien, Epic Traditions and Golden-Age Myths," in *J. R. R. Tolkien*, ed. Harold Bloom (New York: Chelsea House, 2008), 11.

77. Tolkien to Milton Waldman, c. 1951, in *Letters*, 143.

78. Henry Resnik, "The Hobbit-Forming World of J. R. R. Tolkien," *Saturday Evening Post*, July 2, 1966, 40, cited in Saler, *As If*, 159.

79. J. R. R. Tolkien, "On Fairy Stories," in *Monsters*, 144; Saler, *As If*, 159.

80. Tolkien to Waldman, 144. Saler discusses Tolkien's anti-modernism and its ties to the Arts and Crafts Movement and French Symbolists in *As If*, 180–84.

81. J. R. R. Tolkien, *Tolkien: On Fairy-Stories; Expanded Edition, with Commentary and Notes*, ed. Verlyn Flieger and Douglas Anderson (London: HarperCollins, 2008), 243, cited in Saler, *As If*, 166.

82. Tolkien, "On Fairy Stories," 151.

83. Ibid., 148; Tolkien to Christopher Tolkien, October 6, 1944, in *Letters*, 96.

84. Huttar, "Tolkien, Epic Traditions," 11; see also Tolkien, *Fellowship*, 292. Tolkien claimed that his fiction could produce "Disgust, Anger, Condemnation, and Revolt" over modernity in readers; Saler, *As If*, 184.

85. Tolkien, "On Fairy Stories," 148; see Saler, *As If*, 184; and Patrick Curry, "Iron Crown, Iron Cage: Tolkien and Weber on Modernity and Enchantment," in *Myth and Magic: Art According to the Inklings*, ed. Eduardo Segura and Thomas Honegger (Zurich: Walking Tree, 2008).

86. Tolkien to Christopher Tolkien, October 6, 1944, in *Letters*, 65.

87. See Saler, *As If*, 165.

88. Tolkien followed earlier philologists—from Thorkelin to Tolkien's teacher Craigie and Tolkien's colleague Gordon—in affirming links between the early English and Scandinavians. William Craigie, for example, refers to the "knowledge of early Scandinavian history and legend which is so clearly manifested in the *Beowulf*"; Craigie, *The Northern Element in English Literature* (Toronto: University of Toronto Press, 1933), 95. As Tolkien puts it in an unfinished 1920s essay on the Norse *Edda*, any arguments about how "the spirit of" those Scandinavian myths is "a branch of a common 'Germanic spirit'" have "some truth: Byrhtwold at Maldon would do well enough in Edda or Saga"; J. R. R. Tolkien, "The Elder Edda," in *The Legend of Sigurd and Gudru'n*, ed. Christopher Tolkien (Boston: Houghton Mifflin, 2009), 23.

89. Tolkien, *Sigurd and Gudru'n*, 17, 24.

90. Tolkien, *"Beowulf,"* 21, citing P. Ker, *The Dark Ages* (London: Blackwood, 1911), 57.

91. Craigie, *Northern Element*, 2; see also William Craigie, *The Icelandic Sagas* (Cambridge: Cambridge University Press, 1913); Andy Brown, *Political Languages of Race and the Politics of Exclusion* (Aldershot: Ashgate, 1999).

92. Tolkien, *Sigurd and Gudru'n*, 32; cf. Saler, *As If*, 165.

93. Tolkien, *Sigurd and Gudru'n*, 26; cf. Saler, *As If*, 165.

94. Huttar, "Tolkien, Epic Traditions."

95. See also Kim, "Question of Race"; Kuchta, "Dyer Straits."

96. Hall's primary text, *Piers Plowman*, hardly conformed to Tolkien's essentialist and mythic program. Far from engaging pagan northern myths, Langland responded profoundly to his contemporary moment. Small wonder, then, that Tolkien never published on *Piers*, given its social and historical urgency.

97. Saler, *As If*, 163.

98. Cecire, *Re-enchanted*, 83, 90. C. S. Lewis assisted Tolkien in that effort (83–107). Consider the distinctly medieval national essence at work in Oxford in Lewis's 1945 novel *That Hideous Strength*; see Ian Carter, *Ancient Cultures of Conceit: British University Fiction in the Post-War Years* (London: Routledge, 1990), 85–87. Prior to Tolkien's arrival, dons like Walter Raleigh and George Gordon were ambivalent toward English literary study at the recently established School of English Language and Literature; see Chris Baldick, *The Social Mission of English Criticism, 1848–1932* (Oxford: Clarendon, 1983), 70–80, 104–6.

99. J. R. R. Tolkien, "The Notion Club Papers," in *Sauron Defeated*, ed. Christopher Tolkien (Boston: Houghton Mifflin, 1992), 227.

100. Saler, *As If*, 175–79; Verlyn Flieger, *A Question of Time: J. R. R. Tolkien's Road to Faërie* (Kent, Ohio: Kent State University Press, 1997), 73–74.

101. J. R. R. Tolkien, "English and Welsh," in *Monsters*, 190, 197.

102. See Saler, *As If*, 178.

103. Tolkien would similarly attribute to Chaucer "instinctive appreciation of the linguistic situation of his day"; seeTolkien, "Chaucer as a Philologist: *The Reeve's Tale*," *Transactions of the Philological Society* 33, no. 1 (1934): 6.

104. On this and related moments in Hall's lecture, see also Kim, "Question of Race."

105. Tolkien, "On Fairy Stories," 129.

106. Tolkien, *Fellowship*, 82.

107. Tolkien, "English and Welsh," 190, 191, 194. In a 1955 letter Tolkien states, "It is, I believe, as much due to descent as to opportunity that Anglo-Saxon and western Middle English and alliterative verse have been both a childhood attraction and my main professional sphere." Tolkien to Houghton Mifflin, June 10, 1955, in *Letters*, 218.

108. Tolkien to Waldman, 144.

109. Ibid., 144–45.

110. Saler, *As If*, 176.

111. Tolkien to Waldman, 145.

112. Tolkien to Stanley Unwin, February 18, 1938, in *Letters*, 31.

113. Critics stress what Young describes as the "tremendously important role philology and language played in the creation of Middle Earth and its inhabitants"; Young, *Race and Popular Fantasy*, 21; see also Shippey, *Road*.

114. Saler, *As If*, 176.

115. John Akomfrah, writer and director, *The Stuart Hall Project*, Smoking Dog Films, 2013; Stuart Hall, "The Formation of a Diasporic Intellectual: An Interview with Stuart Hall," interview by Kuan-Hsing Chen, in Chen and Morley, *Critical Dialogues*, 486.

116. Stuart Hall, "Whose Heritage? Un-settling 'The Heritage,' Re-imagining the Post-Nation," *Third Text*, 49 (1999–2000): 5.

117. Ibid., 26, emphasis original.

118. Hall, "Formation," 493.

119. Hall and Schwarz, *Familiar Stranger*, 157; William Camden, *Britannia*, cited in John Dougill, *Oxford in English Literature: The Making, and Undoing, of "The English Athens"* (Ann Arbor: University of Michigan Press, 1998), 36. Dougill describes how Camden inaugurated nationalistic celebrations of Oxford that assumed not just gothic but also classicizing forms and sometimes a mixture of both.

120. Matthew Arnold, "Thyrsis" and "Preface," in *Essays in Criticism* (1865), cited in Dougill, *Oxford*, 150–51.

121. William Wordsworth, "Oxford, May 30, 1820," cited in Dougill, *Oxford*, 142–43; Ian Carter, *Ancient Cultures of Conceit* (London: Routledge 1990), 40–51.

122. Stuart Hall, *Personally Speaking: A Long Conversation with Stuart Hall*, interview by Maya Jaggi, dir. Mike Dibb (Northampton, Mass.: Media Education Foundation, 2009), 8, https://mediaed.org/transcripts/Stuart-Hall-Personally-Speaking-Transcript.pdf; A. R. Woolley, *Oxford: University and City* (London: Art and Technics, 1951), 17.

123. Stuart Hall and Les Back, "At Home and Not at Home," *Cultural Studies* 23, no. 4 (2009): 669.

124. Hall, "Whose Heritage?," 4.

125. As Young puts it, citing the American Anthropological Association 1988 statement on race, people "are born with the ability to learn any language or culture"; Young, *Race and Popular Fantasy*, 7.

126. Ahmed, "Phenomenology"; Hall, "Local and the Global."

127. Hall, "Local and the Global," 24.

128. Ibid. On the idea of "vernaculars" like English and white supremacy in medieval studies, see Shyama Rajendran, "Undoing 'the Vernacular': Dismantling Structures of Raciolinguistic Supremacy," *Literature Compass* 16 (2019): 1–13.

129. Stuart Hall and Doreen Massey, "Interpreting the Crisis," *Soundings* 44 (2010): 57, original emphasis.

130. Stuart Hall, "Gramsci's Relevance for the Study of Race and Ethnicity," *Journal of Communication Inquiry* 10, no. 2 (1986): 14 (original emphasis).

131. Ibid., 13.

132. Ibid., 13–14.

133. Stuart Hall, "*Policing the Crisis*: Preface to the 35th Anniversary Edition," in *Essential Essays*, vol. 1, *Foundations of Cultural Studies*, ed. David Morley (Durham, N.C.: Duke University Press, 2019), 368.

134. On British immigration policy, see Kathleen Paul, *Whitewashing Britain: Race and Citizenship in the Postwar Era* (Ithaca: Cornell University Press, 1997).

135. Margaret Byron, *Post-War Caribbean Migration to Britain: The Unfinished Cycle* (Aldershot: Ashgate, 1994); Ceri Peach, *West Indian Migration to Britain: A Social Geography* (Oxford: Oxford University Press, 1968).

136. Vijay Mishra, "Multiculturalism (2010–2011)," *The Year's Work in Critical and Cultural Theory* 21 (2013): 3; see also Annette Henry, "'Nostalgia for What Cannot Be': An Interpretive and Social Biography of Stuart Hall's Early Years in Jamaica

and England, 1932–1959," *Discourse: Studies in the Cultural Politics of Education* 36, no. 2 (2015): 231–32.

137. A. J. Spooner, "Migration and the City of Oxford" (DPhil thesis, University of Oxford, 1979), 30. Hall tacitly confirms that he left Oxford in 1957; Stuart Hall, "Stuart Hall by Caryl Phillips," interview, *Bomb Magazine* 58, January 1, 1997, https://bombmagazine.org/articles/1997/01/01/stuart-hall-by-caryl-phillips/.

138. Spooner, "Migration," 31.

139. Catherine Hall and Sonya Rose, *At Home with the Empire: Metropolitan Culture and the Imperial World* (Cambridge: Cambridge University Press, 2008), 4.

140. Bill Schwarz, "Introduction: Crossing the Sea," in *West Indian Intellectuals in Britain*, ed. Bill Schwarz (Manchester: Manchester University Press, 2003), 7.

141. Tolkien did discuss Africa in, for example, his letters but primarily in white northern European terms as where he spent his earliest years and the site of his son Christopher's air force training. See, for example, Tolkien to Christopher Tolkien, June 10, 1944, in *Letters*, 85; Tolkien to the editor of the "Observer," January 16, 1938, in *Letters*, 30.

142. Tolkien to Christopher Tolkien, October 6, 1944, in *Letters*, 65.

143. Allen Tate, "The New Provincialism," *Virginia Quarterly Review* (1945): 264–65; see also Harilaos Stecopoulos, *Telling America's Story to the World: Literature, Internationalism, Cultural Diplomacy* (Oxford: Oxford University Press, 2023), 24–26.

144. Saler, *As If*, 172.

145. Ibid., 173–75; Andy Duncan, "Senator Bilbo," *PodCastle* (podcast) 32, November 4, 2008, https://podcastle.org/2008/11/04/pc032-senator-bilbo/; Robert Gehl, "Something Is Stirring in the East: Racial Identity, Confronting the 'Other,' and Miscegenation in *Othello* and *The Lord of the Rings*," in *Tolkien and Shakespeare: Essays on Shared Themes and Language*, ed. Janet Brennan Croft (Jefferson, N.C.: McFarland, 2007), 254–55.

146. Tolkien, *Fellowship*, 12

147. Tolkien, *Fellowship*, 176–77.

148. J. R. R. Tolkien, *The Return of the King* (New York: Del Rey, 1973), 307.

149. Matthew Vernon describes a similar dynamic in the wake of Barack Obama's election on the part of far-right medievalisms, which bespeak "a fear of impending change, a fear of a movement beyond the 'clarity' of the past, a fear of blackness"; Vernon, *The Black Middle Ages: Race and the Construction of the Middle Ages* (Cham, Switzerland: Palgrave-Macmillan, 2018), 15).

150. Tolkien to W. H. Auden, June 5, 1955, in *Letters*, 213; Tolkien to Bretherton, 347. Texts like Olaus Rudbeck's *Atlantica* (1702), Ignatius Donnelly's *Atlantis* (1882), and Helena Blavatsky's *The Secret Doctrine* (1888) popularized Atlantis and generated claims including speculations about a Nordic Atlantis.

151. Tolkien, *Return*, 344.

152. Tolkien, *Return*, 346–47.

153. Tolkien, *Return*, 259.

154. Tolkien to Christopher Tolkien, January 18, 1945, in *Letters*, 108.
155. Tolkien to Auden, 212–13.
156. Verlyn Flieger, *A Question of Time: J. R. R. Tolkien's Road to Faërie* (Kent, Ohio: Kent State University Press, 1997), 74–75.
157. Tolkien to Auden, 213; Tolkien to Bretherton, 347.
158. Tolkien, *Return*, 354.
159. Verlyn Flieger, "Do the Atlantis Story and Abandon Eriol-Saga," *Tolkien Studies* 1, no. 1 (2004): 45.
160. Zig Layton-Henry, *The Politics of Immigration: Immigration, "Race," and "Race" Relations in Post-War Britain* (Oxford: Blackwell, 1992), 13.
161. Brown, *Political Languages*, 131.
162. "Immigration into Britain," To the Editor, *Times*, January 20, 1955, 9.
163. Thomas Utley, *Enoch Powell: The Man and His Thinking* (London: Kimber, 1968), 179–90; Margaret Thatcher, interview by Gordon Burns, *World in Action*, Granada Television, January 27, 1978, https://margaretthatcher.org/document/103485.
164. On *Savacou*, see Alison Donnell, *Twentieth-Century Caribbean Literature: Critical Moments in Anglophone Literary History* (London: Routledge, 2006), 27.
165. Stuart Hall, "Black Men, White Media," *Savacou* 9, no. 10 (1971): 97.
166. Hall, "Local and the Global," 19.
167. Tolkien to G. B. Smith, August 12, 1916, in *Letters*, 8; Tolkien to Rhona Beare, no date, in *Letters*, 288; Tolkien, *Fellowship*, 52.
168. Tim Adams, "The Interview: Cultural Hallmark," *Observer*, September 12, 2007, https://theguardian.com/society/2007/sep/23/communities.politicsphilosophyandsociety.
169. Stuart Hall, "Local and the Global," 20.
170. Ibid., 22.
171. Ibid.
172. Tolkien to Houghton Mifflin, 219; Tolkien to Michael Tolkien, March 18, 1941, in Tolkien, *Letters*, 54.
173. Hall, "Whose Heritage?," 5. See also Davies, "Middle Ages as Property," 146–47.
174. Saler, *As If*, 163.

4. Stuart Hall's *Piers Plowman*

1. Stuart Hall, "The Spectacle of the Other," in *Representation: Cultural Representations and Signifying Practices*, ed. Stuart Hall (London: Open University Press, 1997), 239.
2. Stuart Hall, "'In But Not Of Europe': Europe and Its Myths," *Soundings* 22 (2002–3): 66, hereafter cited parenthetically by page number.
3. Stuart Hall, "The West and the Rest: Discourse and Power," in *Formations of Modernity*, ed. Stuart Hall and Bram Gieben (Cambridge: Polity Press, 1992), hereafter cited parenthetically by page number.

4. Stuart Hall with Bill Schwarz, *Familiar Stranger: A Life between Two Islands* (Durham, N.C.: Duke University Press, 2017), 156, hereafter cited parenthetically by page number.

5. On Hall's thesis, "Europe versus America: Cultural and Moral Themes in the International Novels of Henry James," see Stuart Hall, *Personally Speaking: A Long Conversation with Stuart Hall*, interview by Maya Jaggi, dir. Mike Dibb (Northampton, Mass.: Media Education Foundation, 2009), 56. Hall gave up his dissertation in 1956 after a trio of events: the invasions of Hungary and the Suez Canal by Soviet and Anglo-French forces, respectively, and Khrushchev's attack, in a speech, on Stalin's criminal actions. The year 1956 prompted Hall's break from not one but two C's: orthodox communism and culture as it was understood in a Leavisite or Arnoldian sense as embodied by great literary texts. Hall tied his renunciation of English graduate work directly to those political upheavals, telling Kuan-Hsing Chen of his dissertation, "I gave it up literally because of 1956"; "I didn't feel it was right for me to go on thinking cultural questions in 'pure' literary terms"; Stuart Hall, "The Formation of a Diasporic Intellectual: An Interview with Stuart Hall," interview by Kuan-Hsing Chen, in *Stuart Hall: Critical Dialogues in Cultural Studies*, ed. David Morley and Kuan-Hsing Chen (London: Routledge, 1996), 499–500.

6. Edward Said, *Culture and Imperialism* (New York: Vintage, 1993), 59–60.

7. Catherine Gallagher, *Telling It Like It Wasn't: The Counterfactual Imagination in History and Fiction* (Chicago: University of Chicago Press, 2018).

8. Saidiya Hartman, "Venus in Two Acts," *Small Axe* 12, no. 2 (2008): 11.

9. Hartman, "Venus in Two Acts." As Professor Dorothy Kim observed when I first presented my findings in fall 2018 at St. Louis University, I (along with Kim) belong to an intellectual "line" of white medievalists tied to Tolkien. Kim, along with my advisor, L. O. Aranye Fradenburg, studied with V. A. "Del" Kolve (1934–2022), who was "one of Tolkien's last probationer B.Litt. students in 1958"; John Bowers, *Tolkien's Lost Chaucer* (Oxford: Oxford University Press, 2019), 10.

10. Michel Foucault, "Lives of Infamous Men," in *The Essential Foucault*, ed. Paul Rabinow and Nikolas Rose (New York: New Press, 2003); E. P. Thompson, *The Making of the English Working Class* (London: Penguin, 1992).

11. Catherine Gallagher and Stephen Greenblatt, *Practicing New Historicism* (Chicago: University of Chicago Press, 2001), 74.

12. Mary Rambaran-Olm, "A Wrinkle in Medieval Time: Ironing Out Issues Regarding Race, Temporality, and the Early English," *New Literary History* 52, no. 3–4 (2021): 387.

13. Claire Alexander, "Stuart Hall and 'Race,'" *Cultural Studies* 23, no. 4 (2009): 458.

14. Stuart Hall, "Politics and Letters," in *Raymond Williams: Critical Perspectives*, ed. Terry Eagleton (Cambridge: Polity, 1989), 57.

15. West Indians sought independence for their homeland and asserted their rights as English citizens in keeping with the British Nationality Act, an unprecedented

1948 legislation that yoked all members of the UK and the Colonies together under a single rubric of citizenship. Hall and Schwarz, *Familiar Stranger*, 164. On British immigration policy, see Kathleen Paul, *Whitewashing Britain: Race and Citizenship in the Postwar Era* (Ithaca: Cornell University Press, 1997).

16. Stuart Hall, "Whose Heritage? Un-settling 'The Heritage,' Re-imagining the Post-Nation," *Third Text*, 49 (1999–2000): 4.

17. Stuart Hall and Les Back, "At Home and Not at Home," *Cultural Studies* 23, no. 4 (2009): 665; Hall and Schwarz, *Familiar Stranger*, 156.

18. Hall and Schwarz, *Familiar Stranger*, 222; Stuart Hall, "The Life and Times of the First New Left," *New Left Review* 61 (2010): 179.

19. Stuart Hall, "Stuart Hall Interview–2 June 2011," interview by Hudson Vincent, *Cultural Studies* 27, no. 5 (2011): 758.

20. There, Leavis acolyte Derek Traversi praises Nevill Coghill for a 1933 article (Coghill, "The Character of Piers Plowman Considered from the B Text," *Medium Aevum* 2 [1933]: 108–35), "which showed conclusively that Langland's poem was not, as it had been held to be, an example of mediaeval anarchy, redeemed only for the persevering philologist and the hardy student of social conditions"; Traversi, *"The Vision of Piers Plowman," Scrutiny* 5, no. 3 (1936): 276.

21. Larry Scanlon, "King, Commons and Kind Wit: Langland's National Vision and the Rising of 1381," in *Imagining a Medieval English Nation*, ed. Kathy Lavezzo (Minneapolis: Minnesota University Press, 2006), 197.

22. Hall and Schwarz, *Familiar Stranger*, 217; Hall and Back, "At Home," 666–67.

23. F. R. Leavis, *The Great Tradition: George Eliot, Henry James, Joseph Conrad* (New York: New York University Press, 1964), 130.

24. Steven Justice, *Writing and Rebellion: England in 1381* (Berkeley: University of California Press, 1996), 102–39. Lawrence Warner contends that the rebels were not citing Langland; Warner, *The Lost History of "Piers Plowman": The Earliest Transmission of Langland's Work* (Philadelphia: University of Pennsylvania Press, 2011), 1–14. But scholars including Scanlon ("King, Commons and Kind Wit") suggest how Langland encouraged such radical affiliations, particularly in the early incarnations of his work. See also Mike Rodman Jones, *Radical Pastoral* (Burlington, Vt.: Ashgate, 2011).

25. William Rhodes, *Work, Waste, Reform: Literature and Political Ecology from Langland to Spenser* (Ithaca: Cornell University Press, 2025); Sarah Kelen, *Langland's Early Modern Identities* (New York: Palgrave, 2007); Helen Barr, *The Piers Plowman Tradition* (London: Dent, 1993); John Bowers, *Chaucer and Langland: The Antagonistic Tradition* (Notre Dame, Ind.: University of Notre Dame Press, 2007).

26. William Benzie, *Dr. F. J. Furnivall: Victorian Scholar Adventurer* (Norman, Okla.: Pilgrim, 1983), 133, 52. Furnivall included *Piers* in his Early English Text Society editions.

27. William Morris, "Feudal England," in *Signs of Change: Seven Lectures Delivered on Various Occasions* (London: Longmans, 1896), 75.

28. John Richard Green, *A Short History of the English People* (London: Macmillan, 1876), 231, 248, v–vi, hereafter cited parenthetically by page number.

29. Anthony Brundage, *The People's Historian: John Richard Green and the Writing of History in Victorian England* (Westport, Conn.: Greenwood, 1994), 1–2, 157–58.

30. S. S. Prawer, *Karl Marx and World Literature* (Oxford: Clarendon, 1976), 383.

31. "Do you have William Langland's Complaint of Piers the Ploughman? If not, you may be able to borrow it from Furnivall for me, or alternatively, as it isn't dear, I could also buy it in the EARLY etc. series"; Karl Marx, "Letter to Eleanor Marx, 1882," in *Karl Marx, Frederick Engels: Collected Works*, trans. Peter Ross and Betty Ross, vol. 46 (London: Lawrence and Wishart, 1996), 371–72. For Marx's notes on the *Short History*, which include a comment that contrasting Langland with Chaucer could help elucidate late medieval English class tensions, see Karl Marx and Friedrich Engels, *Über Kunst und Literatur*, ed. Manfred Kliem, vol. 1 (Berlin: Dietz 1967), 380.

32. George Philip and Son, "The Piers Plowman Social and Economic Histories," advertisement in *History*, n.s., 9 (1924–25): front cover, verso; E. H. Spalding, ed., *The Piers Plowman Social and Economic Histories*, 7 vols. (London: George Philip and Son, 1926–30).

33. A. L. Morton, *A People's History of England* (London: Gollancz, 1938), 119.

34. Joanna Bullivant, *Alan Bush, Modern Music, and the Cold War: The Cultural Left in Britain and the Communist Bloc* (Cambridge: Cambridge University Press, 2017), 180. Bush co-wrote *Wat Tyler* with his spouse, Nancy.

35. Hall includes Hilton among the "communist humanis[ts]" who formed one of the "two related but different traditions" out of which the British New Left emerged; Hall, "Life and Times," 178. Hilton was a writer affiliated with the *New Reasoner*, an antecedent of the *New Left Review* (182–83). On the CPHG, see Bill Schwarz, "'The People' in History: The Communist Party Historians' Group, 1946–56," in *Making Histories: Studies in History-Writing and Politics*, ed. Richard Johnson et al. (London: Hutchinson, 1982), 44–95.

36. Aglaia Kasdagli, "Medieval History and Marxism in England, 1950–1956," *Past and Present* 242 (2019): e19.

37. Hyman Fagan, *Nine Days That Shook England: An Account of the English Peoples' Uprising in 1381* (London: Gollancz, 1938), 118.

38. Rodney Hilton, introduction to *The English Rising of 1381*, ed. Rodney Hilton and Hyman Fagan (London: Lawrence and Wishart, 1950), 82.

39. Bowers suggests that anxieties regarding anti-Catholic sentiment underpinned Tolkien's avoidance of Langland in *Tolkien's Lost Chaucer*, 118.

40. A possible exception is Furnivall (1825–1910), cofounder of the London Working Men's College. Carolyn Dinshaw suggests that Furnivall's "amateurism associated him with classed and racialized others" in *How Soon Is Now? Medieval Texts, Amateur Readers and the Queerness of Time* (Durham, N.C.: Duke University Press, 2012), 31–32.

41. On the Whiggish Teutonic democracy of John Richard Green, Edward Freeman, William Stubbs, and other historians, see J. W. Burrow, *A Liberal Descent: Victorian Historians and the English Past* (Cambridge: Cambridge University Press, 1983). As the example of Freeman indicates, certain historians claimed the Teutonism of not just the Anglo-Saxons but also the Normans as grounds for the ongoing Germanic character of the English; see Anthony Brundage and Richard Cosgrove, *British Historians and National Identity: From Hume to Churchill* (Cambridge: Cambridge University Press, 2014), 95–108.

42. On the Teutonism of Morris, Marx, Engels, and others, see Anna Vaninskaya, *William Morris and the Idea of Community: Romance, History and Propaganda, 1880–1914* (Edinburgh: Edinburgh University Press, 2010).

43. Friedrich Engels, *Origins of the Family, Private Property, and the State*, trans. Ernest Untermann (Chicago: Kerr, 1902), 217, citing Lewis Morgan. See also Vaninskaya, *William Morris*, 108.

44. Dennis Dworkin, *Cultural Marxism in Postwar Britain: History, the New Left and the Origins of Cultural Studies* (Durham, N.C.: Duke University Press, 1997), 51.

45. Ibid., 18–19, 23, 32–33, 38–44; Schwarz, "'The People,'" 55–56, 71–74; Hall, "Life and Times," 182–83.

46. Morton, *People's History*, 119. Reflecting its popular-front roots, the CPHG formed in 1946 with the intention to discuss a new edition of Morton's book.

47. Dworkin, *Cultural Marxism*, 39.

48. Rodney Hilton, "Peasant Movements in England before 1381," *Economic History Review* 2, no. 2 (1949): 136. See also Hilton and Fagan, *English Rising*, 81; Dworkin, *Cultural Marxism*, 40.

49. Paul Gilroy, "British Cultural Studies and the Pitfalls of Identity," in *Black British Cultural Studies: A Reader*, ed. Houston Baker Jr., Manthia Diawara, and Ruth Lindeborg (Chicago: University of Chicago Press, 1996), 233. Roxy Harris discusses how those blind spots were part of a larger white tradition that extends at least back to Leavis, Eliot, and Arnold and persisted after the creation of the Centre for Contemporary Cultural Studies; Harris, "Black British, Brown British and British Cultural Studies," *Cultural Studies* 23, no. 4 (2009): 483–512.

50. Alexander, "Stuart Hall," 469.

51. Stuart Hall, "Culture, Community, Nation," *Cultural Studies* 7, no. 3 (1993): 355–56, emphasis original.

52. Stuart Hall, "The Local and the Global," in *Culture, Globalization and the World-System: Contemporary Conditions for the Representation of Identity*, ed. Anthony King, (Minneapolis: University of Minnesota Press, 1991), 22; Hall, "Whose Heritage?," 7.

53. Hall, "Culture, Community, Nation," 359.

54. Ibid., 359–60. See also Paul Gilroy, *There Ain't No Black in the Union Jack: The Cultural Politics of Race and Nation* (Chicago: University of Chicago Press, 1991), 50.

55. Alexander, "Stuart Hall," 464.

56. Hall, "Life and Times," 179.
57. Hall, "Life and Times," 178.
58. Ibid., 183, 187, 178.
59. Ibid., 195.
60. Stewart [sic] M. Hall, "Our Literary Heritage," *Sunday Gleaner*, January 3, 1954, 5.
61. J. E. Clare McFarlane, "Our Literary Heritage," part one, *The Daily Gleaner*, December 3, 1953, 8; "Our Literary Heritage," part two, December 4, 1953, 8.
62. Derek Walcott, *The Journeyman Years: Occasional Prose, 1957–1974*, ed. Gordon Collier, vol. 1 (Amsterdam: Rodopi, 2013), 188. On the League, which was founded in 1927 by McFarlane, see Laurence Breiner, *An Introduction to West Indian Poetry* (Cambridge: Cambridge University Press, 1998), 63–67.
63. T. S. Eliot, "Tradition and the Individual Talent," *Egoist* 6 (1919): 55.
64. Eliot, "Tradition," 54–55, 72–73.
65. Eliot, "Tradition," 55.
66. C. L. R. James, "African and Afro-Caribbeans: A Personal View," *Ten.8*, 6 (1984): 55.
67. Stuart Hall, "Thinking Diaspora: Home Thoughts from Abroad," in *Postcolonialisms: An Anthology of Cultural Theory and Criticism*, ed. Gaurav Desai and Supriya Nair (New Brunswick, N.J.: Rutgers University Press, 2005), 556. See also Amiri Baraka, *Black Music* (New York: William Morrow, 1968), 176–207; Houston Baker, *Modernism and the Harlem Renaissance* (Chicago: University of Chicago Press, 1987).
68. See Leavis's celebration of writers who are "peculiarly alive in their time — peculiarly alive to it" in *Great Tradition*, 22, emphasis original.
69. See also Hall and Schwarz, *Familiar Stranger*, 140.
70. See Ernesto Laclau and Chantal Mouffe, *Hegemony and Socialist Strategy* (London: Verso, 1985); Judith Butler, *Bodies That Matter* (London: Routledge, 1993).
71. Hall, "Culture, Community, Nation," 356.
72. Ibid; Hall, "Whose Heritage?," 6.
73. Hall, "West and the Rest," 313, emphasis original; Hall, "Whose Heritage?," 25.
74. Hall, "Whose Heritage?," 6.
75. Hall, "Europe and Its Myths," 65, emphasis original.
76. The excerpt is taken from Michael Mann, "European Development: Approaching a Historical Explanation," in *Europe and the Rise of Capitalism*, ed. Jean Baechler et al. (Oxford: Blackwell, 1988), 10–15, and cited as "Reading A" in Hall, "West and the Rest," 321–25. A modified version of "West and the Rest" appears in *Modernity: An Introduction to Modern Societies*, ed. Stuart Hall, David Held, Don Hubert, and Kenneth Thompson (Oxford: Blackwell, 1996), 184–228. Hall incorporates an abbreviated citation of Mann (which retains Mann's Langland citation) directly into that 1996 edition (197–99).
77. Stuart Hall, introduction to Hall and Gieben, *Formations*, 8.
78. Ibid., 9–10.

79. Ibid., 11.
80. Ibid., 16.
81. Hall cites Ronald Latham, ed. *Marco Polo: The Travels* (Harmondsworth: Penguin, 1958), 8. While Hall stresses how external threats tend to promote internal cohesion, in recent decades, scholars have demonstrated the interpenetration of the Christian West and Muslim culture during the medieval period. See, for example, Christine Chism, "Arabic in the Medieval World," *PMLA* 124, no. 2 (2009): 624–31, and María Rosa Menocal, *The Arabic Role in Medieval Literary History: A Forgotten Heritage* (Philadelphia: University of Pennsylvania Press, 2004). Hall's complex relationship to that scholarship emerges in the foundational role of his work on the local and the global in scholarly publications, including Janet Abu-Lughod, *Before European Hegemony: The World System AD 1250–1350* (Oxford: Oxford University Press, 1989).
82. "A4 unlined loose-leaf refill pad labelled 'Exploration Notebook, New Golden Land/The Man-Eating Myth'" and "A4 unlined loose-leaf refill pad labelled 'Age of Exploration Notebook, Age of Exploration/Aristotle and the American Indians/The Las Casas Debate,'" Stuart Hall Archive US 121, Box 33, Cadbury Research Library: Special Collections, University of Birmingham. The notebooks draw on secondary sources including Hugh Honour, *The New Golden Land: European Images of America from the Discoveries to the Present Time* (New York: Pantheon, 1976).
83. Hall cites Hartmann Schedel, *Nuremberg Chronicle*, fol. xi v; see "The Second Age of the World," fol. Xi v, in *First English Edition of the Nuremberg Chronicle*, trans. Kosta Hadavas (Madison: University of Wisconsin–Madison, 2023), https://search.library.wisc.edu/digital/A3SXNV3NHBQLFQ8J/fulltext/AVRCR3XF2WYPVY9Enur1_00153#thumb.
84. Hall, "West and the Rest," 298.
85. "Exploration Notebook," "Age of Exploration Notebook." Hall cites Honour, *New Golden Land*, 3.
86. "Exploration Notebook," "Age of Exploration Notebook."
87. With its evocation of the "thousand legendary encounters" that determined the information produced by the first "real" contact with the Americas, Hall's language looks back to Fanon on how the Black other is "woven out of a thousand details, anecdotes, and stories" and ahead to Jennifer Morgan's discussion of how, thanks to medieval texts including *Mandeville's Travels*, "The meanings attached to the female African body were inscribed well before the establishment of England's colonial American plantations"; see Frantz Fanon, *Black Skin, White Masks*, trans. Richard Philcox (New York: Grove, 2008), 91; Jennifer Morgan, *Laboring Women: Reproduction and Gender in New World Slavery* (Philadelphia: University of Pennsylvania Press, 2004), 16–17.
88. Hall, "Local and the Global," 21.
89. Stuart Hall, "Culture, the Media, and the 'Ideological Effect,'" in *Mass Communication and Society*, ed. James Curran, Michael Gurevitch, and Janet

Woollacott (London: Arnold, 1977), 327. Future parenthetical page citations appear in the text.

90. Ibid.

91. Stuart Hall, "The Problem of Ideology—Marxism Without Guarantees," *Journal of Communication Inquiry* 10, no. 2 (1986): 43, emphasis original.

92. Stuart Hall, "Cultural Studies: Two Paradigms," *Media, Culture and Society* 2 (1980): 67; Hall, "Problem of Ideology," 43; Hall, "Two Paradigms," 36.

93. Stuart Hall, "Culture's Revenge," interview by Laurie Taylor, *New Humanist* 121, no. 2 (2006), https://newhumanist.org.uk/articles/960/cultures-revenge-laurie-taylor-interviews-stuart-hall.

94. Stuart Hall, "Race, Articulation, and Societies Structured in Dominance," in *Sociological Theories: Race and Colonialism* (Paris: UNESCO, 1980), 305–45.

95. David Scott, "Stuart Hall's Ethics," *Small Axe* 17 (2005): 13-14. See also Brett St. Louis, "On 'The Necessity' and the 'Impossibility' of Identities: The Politics and Ethics of 'New Ethnicities,'" *Cultural Studies* 23, no. 4 (2009): 579; Melissa Gregg, *Cultural Studies' Affective Voices* (New York: Palgrave Macmillan, 2006), 55–81.

96. Gayatri Spivak, "Thinking Cultural Questions in 'Pure' Literary Terms," in *Without Guarantees: In Honour of Stuart Hall*, ed. Paul Gilroy, Angela McRobbie, and Lawrence Grossberg (London: Verso, 2000), 335. Hall's scathing indictment of the British media resonates with Toni Morrison's damning observation about Black racialization. Morrison dryly notes how none of the cultures of the U.S., South America, England, France, and other European sites "has been able to persuade itself for long that criteria and knowledge could emerge outside the categories of domination"; Toni Morrison, *Playing in the Dark: Whiteness and the Literary Imagination* (Cambridge, Mass.: Harvard University Press, 1992), 7.

97. Stuart Hall, "New Ethnicities," in Morley and Chen, *Critical Dialogues*, 444. Future parenthetical page citations appear in the text.

98. On Hall's dialectical movement between rejecting essential identities and acknowledging the need for "identity as a strategic resource and political 'positioning,'" see St. Louis, "On 'The Necessity,'" 561.

99. Nicolette Zeeman, *The Arts of Disruption: Allegory and "Piers Plowman"* (Oxford: Oxford University Press, 2020), 17.

100. See the works cited in Zeeman, *Arts of Disruption*, 122. I attach labels like "formalist" to Middleton et al. to acknowledge their critical diversity; those descriptors fail to approximate to those scholars' own complex critical investments.

101. Zeeman, *Arts of Disruption*, 122, citing David Aers, *Beyond Reformation? An Essay on William Langland's "Piers Plowman" and the End of Constantinian Christianity* (Notre Dame, Ind.: University of Notre Dame Press, 2015), 98; Hall, "Problem of Ideology," 43, emphasis original.

102. References to *Piers Plowman* are taken from William Langland, *The Vision of Piers Plowman: A Complete Edition of the B-Text*, ed. A. V. C. Schmidt (London: Everyman, 1978); and *Piers Plowman: An Edition of the C-text*, ed. Derek Pearsall (Berkeley: University of California Press, 1978). I have modernized thorns and yoghs in Pearsall's edition.

103. Stuart Hall, *The Hard Road to Renewal: Thatcherism and the Crisis of the Left* (London: Verso, 2021), 163.

104. Ibid. Cf. Mark Schmitt, *Spectres of Pessimism: A Cultural Logic of the Worst* (Cham, Switzerland: Palgrave, 2023), 40.

105. Anne Middleton, "William Langland's 'Kynde Name': Authorial Signature and Social Identity in Late Fourteenth-Century England," in *Chaucer Langland, and Fourteenth-Century Literary History*, ed. Steven Justice (Farnham: Ashgate, 2013), 259.

106. D. Vance Smith, "*Piers Plowman* and the National Noetic of Edward III," in Lavezzo, *Imagining a Medieval English Nation*, 246.

107. Ibid., 236.

108. Scanlon, "King, Commons and Kind Wit," 208.

109. Ibid., 204, 212.

110. Traugott Lawlor, *The Penn Commentary on "Piers Plowman,"* vol. 4, *C Passus 15–19; B Passus 13–17* (Philadelphia: University of Pennsylvania Press, 2018), 239.

111. Emily Steiner, *Reading "Piers Plowman"* (Cambridge: Cambridge University Press, 2013), 162.

112. John Burrow, *English Poets in the Late Middle Ages: Chaucer, Langland, and Others* (New York: Routledge, 2012), 8.

113. Lawlor, *Penn Commentary*, 251–52.

114. Hall, "Local and the Global," 21; Hall and Schwarz, *Familiar Stranger*, 215.

115. Lawlor, *Penn Commentary*, 267.

116. For instance, Nicolette Zeeman, *Arts of Disruption*, 13.

117. Simon Meecham-Jones, "Where Was Wales? The Erasure of Wales in Medieval English Culture," in *Authority and Subjugation in Writing of Medieval Wales*, ed. Ruth Kennedy and Simon Meecham-Jones (New York: Palgrave Macmillan, 2008), 30.

118. Cf. Langland's description of Wales and England as part of a single "marche" or borderland of Christian Europe (B.15.444).

119. R. R. Davies, *The First English Empire: Power and Identities in the British Isles, 1093–1343* (Oxford: Oxford University Press, 2000), 113–41.

120. Hall, "Two Paradigms," 67.

121. Hall, "Culture, the Media," 346.

122. See also Langland's representation of white-black dualisms in B.10.433, B.15.112–13, and C.20.214–15. Exemplifying what Cord Whitaker describes as a "late medieval impulse towards dynamic binarism" that proved "central to the development of race-thinking," those passages query the color white yet remain firmly within the structured dominance of a Christian ideological field; Whitaker, *Black Metaphors: How Modern Racism Emerged from Medieval Race Thinking* (Philadelphia: University of Pennsylvania Press, 2019), 65. When Langland points out how whiteness may cover over filth and how whiteness needs blackness to signify, he doesn't take us beyond "white and black" itself as a cognitive opposition. By retaining the very grounds of the debate in the first place, such moments only cement the overall workings of Christian whiteness, where white versus black

remains central to the way Christianity functions as a discourse that produces knowledge of things and lays out the terms necessary for understanding anything.

123. Suzanne Conklin Akbari, "The non-Christians of *Piers Plowman*," in *The Cambridge Companion to "Piers Plowman*," ed. Andrew Cole and Andrew Galloway (Cambridge: Cambridge University Press, 2014), 175. British author Maureen Duffy would, in her unpublished play *Pearson* (1956–62) and her 2017 poem *Past Present*, put Langland's plowman into contact with West Indians and other non-European groups; see Michael Johnston and Lawrence Warner, "'The Pure and Perfect Book': Marilynne Robinson, Maureen Duffy and the Heirs of *Piers Plowman*," *Yearbook of Langland Studies* 35 (2021): 75, 86. On the portrayal of others in *Piers*, see also Geraldine Heng, "A Global Middle Ages," in *A Handbook of Middle English Studies*, ed. Marion Turner (New York: Wiley-Blackwell, 2013), 420; Frank Grady, *Representing Righteous Heathens in Late Medieval England* (New York: Palgrave, 2005), 17–44; and Elisa Narin van Court, "The Hermeneutics of Supersession: The Revision of the Jews from the B to the C text of *Piers Plowman*," *Yearbook of Langland Studies* 10 (1996): 43–87.

124. Hall cites J. M. Roberts, *The Triumph of the West* (London: BBC, 1985), 122. See note 81 above on the interpenetration of the Christian West and Muslim culture during the medieval period.

125. Karla Mallette shows how some southern European nineteenth- and early twentieth-century counter-Orientalists recognized those influences, generating "a model of modernity created by Arabs and Europeans in concert and to which Arabs and Europeans both continue to contribute"; Mallette, *European Modernity and the Arab Mediterranean: Toward a New Philology and a Counter-Orientalism* (Philadelphia: University of Pennsylvania Press, 2010), 5.

126. Hall, "New Ethnicities," 444; see also St. Louis, "On the 'Necessity,'" 563.

5. High Theory, Low Feelings: Gloria Naylor's *Bailey's Cafe*

1. I follow U.S. convention in using the term "post-structuralism," although it was never accepted widely by continental theorists.

2. Jonathan Culler, *Structuralist Poetics: Structuralism, Linguistics and the Study of Literature* (London: Routledge, 1975), 32.

3. Michel Foucault, "What Is an Author?," in *Foucault, Language, CounterMemory, Practice*, trans. Donald Bouchard and Sherry Simon (Ithaca: Cornell University Press, 1977), 116; Fredric Jameson, *Postmodernism, or The Cultural Logic of Late Capitalism* (Durham, N.C.: Duke University Press, 1991), 15.

4. Paul Zumthor, *Essai de poetique medieval* (Paris: Seuil, 1972), trans. Philip Bennett as *Toward a Medieval Poetics* (Minneapolis: 1992).

5. In the U.S., theory first made waves in English literary criticism among scholars of British Romanticism in the 1970s—for instance, J. Hillis Miller, "The Still Heart: Poetic Form in Wordsworth," *New Literary History* 2, no. 2 (1971): 297–310; Harold Bloom, *The Ringers in the Tower: Studies in Romantic Tradition*

(Chicago: University of Chicago Press, 1971); Bloom et al., *Deconstruction and Criticism* (New York: Continuum, 1984).

6. The 1986 conference included a session on *Deconstructing the Canterbury Tales*, where panelists argued "Pro" and "Con" positions; see Beryl Rowland et al, "New Chaucer Society: Fifth International Congress," *Studies in the Age of Chaucer, Proceedings* 2 (1986): 189–95; also in *Studies*, see Peggy Knapp, "Deconstructing the Canterbury Tales: Pro," 73–81, and Trawgott Lawler, "Deconstructing the Canterbury Tales: Con," 83–91.

7. Paul Freedman and Gabrielle Spiegel link how "American medievalists . . . were slow to take up the challenge of postmodernism" to both "the persistence" of a Jeffersonian "discourse of continuity and progress that had marked the American relation to its patently absent past" and "negative interest" to those deemed other to modernity; Freedman and Spiegel, "Medievalisms Old and New: The Rediscovery of Alterity in North American Medieval Studies," *American Historical Review* 103, no. 3 (1998): 694. The late arrival of medievalists to the theory scene is ironic insofar as medieval studies helped lay the groundwork for theory; see Bruce Holsinger, *The Premodern Condition: Medievalism and the Making of Theory* (Chicago: University of Chicago Press, 2005); John Ganim, "Medieval Literature as Monster: The Grotesque before and after Bakhtin," *Exemplaria* 7, no. 1 (1995): 27–40; Amy Hollywood, *Acute Melancholia, and Other Essays: Mysticism, History, and the Study of Religion* (New York: Columbia University Press, 2016); and Erin Labbie, *Lacan's Medievalism* (Minneapolis: University of Minnesota Press, 2006).

8. Robert Jordan, *Chaucer's Poetics and the Modern Reader* (Berkeley: University of California Press, 1987), 2.

9. H. Marshall Leicester Jr., *The Disenchanted Self: Representing the Subject in the* Canterbury Tales (Berkeley: University of California Press, 1990), 401.

10. Ibid., 28.

11. Lee Patterson, "On the Margin: Postmodernism, Ironic History, and Medieval Studies," *Speculum* 65, no. 1 (1990): 90.

12. Peggy Knapp, *Chaucer and the Social Contest* (1990; repr. New York: Routledge, 2011), 2.

13. Ibid., 141.

14. Carolyn Dinshaw, *Chaucer's Sexual Poetics* (Madison: University of Wisconsin Press, 1989), 16.

15. Leicester, *Disenchanted Self*, 402; Dinshaw, *Chaucer's Sexual Poetics*, 183–84.

16. Ibid., 25, 117.

17. Naylor insisted that "cafe" be spelled without an accent, perhaps because of the South African spelling of the word and its transnational associations; *OED*, s.v. "café."

18. Bailey also recalls Frederick Douglass's maternal line: his mother, Harriet Bailey, and grandmother Betsy Bailey; see Frederick Douglass, *Narrative of the Life of Frederick Douglass, an American Slave, Written by Himself* (Boston: Harvard University Press, 1988), 24.

19. Charles Wilson, "Medievalism, Race, and Social Order in Gloria Naylor's *Bailey's Cafe*," *Studies in Medievalism* 10 (1998): 85.

20. Matthew Vernon, *The Black Middle Ages: Race and the Construction of the Middle Ages* (Cham, Switzerland: Palgrave, 2018), 242.

21. Ibid., 235.

22. Ibid., 213, 240.

23. Suzanne Edwards, "'Burn All He Has, but Keep His Books': Gloria Naylor and the Proper Objects of Feminist Chaucer Studies," *Chaucer Review* 54, no. 3 (2019): 233, 240.

24. Gloria Naylor, "Gloria Naylor," interview by Donna Perry, in *Conversations with Gloria Naylor*, ed. Maxine Lavon Montgomery (Jackson: University of Mississippi, 2004), 99. By "structuralist," Naylor meant post-structuralist. On terminology, see note 1 in this chapter.

25. Naylor's correspondence confirms that she worked on *Bailey's* at Cornell: "My fellowship here has given me a chance to catch my breath and gather my resources for the next 'novel'"; Naylor to Kimberly Benston, November 13, 1988, Gloria Naylor Archive, Box 12, Folder 6, Sacred Heart University, Fairfield, Conn.; "The next novel . . . is partly what Cornell was all about for me"; Naylor to Carrie Cohen, December 7, 1989, Gloria Naylor Archive, Box 12, Folder 7).

26. Joel Fineman, "The Structure of Allegorical Desire," in *Allegory and Representation*, ed. Stephen Greenblatt (Baltimore: Johns Hopkins University Press, 1981), 32.

27. Kathleen Forni, *Chaucer's Afterlife: Adaptations in Recent Popular Culture* (Jefferson, N.C.: MacFarland, 2013), 116.

28. Edwards, "'Burn All,'" 246.

29. Stuart Hall, "New Ethnicities," in *Critical Dialogues in Cultural Studies*, ed. David Morley and Kuan-Hsing Chen (London: Routledge, 1996), 444.

30. Ibid., 445.

31. Karen Joy Fowler, review of *Bailey's Cafe*, *Chicago Tribune*, October 4, 1992, in *Gloria Naylor: Critical Perspectives; Past and Present*, ed. Henry Louis Gates Jr. and K. A. Appiah (New York: Amistad, 1993), 26; Dan Wakefield, review of *Bailey's Cafe*, *New York Times Book Review*, October 4, 1992, 30.

32. Gloria Naylor, *Bailey's Cafe* (New York: Vintage, 1993), 28, hereafter cited parenthetically by page number.

33. Henry Louis Gates Jr., *The Signifying Monkey: A Theory of Afro-American Literary Criticism* (New York: Oxford University Press, 1988); Claudia Smith Brinson, "Pick a Spot: Novelist Naylor Explores Landscape of the Imagination," *The State*, Columbia, South Carolina, November 22, 1992, Section F, 8; Gloria Naylor Archive, Sacred Heart University, Box 5, Folder 19.

34. Miss Maple/Stanley certainly could be embraced as a trans figure. My concern, however, is with his ongoing relationship to gender and patriarchy in Naylor's novel.

35. Michael Awkward, *Inspiriting Influences: Tradition, Revision and Afro-American Women's Novels* (New York: Columbia University Press, 1989), 102, 172.

36. For an overview, see Marc Redfield, *Theory at Yale: The Strange Case of Deconstruction in America* (New York: Fordham University Press, 2015).

37. Theory-driven work at Yale extended well beyond the white male group of de Man et al. Afro-American Studies faculty including Hall mentee and visiting scholar Hazel Carby, Ghanaian-British philosopher Anthony Appiah, Nigerian writer-critic Wole Soyinka, and American critics Kimberly Benston, Henry Louis Gates, Michael Cooke, Houston Baker, and Robert Stepto all assumed, in various ways, a theoretical bent. Riffing on the masculinist Romanticism of Yale post-structuralists, a white feminist cohort that included Barbara Johnson, Shoshana Felman, Margaret Homans, and Margaret Ferguson, which came to be called "The Brides of Deconstruction," performed post-structuralist engagements with the sex/gender system and Lacanian psychoanalysis; see Gregory Jones-Katz, "'The Brides of Deconstruction' and the Transformation of Feminism in the North American Academy," *Modern Intellectual History* 17 (2020): 413–22.

38. Kimberly Benston, email message to author, December 18, 2021.

39. Henry Louis Gates Jr., "Reading 'Race,' Writing and Difference," *PMLA* 123, no. 5 (2008): 1535.

40. Paul de Man's first academic position was at Cornell. In 1971, Cornell faculty founded the journal *diacritics*, a major venue for the circulation of French philosophy.

41. Gates and Naylor both were born in September 1950.

42. Elizabeth Alex, "Pursuing the Pages of History," *Washington Post*, August 10, 1983, https://www.washingtonpost.com/archive/lifestyle/1983/08/10/pursuing-the-pages-of-history/e0369a4a-a961-40f3-b686-cf6b64e6b1e6/; Henry Louis Gates Jr., "An Interview with Henry Louis Gates, Jr.," by Charles Rowell, *Callaloo* 14, no. 2 (1991): 452. While the coauthored book never appeared, Gates did publish in 1993 a coedited volume on Naylor (Gates and Appiah, *Gloria Naylor*) and wrote an important structuralist reading of *Linden Hills*, "Significant Others," *Contemporary Literature* 29 (1988): 606–23.

43. Alex, "Pursuing the Pages."

44. While he highlights Naylor's relation to not the academy but rather her Black female contemporaries, Gates stresses how readers may have underestimated the depth and nuance of Naylor's post-structuralism in "Significant Others."

45. Rita Felski, email to Jonathan Culler, February 16, 2020, forwarded by email to author, February 16, 2020.

46. Barbara Christian, "The Race for Theory," *Cultural Critique* 6 (1987): 51–63.

47. Joyce A. Joyce, "The Black Canon: Reconstructing Black American Literary Criticism," *New Literary History* 18, no. 2 (1987): 335–44.

48. Donna Landry, email to author, April 6, 2022.

49. Omofolabo Ajayi-Soyinka, in discussion with the author, November 11, 2023.

50. Christian, "Race for Theory," 52.

51. W. E. B. Du Bois, *The Souls of Black Folk*, ed. Brent Hayes Edwards (Oxford: Oxford University Press, 2007), 8.

52. Philip Page, "Living with the Abyss in Gloria Naylor's *Bailey's Cafe*," *CLA Journal* 40, no. 1 (1996): 23.

53. Hazel Carby, *Reconstructing Womanhood: The Emergence of the Afro-American Woman Novelist* (Oxford: Oxford University Press, 1987), 6.

54. Hortense Spillers, "Mama's Baby, Papa's Maybe: An American Grammar Book," *diacritics* 17, no. 2 (1987): 64–81.

55. A volume that directly emerged from that milieu is Donna Landry and Gerald MacLean, eds., *Materialist Feminisms* (Oxford: Blackwell, 1993). Penned by two Society for the Humanities fellows and featuring readings of Spillers, Naylor, and Michelle Barrett (another fellow), it contended that "a commitment to theory can and should represent an engagement with contemporary struggles around the categories and political realities of feminism, new forms of socialism, anti-racist and" other liberation struggles (xiii). This is not to say that the theory-driven climate at Cornell was always conducive to bonding among women of color. Most notable is the clash that took place between Spivak and Ajayi at the Feminisms and Cultural Imperialism conference; see Omofolabo Ajayi-Soyinka, "Black Feminist Criticism and Drama: Thoughts on Double Patriarchy," *Journal of Dramatic Theory and Criticism* (1993): 174.

56. Gloria Naylor to Donna Perreault, letter, April 27, 1992, Gloria Naylor Archive, Box 5, Folder 21. See also Sylvie Chavanelle, "Gloria Naylor's *Bailey's Cafe*: The Blues and Beyond," *American Studies International* 36 (1998): 58–73; and Keith Byerman, *Remembering the Past in Contemporary African American Fiction* (Chapel Hill: University of North Carolina Press, 2005), 75–93.

57. On *Bailey's* and the Bible, see Sharon Felton and Gloria Naylor, "The Human Spirit Is a Kick-Ass Thing," in Montgomery, *Conversations*, 143. On *Bailey's* self-reflexive citation of Naylor's prior novels, see Maxine Montgomery, "Gloria Naylor's *Bailey's Cafe*: Selling Sex in the Cultural Marketplace," in *Gloria Naylor's Fiction: Contemporary Explorations of Class and Capitalism*, ed. Sharon Lewis and Ama Wattley (Newcastle upon Tyne: Cambridge Scholars, 2017), 61; Page, "Living with the Abyss"; Karen Schneider, "Gloria Naylor's Poetics of Emancipation: (E)merging (Im)possibilities in *Bailey's Cafe*," in *Gloria Naylor's Early Novels*, ed. Margot Anne Kelley (Gainesville: University of Florida Press, 1999), 4; Kelley, introduction to *Gloria Naylor's Early Novels*, xv–xvii.

58. Naylor the post-structuralist highlights the misrecognitions that signification entails by having the anonymous host explain that he allows customers to mistakenly think his name is Bailey "because the name Bailey's Cafe" is "painted across the front window" of the establishment (27–28).

59. Naylor closes the novel with the birth at the cafe of an intertextual figure, George, who appears in *Mama Day* (1988) as a young lover tragically invested in western perspectives.

60. Jonathan Culler's publications disseminated structuralist semiotics to an audience that extended well beyond its primary practitioners; see *Structuralist Poetics: Structuralism, Linguistics and the Study of Literature* (1975; London and

New York: Routledge, 2002); the MLA James Russell Lowell prize winner, *The Pursuit of Signs: Semiotics, Literature, Deconstruction* (Ithaca: Cornell University Press, 1981); and *Framing the Sign: Criticism and Its Institutions* (Norman: University of Oklahoma Press, 1988).

61. Naylor, "Gloria Naylor," 239. By "structuralist" Naylor also clearly meant deconstructionist and post-structuralist.

62. Ibid.

63. Gloria Naylor, "The Evolution of a Writer's Voice," reading sponsored by the Society for the Humanities, recorded November 21, 1988, in Cornell University, Ithaca, N.Y., Cornell University Tape Collection, CUL_Lectures_CU_2994_AM _1_1.mp3 and CUL_Lectures_CU_2994_AM_1_2.mp3, https://ecommons.cornell.edu/handle/1813/43496.

64. Roman Jakobson, "Phonemic Patterning," in *Fundamentals of Language*, ed. Roman Jakobson and Morris Halle *(The Hague: Mouton, 1971)*, 50–66.

65. Culler, *Pursuit of Signs*, 11–12.

66. Jonathan Culler, *On Deconstruction: Theory and Criticism after Structuralism* (Ithaca: Cornell University Press, 2007), 205.

67. On Naylor's lyric, see also Maxine Lavon Montgomery, *The Fiction of Gloria Naylor: Houses and Spaces of Resistance* (Knoxville: University of Tennessee Press, 2010), 54.

68. Toni Morrison, *Sula* (New York: Vintage, 2004), 174.

69. On Naylor's complex engagement with literary history, see Awkward, *Inspiriting Influences*, esp. 38; Cheryl Wall, "Extending the Line: From 'Sula' to 'Mama Day,'" *Callaloo* 23, no. 4 (2000): 1449–63; Missy Dehn Kubitschek, "Toward a New Order: Shakespeare, Morrison, and Gloria Naylor's *Mama Day*," MELUS 19, no. 3 (1994): 75–90; Dorothy Perry Thompson, "Africana Womanist Revision in Gloria Naylor's *Mama Day* and *Bailey's Cafe*," in Kelley, *Gloria Naylor's Early Novels*, 89–111; and Susan Meisenhelder, "False Gods and Black Goddesses in Naylor's *Mama Day* and Hurston's *Their Eyes Were Watching God*," *Callaloo* 23 (2000): 1440–48.

70. Geoffrey Chaucer, *The Canterbury Tales*, I.1–2, in *The Riverside Chaucer*, 3rd ed., gen. ed. Larry Benson (Oxford: Oxford University Press, 1987); Fineman, "Structure," 36, 38. Future citations of Chaucer are by fragment and line number and appear in parentheses in the text.

71. Gloria Naylor, interview by Tom Vitale, *Morning Edition*, National Public Radio, September 22, 1992. See also Gloria Naylor, "A Conversation with Gloria Naylor," interview by Virginia Fowler, in Montgomery, *Conversations*, 126, 130–31; Gloria Naylor to Davida Kilgore, July 9, 1990, letter, Gloria Naylor Archive, Box 12 Folder 8; Brinson, "Pick a Spot."

72. Naylor, interview by Vitale; Brinson, "Pick a Spot."

73. Jennifer Morgan, *Laboring Women: Reproduction and Gender in New World Slavery* (Philadelphia: University of Pennsylvania Press, 2004), 15, 29.

74. Spillers, "Mama's Baby," 69, 65.

75. Hortense Spillers, "A Hateful Passion, a Lost Love," *Feminist Studies* 9, no. 2 (1983): 298.

76. Steven Kruger, "The Prioress's Tale," in *The Cambridge Companion to the Canterbury Tales*, ed. Frank Grady (Cambridge: Cambridge University Press, 2020), 188, 182. Kruger goes on to stress instabilities that undermine the Christian-Jewish opposition in Chaucer's text.

77. My discussion of the Prioress is indebted to L. O. Aranye Fradenburg's "Criticism, Antisemitism, and *The Prioress's Tale*," *Exemplaria* 1, no. 1 (1989): 69–115. Until Fradenburg's intervention, published in the inaugural issue of *Exemplaria*, scholars as early as Matthew Arnold—in a move that mirrors "the silent sobriety" of Chaucer's pilgrims—had elided "pain, and narrative, and criticism" to affirm the universalizing Christian structurality of Chaucer's narrative (97). Marshaling a critical arsenal that includes Barbara Johnson, Elaine Scarry, Julia Kristeva, and Geoffrey Hartman, Fradenburg demonstrates how "'modern' theory" makes "a critical difference" in reading the *Prioress's Tale* (70–72). While other medievalists inhabit the Christian discourse of Chaucer's work, Fradenburg analyzes its antisemitic elements and their lethal effects. Fradenburg addresses her piece toward her fellow medievalists, calling for an oppositional response to Chaucer that *Bailey's* answers.

78. Gloria Naylor, "Love and Sex in the Afro-American Novel," *Yale Review* 78, no. 1 (1989): 27.

79. Montgomery, "Gloria Naylor's *Bailey's Cafe*," 64.

80. Saidiya Hartman, *Lose Your Mother: A Journey Along the Atlantic Slave Route* (New York: Farrar, Straus and Giroux, 2007), 6.

81. Robert Stepto, *From Behind the Veil: A Study of Afro-American Narrative* (Urbana: University of Illinois Press, 1991), xv.

82. Naylor, "Love and Sex," 19.

83. Ibid., 31.

84. On Sadie's two names, see also Claudia Drieling, *Constructs of "Home" in Gloria Naylor's Quartet* (Würzburg: Königshausen & Neumann, 2011), 238.

85. Fradenburg, "Criticism," 89.

86. Ibid., 92.

87. Naylor, interview by Vitale.

88. Fradenburg, "Criticism," 97.

89. Gloria Naylor to Veronica, letter, December 1991, Gloria Naylor Archive, Box 12, Folder 9.

90. A site that refigures both the relation of African Americans to cotton production and the Wife of Bath's relation to cloth-making, the farm provides a version of the isolation from U.S. racism offered by Willow Springs in *Mama Day*.

91. Vernon, *Black Middle Ages*, 238.

92. While Sadie desperately seeks her mother's approval, Stanley criticizes his adoring father as effetely bookish. In a resignification of the Wife of Bath's critique of lecherous friars in her tale, Maple explains that "manhood is a pervasive

preoccupation when you're an adolescent boy, and you tend to see a fairy under every bush. I definitely saw one lurking under Iago, Brutus, that whining Hamlet"; Naylor, *Bailey's Cafe*, 174.

93. On Aesop, see Jacqueline de Weever, *Aesop and the Imprint of Medieval Thought: A Study of Six Fables as Translated at the End of the Middle Ages* (London: McFarland, 2011); Frank Snowden, *Blacks in Antiquity: Ethiopians in the Greco-Roman Experience* (Boston: Harvard University Press, 1976), 88. I predicate my reading on the idea that "Dunbar" does not refer to the medieval Scottish poet, though it might (and thus would prompt a different interpretation).

94. The father's complex relation to gender norms involves rejecting "ideas of machismo" encoded in male and female clothing; Montgomery, *Fiction of Gloria Naylor*, 70. I suggest that the father's play with signs of masculinity and femininity echoes Chaucer's performance of his own (phallic) gender fluidity in the *Canterbury Tales*.

95. Fineman, "Structure," 56, 57, 59.

96. Christopher Norris, *What's Wrong with Postmodernism: Critical Theory and the Ends of Philosophy* (Baltimore: Johns Hopkins University Press, 1990), 194–207.

97. Hazel Carby describes Gates's fraught relationship to the white environment at Yale English in *Cultures in Babylon: Black Britain and African America* (London: Verso, 1999), 232–36. Gates has described how he sought at Yale to show the "skeptics there that African and African American cultures could support the apparatus of literary theory" and was supported by the Algerian French Derrida and Italian semiotician Umberto Eco, who taught at Yale from 1980 to 1981; Gates, "Interview," by Rowell 448.

98. Charles Mills, *The Racial Contract* (Ithaca: Cornell University Press, 1997).

99. As Edwards puts it, these two sequences affirm how "white people police black ownership of" the "literary canon, in the dual senses of physical control of the books and interpretive authority"; "'Burn All,'" 244.

100. Fineman claims that the Wife doesn't resist but rather riffs on the masculinist structurality of Chaucer's work; "Structure," 59. By the time Naylor was working on *Bailey's*, several medievalists would maintain, to varying degrees, that the Wife's performance subverts patriarchal discourse; see Barrie Ruth Strauss, "The Subversive Discourse of the Wife of Bath: Phallocentric Discourse and the Imprisonment of Criticism," *English Literary History* 55, no. 3 (1988): 551; Dinshaw, *Chaucer's Sexual Poetics*, 115; L. O. Aranye Fradenburg, "The Wife of Bath's Passing Fancy," *Studies in the Age of Chaucer* 8 (1986): 56. A more pessimistic reading appears in Susan Crane, "Alison's Incapacity and Poetic Instability in the *Wife of Bath's Tale*," *PMLA* 102, no. 1 (1987): 25–27.

101. Space prevents me from addressing other crucial elements of this episode, among them the manner in which the Gatlins' attack prompts Stanley's annihilating awareness of the Lacanian real when a knife "ripped through his" father's "boxer shorts." "At the sight of one of [the father's] testicles hanging beneath the torn cloth," Stanley feels "something heavy and sick lodge in my throat" and

goes on to feel "my chest ... tightening, my head ... throbbing," and sense that "there would be pieces of me all over the" storage room (181). Later, Stanley newly appreciates his father when he overcomes the Gatlins via a battle that is shot through with resignifications of the Wife of Bath and especially her battle with Jankin. As Vernon shows, the fight also contests the "outrageous caricature" of drag Hortense Spillers identifies as part of the "'social pathology'" associated with Black male bodies; Vernon, *Black Middle Ages*, 277–78.

102. Maple resembles Chaucer's pilgrim the Nun's Priest, a man who lives with nuns.

103. Tyrone Simpson II persuasively interprets "Maple's spectacular troubling of his gender identity" as a critique "about masculine mimicry—about emulating white men" that "intimates that a deeper, more public identification with the feminine is essential for heteronormative black men to feel and be 'blessedly free' from the existential strictures that seek to shackle them"; Simpson, *Ghetto Images in Twentieth-Century American Literature: Writing Apartheid* (New York: Palgrave Macmillan, 2012), 176–77.

104. Cf. Aristotle, *Meteorologica*, trans. H. D. P. Lee (Boston: Harvard University Press, 1952), 187; Debra Strickland, *Saracens, Demons and Jews: Making Monsters in Medieval Art* (Princeton: Princeton University Press, 2003), 79.

105. *Boece*, Metrum 6, in Benson, *Riverside Chaucer*, 417–18.

106. Chaucer's *Boece* contrasts Zephirus with the ill effects on plant life of the south wind (here called by its Latin name, Auster): "Whan the wode waxeth rody of rosene foures in the fyrst somer sesoun thurw the breeth of the wynd Zephirus that waxeth warm, yif the cloudy wynd Auster blowe felliche, than goth awey the fairnesse of thornes"; *Metrum* 3, in Benson, *Riverside Chaucer*, 411. On medieval beliefs regarding heat in Africa, see John Block Friedman, *The Monstrous Races in Medieval Art and Thought* (Syracuse: Syracuse University Press, 2000), 64–65; Suzanne Conklin Akbari, *Idols in the East: European Representations of Islam and the Orient, 1100–1450* (Ithaca: Cornell University Press, 2009), 43–45.

107. Champagne would call to any Chaucerian's mind Cecily Chaumpaigne, the woman linked to Chaucer's rape accusation, thus indicating the feel-bad prospect that Chaucer may have committed sexual assault.

108. Cf. Wilson, "Medievalism," 81–82.

109. Felton and Naylor, "Human Spirit," 253; see also 139, 142–43; and Byerman, *Remembering the Past*, 86.

110. Edwards, "'Burn All,'" 231.

6. Tradition and the Individual Black Talent: Contesting Malory and Modernism in *The Fisher King*

1. Hortense Spillers, *Black, White, and in Color: Essays on American Literature and Culture* (Chicago: University of Chicago Press, 2003), xiv.

2. Paul Gilroy, *The Black Atlantic: Modernity and Double Consciousness* (London: Verso, 1993), 56. On Marshall's transnational politics, see Kevin Gaines,

"From Center to Margin: Internationalism and the Origins of Black Feminism," in *Materializing Democracy: Toward a Revitalized Cultural Politics*, ed. Russ Castronovo and Dana Nelson (Durham, N.C.: Duke University Press, 2002), 294–313.

3. Paule Marshall, "An Interview of Paule Marshall," by Daryl Cumber Dance, in *Conversations with Paule Marshall*, ed. James Hall and Heather Hathaway (Jackson: University Press of Mississippi, 2010), 101.

4. Paule Marshall, "Shaping the World of My Art," *New Letters* 40 (1973): 110–11.

5. Simon Gikandi, *Writing in Limbo: Modernism and Caribbean Literature* (Ithaca: Cornell University Press, 2018), 169.

6. Ibid., 175.

7. Ibid., 177–78.

8. Paule Marshall, "The *Booklist* Interview: Paule Marshall," by Donna Seaman, in Hall and Hathaway, *Conversations*, 128.

9. Paule Marshall, "A MELUS Interview: Paule Marshall," by Joyce Pettis, in Hall and Hathaway, *Conversations*, 94; Marshall, "Interview," by Dance, 99; Paule Marshall, "Holding onto the Vision: Sylvia Baer Interviews Paule Marshall," in *Conversations*, 121–22.

10. Paule Marshall, *Brown Girl, Brownstones*, afterword by Mary Helen Washington (New York: Feminist Press, 1981), 261.

11. See Marshall, "Shaping the World," 105; Marshall, "Interview," by Pettis, 87; Marshall, "Interview," by Dance, 113; Paule Marshall, "Talk as a Form of Action: An Interview with Paule Marshall," by Sabine Bröck, in Hall and Hathaway, *Conversations*, 60; Paule Marshall, "Re-creating Ourselves All Over the World: A Conversation with Paule Marshall," interview by Molara Ogundipe-Leslie, in *Conversations*, 31–32, 39.

12. Stewart [sic] M. Hall, "Our Literary Heritage," *Sunday Gleaner*, January 3, 1954, 5.

13. Stuart Hall, Alex Jacobs, Charles Taylor et al., "Discussion on Commitment," *New Left Review/Universities and Left Review*, Stuart Hall Archive U.S. 121, Box 69, Cadbury Research Library: Special Collections, University of Birmingham.

14. Ezra Pound, *Make it New: Essays* (New Haven: Yale University Press, 1935).

15. David Matthews, "Scholarship and Popular Culture in the Nineteenth Century," in *A Companion to Arthurian Literature*, ed. Helen Fulton (London: Blackwell, 2009), 356; Thomas Hahn and Leah Haught, "Thomas Malory," *Oxford Bibliographies Online*, http://www.doi.org/10.1093/OBO/9780199846719-0135.

16. Spillers, *Black, White, and in Color*, 29.

17. Paule Marshall, "The Art and Politics of Paule Marshall: An Interview," by James Hall and Heather Hathaway, in Hall and Hathaway, *Conversations*, 166.

18. Paule Marshall, "Meditations on Language and the Self: A Conversation with Paule Marshall," interview by Melody Graulich and Lisa Sisco, in Hall and Hathaway, *Conversations*, 140.

19. My argument supports scholarly claims about the feel-bad elements of *The Fisher King*. See Petal Samuel on Marshall's portrayal of an oppressive "aural

discipline" in "The Profane Ear: Regimes of Aural Discipline in Paule Marshall's *The Fisher King*," *Anthurium: A Caribbean Studies Journal* 14, no. 1 (2017), https://anthurium.miami.edu/articles/10.33596/anth.332. My argument complicates the "feel-good" interpretations of Celia Wallhead, "Myth, Ritual and Racial Identity in Paule Marshall's *The Fisher King*," *Revista canaria de estudios ingleses* 45 (2002): 205–14; Rebeca Gualberto Valverde, "'Himself Armed with a Lance': Mythologizing Transmigrant Experience in Paule Marshall's *The Fisher King*," *Revista de Estudios Norteamericanos* 15 (2011): 69–82; Caroline Rosenthal, *New York and Toronto Novels after Postmodernism: Explorations of the Urban* (Rochester, N.Y.: Camden House, 2011), 146–52; Moira Ferguson, *A Human Necklace: The African Diaspora and Paule Marshall's Fiction* (Albany: SUNY Press, 2013).

20. T. S. Eliot, "Notes," *The Waste Land*, in *The Waste Land: Authoritative Text, Contexts, Criticism*, ed. Michael North (New York: Norton, 2001), 21. On Weston and Eliot, see Jonathan Ullyott, *The Medieval Presence in Modernist Literature: The Quest to Fail* (Cambridge: Cambridge University Press, 2015), 47–81.

21. Eliot, *Waste Land*, lines 19–30.

22. Cleanth Brooks, "*The Waste Land*: An Analysis," *Southern Review* 3 (1937–38): 134–35. Eliot also cites Isaiah 32:2.

23. Jessie Weston, *From Ritual to Romance* (Cambridge: Cambridge University Press, 1920), 107; see also 127.

24. T. S. Eliot, "Tradition and the Individual Talent," *Egoist* 6 (1919): 55.

25. Weston, *Ritual to Romance*, 23.

26. Ibid., 17.

27. Clive, whom Tim Watson aptly describes as a "disaffected second-generation Barbardian," might share Eliot's angst-ridden investment in traditional western notions of safety and fertility; Tim Watson, "African and Caribbean Modernist Fiction," in *The Novel in Africa and the Caribbean since 1950*, ed. Simon Gikandi (Oxford: Oxford University Press, 2016), 328.

28. Marshall, "Interview," by Dance, 99.

29. Marshall, "Interview," by Pettis, 94.

30. Marshall, "Interview," by Seaman, 128.

31. Ferguson, *Human Necklace*, 98. The "introductory crawl" of the film describes the "Old South" as a "pretty world" where "Gallantry took its last bow. Here was the last ever to be seen of Knights and their Ladies Fair. Of Master and of Slave"; Alexandra Cook, "Critical Medievalism and the New South: Red Rock and *Gone with the Wind*," *South Central Review* 30, no. 2 (2013): 32. *Gone with the Wind* evinces how the medieval Arthuriana first mobilized below the Mason-Dixon line on behalf of slavery circulated well after emancipation; see Matthew Vernon, *The Black Middle Ages: Race and the Construction of the Middle Ages* (Cham, Switzerland: Palgrave, 2018), 103–57; Charles Wilson Jr., "Medievalism, Race, and Social Order in Gloria Naylor's *Bailey's Cafe*," *Studies in Medievalism* 10 (1998): 74–91.

32. Barbara Christian, "The Race for Theory," *Cultural Critique* 6 (1987): 52. On jazz and *The Fisher King*, see Samuel, "Profane Ear"; Patricia Lespinasse,

"'Her Special Music': Wild Women and Jazz in Paule Marshall's *The Fisher King*," *Anthurium: A Caribbean Studies Journal* 14, no. 1 (2017): 1–16; John Lowney, "'A New Kind of Music': Jazz Improvisation and the Diasporic Dissonance of Paule Marshall's *The Fisher King*," *MELUS* 40, no. 1 (2015): 99–123; Jürgen Grandt, *Gettin' Around: Jazz, Script, Transnationalism* (Athens: University of Georgia Press, 2018).

33. Paule Marshall, *The Fisher King* (New York: Scribner, 2000), 92. Subsequent page citations from this edition appear parenthetically in the text.

34. Marshall, "Interview," by Dance, 98.

35. "The Nkiru Center presents Paule Marshall, author of *The Fisher King*," Medgar Evers College Film and Video Archive, Medgar Evers College, Brooklyn, N.Y., October 20, 2000, https://mecfilmarchive.commons.gc.cuny.edu/2000/10/20/paule-marshall-visits-medgar-evers-college/. Sonny's encounter with that "European agenda" in the 1980s, fifty years after Marshall's schooling, infers her pessimism about a more diverse curriculum for contemporary Black students.

36. T. S. Eliot, "*Le Morte Darthur*," *Spectator* 152 (February 23, 1934): 278. On Malory and Eliot, see T. J. Lustig, *Knight Prisoner: Thomas Malory Then and Now* (Eastbourne: Sussex Academic Press, 2014), 129–31.

37. Andrew Lynch, "*Le Morte Darthur* for Children: Malory's Third Tradition," in *Adapting the Arthurian Legends for Children: Essays on Arthurian Juvenalia*, ed. Barbara Tepa Lupack (New York: Palgrave Macmillan, 2004), 12. Pages 23–27 discuss post-1914 adaptations—one of which may have been assigned to Marshall. See also Norris Lacy, "The Arthur of the Twentieth and Twenty-First Centuries," in *The Cambridge Companion to Arthurian Legend*, ed. Elizabeth Archibald and Ad Putter (Cambridge: Cambridge University Press, 2010), 120–35.

38. On the transnational components of the Fisher King legend and Marshall, see Wallhead, "Myth"; Valverde, "'Himself Armed'"; Rosenthal, *New York*. There are compelling reasons to consider *The Fisher King* and an international medieval Arthur. As Nahir Otaño Grazia stresses, the full story of medieval Arthurian lore shifts us "from a national setting and a Eurocentric point of view" to a more global and international perspective; Otaño Grazia, "Arthur's Heirs: Comparing the Nordic and Spanish Tristan," *Anales de Historia Medieval de la Europa Atlántica* 2 (2015): 186. Marshall's Black diasporic approach resonates with the multiplicity and diversity of Arthurian legend during the Middle Ages—for instance, Wolfram's *Parzival*'s sympathetic depictions of the African queen Belakane, mother of Parzival's half-brother Feirefiz; and the early narration of double consciousness in *Moriaen*, a work about Percival's nephew, the Black knight Moriaen; see Geraldine Heng, *The Invention of Race in the European Middle Ages* (Cambridge: Cambridge University Press, 2018), 210–14, 203.

39. Colin Richmond, "Malory and Modernity: A Qualm about Paradigm Shifts," *Common Knowledge* 14, no. 1 (2008): 35.

40. Eugène Vinaver, introduction to *Works*, by Thomas Malory, 2nd ed. (Oxford: Oxford University Press, 1971), vii.

41. Dorsey Armstrong, *Sir Thomas Malory's "Morte Darthur": A New Modern English Translation* (Anderson, S.C.: Parlor Press, 2009), ix. See George Saintsbury, *The English Novel* (London, 1913), 8, 25, 28–33; Ernest Baker, *The History of the English Novel*, vol. 1 (New York: Barnes and Noble, 1950), 193; John Steinbeck, *The Acts of King Arthur and His Noble Knights* (New York: Penguin, 2007), 326; Andrew Hadfield, "Renaissance Narrative," in *Encyclopedia of the Novel*, ed. Paul Schellinger (Chicago: Fitzroy and Dearborn, 1998), 1090.

42. See David Staines, *Tennyson's Camelot: The "Idylls of the King" and Its Medieval Sources* (Waterloo, Ont.: Wilfrid Laurier University Press, 1982); Kim Moreland, *The Medievalist Impulse in American Literature: Twain, Adams, Fitzgerald and Hemingway* (Charlottesville: University Press of Virginia, 1996), 28–76; Alan Lupack and Barbara Tepa Lupack, *King Arthur in America* (Cambridge: Brewer, 1999). Marshall describes her "very heavy Thomas Mann and Joseph Conrad period," which probably involved reading works such as Conrad's *Chance* and Mann's *The Magic Mountain*, which both engage grail lore; Paule Marshall, "In Celebration of Our Triumph," interview by Alexis De Veaux, in Hall and Hathaway, *Conversations*, 52.

43. Eliot, "*Le Morte Darthur*," 278.

44. "Nkiru Center presents Paule Marshall."

45. Talking Points File, Item Two, Page Three, Paule Marshall Papers.

46. Talking Points File, Item Three, Page Two, Paule Marshall Papers.

47. Talking Points File, Item One, Page Three, Paule Marshall Papers.

48. Sir Thomas Malory, *Le Morte Darthur*, ed. P. J. C. Field, vol. 1 (Cambridge: Brewer, 2013), cited here and throughout parenthetically by page and line number.

49. "Nkiru Center presents Paule Marshall."

50. Jill Mann, "Malory and the Grail legend," in *A Companion to Malory*, ed. Elizabeth Archibald and A. S. G. Edwards (Cambridge: Brewer, 1996), 216.

51. "He ys of all partyes comyn of the beste knyghtes of the worlde and of the highest linage: for Sir Launcelot ys com but of the eyghth degré frome Oure Lorde Jesu Cryst, and thys Sir Galahad ys of the nineth degré frome Oure Lorde Jesu Cryst. Therefore I dare sey they be the grettist jantillmen of the world" (Malory, *Morte*, 673.20–25).

52. Martin Shichtman, "Percival's Sister: Genealogy, Virginity, and Blood," *Arthuriana* 9, no. 2 (1999): 12–13.

53. Marshall's characters also expand on Malory's thematization of age and illness; virtually all her major adult characters are latter-day versions of Evelake—that is, elderly injured people. While aged Black men, such as Edgar Payne and Abe Kaiser, figure in the novel, old women take center stage. Marshall's stress on aged women is such that the first three words of the novel are "The old woman," in reference to Ulene (13). When Florence tells Sonny, "I been holding on waiting for you" (41), Marshall riffs on Evelake, who lives hundreds of years, waiting for Galahad.

54. Marshall, "Shaping the World," 103.

55. Rosenthal, *New York*, 149–50.

56. Marshall, "Art and Politics," 167.

57. Ibid., 162.

58. Marshall, "Art and Politics," 166; Lori Leibovich, "Sounds Good Feel Bad," Review of Paule Marshall, *The Fisher King*, November 26, 2000, *New York Times*, BR 21.

59. Caroline Eckhardt, "Prophecy and Nostalgia: Arthurian Symbolism at the Close of the Middle Ages" in *The Arthurian Tradition: Essays in Convergence*, ed. Mary Flowers Blackwell and John Bugge (Tuscaloosa: University of Alabama Press, 1988), 123.

60. "'Wherefore hit shall greve me right sore, the departicion of thys felyship, for I have had an old custom to have hem in my felyship.' And therewith the teerys felle in hys yen"; Malory, *Morte*, 674.35–675.1–3.

61. Malory, *Morte*, 672.5, 694.35, 701.18–19, 747.1, 746.16, 675.16. Space prevents me from engaging the complex figure of Sir Palomides. On that emotional non-Christian knight, see Kavita Mudan Finn, "'Many Straunge Sygnes and Tokyns': The Affective Power of Thomas Malory's Palomides," *Arthuriana* 31, no. 2 (2021): 108–23.

62. Rosenthal, *New York*, 148.

63. Jennifer Nash, *Black Feminism Reimagined: After Intersectionality* (Durham, N.C.: Duke University Press, 2019), 3.

64. *OED*, s.v. "hold."

65. *OED*, s.v. "hold in." On the figure of the hold, see Christina Sharpe, *In the Wake: Blackness and Being* (Durham, N.C.: Duke University Press, 2016); and Stefano Harney and Fred Moten, *The Undercommons: Fugitive Planning and Black Study* (Wivenhoe, UK: Minor Compositions, 2013).

66. Sianne Ngai, *Ugly Feelings* (Cambridge, Mass.: Harvard University Press, 2005), 3.

67. Marshall, "Shaping the World," 110.

68. James Baldwin, "Sonny's Blues," in *The Jazz Fiction Anthology*, ed. Sascha Feinstein and David Rife (Bloomington: Indiana University Press, 2009), 17–18.

69. Lespinasse, "'Her Special Music,'" 14–15.

70. Among the many important studies of Black women writers and literary history is Cheryl Wall, *Worrying the Line: Black Women Writers, Lineage, and Literary Tradition* (Chapel Hill: University of North Carolina Press, 2005).

71. Sara Ahmed, "A Phenomenology of Whiteness," *Feminist Theory* 8, no. 2 (2007): 150.

72. Sara Ahmed, *The Cultural Politics of Emotions* (Edinburgh: Edinburgh University Press, 2014), 191.

73. Hall, "Our Literary Heritage," 5. Hall also responds to the West Indian–centric view of his interlocutor (see Chapter 4).

74. Eliot, "Tradition," 55.

75. Rosenthal, *New York*, 132; Grandt, *Gettin' Around*, 105.

76. Ibid., 103.

77. Lespinasse, "'Her Special Music,'" clarifies the centrality of Hattie and her artistry to the novel, on which Mary Helen Washington further elaborates in her forthcoming biography of Marshall for the Yale University Press Black Lives series.

78. The Broadway milieu to which Sonny-Rett responds has important and long-standing African American dimensions. Starting in 1898, musicals appeared on Broadway by Black writers and musicians such as Bob Cole, John Rosamond Johnson, and James Weldon Johnson. *Clorindy: The Origin of the Cake Walk* inaugurated that era. A one-act musical whose songs were published by Tin Pan Alley, *Clorindy* was composed by Will Marion Cook with lyrics by Paul Laurence Dunbar. That short-lived period of Black musical theater ended by 1911.

79. Richard Dyer, *Only Entertainment* (London: Routledge, 1993), 43.

80. Ibid., 36–45.

81. Rosenthal, *New York*, 157; Ralph Ellison, *Shadow and Act* (New York: Random House, 1964), 234.

82. Lespinasse, "'Her Special Music,'" 9.

83. "*The Fisher King* features dramatic scenes of jazz improvisation, and, like the process in which Sonny-Rett transforms popular songs through his improvisatory interpretations, the novel's narrative structure adapts and transforms Western myths of the Fisher King"; Lowney, "'New Kind of Music,'" 99–100.

84. *OED*, s.v. "put."

85. "There was no knyght that myght speke one worde a grete whyle, and so they loked every man on other as they had bene doome" (Malory, *Morte*, 673.35–674.1–2).

86. "The holy vessell departed suddeynly, that they wyst nat where hit becam. Than had they all breth to speke" (Malory, *Morte*, 674.7–8).

87. "And at the lyftyng up there cam a vigoure in lyknesse of a chylde, and the vysayge was as rede and as bright os ony fyre, and smote hymselff into the brede, that all they saw hit that the brede was fourmed of a fleyshely man" (Malory, *Morte*, 783.1–4).

88. *OED*, s.v. "grail"; R. E. Latham, *Dictionary of Medieval Latin from British Sources*, s.v. "gradale," https://logeion.uchicago.edu/gradale; Frédéric Godefroy, *Dictionnaire de l'ancienne langue française*, s.v. "graal," https://micmap.org/dicfro/search/dictionnaire-godefroy/graal.

89. Tom Dalzell et al., *The New Partridge Dictionary of Slang and Unconventional English* (Oxford: Routledge, 2012), s.v. "bucket of blood."

90. Marshall, "Interview," by Pettis, 87; Marshall, "Interview," by Dance, 113. See also Marshall, "In Celebration," 52; Marshall, "Shaping the World," 105; Marshall, "Talk as a Form of Action," 60; Paule Marshall, "Re-creating Ourselves," 31–32, 39.

91. By the time Marshall arrived at Hunter, Newstead had published her Columbia University Press book and essays in *PMLA* and elsewhere on the Celtic origins of the Fisher King legend. See Gale Segal, "Voicing Silenced Rituals: The Unearthing of the Life Story of Arthurian Legend by Helaine Newstead," in *Women*

Medievalists and the Academy, ed. Jane Chance (Madison: University of Wisconsin Press, 2005), 683–96.

92. Cheryl Harris, "Whiteness as Property," *Harvard Law Review* 106, no. 8 (1993): 1709–91.

93. Kobena Mercer, "Black Hair/Style Politics," *New Formations* 3 (1987): 33–54. Further citations appear parenthetically in the text.

94. Marshall, "Art and Politics," 169.

95. Marshall, "In Celebration."

96. Mary Helen Washington, ed., *Black-Eyed Susans / Midnight Birds: Stories by and about Black Women* (New York: Anchor, 1989), 82.

97. Marshall, "Interview," by Dance, 115.

98. Paule Marshall, "Interview with Paule Marshall," by Sandi Russell, in Hall and Hathaway, *Conversations*, 83, my emphasis.

99. Christian, "Race for Theory," 52.

100. See Wallhead, "Myth," 211.

101. See the title of Marshall's autobiography, *Triangular Road: A Memoir* (2009), and her comment that her roots in "Africa, Barbados, Brooklyn" make her "a tri-part person" concerned with "the triangular nature of our inheritance and our place in the world"; quoted in Felicia Lee, "Voyage of a Girl Moored in Brooklyn," *New York Times*, March 11, 2009, https://www.nytimes.com/2009/03/12/books/12paul.html. See also Valverde, "Himself Armed," 73; Lowney, "'New Kind of Music,'" 102; Marie Foster Gnage, "Reconfiguring Self: A Matter of Place in Selected Novels by Paule Marshall," in *Middle Passages and the Healing Place of History: Migration in Black Women's Literature*, ed. Elizabeth Brown-Guillory (Columbus: Ohio State University Press, 2006), 113–15.

Appendix: Stuart Hall's First Publication

1. Open quote appears in source.

2. British social scientist Thomas Simey (1906–69) authored *Welfare and Planning in the West Indies* (Oxford: Clarendon Press, 1946). Eric Williams (1911–81) was the first prime minister of Trinidad and Tobago and a historian who authored *Capitalism and Slavery* (Chapel Hill, N.C.: University of North Carolina Press, 1944) and many other works on the West Indies.

Index

Abushouk, Lina, 114
Achi, Andrea, 79
Adams, James Eli, 290n48
Adorno, Theodor, Tolkien and, 122
Aers, David, 171
Aeschylus, Eliot on, 225
Aesop, 204–5
Ahmed, Saladin, 115
Ahmed, Sara, 2, 5, 7–8, 19, 22, 25, 90, 113, 116–117, 131, 232–33, 269n19, 266n98; Williams and, 7
Ajayi-Soyinka, Omofolabo, 190
Akbari, Suzanne Conklin, 91, 273n20; on Langland, 177
Akomfrah, John, Hall on, 170
Alberti, Leon Battista, 93
Alexander, Claire, 13, 144
Alexander, Michelle, 77
alliterative *Morte Arthure*, Patterson on, 68–69; James Simpson on, 73
Althusser, Louis, 89, 117; Hall and, 169
Altschul, Nadia, 16
Andrews, Tarren, 23
Ariosto, Ludovico, 93
Armstrong, Dorsey, 224
Arnold, Matthew, 129–30, 255, 301n49, 312n77
Asad, Talal, 93, 259n3
Augustine of Hippo, 46, 92, 99, 103; Jameson and, 53–55
The Autumn of the Middle Ages (Huizinga), 56–61, 95–98. *See also* Huizinga
Awkward, Michael, on Naylor, 188

Bailey's Cafe (Naylor), 28–31, 33, 183–215
Baker, Houston, 207, 309n37; Hall and, 155
Baldwin, James, Marshall and, 231–32
Bale, John, Simpson on, 73
Balfour, Arthur James, 96
Baraka, Amiri, Hall and, 155
Bataille, Georges, Holsinger on, 71–72
Baudelaire, Charles, Berman on, 51
Bédier, Joseph, 16
Benjamin, Walter, Hall on, 158–59, 171
Benston, Kimberly, 188–89
Beowulf, Grundtvig on, 120; Hall and, 5; Kemble and, 121; Naylor and, 206; Tolkien on, 1, 15, 31, 126–28, 149, 150
"*Beowulf*: The Monsters and the Critics" (Tolkien) 114, 119, 123–26
Berlant, Lauren, 2, 5, 7–8
Berman, Marshall, 40, 46, 50–53, 55–56, 98–99; on Baudelaire, 51; Burckhardt and, 51–52; Du Bois and, 83–84; on Foucault, 50–51; on Goethe, 51–52; Greenblatt and, 52; Jameson and, 53, 55; on Marx, 46, 49–51; on Nietzsche, 51; Patterson and, 68; on Weber, 50–51
Bernard of Clairvaux, 92, 101
Biddick, Kathleen, 8, 80, 92–93
Biden, Joseph, 18
"Black Men, White Media" (Hall), 137–38
Blake, William, 255
Blavatsky, Helena, 296
Bloom, Harold, 188
Bourdieu, Pierre, Holsinger on, 72

Bouwsma, William, 95
Bowers, John, 300n39
Boyarin, Daniel, on Paul, 99–100
Bracciolini, Poggio, 44
Brooks, Cleanth, 118, 220
Brooks, Gwendolyn, Marshall and, 242
Brown, Andy, 136
Brown, Marshall, 2
Brown Girl, Brownstone (Marshall), 217, 221, 244
Burbank, Luther, 64
Burckhardt, Jakob, 17, 30, 41–44, 93–95, 97, 99, 101–5, 284–85n78; Berman and, 51–52; Bynum and, 29, 69–70; Chaucer and, 91; Cold War intellectuals and, 67; Du Bois and, 83, 99, 101–3, 286n98; Greenblatt and, 40, 44–45, 273n21; Hall and, 159, 165; Hanning and, 67; Haskins and, 61–63; Hegel and, 105; Holsinger and, 72; Huizinga and, 58–59, 95–97; Jameson and, 53–55, 59; Lupton on, 42, 94, 286–87n111; Malory and, 91; Marshall and, 232; Marx and, 46, 50, 274–75n127; Naylor and, 204–5; Paul and, 101–5; post-structuralism and, 181; Simpson and, 73; Southern and, 65–66; Thorndike and, 64; Tolkien and, 111–112, 121–24; de Wette and, 101–2; Wynter and, 80, 86–87
Burrow, John, 173
Bynum, Carolyn Walker, 39–40, 69–71; Burckhardt and, 29, 69–70; Greenblatt and, 70; Huizinga and, 29, 40, 56, 69–71; Valéry and, 71; Watson on, 37
Byron, Lord, 254

Carby, Hazel, 116, 190–91, 309n37; on Gates, 313n97
Cecire, Maria Sachiko, 112, 114, 124
Certeau, Michel de, Holsinger on, 72
Chaganti, Seeta, 79
Chakrabarty, Dipesh, 12
Chance, Jane, 109
Chaucer, Geoffrey, 30, 32, 33, 88–89; Burckhardt and, 91; Dinshaw on, 182–85; Fradenburg on, 201, 262–63n40, 282n49, 312n77; Hall on, 118, 153–54, 159, 161, 254–55; Robert Jordan on, 182; Peggy Knapp on, 182–83; Leicester on, 182–85; Malory and, 88, 91; Michael Mann on, 160–61; Naylor on 183–215; Weber and, 183
Cheng, Anne Anlin, 5, 26, 33
The Chosen Place, the Timeless People (Marshall), 217
Chow, Rey, 191

Chrétien de Troyes, Hanning on, 67; Patterson on, 68
Christian, Barbara, 24, 33, 189, 207, 223; Marshall and, 246
Cohen, Jeremy, 92; on Paul, 99–100
Cole, Andrew, 72
Coleridge, Samuel Taylor, 65
Conrad, Joseph, Huizinga and, 58; Marshall and, 217
Craigie, William, Tolkien and, 121, 123, 293n88
Crane, Susan, 313n100
Crang, Mike, 263n46
Crenshaw, Kimberlé, 265n66
Culler, Jonathan, 181, 310n60; Naylor and, 191–95
"Culture, Community, Nation" (Hall), 151, 157
"Culture, Media, and the 'Ideological Effect'" (Hall), 26, 169–70

Dainotto, Roberto, 285n79
D'Arcens, Louise, 72
Dark Princess, (Du Bois), 105
Daston, Lorraine, 2
Davis, Kathleen, 12, 16, 80
Davis, Lennard, 81
de Grazia, Margreta, 4, 29
Derrida, Jacques, 181, 182, 188, 189, 313; Gates and, 313n97; Hall on, 160; on Heidegger, 104; Holsinger on, 71; Kant and, 207
de Weever, Jacqueline, 20, 85, 185
Dinshaw, Carolyn, 9–10, 182–83, 185, 300n40; on Chaucer, 182–85; Lacan and, 182; Naylor and, 184
Donnelly, Ignatius, 296n150
Dougill, John, 295n19
Douglass, Frederick, 17–18, 81, 103
Du Bois, W. E. B., 10, 29, 30, 76, 142, 165, 190, 279n2, 286n98, 280n14, 287n11; Berman and, 83–84; Burckhardt and, 83, 99, 101–3, 286n98; Fineman and, 205; Foucault and, 83; Gilroy on, 77; Hall and, 156, 165; Hegel and, 77; Heng and, 85; Huizinga and, 97, 98; Marshall and, 232; Marx and, 83, 99; Morgan and, 84; Naylor and, 185, 204–5, 207; Paul and, 105; Tolkien and, 140; Vernon on, 282n50; Weber and, 83; Wynter and, 80, 87, 91. See also *Dark Princess*, *The Souls of Black Folk*, "The Souls of White Folk"
Duff, Alexander, 17
Duffy, Eamon, 278n105
Dunbar, Paul Laurence, Marshall and, 242

INDEX

Dyer, Richard, 39, 45, 49, 90, 103–4, 116–117, 121, 235

Eckhardt, Caroline, 228–29
Eco, Umberto, Gates and, 313n97
Edwards, Suzanne, on Naylor, 184, 186, 215
Ehrmann, Jacques, on Huizinga, 97, 286n91
"The Elder *Edda*" (Tolkien), 121, 123–24, 293n88
Eliot, T. S., 1, 220–21, 240, 301n49; on Aeschylus, 225; Hall and, 120, 142, 159; Hall on, 154–57, 254; on Homer, 225; Huizinga and, 57, 60; Malory and, 229; Marshall and, 224–25, 228, 242; Marshall on, 32, 216–19; 221–22, 232–37; on Shakespeare, 154; Tolkien and, 157; Weston and, 220–21; Wolfram and, 220, 221, 240, 317n38. *See also* "Tradition and the Individual Talent," *The Waste Land*
Ellard, Donna Beth, 8, 15
Ellington, Duke, Naylor and, 203
Ellison, Ralph, Marshall and, 236–37
Engels, Friedrich, 300n31, 301n42
"English and Welsh" (Tolkien) 125, 128
Equiano, Olaudah, 81, 103
"Europe and its Myths" (Hall), 141, 156–59, 161, 163–66; Langland and, 171, 173, 175
"Exploration Notebook" (Hall), 161–64

Fabian, Johannes, 12, 38, 78
Fagan, Hyman, 148
Fahey, Richard, 266n84
"On Fairy Stories" (Tolkien) 122, 126
Familiar Stranger (Hall), 5–6, 112–114,118–119, 130–31, 142
Fanon, Frantz, 10, 20, 26, 90, 98, 113, 137, 232, 263n46, 303n87
The Fateful Triangle (Hall), 13–14
Faulk, Seb, 260n17
Fawaz, Ramzi, 110
The Fellowship of the Ring (Tolkien), 109–110, 111, 127, 133–34, 138, 290n49
Felman, Shoshana, 309n37
Felski, Rita, 2, 10–12, 28, 43, 81, 189, 291n58
Ferguson, Margaret, 309n37
Ferguson, Wallace, 4, 42–43, 61
Fickle, Tara, on Huizinga, 97, 285n85
Fimi, Dimitra, 114, 115
Fineman, Joel, 195, 205, 213
Finn, Kavita Mudan, 10, 319n61
The Fisher King (Marshall), 218–47
Fleissner, Jennifer, 12
Flieger, Verlyn, 135, 136
Foner, Eric, 276n76

Foucault, Michel, 2, 68, 81, 143, 164, 181; Berman on, 50–51; Du Bois and, 83; Hall and, 163; Holsinger on, 71; Jameson and, 40
Forni, Kathleen, 185
Fradenburg, L. O. Aranye, 3, 8, 263n40, 277n89, 312n77; on Chaucer, 201, 282n49, 313n77; Tolkien and, 298n9
Fraiman, Susan, 2
Freedman, Paul, 2, 62, 277n90, 307n7
Freud, Sigmund, 135–36
Friedman, John Block, 141, 161
Friedman, Susan Stanford, 11–12

Gabriele, Matthew, 260n17
Galison, Peter, 2
Gallagher, Catherine, 143
Gates, Henry Louis Jr., 187–190, 207; Carby on, 313n97; Derrida and, 313n97; Eco and, 313n97; Naylor and, 189
Gikandi, Simon, 17, 20; on Marshall, 217
Gilman, Sander, 18–19
Gilroy, Paul, 30, 81, 82, 85, 88, 216, 280n22; on the British New Left, 150; on Du Bois, 77; Hall on, 152
Goethe, Johann Wolfgang von, Berman on, 51–52
Gone with the Wind, Marshall and, 222
Gooding-Williams, Robert, 77, 279n3
Gordon, E. V., Tolkien and, 121–23, 127, 293n88
Gramsci, Antonio, Hall and, 15, 26, 144, 168, 171–72, 177, 190; Hall on, 131
"Gramsci's Relevance for the Study of Race and Ethnicity" (Hall), 131–32
Green, John Richard, 147–48, 149, 157, 173
Greenblatt, Stephen, 39, 44–45, 56, 143; Berman and, 52; Burckhardt and, 40, 44–45, 273n21; Bynum and, 70; Marx and, 46; Simpson and, 73; Southern and, 65
Gregory the Great, 175
Grandt, Jürgen, on Naylor, 234
Grimm, Jacob, Tolkien and, 121
Grimm, Wilhelm, Tolkien and, 121
Grundtvig, N. F. S., on *Beowulf*, 120; Tolkien and, 120, 123

Haidu, Peter, 22
Hall, Catherine, 133
Hall, Stuart, 13–15, 19–20, 22, 89, 116, 141–78, 190, 296n137; on Akomfrah, 170; Althusser and, 169; Baker and, 155; Baraka and, 155; on Benjamin, 158–59, 171; the British Left and, 147–52, 155–56, 163,

Hall, Stuart *(continued)*
  300n35; Burckhardt and, 159, 165; on Chaucer, 118, 153–54, 159, 161, 254–55; Communist Party Historians' Group and, 150; on Derrida, 160; Du Bois and, 156, 165; on Eliot, 154–56; Foucault and, 163; on Gilroy, 152; Gramsci and, 15, 26, 144, 168, 171–72, 177, 190; on Gramsci, 131; Hilton and, 148, 300n35; C.L.R. James and, 81, 155; Henry James and, 142, 146–47, 298n5; on Henry James, 256, 298n5; Langland and, 141–47, 156, 159–61, 168, 170–78; Leavis and, 118–119, 124, 128, 146, 156, 256, 302n68; on Mandeville, 163–64; Michael Mann and, 159–61, 163; Marshall and, 33, 218, 236–37; on Marx, 167–69, 172; on McFarland, 153–56, 253–57; Morrison and, 304n96; on Muslims, 177, 303n81; Naylor and, 33, 185–86, 206; on Pound, 155–57; Said and, 163–64; Scott on, 169; on Shakespeare, 254–55; Spivak on, 26–27, 169; Tolkien and, 5–6, 30–31, 112–15, 117–120, 125–40, 142, 145–46, 148–49, 155, 163–64, 177–78, 206, 293n96, 290n37; on Weber, 167–68; Wynter and, 165. *See also* "Black Men, White Media," "Culture, Community, Nation," "Culture, Media, and the 'Ideological Effect,'" "Europe and its Myths," "Exploration Notebook," *Familiar Stranger*, *The Fateful Triangle*, "Gramsci's Relevance for the Study of Race and Ethnicity," *The Hard Road to Renewal*, "Life and Times of the New Left," "The Local and the Global," "New Ethnicities," "Our Literary Heritage," "The Problem of Ideology—Marxism without Guarantees," "Race, Articulation, and Societies Structured in Dominance," "The Spectacle of the Other," "Thinking Diaspora," "The West and the Rest," "Whose Heritage?"
Hanning, Robert, 67–8, Burckhardt and, 67; on Chrétien, 67; Huizinga and, 68; on *Le Mort le Roi Artu*, 68
The Hard Road to Renewal (Hall), Langland and, 172
Hardy, Thomas, Marshall and, 217
Harpham, Geoffrey, 120
Harris, Cheryl, 20, 26, 27, 242
Harris, Roxy, 301n49
Harris, Stephen, 120
Hartman, Geoffrey, 188, 312n77
Hartman, Saidiya, 20, 26, 27, 143, 200, 267n91
Harvey, David, 3, 48

Haskins, Charles Homer, 29, 40, 56, 61–63; Burckhardt and, 61–63; Heng and, 85–86; Huizinga and, 62–63; Michael Mann and, 160; Marx and, 63; Patterson and, 68; Southern and, 66–67; Thorndike and, 64
Hegel, Georg, 105; Burckhardt and, 105; Du Bois on, 77; Jameson and, 54
Heidegger, Martin, Derrida on, 104
Heng, Geraldine, 6, 20, 85, 86, 89
Henriques, Anuradha, 114
Henry VIII, Simpson on, 73–75, 88
Herder, Johann Gottfried, Huizinga and, 95, 285n81; Tolkien and, 120
Hereford world map, 92
Hildebrand of Sovana (Pope Gregory VII), 65, 86
Hill, Anita, 204
Hilton, Rodney, 148–52, 157; Hall and, 148, 300n35
Hite, Molly, 189
The Hobbit (Tolkien) 109–112, 115–117, 128
Hodge, John, 103
Hoffman, Donald, 90
Holsinger, Bruce, 72, 74, 273n26; on Bataille, 71–72; on Bourdieu, 72; Burckhardt and, 72; on Derrida, 71; on Foucault, 71; Huizinga and, 72
Homans, Margaret, 309n37
Homer, Eliot on, 225
Homo Ludens (Huizinga), 97
Horkheimer, Max, Tolkien and, 122
Howard, Henry, Simpson on, 73
Hsy, Jonathan, 10, 56, 261n17, 265n72, 267n86, 289n34
Hughes, Langston, Marshall and, 225
Huizinga, Johan, 29, 40, 56–61, 96–98, 275n48; Burckhardt and, 58–59, 95–97; Bynum and, 29, 40, 56, 69–71, 277n95; Conrad and, 58; Du Bois and, 97, 98; Eliot and, 57, 60; Ehrmann on, 97, 286n91; Fickle on, 286n93; French symbolists and, 59; Hanning and, 68; Haskins and, 62–63; Herder and, 95, 285n81; Holsinger and, 72; Jameson and, 59; Kern and, 96; Lawrence and, 58; Marx and, 57; Müller and, 96; Rimbaud and, 59; Shelley and, 58; Simpson and, 74–75; Southern and, 65–66; Tolkien and, 111–112, 122, 127; Valéry and, 59; Wordsworth and, 58. See also *The Autumn of the Middle Ages*, *Homo Ludens*
Hurston, Zora Neale, Marshall and, 225
Huysmans, J. K., 275n50

INDEX

Ingham, Patricia Clare, 278n96
Isidore of Seville, 92

Jackson, Peter, 109
Jakobson, Roman, Naylor and, 193, 205
James, C. L. R., 81; Hall and, 155
James, Henry, Hall and, 142, 146–47, 298n5; Hall on, 256, 298n5
James, Marlon, 110, 115
Jameson, Fredric, 2, 39, 40, 45–46, 53–56, 59, 71, 75, 181, 274n132; Augustine and, 53–55; Berman and, 53, 55; Burckhardt and, 53–55, 59; Foucault and, 40; Hegel and, 54; Huizinga and, 59; Marx and, 53–55; Nietzsche and, 53; Weber and, 40
Jauss, Hans Robert, 3, 11
Johnson, Barbara, 309n37
Johnson, James Weldon, Marshall and, 225
Johnston, Michael, 306n23
Jones-Katz, Gregory, 309n37
Joplin, Scott, Naylor and, 191, 214
Jordan, Robert, 182, 183
Jordan, Winthrop, 85
Joyce, James, Marshall and, 217, 242
Joyce, Joyce A. 190, 207
Julian of Norwich, Watson on, 37

Kabir, Ananya Jahanara, 16–17, 95–96
Kant, Immanuel, 2; Derrida and, 207; Mills on, 207–8; Naylor on, 206–8, 212
Kao, Wan-Chuan, 6, 10, 21, 285n81
Kaplan, M. Lindsay, 92, 251
Keats, John, 129, 153, 154
Kemble, John Mitchell, *Beowulf* and, 121; Tolkien and, 15, 121, 290n48
Kempe, Margery, Simpson on, 73
Kern, Henrik, Huizinga and, 96
Kim, Dorothy, 289n36; Tolkien and, 298n9
Kincaid, Jamaica, 26
King, Deborah, 265
Klee, Paul, 158–59
Knapp, Ethan, 72, 118
Knapp, Peggy, 182–83
Knights, L. C., Hall and, 118
Kolve, V. A., Tolkien and, 298n9
Kruger, Steven, 196, 312n76

Labbie, Erin, 72
Lacan, Jacques, 183, 189; Dinshaw and, 182; Holsinger on, 72; Naylor and, 313
Laclau, Ernesto, 38, 157
La Mort le Roi Artu, Hanning on, 68
Lampert-Weissig, Lisa, 9, 85, 101
Landry, Donna, 190, 310n55

Langland, William, Aers on, 171; British Left and, 73, 147–50; Hall and, 5, 31, 112, 130, 142–52, 156, 161, 170–78; Michael Mann on, 159–61; Middleton on, 171, 172; Scanlon on, 146, 173; Simpson on, 73; Smith on, 171, 172; Tolkien and, 175–76, 177–78, 293n96, 300n39; Tolmie on, 171; Weber and, 171; Zeeman on, 170–71
Latour, Bruno, 12, 21
Lavezzo, Kathy, 269n109; Tolkien and, 298n9
Lawrence, D. H., Huizinga and, 58
Lears, T. Jackson, 278n96
Leavis, F. R., 5; Hall and, 118–119, 124, 128, 146, 156, 256, 302n68
Leavis, Q. D., Hall and, 118
Le Goff, Jacques, Wynter and, 86
Leibovich, Lori, 228
Leicester, Jr., H. Marshall, on Chaucer, 182–85
Leland, John, Simpson on, 73
Lespinasse, Patricia, 232, 237
Lewis, C. S., Tolkien and, 113, 115, 294n98
"Life and Times of the New Left" (Hall), 152
Linden Hills (Naylor), 223
Lipsitz, George, 269n109
Lloyd, Edward, 18
"The Local and the Global" (Hall), 115, 131, 138–39, 151, 164, 166
The Lord of the Rings trilogy (Tolkien), 109–112, 115–117. See also *The Fellowship of the Ring*, *The Return of the King*
Lorde, Audre, 28
"Love and Sex in the Afro-American Novel" (Naylor), 197
Love, Heather, 5, 25, 33
Löwith, Karl, 93
Lowney, John, 320n93
Lupton, Julia Reinhard, 99, 102–3, 284n73; on Burckhardt, 42, 94, 286–87n111
Lydgate, John, Simpson on, 73

MacLean, Gerald, 310n55
Mallette, Karla, 268n101, 306n25
Malory, Thomas, 30, 32–33, 80, 89–91; Burckhardt and, 91; Chaucer and, 88, 91; Eliot and, 219, 229; Eliot on, 224–25; "Lost Cause" Southerners and, 219; Jill Mann on, 90, 226; Marshall and, 216–46; Richmond on, 224; Shichtman on, 226; Simpson on, 73; Steinbeck and, 224; Tennyson and, 224; Twain and, 224; Vinaver on, 90, 224
de Man, Paul, 183

Mandeville, John, Hall on, 163–64; Morgan on, 84
Mann, Jill, on Malory, 90, 226
Mann, Michael, 142, 159–61, 168, 177; on Chaucer, 160–61; on Langland, 159–61
Mann, Thomas, Marshall and, 217, 242
Marcuse, Herbert, 26
Marriott, David, 26–27
Marshall, Paule, 6, 28, 31–33; Baldwin and, 231–32; Gwendolyn Brooks and, 242; Burckhardt and, 232; Christian and, 246; Conrad and, 217, 242; Dunbar and, 242; Eliot and, 224–25, 228, 242; on Eliot, 32, 216–19, 221–22, 232–37; Ellison and, 236–37; Gikandi on, 217; *Gone with the Wind* and, 222; Hall and, 33, 217, 218, 233–34, 236–37; Hardy and, 217; Hurston and, 225; Hughes and, 225; James Weldon Johnson and, 225; James Joyce and, 217; 242; Lespinasse on, 232, 237; Malory and, 218–19; Thomas Mann and, 217, 242; McDaniel and, 222; Mercer and, 243; Naylor and, 217, 218, 222–23, 233, 244; Newstead and, 242; Ngai and, 230; Rosenthal on, 227, 234, 237; Spillers on, 216, 217, 219; Washington on, 244. See also *Brown Girl, Brownstone*; *The Chosen Place, the Timeless People*; *The Fisher King*
Martin, Biddy, 189
Marie de France, Tolkien on, 124
Marx, Karl, 25, 29, 39, 40, 45–49, 54, 55, 56; Berman on, 46, 49–50, 68; Burckhardt and, 46, 50, 274–75n27; Du Bois and, 83, 99; Greenblat and, 46; Hall on, 167–69, 172; Haskins and, 63; Huizinga and, 57; Jameson and, 53–55; Tolkien and, 122
McDaniel, Hattie, Marshall and, 222
McFarlane, J. E. Claire, 153–54; Hall on, 153–56, 253–57
McNamara, Jo Ann, 22
Medici, Lorenzo de', 93
Meecham-Jones, Simon, 175
Meloni, Giorgia, Tolkien and, 110
Menocal, María Rosa, 303n81
Mercer, Kobena, Marshall and, 243
Meyer-Lee, Robert, 89
Middleton, Anne, 89; on Langland, 171, 172
Mignolo, Walter, 81–82
Miller, D. A., 25
Miller, J. Hillis, 188
Mills, Charles, 207
Miyashiro, Adam, 16, 268n101

Mohanty, Chandra, 191
Montesquieu, 105
Montgomery, Maxine Lavon, on Naylor, 197, 313n94, 311n67
Moore, R. I., 22
Morgan, Jennifer, 84–85, 142, 196; Du Bois and, 84; on Mandeville, 84; Naylor and, 185, 196
Morris, William, 129, 147, 149, 151, 173
Morrison, Karl, 271n1
Morrison, Toni, 33, 194; Hall and, 304n96
Morton, A. L., 148, 150, 173, 301n46
Morton, Timothy, 81
Mouffe, Chantal, 38
Müller, Max, Huizinga and, 96

Nash, Jennifer, 5, 26, 28, 229
Naylor, Gloria, 6; Awkward on, 188; *Beowulf* and, 206; Burckhardt and, 204–5; on Chaucer, 183–215; Culler and, 192–95; on Culler, 192; Dinshaw and, 184; Du Bois and, 185, 204–5, 207; Edwards on, 184, 186, 215; Ellington and, 203; Gates and, 189; Grandt on, 234; Hall and, 33, 185–86, 206; Saidiya Hartman and, 200; Hill and, 204; Jakobson and, 193, 205; Joplin and, 191, 214; on Kant, 206–8, 212; Lacan and, 313; Leicester and, 184, 185; Marshall and, 217, 218, 222–23, 233, 244; Montgomery on, 197, 313n94, 311n67; Morgan and, 185, 196; Morrison and, 194–95; on Shakespeare, 208–9, 212; Spillers and, 196, 199; Stepto and, 200; Tolkien and, 206; Vernon on, 184, 195, 204, 314n101; de Weever and, 185; Whitaker and, 185; Charles Wilson on, 184; Wynter and, 185. See also *Bailey's Cafe, Linden Hills*, "Love and Sex in the Afro-American Novel"
"New Ethnicities" (Hall), 170, 178
Newstead, Helaine, Marshall and, 242
Ngai, Sianne, 5, 7–8, 26; Marshall and, 230
Nietzsche, Friedrich, Berman on, 51, 68; Jameson and, 53
Norako, Leila, 111
The Notion Club Papers (Tolkien), 125

Odo of Châteauroux, 101
Olson, Paul, 263n40
Otaño Gracia, Nahir, 317n38
Otterspeer, Willem, 59, 97
"Our Literary Heritage" (Hall), 152–57, 233–34, 253–57

INDEX

Panofsky, Erwin, 260n14
Patterson, Lee, 56, 68, 182; on the alliterative *Morte*, 68–69; Berman and, 68; on Chrétien, 68; Marx and, 68; on *Roman d'Enéas*, 68
Patterson, Orlando, 270
Paul of Tarsus (Saint Paul), 80–81, 98–105; Boyarin on, 99–100; Burckhardt and, 101–5; Jeremy Cohen on, 99
Perry, David, 260–62n17
Petrus Alphonsi, 92
Pico della Mirandola, Giovanni, 80; Wynter on, 87–88
Pound, Ezra, 156, 157, 218; Hall on 155, 254, 257
Powell, Enoch, 137
Prendergast, Thomas, 8–9, 96, 272n10
"The Problem of Ideology—Marxism without Guarantees" (Hall), 168
Puar, Jasbir, 265n66

"Race, Articulation, and Societies Structured in Dominance" (Hall), 15, 117, 169
Rambaran-Olm, Mary, 15–16, 39, 76, 77, 143–44, 260n17, 271–72n7, 289n36
Rampersad, Arnold, 77
Rask, Rasmus, 121
Reed, Jr., Adolph, 77
Reid, Robin, 111
Renan, Ernest, Tolkien and, 120
The Return of the King (Tolkien), 134–36
Rhodes, William, 147
Richmond, Colin, on Malory, 90, 224
Rimbaud, Arthur, Huizinga and, 59
Rios Maldonado, Mariana, 112
Robinson, Cedric, 85
Roman d'Enéas, Patterson on, 68
Rosenthal, Caroline, on Marshall, 227, 234, 237
Rubin, Miri, 22

Said, Edward, 12, 21, 38, 78, 94, 96, 143; Hall and, 163–64
Saler, Michael, 114, 122, 128, 133, 293n80
Samuel, Petal, 315n19
Samuel, Raphael, 146
Scanlon, Larry, on Langland, 146, 173
Schedel, Hartmann, 303n83
Schwarz, Bill, 113, 133
Scott, David, on Hall, 169
The Seafarer, Hall and, 5
Sévère, Richard, 20
Sexton, Jared, 26

Shakespeare, William, 9, 208–9; Eliot on, 154; Hall on, 254–55; Naylor on, 208–9, 212; Tolkien and, 133
Sharpe, Christina, 319n65
Shelley, Percy, 129, 255; Huizinga and, 58
Shichtman, Martin, on Malory, 226
Shippey, Tom, 109
The Siege of Jerusalem (poem), 92
Simons, Walter, 274n40, 275n48
Simpson, James, 40, 72–75, 88, 278n105; on the alliterative *Morte Arthure*, 73; on Bale, 73; Burckhardt and, 73; Greenblatt and, 73; on Henry VIII, 73–75, 88; on Howard, 73; Huizinga and, 74–75; on Kempe, 73; on Langland, 73; on Leland, 73; on Lydgate, 73; on Malory, 73; on Wyatt, 73
Simpson, Tyrone II, 314n103
Sir Gawain and the Green Knight, Hall and, 5, 130; Tolkien and, 119
Small, Graeme, 95
Smith, D. Vance, 72; on Langland, 171, 172
The Souls of Black Folk (Du Bois) 76–79, 105, 280n14
"The Souls of White Folk" (Du Bois), 77–78, 82–84
Southern, R. W., 40, 65–67, 85, 86, 126, 283n61; Burckhardt and, 65–66; Greenblatt and, 65; Haskins and, 66–67; Huizinga and, 65–66; Tolkien and, 126
Spearing, A. C., 73
"The Spectacle of the Other" (Hall), 31, 141–42, 161
Speirs, John, Hall and, 118–19, 291n57
Spiegel, Gabrielle, 2, 62, 277n90, 307n7
Spillers, Hortense, 5, 10, 20, 24, 26, 191, 196, 199, 216, 217, 219, 267n91, 310n55, 314n101
Spivak, Gayatri, 191, 310n55; on Hall, 26–28, 169
Steinbeck, John, Malory and, 224
Steiner, Emily, 173
Stepan, Nancy Leys, 18–19
Stepto, Robert, 77, 200, 309n37
Stimpson, Catharine, 111, 115
Strauss, Barrie Ruth, 313n100
Sturges, Robert, 20
Sundquist, Eric, 77
Symes, Carol, 57

Tally, Robert, 274n32
Tate, Allen, 133
Taylor, Charles, 93, 146
Tennyson, Alfred Lord, Malory and, 224
Thatcher, Margaret, 137

Thompson, Denys, 118
Thompson, E. P., 147, 148,
Thorkelin, Grímur, Tolkien and, 120, 123, 293, 293n88
Thorndike, Lynn, 64–65, 86; Burckhardt and, 64
Thorpe, Benjamin, Tolkien and, 15, 121
Tolia-Kelly, Divya, 263n46
Tolkien, Christopher, 136
Tolkien, J. R. R., 9, 109–40, 291n54, 293n84, 296n141; Adorno and, 122; Burckhardt and, 111–112, 121–24; Craigie and, 121, 123, 293n88; Eliot and, 157; Fradenburg and, 298n9; Gordon and, 121–22, 127, 293n88; Green and, 157; Grimm brothers and, 121; Grundtvig and, 120; Hall and, 5–6, 30–31, 112–115, 117–120, 125–40, 142, 145–46, 148–49, 155, 163–64, 177–78, 206, 293n96, 290n37; Herder and, 120; Hilton and, 157; Horkheimer and, 122; Huizinga and, 111–112, 122, 127; Marlon James on, 107, 115–16; Kemble and, 121; Kim and, 298n9; Kolve and, 298n9; Langland and, 175–76, 177–78, 293n96, 300n39; Lavezzo and, 298n9; F. R. Leavis and, 124; on Marie de France, 124; Marx and, 122; Meloni and, 110; Naylor and, 206; Pound and, 157; Renan and, 120; Shakespeare and, 133; Southern and, 126; Thorkelin and, 293n88; Thorpe and, 121; Weber and, 122–23; Raymond Williams and, 157. See also *Beowulf*, "*Beowulf*: The Monsters and the Critics," "The Elder *Edda*," "English and Welsh," "On Fairy Stories," *The Fellowship of the Ring*, *The Hobbit*, *The Lord of the Rings* trilogy, *The Notion Club Papers*, *The Return of the King*, *Sir Gawain and the Green Knight*
Tolmie Sarah, on Langland, 171
"Tradition and the Individual Talent" (Eliot) 154–55, 218, 221, 233–35
Treichler, Paula, 189
Trigg, Stephanie, 8–9, 96, 272n10
Twain, Mark (Samuel Clemens), 209; Malory and, 224

Ullmann, Walter, 67, 85, 86, 276n77, 276–77n80
Ullyott, Jonathan, 316n20

Valéry, Paul, Bynum and, 71; Huizinga and, 59

Valverde, Rebeca Gualberto, 315–16n19, 317n38
van Court, Elisa Narin, 306n23
Vaninskaya, Anna, 301n42
Verlaine, Paul, 275n50
Vernon, Matthew, 18, 79, 265n72, 280n14, 296n149, 316n31; on Du Bois, 282–83n50; on Naylor, 184, 195, 204, 314n101
Vinaver, Eugène, on Malory, 90, 224
Vizenor, Gerald, 81

Walcott, Derek, 153, 233, 257
Wall, Cheryl, 319n70
Wallace, David, 74
Wallhead, Celia, 317n38, 316–17n19
The Wanderer, Hall and, 5
Warner, Lawrence, 299n24, 306n123
Warren, Calvin, 26–27, 33
Warren, Michelle, 15–17, 79
Washington, Mary Helen, on Marshall, 244, 320n77
The Waste Land (Eliot) 57, 60, 217–18, 220–22, 224–25, 229
Watson, Nicholas, 40, 69; on Bynum, 37; on Julian of Norwich, 37
Weber, Max, 22, 71, 105, 182, 183; Berman on, 50–51; Chaucer and, 183; Du Bois and, 83; Hall on, 167–68; Jameson and, 40; Langland and, 171; Leicester on, 182; Michael Mann on, 160; Tolkien and, 122–23
Weheliye, Alexander, 5; on Wynter, 24, 86
"The West and the Rest" (Hall), 159–68, 259n3, 302n76; Langland and, 173–74, 177; Naylor and, 185
Weston, Jessie, Eliot and, 220–21
de Wette, Wilhelm, Burckhardt and, 101–2
Wilderson, Frank, 26–27, 270n119
Whitaker, Cord, 6, 10, 79, 85, 185; Langland and, 305n122
White, Hayden, Hall on, 160
Whitehead, Jane, 190
"Whose Heritage?" (Hall), 139–40, 151, 157–59; Langland and, 174
Wiegman, Robyn, 22, 269n109
Wilderson, Frank, 26, 27, 263n46, 270n119
Williams, Deanne, 95–96
Williams, Eric, 256, 321
Williams, Raymond, 7, 151–52, 157; Ahmed and, 7; Hall on, 151–52; Tolkien and, 157
Wilson, Charles, 184
Wilson, Woodrow, 61
Winant, Howard, 76

Wolfram von Eschenbach, Eliot and, 220, 221, 240, 317n38
Woodside, Alexander, 11
Wordsworth, William, 129, 153, 154; Huizinga and, 58
Wright, Michelle, 77
Wright, Richard, 81
Wyatt, Thomas, Simpson on, 73
Wynter, Sylvia, 5, 6, 10, 24, 29, 30, 80, 85–88, 91, 165, 185, 247, 281n26; Burckhardt and, 80, 86–87; Chaucer and, 91; Du Bois and, 80, 87, 91; Hall and, 165; Le Goff and, 86; Malory and, 91; Naylor and, 185; on Pico della Mirandola, 87–88; Weheliye on, 24, 86

Yancy, George, 77
Young, Helen, 114, 115, 116, 294n113, 290n43, 295n125

Zeeman, Nicolette, on Langland, 170–71
Zumthor, Paul, 181

Kathy Lavezzo is Professor of English at the University of Iowa. She is the author of *Angels on the Edge of the World: Geography, Literature, and English Community, 1000–1534* and *The Accommodated Jew: English Antisemitism from Bede to Milton* and is the editor of *Imagining a Medieval English Nation*.

www.ingramcontent.com/pod-product-compliance
Lightning Source LLC
Chambersburg PA
CBHW020351080526
44584CB00014B/986